P9-AOK-982

THE FAMILY AND INHERITANCE

The Family

and Inheritance

Marvin B. Sussman

Judith N. Cates

David T. Smith

With the collaboration of Lodoska K. Clausen

Russell Sage Foundation / New York / 1970

FERNALD LIBRARY
COLBY-SAWYER COLLEGE
NEW LONDON, N. H. 03257

PUBLICATIONS OF RUSSELL SAGE FOUNDATION

Russell Sage Foundation was established in 1907 by Mrs. Russell Sage for the improvement of social and living conditions in the United States. In carrying out its purpose the Foundation conducts research under the direction of members of the staff or in close collaboration with other institutions, and supports programs designed to improve the utilization of social science knowledge. As an integral part of its operations, the Foundation from time to time publishes books or pamphlets resulting from these activities. Publication under the imprint of the Foundation does not necessarily imply agreement by the Foundation, its Trustees, or its staff with the interpretations or conclusions of the authors.

KFO
142
.S9

© 1970
RUSSELL SAGE FOUNDATION

Printed in the United States of America

Library of Congress Catalog Card Number: 74–104183

Standard Book Number: 87154–873–9

Preface

SINCE WORLD WAR II, large sums of money have been made available to behavioral scientists for research on a variety of subjects. More than a few sociologists believe that the discipline has been corrupted in the sense that it is doing far too much applied research at the expense of basic inquiries. Since World War II, sociologists have become involved with the problems of air pollution, automobile safety, mental health, rehabilitation, the education of professionals, the control of the deviant, riots, and transportation, to name only a few substantive problems. The pursuit of basic sociological knowledge—explanations of the workings of groups, institutions, and societies–has been secondary according to the sociologists who hold this view. To them, sociology as a basic discipline is becoming disestablished. Sociology is becoming a soft applied science.

Furthermore, because government agencies and private foundations pay for sociological investigations, these organizations decide which theoretical perspectives and accompanying research processes are to be developed and used. In short, behavioral scientists today are controlled by those who handle the purse strings: colleagues who are working for powerful government agencies and large tax-exempt foundations, and administrators who seek practical solutions to everyday problems.

A neglected side of this argument, and one which we support, is that because of the abundance of money available for research in a variety of areas, today's investigator has options that he never had when money was scarce or unavailable. He has options of two kinds. One is that he may choose among a number of substantive problems, a choice that is compatible with his value system and that provides opportunities for obtaining knowledge which may be useful in determining policies and practices of organizational systems within a society. A second option is that he may select a specific problem that optimizes conditions under which the researcher can explore basic questions of relevance to sociological theory. If he is working in the field of transportation or air pollution, he can examine questions in these areas that will allow for testing hypotheses derived from ecological and urban behavior theories. If, for example, he is working on family problems such as foster care, premarital pregnancy, or the single-parent family, he can examine any of these issues in reference to certain propositions of intrafamily dynamics or interfamily-societal system relationships. Studies on the making of a lawyer can employ hypotheses applicable to the sociology of professions, especially those hypotheses concerned with the socialization of the novice into a professional career.

Any such funded project will provide different degrees of freedom and opportunities to explore relevant sociological hypotheses. Essentially, today's investigator has more options and fewer constraints than the researcher in 1950 had in harmonizing relevant sociological concerns with the search for solutions to the problems that currently beset human society.

Thus provided with these options, the investigator is faced with important decisions. Which research should he choose to undertake, and how much time should he spend on it? The availability of alternatives of research-supported projects means a careful assessment of all possibilities in order to optimize the choice of a project that will be academically respectable, satisfying to the personal needs of the investigator, and above all, a contribution to society. It is obvious that with a limited number of years available for productive research, the social scientist must select problems critical to the development of behavioral theory and on the cutting edge of knowledge in his field. A science is constructed by building blocks of research very much as a mason constructs a wall. It is the responsibility of every scientist to cement a block or two and build the wall of theory, of testable and tested propositions, a little bit wider and taller. The over-all objectives are to obtain a more complete understanding of the phenomena being observed and, hopefully, to use this new knowledge in creative and effective ways.

The time dimension in the motivation of the scientist to undertake a specific research project should not be underestimated. The fact that money is available has tended to cause this primary motivation to be ignored. A researcher who makes a mark in his field and who has the respect of his colleagues is primarily concerned with the expenditure of time. He will use money to develop his discipline, to test hypotheses, and to raise questions about existing research. He will seek within substantive areas the conditions under which he can examine relevant constructs derived from a variety of theories found in his field.

We decided to study inheritance, family relationships, lawyers, and the probate court system—an area designed to be of interest to both sociologists and members of the legal profession. Thus, the project reported in this book is an attempt to undertake cross-disciplinary work between sociology and law; it is a piece of research by a joint team consisting of two sociologists and a lawyer. It is our firm belief that we are investigating an area of mutual interest. The entire book represents the combined efforts of all three team members.

Dr. Marvin B. Sussman, Professor and Chairman of the Department of

Sociology, Case Western Reserve University, was the principal investigator of this project. Co-investigators were Dr. Judith N. Cates of the American Psychological Association, Washington, D.C., and Professor David T. Smith of the University of Florida College of Law, former faculty members of the Department of Sociology and School of Law, Case Western Reserve University, respectively, during the course of the project. Collaborating with the authors was Lodoska K. Clausen, Research Co-ordinator, whose tireless efforts and many contributions deserve special commendation.

We are deeply indebted to many persons for making our enterprise possible, especially our able interviewers who, like the mailman, at times endured snow, rain, heat, and gloom of night. They are: Marsha Blech, Audrey Cline, Judith Marsh, Jo Anne Randall, Mignon Schultz, and Sandra Zalin. Special appreciation is extended to Allison Dunham, Professor of Law at the University of Chicago and former Executive Director, National Conference of Commissioners on Uniform State Laws, and to Richard V. Wellman, Professor of Law at the University of Michigan, for their review of our preliminary manuscript and their helpful criticisms of its parts. We are grateful also to Dr. Marie R. Haug of the Department of Sociology, Case Western Reserve University, for reviewing the manuscript. Alan P. Chesney rendered needed assistance on specific areas of concern, and Walter Schultz assisted in data processing. We wish to thank the secretarial pool of the Department of Sociology, headed by Diane P. Ferris, for cheerfully typing and retyping the materials that now comprise this book. Anne Worth deserves special recognition for her aid in the final editing of the manuscript. Finally, our thanks are due the decedents' survivors and attorneys whose interviews provided us with much of the data, and to Russell Sage Foundation for the generous financial support that made this book possible.

MARVIN B. SUSSMAN
JUDITH N. CATES
DAVID T. SMITH

Contents

Preface

CHAPTER 1: The Family and Inheritance Study in Perspective 1

Introduction 1

The Concept of Testamentary Freedom 4

Family Continuity 9

The Interest of Society, Probate Court, and Lawyers in Inheritance 10

Contents 11

CHAPTER 2: Inheritance and the Legal Process 16

Intestate Succession 16

The Normal Pattern

Interpretative factors in the normal pattern

Deviations from the Norm: Some Special Problems

Testate Succession 23

Execution Requirements / The Will and the Family

The Will Substitutes 27

Gifts / Trusts / Life Insurance / Joint Ownership

Conclusion 35

CHAPTER 3: Perspectives and Design of Inheritance Study 36

Previous Probate Studies 37

Theoretical Perspectives 40

Study Design 44

Public Records / Survivor Interviews / Case Loss /
The Lawyer and the Inheritance System / Lawyer Sample

Conclusion 60

CHAPTER 4: Testacy Versus Intestacy 62

Proportion of Testate Cases 62

Decedent Sample / Survivor Population

Frequency of Testacy 64

Age / Location in Family Network

Sex / Type of surviving kin / Size of kin group

Economic Class

Decedent sample / Survivor population

Social Status

Decedent sample / Survivor population

Conclusion 81

CHAPTER 5: Conceptions of Justice: The Testator 83

Spouse and/or Lineal Kin Survived 86

Spouse Was the Sole Survivor / Spouse and Lineal Kin Were the Survivors / Lineal Kin Were the Survivors

Parents were the sole survivors / Minor children were the survivors / Adult children were the survivors / Children and grandchildren were the survivors

Collateral Kin Were the Survivors 103

Estranged Families

Nonrelated Inheritors 108

No Known Next of Kin Survived / Family of Procreation Survived / Family of Orientation Survived

Bequests to Charities 113

Decedent Sample / Survivor Population

Conclusion 118

CHAPTER 6: Conceptions of Justice: The Heirs 121

Redistribution in the Testate Case 122

Redistribution in the Intestate Case 125

Spouse Was the Only Survivor / Spouse and Lineal Kin Were the Surviving Next of Kin

Remarriage and estate fragmentation / Special problems of spouse and surviving minor children

Lineal Kin Were the Only Surviving Next of Kin

Minor children / Adult and minor children / Adult children

Parents Were the Sole Surviving Next of Kin / Collateral Kin Survived / Laughing Heirs / No Known Next of Kin Survived

Conclusion 143

CHAPTER 7: The Inheritance 146

Fairness 146
Disinheritance 149
Inheritors 153
Mementos / Use of the Inheritance
Savings / Living expenses / Real estate / Durable goods / Bills / Education of children / Vacation
The Meaning of the Inheritance
Conclusion 170

CHAPTER 8: Economic and Legal Aspects of Estates 173

Size of the Estate 173
Large Estates / Small Estates
Release of assets / Other small cases
Extra-probate Assets 177
Insurance as an Extra-probate Asset
Debts 180
Funeral / Allowance and Exemption / Other Debts / Will Contests and Personal Claims: Settlement Aspects
Inferences with Regard to Economic Aspects 188
Testamentary Devices of Control 188
Trusts / Guardianship / Life Estates / Conditional Bequests / Contingency Provisions
Frequency of contingent provisions / Effect of contingent provisions
Inferences with Regard to Testamentary Devices of Control
Conclusion 200

CHAPTER 9: Will Making 201

Client 201
Reasons for Testacy / Testamentary Freedom
Legal sophistication of will makers / Qualifications of freedom
Analysis and Implications of Client Attitudes Toward Will Making
Lawyer 214
Image of the Client / Drafting the Will / Encroachment / Generalizations Regarding Lawyers and the Will-making Process
Conclusion 225

CHAPTER 10: Estate Settlement:
Purpose and Function of Probate Court 227
Probating the Will 227
Administering the Estate 231
Family Member as Personal Representative / Lawyer as Personal Representative / Corporation as Executor / Elements of Estate Administration / Time Involved in Estate Administration / Expenses of Estate Administration
Conclusion 245

CHAPTER 11: Estate Settlement:
Client Attitudes Toward the Probate Process 247
The Probate Court 248
The Lawyer 252
Appraisers 258
The Executor or Administrator 259
Time Taken for Estate Settlement 260
Attitudes Toward Estate Settlement in General and Fees in Particular 262
General Attitude Scale / Fee Attitude Scale
Determinants of Attitudes Toward Settlement 263
Conclusion 265

CHAPTER 12: Estate Settlement:
Lawyer Attitudes Toward the Probate Process 267
The Ideal Client 268
Estate Settlement Problems 269
The Lawyer's Compensation 274
The Probate System 276
Conclusion 284

CHAPTER 13: Findings, Implications, and Analysis 286
Findings 286
Prerequisites for Comprehensive Inheritance Study / Testacy and Its Attributes / Patterns of Distribution / Meanings and Uses of Inheritance / Economic and Legal Factors in Estate Settlement / Will-making Practices and Attitudes Among Survivors / Lawyers and Probate Work / Estate Administration: Factors and Attitudes

The Implications of the Study Findings for Initiating Changes in Legislation and Public and Legal Education in Probate Work 296

Legislative Reform / Public Education / Implications for Lawyers and Legal Education / Needed Research

Reflections 310

Functions of Inheritance and Testamentary Freedom

APPENDIX A: Statutes from the Ohio Revised Code 317

APPENDIX B: Rating Scale for Homes in Cuyahoga County 323

APPENDIX C: Description of the Lawyer Sample 325

APPENDIX D: Life Cycle and Testacy 330

APPENDIX E: General Tables 334

APPENDIX F: Code of Conduct for Cleveland Banks Regarding Estate Planning 339

APPENDIX G: Probate Court Rules 341

Glossary 349

Bibliography 355

Index 363

Chapter 1

The Family and Inheritance Study in Perspective

Introduction

WITH THE GROWTH of complex industrialized societies, inheritance has been de-emphasized as a factor in establishing the individual's or the family's status, power, security, and economic position within the society. The large-scale development of corporate structures as concomitants of modernization provides for the continuity of economic life over generational time. The patterns of family inheritance fit within this corporate structure. Assets that are now transmitted within families and from one generation to the next are for the most part not in the form of real estate holdings or herds of cattle but are likely to be in the form of stocks, bonds, income from insurance policies, and small real property holdings (such as the family home) which are easily sold or transferable. The corporate structure provides for a large number of owners, and the death of a stockholder, except under very extreme circumstances, has little effect upon the continued operations of the corporation. At death, these equities are transferred to successors who can then dispose of them or assume the ownership of them as once held by the decedent in the corporate structure. Actually, these equities are never without an owner or are destroyed during this transfer. At this period of transition, the personal representative acquires ownership in a fiduciary capacity until the estate is distributed. The activities of the corporate structure are modified hardly at all.

With modernization has also come the development of society-wide welfare, social security, educational, and health-care systems that provide basic services for the very young and the retired, services that would normally be provided by the family or kinship group. A universal system of taxation furnishes support for the old and young nongainfully employed workers in the labor market and is the basis of society-wide economic transfers from one generation to the next. It is apparent that such economic transfers and income redistribution have been largely a function of governmental and political superstructures of modern societies and have overshadowed the family's efforts to arrange for the economic maintenance of its members. One consequence is the reduced importance of the function of inheritance in providing the family with the necessary assets to sustain its members over generational time, to educate its dependent youth, and to care for its ill or aged members.

The trend toward universal and society-wide support and care systems began at the turn of this century, and the quality and extent of these systems are linked to the rate and level of modernization achieved in such areas as economics, politics, leisure, and religion. The statistical data on life and work expectancy at birth over the period from 1900 to 1960 provide proof of this trend without indicating the reasons for it. It is found increasingly over this sixty-year period that gainfully employed individuals who are between the ages of 18 and 55 provide the economic support for the retired and the very young. In addition, the age of retirement has been set and reset at a lower age over the years, thus removing from the work force many individuals who would prefer to remain in it. The period of dependency of youth has been extended with the development and extension of the period of training in society-wide publicly supported educational systems. In the United States, life expectancy and work-life expectancy at birth in the years from 1900 to 1960 increased markedly; life expectancy increased from 48.2 years in 1900 to 66.6 years in 1960, and work-life expectancy increased from 32.1 years in 1900 to 41.4 years in 1960. During the same period, the proportion of individuals outside the labor force increased from 16.1 per cent in 1900 to 25.2 per cent in 1960; this increase suggests that the very young and the very old are being supported by a smaller percentage of the working population engaged in gainful employment.[1] This situation is the result of the continuous introduction of automatic processes in industry, improved health care, education, and training for occupational placement. The result is the high production of goods and services over and above those needed for societal survival as reflected in the average 9 per cent increase in the gross national product over the past decade. Mortality rates have lowered since 1900, and more individuals born in 1960 will live to the age of 70 than those born in 1900. Associated with these developments and trends is heavy investment in society-wide institutional bureaucratic systems that provide medical services, hospital care, housing, income, and a variety of services for maintenance of individuals during their nongainfully employed years.

These systems of maintenance and care have diminished the obvious importance of inheritance as one process for sustaining the economic well-being of the family. Also, the corporate structure of modern economic systems reduces the necessity for an orderly intergenerational transfer of equity within family and kinship lines in order to enhance the continuity of the economic system, a prerequisite in the preindustrial period.

1. Seymour L. Wolfbein, *Changing Patterns of Working Life*, United States Department of Labor (Washington, D.C.: Government Printing Office, 1963), p. 10.

Although the importance of inheritance to the economic maintenance of the family in modern times has diminished, and property holdings of families, kinship groups, or lineages have very little effect upon the workings of the economic market, the transfer of property, especially in modern industrial countries, is still a vital function. Inheritance may be viewed as an individually based or society-wide transfer.[2] Financial support of social security, welfare, and education by persons in their middle years may be interpreted as a legacy for the younger and older generations; these are society-wide transfers. Bequeathing one's property to another in a will is an individually based transfer.

This study deals with inheritance as an individual transfer involving two social systems and three principal actors. The systems are the family kinship network and the probate court; the actors are the decedent, the survivor, and the lawyer. The study explores the exercise of testamentary freedom (the right of a person to name his successors, within certain legal boundaries and cultural prescriptions) in relation to acts of familial responsibility and intergenerational behavior that are congruent with the aims of family continuity. Wills and other individual-transfer devices allow the individual options for distributing his property, options that social security and other society-wide transfers do not allow.

Still another reason for focusing on inheritance as an individual transfer is the relevance of property disposition to the study of the structure, meaning, and significance of members' interaction within urban kinship systems. The study of property transfers provides one basis for examining reciprocities consisting of uneven exchanges of goods and services between individuals and families in kin family networks, serial reciprocity and serial service, and bargaining and pay-offs. These are necessary conditions and processes for the persistence of the network over time as a viable voluntary organization, one that is capable of competing with other organizations and institutions for the active participation, loyalty, and identification of its members.[3]

In order to complete the perspective of the family and inheritance study, the concept of testamentary freedom, the relationship of continuity of the family system to inheritance and the exercise of testamentary freedom, and the interests of society, lawyers, and the probate system in inheritance are covered in greater detail. Finally, questions relevant to testamentary freedom, family relationships, and the probate process are raised.

2. For a discussion of society-wide transfers (both government and industrial security programs), see Juanita M. Kreps, "The Economics of Interpersonal Relationships," *Social Structure and the Family,* ed. Ethel Shanas and Gordon F. Streib (Englewood Cliffs, N.J.: Prentice-Hall, Inc., 1965), pp. 267–288.

3. An extensive discussion of the theoretical bases of the family kin network is found in Marvin B. Sussman, "Adaptive, Directive and Integrative Behavior of Today's Family," *Family Process* 7 (September, 1968): 239–250.

The Concept of Testamentary Freedom

Edmund Burke once said, "The power of perpetuating our property in families is one of the most valuable and interesting circumstances belonging to it, and that which tends the most to the perpetuation of society itself."[4] The likelihood of perpetuating property within family systems is potentially diminished by the presence of testamentary freedom, which allows the testator to will property away from the family in favor of outsiders. The exercise of this freedom without considering the context in which it occurs appears to be in sharp contradiction with the major intent of inheritance: to provide continuity to family systems and to maintain the social structure. Yet testamentary freedom is an accommodation mechanism in American society. It functions to meet multiple demands: those of continuity; a multilineal descent system; values that espouse freedom, democracy, and rationality; and a complex and highly differentiated modern industrial society.

Essential questions are: How "free" is the individual in exercising testamentary freedom? How has testamentary freedom been able to exist for so long in this society? How is the right of the individual to dispose of his property in a manner deemed fitting to him reconciled with the expectation that he act in a responsible fashion, especially in matters involving the well-being of the family?

Freedom, like justice, is a relative condition. One starts with the problem of definition, and even if one reaches a high degree of consensus among members of a society over what freedom or justice is, one rarely finds either of these conditions in an absolute sense. There are numerous situations that compromise the expression of complete freedom or the exercise of absolute justice. Freedom is expressed and justice is meted out within a context of values, structural prerequisites, normative demands, and social realities that human beings have created for themselves.

Succession law reveals an uneasy compromise among the interests of the individual, the family, and the community. Because man cannot live alone and determine for himself exactly what he wants to do in a given situation, such a compromise puts controls over the exercise of testamentary freedom. To understand the resulting limitations, it is necessary to consider a series of related questions: What kinds of property are not subject to testation? Is it likely that the needs of the community will be considered before the needs of the family? How much property is subject to the will of the testator? Namely, what kinds of property does he have control over that are judged not vital to the survival of the community or the family? Lastly, can the testator include or exclude any person he desires?

4. Edmund Burke, *Reflections on the French Revolution and Other Essays* (New York: E. P. Dutton & Co., Inc., 1910), p. 49.

5

The Concept of Testamentary Freedom

Assets garnered through forced savings—for example, some company and union insurance and benefit programs and programs sponsored by the government under social security legislation—are not available to be freely distributed by the testator. These valuable rights in job-related death or survivorship benefits specify recipients; and in almost all instances, these assets are allocated to surviving spouses and children. There is a marked increase in such benefit programs in modern societies, whereby the decedent's successors are predetermined by statutes, and the implementation of the transfer of such assets is done automatically and impersonally by a bureaucratic public or quasi-public agency.

The testator of a small estate is effectively restricted in his freedom to distribute because the estate can be consumed entirely in payment of debts or by the exemption, year's allowance, and other provisions awarded to the widow, widower, or children. Limited assets induce forced succession even though the testator might have had other things in mind.

The more wealthy testator can to some degree choose his successors and distribute his estate in a manner in keeping with his desires; he has the greatest opportunity to express testamentary freedom. But even in this instance, state and federal estate taxes prevent him from freely disposing of all his assets. The progressive tax on estates forces the testator to leave an increasingly larger proportion of his estate to the public. All he can do is to determine the manner in which he serves the public, either through progressively increasing estate taxes (depending upon the size of his estate) or through tax-free gifts to charity. For both the wealthy and the poor, necessity is an underlying principle in determining what may be distributed and to whom. For the rich, necessity is determined by the public, which says in effect that the more a person leaves to his successors, the greater should be the share that will be given back to the society in which he had the opportunity to accumulate or obtain such wealth. The individual can determine how the public will be appeased. He obviously has a larger share of equity remaining to distribute according to his desires. For the less well-to-do person, the requirements of his family may dictate his will in order to provide the assets for maintenance of the family over time. For both the rich and the poor, government and industrial security programs are developing across the board in which takers are designated and individuals are protected against the exigency of death and disablement; testators have little or nothing to say about who will be the recipients of these equities after death.[5]

Such legal restrictions support widely held societal notions regarding the individual's responsibility for members of his family and his own competence to act appropriately in accord with such responsibilities. For these reasons, the law is very concerned about the mental state of individuals and seeks to pro-

5. See discussion of society-wide transfers by Kreps, op. cit.

vide safeguards to ensure that the individual was not under any restraint in making a will (that is, under duress, undue influence, or the victim of fraud). The doctrine of sound mind was introduced in order to provide standards for measuring the capabilities of an individual to exercise testamentary freedom. The legal definition of a sound mind for testamentary capacity is that a man must know what he possesses, must know the natural objects of his bounty, and must understand the nature of the business in which he is engaged. One of the more fascinating problems is how to develop a simple method of evaluating an individual's soundness of mind. It appears that courts and juries determine soundness of mind not simply by determining what a man owns and what is his knowledge about his successors but also by judging such matters as whether he neglects his family, deeming such abandonment as unnatural and deducing that unnaturalness equals unsoundness.

The soundness-of-mind principle is supported by the possibilities of forced guardianship in cases where an individual is judged incapable of looking after his property. In instances where the estate is very large or complex because of varied assets and the possessor lacks managerial competence, a guardianship may be effected. Court decisions have tended to favor not only the "helpless dependent" but also any family member. Potential successors who feel that they are going to be denied their legacy and are being "taken" by actual or perceived threats of estate disposition, because of poor management before the death of the testator, are apt to ask for court action to establish a guardianship, and generally they are favorably heard.[6]

The current societal posture toward testamentary freedom is predicated on values which assure that caring for one's own kin and orderly social relationships among family members are highly desirable. Testamentary freedom is highly correlated with the condition of sufficient assets. A person has to have equity in order to be able to dispense it. Individuals who are well-to-do usually have sufficient assets to take care of the natural objects of their bounty and also to give to others. Frequently, their spouses and children are not in great need of their beneficence. In many instances, wives will have legacies from their own side of the family, and children may in part have been taken care of by grandparents. Well-to-do individuals are in the best position to meet their familial responsibilities and to a large degree fulfill community expectations, based on an assessment of the financial and status needs of their potential descendants. If spouses and children are amply provided for from other sources, such as legacies and trusts, or are potential inheritors from grandparents and members of their own familial line and will thus be enabled to maintain sufficiently their position and status within the community, then testators have an alternative

6. "The Disguised Oppression of Involuntary Guardianship: Have the Elderly Freedom to Spend?" *Yale Law Journal* 73 (1964): 676–692.

for distribution of their assets and are more likely to exercise testamentary freedom. The allocations that they would make to institutions and nonrelated individuals would meet with no disapproval because they would have fulfilled community expectations of taking care of their next of kin.

For most individuals, will making is related to the desire to exercise testamentary freedom under conditions that warrant its use. It is possible to say that the making of a will is tantamount to testamentary freedom. In an ideological sense, it is. In practice, however, will makers conform, by and large, to cultural prescriptions of familial responsibility over generational time. The will provides a mechanism for exercising preferred choices if conditions and circumstances are appropriate.

The existence of a multilineal family-descent system, a nuclear family structure voluntarily organized into kin networks, and a relatively high rate of social and geographical mobility of nuclear units are conditions that favor, and perhaps even require, testamentary freedom as part of any inheritance process.

Testamentary freedom allows the individual more choices in the selection of his lineal kin as well as additional opportunities to be chosen by others as part of a family line. This method of free selection is essential in a society that traces its ancestry through a multilineal kinship system. An individual born in this society can claim as his ancestors or be claimed as a descendant initially along four major lines representing those of his grandparents. If he goes back three generations, there are eight possible lines; four generations, sixteen possible lines, and so forth. The variability of the multilineal kinship system implies that a person can select any ancestral line or be selected to be a member of one for a variety of reasons. Testamentary freedom makes a rather complicated lineage system less complicated by forcing individuals to select one or a small number of descent lines because the system requires that either beneficiaries be named in wills or they will be named under intestate distribution.

Inheritance, in the broad sense, has existed in all civilizations and preliterate societies known to man. Intergenerational transfers are a common phenomenon in all societies, and the inheritance process is one major technique for effecting these transfers. There has been, and is, great variation, however, in the use of testamentary freedom. There appears to be a high correlation between its exercise and the rise in societal complexity. Parallel with this increase is a development and extension of society-wide systems of welfare, social security, insurance, and so forth, which are basically economic transfers (forms of inheritance) along generational lines.

This is not to say that testamentary freedom came into being with industrialization, and there is some reason to believe that there are important exceptions to the correlation of modernization and testamentary freedom. There is historical evidence of the use of testamentary freedom in ancient Greece and Rome and in Anglo-Saxon England before 1066, especially when the individual had no descendants. France, on the other hand, has severely prescribed distribution of an estate at death. With few exceptions, beneficiaries are immediate family members. The economy of France until very recently was built around family enterprises, and the restriction on testamentary freedom may be an accommodation to this economic condition. Present French economy, resembling more the corporate structure of the United States, may bring about changes in existing restrictions on testamentary freedom. Also, as the state itself assumes more responsibility for the care of the young and the old, conditions are increasingly conducive to the extensive exercise of testamentary freedom. The severe restrictions on testamentary freedom in France have not been conducive to the development of charitable foundations and agencies having the functions of public service and research. The government has control over research and social-betterment programs. The implications of this are worth a speculative essay. For the purposes of this study, the point is that testamentary freedom and its exercise are intricate parts of the economy, political ideology, and social systems of a society.

Testamentary freedom may be perceived by the testator as a way to "right a wrong" done to an individual, to improve the family's capability of surviving as a unit, to maintain a surviving member over time, to reward a deserving person, or to punish the undeserving. Testamentary freedom, in this sense, can function to support the family and social order and especially those values that undergird intimate relationships: affection, service, reciprocity, exchange, and identification. Extensive use of testamentary freedom to provide for nonfamily or kin members by disinheriting closely related family members, on the other hand, would raise serious questions about the functions of testamentary freedom in modern society. If, for example, it had been discovered in this study that there is widespread naming in wills of nonrelated persons in lieu of kin, particularly individuals who provided few services and little affection or friendship, then it would be necessary to question whether inheritance is intended to enhance intergenerational family continuity, provide for the smooth transition of power via intergenerational transfers, function as an important mechanism by which the older generation can maintain power within the family, or whether inheritance has a role in maintaining the social structure.

If inheritance provides survivors in this study with more than property, if inheritance symbolizes a transfer of love, affection, and identification, and if testamentary freedom is employed to name as beneficiaries nonfamily individuals or particular family members who provided emotional services, then it is possible to enumerate more systematically the conditions under which intergenerational family continuity can be maintained. Such a finding would suggest focusing on the family as an interaction system and studying the quality and character of interactions. The money involved in inheritance and the power and use it represents may be the least important variables in explaining intergenerational behavior.

Family Continuity

Intergenerational family continuity is one important linkage, perhaps the most important, of the nuclear family kinship network in American society. It pertains to ongoing relationships between parents, children, and grandchildren. Reciprocity, exchange, expectations, and services are some of the conditions, acts, and perceptions that determine continuity.[7] Data from this study of intergenerational transfers of property within kinship networks may provide clarification of the relationship between variables such as family size, occupation, education, ages of members, sex distribution and patterns of service, exchange, expectations, and reciprocities.

Reciprocity and exchange are fundamental to all social relationships. The bases of social relationships within the family are found in help patterns involving the exchange of unequal amounts and of different orders. Yet the giving and taking in meeting the needs of individual family members as well as the needs of whole families are basic for the continuity of nuclear family relationships, whether along generational or bilateral kinship lines. The anticipation of inheritance and the rightful claim to a large share of the inheritance precipitate the provision of services to those who have money to leave by relatives who expect to be compensated for providing care throughout the lifetime of the testator, but especially in his last years. Thus, within the family system it may be that inheritance is an important stimulus for making manifest reciprocity and exchange mechanisms that become the essential links in any viable social system.

In complex modern societies like ours, we have developed many other institutional systems and programs that materially support families. These range from welfare programs to outright subsidies and the pattern of intergenerational transfers that has already been discussed. The increasing program coverage and number of individuals involved in these society-wide generational economic transfers, a universal form of inheritance transmission, may condition the bases upon which individual dispositions are made. Inheritance transfers may be less a consequence of acts of serial reciprocity, based upon what specific individuals of one generation in a family do for others of another generation, but more a function of serial service.[8] Serial service involves an expected generational transfer that occurs in the normal course of events. It is expected that parents have to help their young children, and middle-aged chil-

7. For a review of this position, see M. B. Sussman and L. G. Burchinal, "Kin Family Network: Unheralded Structure in Current Conceptualizations of Family Functioning," *Marriage and Family Living* 24 (1962): 231–240; M. B. Sussman and L. G. Burchinal, "Parental Aid to Married Children: Implications for Family Functioning," *Marriage and Family Living* 24 (1962): 320–332; M. B. Sussman, "Relationships of Adult Children with Their Parents in the United States," *Family, Intergenerational Relationships and Social Structure,* ed. Ethel Shanas and Gordon E. Streib (Englewood Cliffs, N.J.: Prentice-Hall, Inc., 1965), pp. 62–92.

8. Wilbert E. Moore discusses this concept in Chapter 13 of *Order and Change* (New York: John Wiley & Sons, Inc., 1967), pp. 245–249.

dren may be called upon to give care or arrange for care of an aged and often ailing parent. This is within the cycle of life, and services of this kind are expected and are not based upon reciprocal acts. Whatever parents have in the way of worldly possessions will in due course be passed on to lineal descendants.

The study of inheritance provides one opportunity to examine this issue of serial reciprocity versus serial service. Is the transfer of property within families and along generational and bilateral kin lines based upon notions of distributive justice (a person receives according to his contribution) or on another principle such as equal distribution to survivors, or on distribution to specifically named heirs and legatees on grounds other than acts of service?

A related issue is that with the growth of society-wide support programs, a longer life span, increasing inflation, and increased consumer spending, the dollar amounts to be inherited by the overwhelming majority of survivors will be relatively small. Consequently, inheritance for many families may turn out to be symbolically more important than the material aid it provides. Undoubtedly, where estates are large, it is impossible to overlook the material assistance given to selected takers. But in most cases, inheritance symbolizes what were at one time the love links and bonds between family members, most often those between marital partners, and between parents and children.

The juxtaposition of family continuity and testamentary freedom is not so incongruous as it first appears. Continuity implies order, succession, transfer, and identification; freedom suggests the right to act, the control of decision making, and (what is often forgotten) responsibility. The inheritance transfers discussed in this study provide the necessary behavior for the description of the conditions under which the normative requirements of testamentary freedom and family continuity are met and of the consequences of the exercise of testamentary freedom for family continuity.

The Interest of Society, Probate Court, and Lawyers in Inheritance

The main reason for the interest of society and its representatives in inheritance is the desire to protect the rights of each individual involved in the economic transfer. These individuals include the decedent, the heir, the legatee, the creditor, and the public.

Another reason probate courts, lawyers, and related functionaries are interested in inheritance is that they must obtain a fair share of inherited wealth for the maintenance of their own institutional systems over time—payment for protecting the rights of the decedent, the heirs, and the legatees and for supervising the administration of justice in matters of inheritance. It is important that the state, through its scheme of fees and taxes, obtain a portion of the inheritance in order to satisfy the needs of the system and consequently maintain the social and economic well-being of all involved.

11

Interest of Society, Probate Court, and Lawyers in Inheritance

Society, through its organized social systems, functions as a third party to almost all except the most personal and intimate transactions that involve individuals in their relationships with other groups and social systems. The intention is not that the state act as a Big Brother in these transactions, but rather that it should provide the processes and mechanisms for managing tasks associated with the initiation or completion of certain functions and role changes during the life span of the individual. The state is legally present at the birth of every individual; it is present when he is drafted into the armed service, when he marries, when he enters many occupations, and when he dies. The state legitimizes these events and many others and provides the means for managing the tasks associated with them. When a person dies, it is the state's responsibility not only to legitimize death by officially recording it but also to prescribe the rules under which the bodily remains are to be disposed of.

Still acting in a third-party role, the state functions as an arbitrator, its main objective being to reduce to a minimum the potentialities for conflict. The state acts as a judge in will-contest cases between alleged heirs and those who are beneficiaries under the disputed will. The state, through its appropriate machinery, is presumed to be objective and provides the decision that becomes final. It settles differences absolutely and completely.

Inheritance is intricately related to the corporate structure and functions of modern societies and is chiefly involved with the economic system. The state functions in matters of inheritance in the best interests of society by defining the outer boundaries within which inheritance may occur. It does not permit distributions that are contrary to the public interest; and where the danger to the public is great, the state may intervene to alter the wishes of the individual in making his last will and testament or to alter the intestate succession. An illustration of the state's role may be seen in current legal safeguards regarding inheritance by named legatees or by takers under intestate succession who reside in iron curtain countries. Such restraints are deemed to be in the best interests of the American public, and consequently the property is placed in an escrow or trust account for safekeeping for the nonresident. In this situation the state voids the expression of testamentary freedom and refuses to implement immediately the statute concerning intestate succession.

Contents

The issues involved in inheritance, testamentary freedom, the probate court, the probate process, and family continuity are examined in Chapters 2 to 13. Chapter 2 presents a review of intestate and testate legislation and practices in the United States, with a specific focus on these conditions in the state of Ohio. This examination of the Ohio statutes regarding succession indicates far more similarity than dissimilarity between Ohio and other states of the Union. Will substitutes employed by testators to transfer assets before and after death are also examined.

The Family and Inheritance Study in Perspective

The Cuyahoga County study is an empirical one, and most of Chapter 3 is concerned with an examination of the hypotheses, design, methodology, techniques, and sampling of three populations. One population is composed of decedents; a second consists of the survivors of these decedents; and a third is a group of practicing lawyers. Each of these populations is studied in relation to specific questions regarding issues of testacy, the probate court, and the court's machinery. In order to estimate the general applicability of these data, other inheritance studies are examined, and some of the critical issues derived from these investigations that were considered in research for this study are presented.

Chapter 4 is concerned with the frequency and distribution of the condition of testacy. Comparisons are made between individuals who are testate and intestate with respect to age, location in the family network, economic class, and social status. Among the questions discussed in Chapter 4 are the following: Given a randomly selected population, what percentage of this group would one expect to be testate? In what age category is one likely to find the greatest number of will makers? Are wills drawn largely because of the imminence of death? What are the major reasons for making a will? What are the differences in the median size of the estate for testate and intestate cases? Do individuals of different occupational backgrounds and levels vary in the condition of testacy? Is education a factor related to the state of testacy?

Chapter 5 deals with the testators' conception of justice. These perceptions are obtained by examining the wills of both decedents and surviving heirs and legatees. An effort was made to relate such concerns over justice to those relationships that existed at one time between the decedent testator and the surviving family and to those relationships that are currently in existence between the will maker and his family. Considered also is the connection between the conception of justice and patterns of interpersonal relationships and processes such as exchange and reciprocity.

In a sample of probate cases such as the cases in the Cleveland study, to what extent and degree does disinheritance occur? More specifically, in those instances where disinheritance occurs, is it the result of emotional outrage and feelings by a testator and thus intended as a mechanism of social control, or is it done for logical and humane reasons such as providing for the welfare of a spouse or minor children by disinheriting others who would normally be expected to take under the will? In cases where there is no immediate family, to what extent is the estate distributed to friends, neighbors, or charities? Bequests to charities are discussed extensively. How much is actually bequeathed to the church and other charitable organizations and under what circumstances? In making a will, what are the expectations of the testator in reference to the services surviving children will provide for the surviving spouse? To what degree do testators deviate from the distribution that would normally occur under intestate succession?

Chapter 6 is basically an extension of Chapter 5, but it concentrates on the survivors' conception of justice. Testate and intestate redistributions are closely examined with reference to family-member relationships and relevant concepts of intergenerational family theory. Attention is focused especially on the reasons given by survivors for redistributing dispositions in both testate and intestate situations. Distributive justice is viewed within the context of service provided to the decedent and expectations of help and care to be given by one or more children to the surviving spouse.

Much has been written about the so-called laughing heir, sometimes called the unworthy taker, who receives an inheritance from what appears to be an unknown source. He takes an estate or a portion of one under intestate succession and "laughs all the way to the bank." How prevalent is this phenomenon, which has been popularized in the mass media? Under intestate succession, to what degree and under what circumstances is equality among takers the principal mode of distribution? What effects does remarriage have upon property disposition generally and intergenerational continuity in particular? How frequently does the transfer of property occur through a two-step process: from the decedent to the surviving spouse and then to descendant and ascendant lineal kin under both testate and intestate succession?

In Chapter 7 the effect of inheritance upon social mobility and economic security is investigated. The sense of fairness expressed by survivors regarding the various forms of property disposition is described. Issues such as disinheritance and the uses and meanings of inheritance for the individual are discussed. Also covered in this chapter is the question of what inheritance does to and for the taker. Does inheritance effect any changes in the life style of the individual or increase his social mobility, or (as it is often expressed) do the rich become richer as a consequence of inheritance? What is the meaning of inheritance to successors? How are mementos distributed among family members? What is the emotional significance of such distributions? Receiving an inheritance, small or large, requires some decision regarding its use. The principal uses made of inheritance are examined according to age, sex, stage of the family life cycle, and type of family structure.

In Chapter 8 attention is directed to the economic characteristics of the decedents' estates, including both assets and liabilities, and to certain legal characteristics of the decedents' wills such as trusts, guardianships, life estates, conditional bequests, and contingency provisions. An attempt is made not only to describe the frequency of these characteristics but also to show how the legal and economic aspects of inheritance are interrelated.

It is often assumed that potential named takers are ignorant of the will or its contents because the testator's declaration is made in an aura of secrecy. This chapter contains some fundamental information about the survivors' knowledge of the will, its provisions, and the size of the estate. It is likely that any will contest will receive widespread publicity. Thus, one important question is,

What percentage of testate cases end up in will contests? What are the circumstances and conditions under which such contests are initiated? Also described in this chapter is the amount of assets found in each estate according to the condition of testacy or intestacy. Extra-probate assets are also reviewed. The importance of insurance as such an asset is carefully examined.

Over the years, there has been a good deal of discussion in the mass media about the high cost of dying. This study presents data on the cost of funerals as it is related to the size of the decedent's estate. Also carefully documented in this chapter are allowances for survivors, how they are determined, and the type and amount of debts of the estate according to conditions of testacy or intestacy.

It has often been claimed that testators make extensive use of testamentary devices of control in order to master or guide the future behavior of descendants. To what extent are trusts, guardianships, life estates, and conditional bequests used as devices of control? Under what conditions are these devices, as well as contingency provisions, employed?

Chapter 9 covers will making. It deals with the personal motives of the will-making individual and examines in great detail the individual's perceptions of the capability of a will to save him and his family time and money. The concept of testamentary freedom is examined in relation to family continuity and how the exercise of testamentary freedom occurs in relation to responsibility for meeting the needs of family members. The belief in and exercise of testamentary freedom are examined in relation to the education, occupation, and income of survivors. Also investigated are the optimum conditions under which testamentary freedom can be properly exercised.

Another major section of this chapter covers the lawyer's role in will making The lawyer is asked to describe the ideal client in this area of practice. What are some of the major problems he has in this area of service, and what are some of the techniques he uses in working out a testament with a client? One important issue is the pay-off for the lawyer from will making. What does it lead to, especially in the face of competition from banks and other economic institutions?

Chapter 10 covers one component of estate settlement: the purposes and functions of the probate court. The rules governing the period of time from the probating of the will to the closing of the case are described. The discussion covers the time between death and filing for probate by condition of testacy and the bases for will contests. When a nonfamily member serves as administrator or executor of the estate, under what conditions is he selected? How frequently does this situation occur in relation to the total sample of cases? How much time does it take to close a case under testate and intestate conditions?

One important area of inquiry concerns the question of whether attorneys milk an estate, especially when they serve as administrator or executor. Careful documentation is given of the expenses of estate administration, covering not only attorneys' fees but court costs, appraisers' fees, and personal representatives' fees.

Chapter 11 is concerned with the client's attitudes toward the probate process. This issue is approached from the client's perception of the role of the functionaries of the probate court in estate settlement. Consequently, a series of scales and attitude questions is employed to tap client satisfaction with the performance of court personnel, lawyers, and appraisers, with fees charged, and to tap general satisfaction with the settlement. Also examined is the clarity of the client's perception of the roles of the executor or administrator and lawyer, as well as his concept of the ideal lawyer. The bases for dissatisfaction that can be found within the communication network of the lawyer, his client, and other beneficiaries are also investigated.

Chapter 12 reviews the lawyers' feelings and perceptions of the probate process and especially their attitudes toward their clients. Examined in depth are the lawyer's conceptions of the ideal client and his expectations of client behavior in order to have a satisfactory experience in both the will making and estate settlement areas. The good and bad estate settlement cases are discussed, as well as the lawyer's expectations regarding fees and his reasons for practicing in the estate settlement area. The advantages and disadvantages of the current probate system are examined from the viewpoint of the lawyer.

Chapter 13 has three sections. The first section is a brief summary of selected findings; the second presents implications of these findings for initiating changes in legislation and in public and legal education concerning probate work. The final section of this chapter contains reflections on the functions of inheritance for family continuity in relation to the concept of testamentary freedom and the viability of testamentary freedom in American society.

Chapter 2

Inheritance and the Legal Process

THE LAW of intestate and testate succession governs the transfer at death of economic interests, frequently from one generation to another. *Intestate* succession occurs when a person dies without a will. If he fails to dispose of all his estate at death by means of a will, he is partially intestate. *Testate* succession refers to the disposition of property at death according to the terms of a will. The so-called will substitutes are devices that may be utilized to avoid, at least in part, the usual process of estate settlement. These substitutes include jointly owned property (bank accounts, stocks, bonds, and real estate), irrevocable and revocable trusts, savings bank trusts, and life insurance. These alternative approaches to succession are the subject of this chapter.

Intestate Succession

The Normal Pattern

Intestate succession is regulated by statute. In each state, laws provide patterns under which intestate property will pass. In general, these intestate laws resemble one another, being based upon the English Statute of Distribution (1670). Although this statute concerned personal property only, its American copies use a single scheme of succession for both real and personal property. Despite variations from state to state, the laws of intestate succession have a certain basic commonality. Most statutes represent a combination of the parentelic and civil-law systems of kin computation. Under the parentelic system, derived from the descent of land under English common law, the entire line of issue (lineal descendants) of the nearest ancestor is preferred to issue of a more remote ancestor. For example, the issue of the intestate's parents, however distant, would take precedence over the issue of grandparents; a decedent's grandnephews and grandnieces would be preferred to uncles or aunts. Under the civil-law system (as utilized in the Ohio Statute of Descent and Distribution), the uncle or aunt would be preferred.[1]

The usual distribution for the immediate family provides the spouse with a third or half of the property and the issue with the balance. If the intestate

1. Under the rules of civil law, generations are counted from the surviving relative (omitting the latter in counting) back to the first common ancestor with the decedent and from that ancestor down to the decedent (including the latter in counting).

leaves no descendants but is survived by a spouse and specified relatives, some states give all to the surviving spouse, while other states include the relatives. It is likely that more than 95 per cent of all intestate cases are within the scope of basic legislation. Perhaps the most satisfactory method of indicating the general pattern of American intestate succession law is to present the Ohio Statute of Descent and Distribution, which is fairly representative of the normal pattern.[2]

It reads as follows:

2105.06 Statute of Descent and Distribution

When a person dies intestate having title or right to any personal property or to any real estate or inheritance in this state, such personal property shall be distributed and such real estate or inheritance shall descend and pass in parcenary, except as otherwise provided by law, in the following course:

(A) If there is no surviving spouse, to the children of such intestate or their lineal descendants, per stirpes;

(B) If there is a spouse and one child or its lineal descendants surviving, one half to the spouse and one half to such child or its lineal descendants, per stirpes;

(C) If there is a spouse and more than one child or their lineal descendants surviving, one third to the spouse and the remainder to the children, equally, or to the lineal descendants of any deceased child, per stirpes;

(D) If there are no children or their lineal descendants, three-fourths to the surviving spouse and one-fourth to the parents of the intestate equally, or to the surviving parent; if there are no parents, then the whole to the surviving spouse;

(E) If there is no spouse and no children or their lineal descendants, to the parents of such intestate equally, or to the surviving parent;

(F) If there is no spouse, no children or their lineal descendants, and no parent surviving, to the brothers and sisters, whether of the whole or of the half blood of the intestate, or their lineal descendants, per stirpes;

(G) If there are no brothers or sisters or their lineal descendants, one half to the paternal grandparents of the intestate equally, or to the survivor of them and one half to the maternal grandparents of the intestate equally, or to the survivor of them;

(H) If there is no paternal grandparents [sic] or no maternal grandparent, one half to the lineal descendants of such deceased grandparents, per stirpes; if there are no such lineal descendants, then to the surviving grandparents or their lineal descendants, per stirpes; if there are no surviving grandparents or their lineal descendants, then to the next of kin of the intestate, provided there shall be no representation among such next of kin;

(I) If there are no next of kin, to stepchildren, or their lineal descendants, per stirpes;

(J) If there are no stepchildren or their lineal descendants, escheat to the state.

As in all states, near relatives are preferred in the Ohio statute to remote relatives. Cousins will receive no inheritance if the decedent is survived by any of

2. Ohio Revised Code 2105.06.

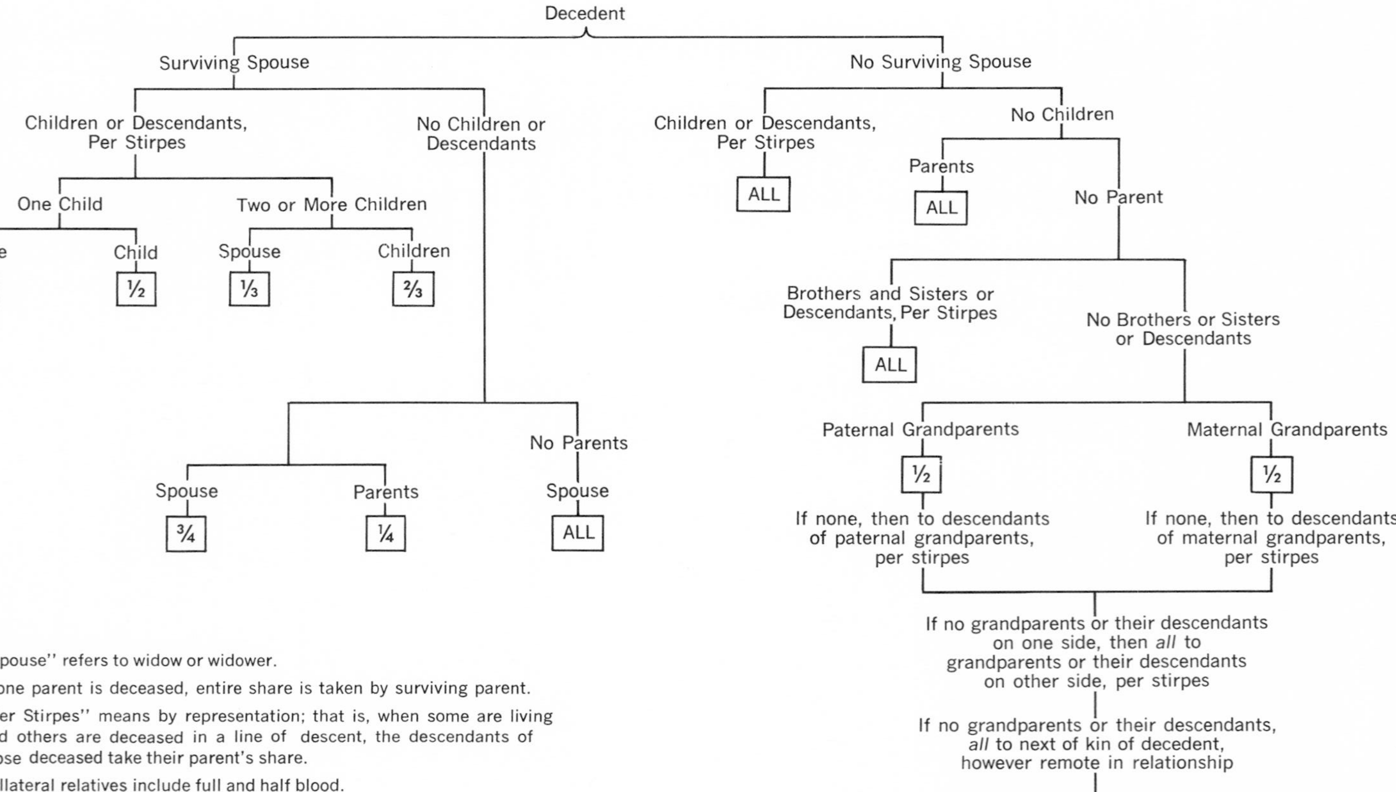

NOTE

1. "Spouse" refers to widow or widower.
2. If one parent is deceased, entire share is taken by surviving parent.
3. "Per Stirpes" means by representation; that is, when some are living and others are deceased in a line of descent, the descendants of those deceased take their parent's share.
4. Collateral relatives include full and half blood.
5. No right of representation among next of kin.

CHART 2–1 STATUTE OF DESCENT AND DISTRIBUTION (Ohio Revised Code 2105.06) the following classes: children, brothers and sisters, nephews and nieces, or uncles and aunts. The Ohio statute is typical in that it gives a fractional share of the estate to the surviving spouse. This share varies according to the number of children or their surviving lineal descendants. Ohio is in the minority of jurisdictions in preferring the intestate's parents along with the spouse if no children or their descendants survive. The Ohio statute clearly identifies the successors through the descendants of grandparents. It is then that the parentelic system terminates and the civil-law system begins, and the next of kin of the deceased are determined by degrees of relationship computed by the rules of civil law.[3] Ohio varies from the norm in that it includes stepchildren in its intestate succession law. If no survivors can be found, the property escheats (that is, reverts) to the state. It is to be noted that intestate succession is inflexible, with no court having the right to alter the pattern. The person who has died intestate has lost the opportunity to pick or choose his successors according to their needs and his notions of fairness or reciprocity.

Intestate property will pass either per capita (by the heads) or per stirpes (by the roots).[4] In a per capita distribution, each taker receives an equal share with the others, in his own right. If an intestate decedent were survived by three children (with no child having predeceased him), each would take one-third of his estate. Any surviving grandchild would take nothing. Distribution per stirpes refers to the transmitting of property in which the nearest lineal descendant of a deceased person takes the share that individual would have taken from the estate of the intestate. Here is an example of the process in its most elementary sense. If the intestate were survived by only two children plus two grandchildren who were the issue of a predeceased child, there would be the following distribution: one-third to each of the surviving children, with the remaining one-third split between the two grandchildren. They would receive their parent's share, that is, would take by representation. In Ohio, representation is not permitted further than lineal descendants of grandparents. Some states allow representation only to the children of the intestate's brothers and sisters; other states include grandchildren or all descendants of brothers and sisters, with some jurisdictions extending representation to the descendants of other or all collaterals.[5] In an increasing number of jurisdictions, there is no problem with remote next of kin. Legislation in these states terminates intestate succession with the issue of grandparents.[6] Escheat occurs if relatives are more remote. These distant kin are known as *laughing heirs.*

3. See Ohio Revised Code 2105.03.

4. See, for example, Ohio Revised Code 2105.11–.13.

5. Thomas E. Atkinson, *Wills,* 2d ed. (St. Paul, Minn.: West Publishing Co., 1953), pp. 69–70. Collaterals are relatives of the decedent who belong to the same ancestral stock but who are not in a direct line of descent or ascent.

6. For example, the state is preferred in Pennsylvania but not in Ohio. Compare Pennsylvania Statutes, title 20, 1.3 with Ohio Revised Code 2105.06.

Interpretative factors in the normal pattern. Not all basic problems may be adequately covered in a general statute of descent and distribution. Other legislation or case law may be necessary for interpretative purposes. There are two typical kinship problems: the meaning of children and the status of half bloods.

Although legitimate natural children are preferred takers in all states, adopted children and illegitimate children create additional problems for the inheritance system. Adoption in the sense of creating a legal relationship of parent and child was not part of the English common law. The first American adoption statute was passed in Massachusetts in 1851. Its purpose was to provide the needy child with parents and a home, rather than to furnish the adopter with an heir.[7] Today all states have adoption statutes. However, provisions related to inheritance are secondary, varied, and in many instances inadequate. A model that does not treat the adopted child as a second-class citizen is followed in Ohio. Upon adoption, the child, for succession purposes, is completely transplanted into the family of his adopting parents. There can be inheritance by, from, and through the child. The adopted child has the same rights as a natural child of the adopting parents and is, with limited exceptions, no longer treated as the child of his natural parents for the purpose of intestate succession. (See Appendix A for Ohio adoption legislation [Ohio Revised Code 3107.13] effective July 1, 1968.)

The illegitimate child under common law had no rights. He was *filius nullius,* the child of no one. He could inherit from no one because he was deemed without parents. The only persons who could inherit from him were his legitimate children or their issue. He was new stock for intestate succession purposes. Such an approach was rationalized under common law as a check on immorality, but the wrong individual was penalized; the innocent child was paying for the sins of his parents. Today in the United States, the illegitimate child can inherit from his mother, although several states impose some restrictions concerning such an inheritance. Ohio is in accord with the majority of jurisdictions in permitting succession between the child and his mother's kindred. Ohio Revised Code 2105.17 states:

> Bastards shall be capable of inheriting or transmitting inheritance from and to the mother, and from and to those from whom she may inherit or to whom she may transmit inheritance, as if born in lawful wedlock.

Provisions are present in state statutes for legitimation of bastards, and the legitimated child is brought within the intestacy statutes for all purposes.

The posthumous child or other qualified descendants of an intestate who were begotten before his death but born thereafter will be capable of inheriting from the intestate.

7. Richard R. Powell, *Real Property,* vol. 6 (New York: Matthew Bender & Co., Inc., 1958), sec. 1004.

Ohio has one statute not generally found in other states. This allows a person to designate an heir-at-law. The person so designated will be treated as a child of the declarant for purposes of intestate succession from him. However, he cannot take through his designator, and the latter cannot inherit from him. (See Appendix A for "Designation of heir-at-law" [Ohio Revised Code 2105.15] legislation.)

Another question that may arise is whether and what share half-blood relatives (for example, half brother or half sister) should inherit? It is the prevailing rule in the United States that relatives of the half blood inherit equally with those of the whole blood. However, legislation may prefer the whole blood relative to the half blood. The half blood may take a smaller share, or his share may be deferred in favor of whole-blood relatives of the same degree. Ohio does not treat the half-blood relative any differently from the whole-blood relative.

Deviations from the Norm: Some Special Problems

There are several areas of law that can alter the normal pattern of intestate succession. One concerns the rights of a slayer in the estate of his victim. There is always potentially present the problem of a felonious killing with an attempt to share in the estate of the decedent. The basic common-law approach is that the slayer may take his share. In the absence of statute, this is the majority view in the United States. Whether the slayer would himself enjoy the fruits of his crime is another question. It would however be his to pass on to his successors. The rationale for such a claim is that the law abhors a forfeiture for crime.

An opposite view held by a strong minority would deny recovery to a person who has killed his ancestor or testator on the theory that he should not profit by his own wrong. Some jurisdictions simply indicate that the slayer takes no title. Other jurisdictions utilize the constructive trust, which provides for the distribution of the estate to other heirs.

The majority of states have statutes that govern this problem. The word "slayer" is used here because the killing may be wrongful but not murder. Ohio Revised Code 2105.19 provides in part:

> No person finally adjudged guilty, either as a principal or accessory, of murder in the first or second degree shall inherit or take any part of the real or personal estate of the person killed whether [by intestate succession], or under the will of such person.[8]

Such legislation is poorly drafted for several reasons. The killer must be convicted of murder in the first or second degree. He would thus profit if convicted

8. Ohio Revised Code 2105.19 further provides that the murderer shall be considered to have preceded in death the person killed. The rights of a bona fide purchaser from the murderer prior to the time he is adjudged guilty are not affected. Also a pardon

of a lesser included offense such as voluntary manslaughter or if he committed suicide before being tried or convicted. Also, it has been contended that the conviction would have to take place in Ohio.[9]

If the facts of a particular case do not fit into a state's statute, the majority of jurisdictions, Ohio included, adhere to the common law. In such a case, the slayer would be permitted to acquire the property of his victim and to retain it in spite of his crime.

A related problem is whether a person should lose property rights as a result of conviction of a crime. The "slayer's statute" is considered part of the law of succession. The vast majority of states, otherwise, do not have any disability statutes regarding transmission or succession of property rights as a result of conviction of a crime. Ohio is with the majority.

A frequent problem arises when two or more persons die in a common disaster. In such a case (for example, an automobile or an airplane accident), there is often no evidence concerning the order of death. As in the question of the slayer's rights, these problems relate to testate as well as intestate succession. How should the property of the decedent pass? The resolution in most states comes from the Uniform Simultaneous Death Act, which provides that if there is no contrary provision in the will (if there is testate succession), "where the title to property or the devolution thereof depends upon priority of death and there is no sufficient evidence that the persons have died otherwise than simultaneously, the property of each person shall be disposed of as if he had survived."[10] A somewhat modified version of such legislation in effect in Ohio (Ohio Revised Code 2105.21) is found in Appendix A.

Under common law, an alien was not able to inherit land, and he could not transmit it by descent; but there was no such disability with respect to personal property. In the United States today, there is much variation in the respective states concerning the rights of aliens. In the absence of legislation, it is possible to take or transmit personal property, but it is not possible to take or transmit realty. In only approximately one-third of the states are disabilities of aliens completely removed. Ohio belongs to this latter group.[11]

The English approach to the descent of land limited inheritance to relatives of the blood of the ancestor who was the first purchaser. This favoring of the branch of the intestate's family from which the realty was inherited is known as the *doctrine of ancestral property*. It has only limited application in the United States today. Although the doctrine was not applicable to personal

---

shall restore to the murderer all succession rights but again will not affect the rights of a bona fide purchaser.

9. See annotation in *American Law Reports,* 2d ed., vol. 39 (Rochester, N.Y.: The Lawyers Co-operative Publishing Co., 1955), p. 499.

10. 9-C Uniform Laws Annotated 160.

11. See Ohio Revised Code 2105.16.

property in England, it may be in the United States if based upon a statute. The American statutes that preserve ancestral property do so when the claimants include half-blood relatives who are not of the blood of the ancestor.

Ohio follows the majority of states in rejecting the archaic notions of ancestral property. Ohio Revised Code 2105.01 reads as follows:

> In intestate succession, there shall be no difference between ancestral and non-ancestral property or between real and personal property.

Yet there is in Ohio a peculiar statute (Ohio Revised Code 2105.10) technically entitled "Descent of estate which came from deceased spouse" (see Appendix A). It is commonly known as the *half-and-half* statute. Its purpose is to preserve equity between the next of kin of two spouses in property that has passed from one spouse to the other in a certain manner. This legislation can be considered the last vestige of ancestral property in a state that has abolished ancestral property.

Testate Succession

Execution Requirements

Basically, the law relating to wills can be simply stated. The will must be in writing, signed by the testator, and generally witnessed by at least two competent attesting witnesses. The testator must be over a stated age, of sufficient mental capacity, and not under any restraint. American law controlling the execution of wills is derived from three English statutes: Statute of Wills (1540), Statute of Frauds (1677), and the Wills Act (1837).

The Statute of Wills required only a written will for the devise of land. In fact, it did not specify that the testator had to write or sign the instrument. Prior to this statute, testamentary power with respect to real property was lacking because of feudal concepts of land ownership. Reliable proof of a will came with the Statute of Frauds, which dealt with both personal and real property. Wills of real property were to be

> in writing, and signed by the party so devising the same, or by some other person in his presence and by his express direction, and shall be attested and subscribed in the presence of said devisor by three or four credible witnesses.

Wills of personal property were required to be in writing although there was no requirement of the testator's signature or of witnesses. Thus personal property under the Statute of Frauds was put on parity with real property under the Statute of Wills. Until the Statute of Frauds was enacted, personal property could be disposed of by oral testament.

Uniform rules for the execution of wills, without distinction between real and personal property, came with the Wills Act. It stated that a will shall be in writing, shall be signed at the foot or end thereof by the testator, or by some other person in his presence and by his direction; and such signature shall be made or acknowledged by the testator in the presence of two or more witnesses present at the same time, and such witnesses shall attest and shall subscribe the will in the presence of the testator.

The provisions of the latter two statutes provided the basic pattern for American legislation. Each state today has provisions for the execution of wills that apply uniformly to both personalty and realty. Legislation also controls the revocation of wills.

Today all but a few states have statutes relating to execution that tend to follow the Wills Act. Ohio is typical of most states. In Ohio,

every last will and testament shall be in writing, but may be handwritten or typewritten. Such will shall be signed at the end by the party making it or by some other person in such party's presence and at his express direction, and be attested and subscribed in the presence of such party, by two or more competent witnesses, who saw the testator subscribe, or heard him acknowledge his signature.[12]

Under Ohio law, "a person of the age of eighteen years, or over, sound mind and memory, and not under restraint may make a will."[13] Legislation in other jurisdictions is similar.

The traditional age for will making was twenty-one, as found in the Wills Act of 1837. Today, however, not more than half of the states require age twenty-one for testamentary capacity. At the time that data for this study were obtained, the age of testamentary capacity in Ohio was twenty-one; it was reduced to eighteen in August, 1965. A person does not have to have average intelligence to make a will. Less than average intelligence will suffice if a person is able to comprehend and remember in a general way (1) those who are the natural objects of his bounty, (2) the nature and extent of his property, and (3) the nature of the act that he is performing. A person is under restraint if the will is the result of fraud, duress, or undue influence.

Some jurisdictions, states mostly in the South and West, allow what is called the *holographic will.* Such a will requires no attesting witnesses, but it must be written by the testator in his own hand. Ohio does not recognize the unattested holographic will. Oral or nuncupative wills are generally allowed with respect to personal property. Such wills must comply with a number of restrictions (see Appendix A for Ohio Revised Code 2107.60, which is a typical statute validating oral wills).

It is to be noted that the law of wills is quite inflexible. The will formalities are mandatory. A will lacking a witness is not worth the piece of paper it is

12. Ohio Revised Code 2107.03. Oral wills allowed with respect to personalty under very limited conditions by Ohio Revised Code 2107.60 are excepted from this provision.
13. Ohio Revised Code 2107.02.

written on, despite the good faith of the decedent. If the will is invalid, intestate succession takes place.

The Will and the Family

What is accomplished with a will? First, it permits in theory the expression of testamentary freedom: a person may make any disposition of his property that he pleases. However, irrespective of such a general rule, public policy in most states gives the surviving spouse certain property rights in the deceased's estate that have priority over the claims of other takers. The will can be renounced, and a *forced share* (usually a fraction of all the assets disposed of by the will) can be taken where no provision or an insufficient provision is made. One authority indicates that "a widow has such an option in all jurisdictions except the Dakotas and a widower in all except eleven states."[14] Ohio, like the majority of jurisdictions, permits the surviving spouse, male or female, to waive the will made by the decedent and to take a share of the estate afforded by statute.[15]

Two common-law expectant interests, dower and curtesy, are apt to be replaced or modified because of modern intestate succession and election statutes. *Dower,* under common law, was the widow's right to a life interest in one-third of the lands that her husband owned during their marriage. *Curtesy* was a somewhat similar right for the husband by which he was entitled to a life estate in all lands owned by his wife at any time during the marriage provided that there was issue born alive capable of inheriting the estate. In Ohio, there is a statutory dower applicable to both spouses to safeguard the surviving spouse against lifetime transfers of realty owned by the decedent where the survivor did not relinquish dower.[16] Such property would not be part of the estate at death and would be outside succession legislation. Certain additional rights are usually granted to a surviving spouse (or only to the widow) either alone or together with minor children. In Ohio, these are the year's allowance,[17] quarantine[18] (the right to live in the home owned by the deceased for a specified period of time), and the right to receive certain property exempt from administration.[19]

Variations in the surviving spouse's rights will be found in the community-property states: Louisiana, Texas, New Mexico, Arizona, California, Nevada, Washington, and Idaho. *Community property* is essentially all property ac-

14. Lowell Turrentine, *Wills and Administration,* 2d ed. (St. Paul: West Publishing Co., 1962), p. 18.
15. See Ohio Revised Code 2107.39.
16. See Ohio Revised Code 2103; curtesy is abolished by section 2103.09.
17. Ohio Revised Code 2117.20.
18. Ohio Revised Code 2117.24.
19. Ohio Revised Code 2115.13.

quired during the marriage except that received gratuitously by gift or by intestate or testate succession. Excluded also from the community-property scheme is whatever a spouse owns before marriage.

The surviving spouse is entitled to at least one-half of the community property, and this right cannot be defeated by the decedent's will. The general rule is that the spouse who dies first may will away the other half. If this half is not so transferred, it passes either to the surviving spouse or to the deceased's descendants, the states being evenly split between these approaches. The decedent has testamentary freedom with respect to his separate property. If he should die intestate, descent and distribution take place in the traditional manner.

The law usually provides ample protection for the surviving spouse of a testate decedent, but it is less than adequate in regard to the rights of children. A child can easily be disinherited or unintentionally excluded from testate succession. In any particular testacy, he may have no rights, despite the fact that he would have been in a preferred position to take of the estate if intestacy had occurred. There are two basic types of legislation in the United States that make the testator's intent immaterial and limit his power to disinherit. The first consists of statutes protecting the spouse from disinheritance. The second involves statutes protecting families against charities. Neither protects the child from the testator.

When does the child receive protection? He will normally be protected from disinheritance in Louisiana, where succession law is civil law based on the Code Napoléon rather than on English common law. In other states, the freedom to disinherit is universal with one exception, the "pretermitted" child who has been unintentionally omitted from the will. The child may be after-born or unintentionally omitted although born before the making of the will. In general, this child may share in the parent's estate. However, legislation pertaining to pretermitted children varies considerably from state to state (see, for example, Appendix A, Ohio Revised Code 2107.34). In Ohio, the after-born (also after-adopted) child who is unprovided for or not intentionally disinherited is protected. However, not every youngster born before the making of the will who is unintentionally omitted has rights. Protection is only afforded to the child who was absent and reported to be dead at the time of the will's execution and who is later found to be alive. This is limited legal protection.

In some states, the legislatures have placed restrictions on testators making charitable dispositions. Such statutes are intended to protect the interests of close relatives. They are the so-called mortmain acts patterned after English legislation controlling the transfer of property to charitable, and especially religious, uses. There are two basic varieties of mortmain acts: (1) wills making gifts to charity must be executed a certain period before the death of the testator, and (2) the proportion of the estate that can be given to charity with no time qualification is limited. A single statute may combine the elements of time and amount as the present Ohio act does.[20] (See Appendix A for Ohio Revised Code 2107.06.) These statutes usually apply only if the testator is survived by designated near relatives and frequently only if, and to the extent that, the relative would gain by invalidating the charitable gift. Mortmain statutes are found today in fewer than half the states.

The Will Substitutes

Will substitutes are legal devices utilized to prevent property from passing by way of testate or intestate succession.[21] The most common will substitutes are gifts, jointly owned property (bank accounts, stocks, bonds, and real estate), irrevocable and revocable trusts, savings bank trusts, and life insurance. Such property will not be probated.

The degree of control that the property owner possesses after creation of a will substitute varies according to use. All ownership rights are lost by the donor of the gift inter vivos or irrevocable trust provided he is not a life beneficiary under the transfer. Other will substitutes generally leave some measure of control with the creator. Tax laws influence the decision to use a will substitute. If tax savings can be effected, the will substitute is frequently employed. For example, an irrevocable transfer in the lifetime of the decedent will not be subject to state and inheritance taxation, although if gratuitous it may incur a gift tax at a lower rate than taxes applicable to transfers at death.

Estate planning involves a balancing of many interests. It is the purpose of this section to describe the most common forms of will substitutes and their rationales rather than to focus on complex estate-planning problems. All are conceptually distinguishable from the will because the transferee receives his interest in the lifetime rather than at the death of the transferor. He may not necessarily ever possess and enjoy such interest, however.

Gifts

The most widely used will substitute is the gift. In fact, the donor may not realize that his subjective intent may be to distribute, ahead of death, a portion of his wealth. The law has categorized two types of gifts: the *gift inter vivos* and the *gift causa mortis*. The former is the ordinary gift between living persons and is immediate and unconditional when made. The latter is made in contemplation of death.

Both types of gifts involve a vesting of title in the donee during the lifetime of the donor, with the property being extracted from the estate for probate and

20. The Ohio mortmain act in effect at the time the project data were gathered was time oriented only. It is found in Appendix A and may be compared with the liberalized version in effect today.

21. An excellent article on the will substitutes is "Estate Planning—Avoidance of Probate," by Professor A. James Casner of the Harvard Law School, in *Columbia Law Review* 60 (1960): 108.

settlement purposes. Gifts inter vivos result in relinquishment by the donor of all dominion and control. It is an unconditional gift made during the lifetime of the donor. On the other hand, the gift causa mortis is a transfer subject to specific subsequent conditions. The transfer does not take final and irrevocable effect until the donor's death. The donor may expressly revoke it until then. The gift is revoked automatically if the donor fails to die of the anticipated peril or if the donor outlives the donee. Gifts causa mortis are limited to personal property; whereas the unconditional gift may be of personal or real property. The necessary elements for the creation of a gift are threefold: intent, delivery, and acceptance. A number of problems may arise concerning the existence of these elements where the question is whether a gift was made or the property is part of the decedent's estate.

The gift causa mortis is less used and is a somewhat marginal nontestamentary transfer. Its key feature is revocability, which primarily distinguishes it from gifts inter vivos. Gifts causa mortis resemble wills in that a measure of control is held by the donor because he reserves the power to revoke. Although the gift causa mortis theoretically is not considered as part of the estate at death, it will be subject to the claims of the decedent's creditors where the estate is insolvent without any showing of fraudulent intent on the part of the donor. Generally, it is taxed as estate property and might be subject to the claims of the surviving spouse where there is an election to take against the will. Gifts made by a person contemplating death are presumed to be causa mortis. However, if it can be shown that the donor's intent was to make an immediate gift without any conditions attached, this presumption is rebutted and the gift is unconditional and inter vivos.

The principle of testamentary freedom can be considered part of the principle of gift because a transfer at death that is gratuitous is a "gift." The principle of reciprocity is involved in both situations if both gifts received during the lifetime or by testate succession represent sequential reciprocity, one generation receiving and the other giving in payment for current or anticipated services.

Trusts

Not all will substitutes are gifts of outright interests. The donor may prefer not to convey outright ownership to his transferee or transferees, and his aims might then be better accomplished by a *trust*.

Professor George Bogert, a leading authority on the law of trusts, defines a trust as "a fiduciary relationship in which one person is the holder of the title to property, subject to an equitable obligation to keep or use the property for the benefit of another."[22] The titleholder is called the *trustee*, and the person receiving the benefit is called the *beneficiary*. The creator of the trust, usually

22. George C. Bogert, *Trusts*, 4th ed. (St. Paul, Minn.: West Publishing Co., 1963), p. 1.

called the *settlor,* may himself become the trustee. But frequently the trustee is a third party; in the majority of cases, a bank. There may also be cotrustees.

The trust usually involves a separation of legal and equitable title, the latter being the beneficial interest. The trustee gets whatever title the settlor had, normally legal title. He holds this bare title and actively manages the property for the beneficiaries, generally distributing the revenue produced according to the terms of the trust. The trust is a means of providing for ownership over generational time, with present interests in some beneficiaries and remainder interests in others. Gifts inter vivos could also split legal ownership into present and future interests, but such a division is uncommon, although normal in the area of trusts. Trusts may be created by will as well as by declaration during a person's lifetime. If created inter vivos, there is no certain form required, although express trusts of real property usually necessitate a written instrument.

The *irrevocable* trust is one type of trust used in estate planning. Here the settlor relinquishes control over his property except to the extent of acting in a fiduciary capacity toward the beneficiaries if he has made himself trustee. Even if the creator reserves to himself a life interest, he cannot any longer control the passing of his property at death if valid remainders have been created in third persons. In the usual case, the irrevocable trust represents an inter vivos transfer of both present and future interests. The settlor of an irrevocable trust has relinquished the power to revoke; he no longer can change his mind; his gift through use of a trust is final.

The irrevocable trust is primarily a tax-saving device, used by persons of substantial means. The legal gift may involve equity of any value, but the trust is not practical where available assets are limited. In summary, the irrevocable trust can be used by a wealthy person to pass property inter vivos, rather than by will, to designated beneficiaries at a tax saving with respect to income and estate taxation. The irrevocable trust is inflexible.

The *revocable* inter vivos trust is perhaps the most flexible estate-planning device. Here the settlor, who is not the trustee, can retain the right to all income for life together with the right to alter, amend, or revoke the trust. He can terminate the trust at any time and take back the property. He can also change the beneficiaries who have the remainder interests. At his death, the corpus or subject matter of the revocable inter vivos trust is not part of the probate estate. It does not pass by testate or intestate succession. Property could be added to it (or to the irrevocable trust) by will, and this property will afterward be distributed according to the terms of the trust. Property so received by will is the result of testate succession.

There is a fine distinction between a will and a revocable trust in reference to individuals with remainder interests. Theoretically, a present interest is created in all beneficiaries, with no interests being created at death. The remainder interest may very likely not be subject to the right of the settlor's surviving spouse to an elective share of the deceased's estate, even if the intent to defraud is present.

In some states, the corpus of the revocable inter vivos trust is treated as part of the estate for election purposes, by virtue of legislation. There may be no real difference in objectives between a declaration of a revocable trust and the execution of a will insofar as control is concerned. The differences are in the structure and implementation of succession intentions. With the trust, present rights vest, and the trustee is under a fiduciary obligation. The power to revoke, when exercised, divests an interest created during the settlor's lifetime. In a similar manner, a will can be revoked. The major difference between a revocable trust and a will is that a will creates an interest at death and is ineffective until then; whereas a trust gives rise to an interest effective before death.

The revocable trust is an estate-planning device most often used by individuals whose estates will exceed $100,000 in value after death. With expected additions to the estate allowed by will, there is no necessity that the trust be funded initially with excessive property. In fact, the corpus of the revocable inter vivos trust may in many cases be only an insurance policy. Unless there is a special reason for a trust, such as maintenance of an incompetent, an outright transfer of property, whether in part by gift before death or all at death, is more feasible for the man of average means.

The *tentative, savings bank,* or *Totten,* trust is a very limited trust. The name Totten comes from the case that gave recognition to this will substitute.[23] The tentative trust is difficult to justify by legal theory, but it is an extremely practical device. It is known as the "poor man's will," since it can be used by an average person and is effective in avoiding probate and administration. It comes into being when a savings account in a bank or loan association is opened by *A* in the form "*A*, in trust for *B*." Where such language is used without further qualification, *A*'s intent is ambiguous. He may have intended an irrevocable trust or no trust. It cannot be considered an ordinary revocable trust because such a trust requires an expressed power of revocation, and in this case none is so stated. Many states hold that the tentative trust is created. An implied power of revocation is deemed to be present: the trust is subject to withdrawals by the depositor (*A*) and can be completely dissipated. Any amount in the account at death belongs to *B*.

Theoretically, what has been created is a present trust. *A* is the settlor and also the trustee. *B* is the beneficiary. The bank is only a debtor owing the amount on deposit, with the technical trust corpus being the claim against the bank for the sum deposited. While the beneficiary gets only what is left in the account on the depositor's death, this property is not considered to pass at

23. In re Totten, 179 N.Y. 112, 71 N.E. 748 (1904).

death. This savings bank trust is easily terminated by withdrawal, by change in the account title, or by an intent to revoke that is properly manifested. There are no management duties on the part of the trustee, who is able to treat the account money as his own until death.

Although all states recognize gifts and irrevocable and revocable trusts, there is a considerable split of authority about the validity of the Totten trust. The general view is that it is not testamentary, but some states say that the beneficiary would receive his interest at death; that is, that the transfer fails and the property becomes part of the decedent's estate. Even in the states where it is recognized as a will substitute, the account money will be considered as estate property for taxation purposes and for creditors' claims in the same manner as the gift causa mortis. It may be treated in the same manner as the normal revocable trust in cases where the surviving spouse is electing to take against the will. If it is so treated, it would not be subject to such an election in the usual case because it is an inter vivos transfer.

Yet there is the matter of public policy. The spouse's right of election has priority over statutes governing execution of wills. Although the will is valid, the spouse is entitled to a forced share if dissatisfied. Should the flimsy poor man's will prevail over the rights of the surviving spouse where the formal will may not? Although this device may pass property as a limited exception to succession at death, should its validity be carried to extremes? There is no general agreement among the states regarding these questions.

Until 1963, Ohio was not sure whether the tentative trust was valid. In that year, a case decided that Ohio did not recognize this will substitute.[24] Property that was passing at death could only be given to a designated individual by a will. The real intent of the depositor was considered testamentary. The judicial law was changed by the Legislature, and the tentative trust became a sanctioned will substitute (Ohio Revised Code 1107.07). This code section (effective January 1, 1968) reads as follows:

1107.07 Deposits in trust for another

(A) Whenever any deposit is made in a bank by any person stated on the depositor's signature card to be in trust for another, and no further notice of the existence and terms of a legal and valid trust is given in writing to the bank, such deposit or any part thereof, together with the dividends or interest thereon, may, in the event of the death of the trustee, be paid to the person named on the bank's records for whose benefit the deposit was made.

(B) Any deposits on the records of a bank on January 1, 1968, or thereafter made in the form and manner set forth in division (A) of this section, shall constitute an intent on the part of the depositor to create a revocable trust for the benefit of the person for whom the deposit was made. Such deposit shall constitute clear and con-

24. In re estate of Hoffman, 175 Ohio St. 363, 195 N.E. 2d 106 (1963).

vincing evidence that one of the terms of such trust is that upon the death of the trustee the then amount of such deposit shall belong to the persons for whose benefit the deposit was made. No other written instrument shall be required to establish such trust or such term. Upon the death of the trustee, no part of such deposit shall pass and descend to his estate unless such estate is the person's for whose benefit such deposit was made.

Not all problems are necessarily resolved by such a statute. Litigation or amended legislation will most likely be necessary to determine the rights of a surviving spouse in tentative trust property in Ohio.

Life Insurance

A very widely used will substitute is *life insurance.* With insurance, a man of modest means can provide protection for his family; and if the policy is made payable to a designated beneficiary or beneficiaries, it will avoid estate administration.

Life insurance is a contractual arrangement. The insured pays premiums, and the insurance company contracts to pay a stated amount to the beneficiary at the death of the insured. The beneficiary is generally a donee or gratuitous taker. Rights of this donee are vested at the time the insurance contract takes effect. The beneficiary gets a present right to collect the proceeds of the policy upon the death of the insured. Thus life insurance constitutes an inter vivos transfer with only one difference: enjoyment of the proceeds is postponed until the insured's death.

Life insurance is a most satisfactory will substitute. The insured has the ability to keep secret both the value of the policy and the beneficiaries. The beneficiaries may be changed whenever the insured so desires. He can cash in the policy or borrow on it. Creditors cannot reach the proceeds upon the insured's death without proof of fraud, and life insurance can have certain tax advantages.

While the proceeds may be paid in a lump sum to the beneficiary or paid in installments under a contract option, insurance is frequently the subject matter of a trust. The beneficiary of the policy is named as the trustee of such an insurance trust. The trustee receives the legal right to collect the value of the policy upon the death of the insured. The trustee will manage these proceeds for the designated trust beneficiaries. The insured can still retain control over the policy to the same extent he could if no trust were created. This trust may be made revocable and amendable. If the only corpus of the revocable trust is the life insurance, there will be no costs of trust administration during the insured's life because the trustee will have no duties until the proceeds are collected.

Sizable estates may be created by the average person through the use of insurance. Life insurance and a trust may together be the best estate-planning device for such an individual, since flexibility and control are present until death.

Joint Ownership

Another frequently used will substitute is generally called *joint ownership of property with right of survivorship.* A person can avoid passing by means of a will property owned in some form of joint ownership with a right of survivorship. Such jointly owned property may be real estate or some form of personal property such as bank accounts, stocks, or bonds. This survivorship feature is permitted in almost every state and applies to both real and personal property. The technical methods of creating joint and survivorship property may, however, differ.

The English common law recognized a variety of concurrent interests in two or more persons. The will substitutes involve the concurrent ownership devices called *cotenancies,* situations where two or more persons simultaneously have equal rights in the possession of real or personal property. Today joint ownership with the right of survivorship is not favored by the law, although it is legally permissible. Transfers to two or more persons will be considered to give rise to the cotenancy known as tenancy in common unless the intent to create joint ownership is shown to be present.

A *tenancy in common* is co-ownership of real or personal property where each cotenant has a separate interest in the property. The tenant's ownership interest is a fractional part of the undivided whole, and all cotenants do not have to have equal fractional interests. Assume a tenancy in common with two cotenants, *A* and *B*. Each may own a one-half interest; but depending on the terms of its creation, *A*'s interest may be one-third and *B*'s two-thirds, or one-tenth and nine-tenths, respectively. The most important aspect of the tenancy in common is that there is no right of survivorship. Upon *A*'s death, his one-half, one-third, or one-tenth will not belong to *B* by joint ownership. *A*'s ownership interest will be in his estate at death to pass by will or intestacy. The tenancy in common may be the most widely found type of contenancy, but it most certainly is not a will substitute. It is not joint ownership with right of survivorship.

Joint tenancy was another type of cotenancy under common law. The technical joint tenancy or a modified version is recognized in the United States. A *joint tenancy* is a form of co-ownership in real or personal property where two or more persons own one interest together, each owner having exactly the same rights in that interest as his cotenant or cotenants. An inherent attribute of the joint tenancy is the right of survivorship. Upon the death of a joint tenant, the remaining tenant or tenants retain ownership. The joint tenant owns no interest that will pass as part of his estate. However during his lifetime, there

FERNALD LIBRARY
COLBY-SAWYER COLLEGE
NEW LONDON, N.H. 03257

is no restriction on the alienation of his interest as a joint tenant. If a joint tenant transfers his interest, the joint tenancy is severed and a tenancy in common is created. If there are two joint tenants, *A* and *B*, and *A* conveys his title to a third party *X*, *B* and *X* become tenants in common, each having a one-half fractional ownership interest. If there were three joint tenants, *A*, *B*, and *C*, with *A* transferring to *X*, the latter would hold a one-third interest as a tenant in common with *B* and *C*, who would hold the remaining two-thirds as joint tenants.

Ohio does not recognize the common-law joint tenancy despite the fact that there is no statute in the state abolishing it. It is possible to create a joint tenancy with right of survivorship, however, that is analogous to the common-law interest. The important point is that the survivorship provision must be stated. If the mere expression "joint tenancy" were used in Ohio, without an expressed provision for right of survivorship, a tenancy in common would be created; whereas in most states, a transfer to "*A* and *B* as joint tenants" would give rise to the joint tenancy. Some states take an approach similar to Ohio's. Joint and other bank accounts with right of survivorship are expressly authorized by the Ohio Code, as are "payable on death" accounts.[25] Neither is subject to probate court jurisdiction.

Tenancy by the entirety is the third cotenancy. This estate is much like the joint tenancy but can exist only between husband and wife. More than two-thirds of the states no longer recognize the tenancy by the entirety.[26] It developed in a period when the married woman had disabilities with respect to property ownership. Ohio does not recognize the tenancy by the entirety. In Ohio, a conveyance to husband and wife would vest in them as tenants in common. If survivorship were expressed, there would be joint ownership with a right of survivorship. In both the joint tenancy and the tenancy by the entirety, the death of one tenant theoretically passes no interest to another tenant. Rather, the deceased tenant's ownership rights simply cease to exist. The basic difference between the joint tenancy and the tenancy by the entirety is that the latter cannot be terminated by husband or wife transferring an ownership interest. Both together however may convey to a third person. They also may change the tenancy by the entirety into a joint tenancy or tenancy in common with little difficulty.

25. Ohio Revised Code 1107.08 (effective January 1, 1968) reads as follows:

(A) When a deposit is made in the name of two or more persons, payable to either, or the survivor, such deposit or any part thereof, or any interest thereon, may be paid to either of said persons, or the guardian of his estate, whether the other is living or not, and the receipt or acquittance of the person paid is a sufficient release and discharge of the bank for any payments so made.

(B) A bank may enter into a written contract with a natural person whereby the proceeds of such person's deposit may be made payable on his death to another natural person in accordance with the terms, restrictions, and limitations set forth in sections 2131.10 and 2131.11 of the Revised Code.

26. See Atkinson, op. cit., p. 165.

Joint ownership with right of survivorship is a frequently used will substitute. It avoids problems that might arise with respect to probate and estate administration. However, it is to be noted that joint ownership may also become a tax trap for the unwary because tax legislation, in general, treats all such property as presumptively belonging to the first owner to die. The burden is on the survivor to prove the extent of his contribution, which if shown is not taxed as part of the deceased's property.[27]

Conclusion

The purpose of this chapter was to describe both the law of intestate and testate succession and the most frequently used will substitutes. Since this study was undertaken in Ohio, Ohio law has been expounded in relation to succession at death and accepted will substitutes. The way in which an Ohio decedent's property passes through probate court is similar to the procedure followed in other jurisdictions. The various will substitutes are basically the same as those found in other states. These will substitutes are more important today than in the past as estate-planning devices because of the multivarious form and size of transferable assets. Ohio can be considered a representative jurisdiction. Although the data for this project came from a probate court in Ohio, a probate court in almost any state could have been the starting point for a similar study.

27. In Ohio, if the joint and survivorship property is held by husband and wife, one-half of the property is taxable in the first decedent's estate regardless of contributions. See Ohio Revised Code 5731.10. Such a law is a boon where the decedent was the contributor but a disaster where the survivor was the contributor.

Chapter 3

Perspectives and Design of Inheritance Study

THE CUYAHOGA COUNTY study was based on a sample of probate court cases closed in 1965. Cuyahoga County, which encompasses the city of Cleveland, is a metropolitan area of 456 square miles, with a population of approximately two million people. It consists of sixty-one townships, villages, and cities, of which Cleveland is the largest, with over 850,000 people. The area is highly urbanized and has diversified industrial, commercial, and business activities. It is the eleventh largest metropolitan area in the United States. Over 97 per cent of its residents live in cities and their suburbs, a pattern that is typical of most metropolitan areas.

When interviewed, most residents of metropolitan areas report that they live in a "typical" modern industrial community. It remains for the urban sociologist and ecologist to determine the validity of this perception. The authors share the feeling of the urban residents interviewed for this study that modern cities resemble one another more than they differ. Each has a social-class system; a diversified economy consisting of multiple and varied industrial, commercial, and business enterprises; occupational specialization; and an array of welfare, recreational, religious, political, social-control, and other social systems that perform specific functions. Most important is the fact that interdependence rather than independence of institutional systems is requisite for the maintenance of the social order in a metropolitan area.

The court is an integral arm of the social-control system in any community, and its objective is largely to maintain order through the process of conflict resolution. It handles all forms of behavior deemed deviant by those in control of the society and generally implements existing laws and statutes concerned with the maintenance of social order and social systems. The probate court is one unit of a highly complex regulatory system charged with the duty of overseeing the distribution of an individual's worldly possessions at death according to established practices buttressed by legal statutes and cultural values. The diversity and complexity of institutional systems in any community and the varied socioeconomic status of its members suggest that any probate court system covering a metropolitan jurisdiction handles estates which are small, moderate, or large in size and which vary extensively in the pattern of property distribution.

According to this theoretical position, inheritance outcomes in metropolitan areas should be somewhat similar even though there are variations in time when the data are collected, in methods of collection, in sample size, and in research design. The contention of this study is that patterns of behavior, in this instance probate practices in each jurisdiction, emerge which are characteristic of the general pattern found in other jurisdictions. Applying the method of comparative analysis to studies that were not conceptualized with this design in mind has some value. It provides a basis for correlating and testing hypotheses. It will also provide greater confidence in the reliability of the data for this study if the findings prove to be in accordance with the other studies, which were completed in other times and places and for other purposes.

Previous Probate Studies

There are three other major United States studies similar to this investigation utilizing probate records. In 1930, Richard R. Powell and Charles Looker published the results of their study of probate and tax records for New York and Kings County between the years 1914 and 1929.[1] The 1950 study by Edward Ward and J. H. Beuscher covered the years 1929, 1934, 1939, 1941, and 1944 for Dane County, Wisconsin.[2] Allison Dunham's 1962 study of probate proceedings in Cook County, Illinois, is based upon the years 1953 and 1957.[3] The New York and Kings County and the Cook County studies are of metropolitan areas similar to Cleveland, Ohio; whereas the Dane County study encompasses a university town (Madison, Wisconsin) and a rural population in the hinterland.

One primary objective of these studies was to indicate the proportion of resident decedents who left wealth to be distributed through probate court during a given time period. The highest proportion found was 47 per cent in Dane County for the year 1941.[4] Powell and Looker found that in 1929 probate was initiated for 30 per cent of the Kings County decedents.[5] Dunham's corresponding figure for the year 1957 is 15 per cent.[6]

Another aim of the studies was to determine the proportion of testate cases in the total sample of probate estates. For the period from 1914 to 1929, Pow-

1. Richard R. Powell and Charles Looker, "Decedents' Estates," *Columbia Law Review* 30 (November, 1930): 919–953.
2. Edward Ward and J. H. Beuscher, "The Inheritance Process in Wisconsin," *Wisconsin Law Review* (1950): 393–426.
3. Allison Dunham, "The Method, Process and Frequency of Wealth Transmission," *Chicago Law Review* 30 (Winter, 1962): 241–285.
4. Ward and Beuscher, op. cit., p. 397.
5. Powell and Looker, op. cit., p. 923.
6. Dunham, op. cit., p. 243.

ell and Looker found that 40 per cent of all probate cases in Kings County were testate.[7] The corresponding figures for Dane County and Cook County are 47 per cent and 58 per cent, respectively.[8] Will making is practiced more extensively among the more recent decedents.

All three studies determined the size and complexity of the estates. Because Powell and Looker obtained their data from tax reports rather than from individual estate records,[9] only the data derived from the Dane and Cook County studies will be used here in making comparisons of size and composition of estates. In Dane County, the mean net worth at the time of death was found to be $11,527.[10] Wills were more frequently found in the larger estates.[11] There were considerable variations among occupational groups in regard to both the size and the composition of the estate. The estates of farmers were primarily composed of real estate, personal property, and cash and bank deposits; whereas professionals and proprietors had relatively more of their assets in stocks, bonds, and insurance. Changes in the composition of the estate were also associated with changes in the size of the estate.[12] In Cook County, the mean testate estate was $41,885, and the mean intestate estate was $7,920.[13] The intestate estates were not only smaller than the testate estates were, but they were also more often composed of a single type of asset, such as a house.[14]

A fourth aim of the Dane and Cook County studies was to describe the patterns of distribution chosen by testators. The most significant deviation from the pattern of intestate distribution was the bequest or devise of the entire estate to the surviving spouse.[15] The final aim of all three studies was to provide information on the time and costs of estate administration.

The authors of these studies believed that probate material was a rich source of data for understanding probate practice and that it might provide information for determining whether the education of lawyers in this area of practice was adequate or whether reform of the probate process was required. These beliefs are shared by the authors of the present study. A number of studies using probate material of assorted populations and disparate samples and with varied objectives have provided interesting findings on will making, patterns of testacy, and distribution of estates. S. H. Britt, using nineteenth-century probate material, and with occupation as an independent variable, hypothesized that testamentary provisions would differ among occupational groups.

7. Powell and Looker, loc. cit.
8. Ward and Beuscher, op. cit., p. 412; Dunham, op. cit., p. 244.
9. Powell and Looker, op. cit., pp. 943–953.
10. Ward and Beuscher, op. cit., p. 401.
11. Ibid., p. 412.
12. Ibid., pp. 407–411.
13. Dunham, op. cit., p. 264.
14. Ibid., p. 266.
15. Ward and Beuscher, op. cit., p. 413; Dunham, op. cit., p. 256.

He was, however, not able to discern occupational differences among the group of testators. For nearly all decedents, the predominant pattern was to leave the entire estate to the immediate family or other relatives, thus preserving the family as a significant social unit.[16]

Time is the major variable employed in Lawrence Friedman's study of Essex County, New Jersey, based upon wills drawn in 1850, 1875, and 1900. The trends by 1900 were: (1) an increase in female testators, (2) a decrease in deathbed wills, and (3) an increased share to the surviving spouse and a decreasing proportion of life estates.[17]

Economists have used probate material to study the accumulation and transfer of wealth. Two English studies, one by Josiah Wedgwood and the other by O. D. Harbury, are in this tradition. Wedgwood chose 99 estates with a gross value of over £200,000 probated in 1924–1925 and 140 estates with a gross value between £10,000 and £20,000 recorded in January–February of 1926.[18] Harbury chose all those with estates over £100,000 in 1956–1957 and a random sample of estates between £50,000 and £100,000 during the same two years.[19] Both these economists demonstrated the function of inheritance in building large fortunes. For both generations, men leaving large estates had fathers who, similarly, had left large estates.

Probate documents are a new source of data for sociologists, and to date, they have been utilized primarily in studies by lawyers and economists. Sociological studies on intergenerational transfers of goods and services have been of inter vivos transactions.[20] The reason for this is the reluctance of some sociologists to utilize data that have originally been collected for nonresearch purposes. However, probate material has one advantage that even fresh empirical data may lack, and that is relative accuracy. The transfer of property on death is of considerable interest to the state and beneficiaries. The public interest is served by collecting inheritance and estate taxes, by displaying in

16. Steuart Henderson Britt, "The Significance of the Last Will and Testament," *Journal of Social Psychology* 8 (August, 1937): 347–353. Britt's group was made up of New Yorkers who had "news obituaries" during the period 1880–1885. He compared 16 manufacturers with 14 physicians and 19 in other occupations.

17. Lawrence Friedman, "Patterns of Testation in the 19th Century: A Study of Essex County (New Jersey) Wills," *American Journal of Legal History* 8 (1964): 34–53.

18. Josiah Wedgwood, *The Economics of Inheritance* (London: George Routledge and Sons, Ltd., 1929).

19. O. D. Harbury, "Inheritance and the Distribution of Personal Wealth in Britain," *Economic Journal* 72 (1962): 845–868.

20. Marvin B. Sussman and Lee Burchinal, "Parental Aid to Married Children: Implications for Family Functioning," *Marriage and Family Living* 24 (1962): 320–332; Harry Sharp and Morris Axelrod, "Mutual Aid Among Relatives in an Urban Population," *Principles of Sociology,* ed. Ronald Freedman et al. (New York: Holt, Rinehart & Winston, Inc., 1956), pp. 433–439; Juanita M. Kreps, "The Economics of Intergenerational Relationships," *Social Structure and the Family,* ed. Ethel Shanas and Gordon E. Streib (Englewood Cliffs, N.J.: Prentice-Hall, Inc., 1965), pp. 267–288.

public records the rights of the new owners, and by keeping breaches of the peace to a minimum through orderly distribution of the estate among beneficiaries and payment of the claims of the creditors.[21]

Although the cited studies have been predominantly exploratory and descriptive, they do show that probate records can be utilized to illuminate certain basic problems: economic and legal change, the relationship of social characteristics of the decedent to capital accumulation and testamentary disposition, and the effect of inheritance upon the capital accumulation of succeeding generations. The limitations of probate records as a basis for studying the transmission of wealth at death are that they tell nothing about capital accumulated by people whose estates are not processed in court and that they disclose little about transfers of capital accumulations made before death.[22] Also, probate records omit such relevant information as the age, occupation, and education of the decedent and his beneficiaries, demographic and social characteristics that are important to the scientist who is using a sociological perspective in studying inheritance.

Theoretical Perspectives

The primary choices an individual has in regard to disposition of his property at death are whether he makes a will or allows his property to be disposed of according to the laws of intestacy. Antecedent to a consideration of patterns of testacy and their effect upon the family is an understanding of the questions, "What proportion of the population make wills?" and "Among which social groups is will making more prevalent?"

No prediction will be made of the proportion of the population that would be testate. Previous studies provide no clue other than indicating extreme variability over time and among different jurisdictions. Better understanding of the factors predisposing individuals toward testacy may eventually contribute to an explanation of variability over time and among jurisdictions.

The common belief is that a will permits the testator the freedom to give his property to whomever he chooses and to use a variety of means in doing so. In fact, the testator does not have unlimited freedom. For instance, in most states the spouse has an indefeasible share. Through a will one may alter the prescribed distribution among next of kin or choose beneficiaries other than kin, that is, friends, employees, and charities. The testator may avoid outright distribution of property and may also make certain stipulations regarding the use and sale of property. He may choose his own executor, rather than allow the court to appoint an administrator. Appointment of guardianship for minor children may also be accomplished in the will. Especially in earlier times, the

21. Ward and Beuscher, op. cit., pp. 394–395.

22. Ibid., p. 395. There are many extralegal devices that can be utilized to avoid the probate process. The basic will substitutes are discussed in Chapter 2.

last will and testament was also the place where the decedent registered his sentiments toward the members of his family.[23] A will gives the decedent the possibility of some mastery and control over his heirs and legatees after death.[24]

In the Middle Ages, intestacy was sinful and understood only in terms of negligence or sudden death.[25] Today, intestacy is still considered by some to be a sign of negligence. According to the following notion, a will can indicate the characteristics of the testator: "It is of the nature of action that a like agent should produce a like action, since everything acts according as it is in act."[26]

A will is a statement of intention and expectation. It does not take effect until after death. In earlier years, deathbed wills were frequent.[27] Despite the human capacity for denial, there is a recognition of the inevitability of death. Since the probability of death increases with age, the recognition of death also should increase with age, and that recognition of death should prove to be an impetus to testation.

"It [the will] is of utmost importance in providing for the security and well-being of family members."[28] The preceding statement is based on the assump-

23. Two books with many examples of curious wills and sometimes vitriolic sentiments are: Virgil Harris, *Ancient, Curious and Famous Wills* (Boston: Little Brown and Company, 1911); and Robert S. Menshin, *The Last Caprice* (New York: Simon & Schuster, Inc., 1963). A testator must be circumspect, however. It has been pointed out that, "The probate of defamatory wills has presented a good many problems. Since the executor is under a duty to probate the will, any defamation can scarcely be charged him; and since the publication has occurred after the death of the testator, there are logical difficulties in the way of holding his estate, including the generally accepted rule that liability for defamation dies with the defamer. For such reasons two American decisions have refused to find any liability at all. Four others have held the estate liable, more or less frankly recognizing that the recovery, whether or not it fits very well into common law principles is necessary as a matter of policy for the protection of those who would otherwise be helpless against the malice of the dead. One possible solution may be for the probate court to strike the defamatory matter from the copy of the will admitted to probate." William L. Prosser, *Torts,* 3d ed. (St. Paul, Minn.: West Publishing Co., 1964), pp. 789–790.

24. For a discussion of the inheritance as means of intergenerational control, see Max Rheinstein, "Motivation of Intergenerational Behavior by Norms of Law," *Social Structure and the Family,* ed. Ethel Shanas and Gordon E. Streib (Englewood Cliffs, N.J.: Prentice-Hall, Inc., 1965), pp. 257–266.

25. Thomas Robinson, *Gavelkind* (London: Henry Battleworth, 1822), p. 25. "Whether a man has died intestate through negligence or through sudden death, the lord nevertheless may not take for himself any of the man's goods (except what is legally owed to him under the title of heriot); he must rather distribute them fairly and justly, according to his judgment, to the wife, children and relatives of the deceased" (translated from the Latin by Robert McMillan, S.J.). It is noteworthy that the intestate's family is not to suffer by his sin or negligence.

26. Aquinas as quoted in Kenneth Burke, *A Grammar of Motives* (Englewood Cliffs, N.J.: Prentice-Hall, Inc., 1945), p. 227.

27. Friedman, op. cit., p. 37.

28. "The Importance of a Will," *Taxes & Estates,* June, 1965, a monthly bulletin published by the Cleveland Trust Company. It is assumed that this bulletin is representative of trust company advertising.

tion that responsibility for others is a motivation for testacy. On the other hand, Le Play argued that testation is associated with free choice and that where the owner cannot freely dispose of at least half his property, the practice of making a will disappears.[29] Except in a few jurisdictions, testamentary freedom is restricted for the married. In Ohio, the surviving spouse can elect against the will and receive from one-third to one-half of the net estate.[30] Previous studies have, however, shown a strong tendency for married testators to leave their entire estates to their spouses. Thus, the married may find their motive for testacy in the smaller share given the spouse under the intestate distribution.

The inheritance laws do differ somewhat in their treatment of the sexes. The female surviving spouse is entitled to a year's allowance, and the male surviving spouse is not. But otherwise, the sexes are treated equally.[31] However, other laws, values, and moral sentiments hold the man and not the woman responsible for the support of the family, and as a consequence males may feel less free to diverge from standards of family responsibility.

For both male and female, it would appear that the type of surviving kin is an important variable. One is more free to choose one's beneficiaries if the nearest surviving kin are cousins than if they are children because one has feelings of greater responsibility toward surviving children than toward surviving cousins.

The size of the kin group may be an important factor in testation. With a large number of next of kin, the inheritance received by any one individual beneficiary would be so small that it would be nearly meaningless. Prevention of this fragmentation may be a motive in testation. Also, the person with many next of kin has alternative beneficiaries available to him without going beyond the kin group, and he may wish to choose among them.

The position of this study is that testacy is associated with the individual's location in the family network. Marital status, sex, type of kin, and size of the kin group are taken as indicators of location in the family network.

A will is "the written instrument, legally executed, by which a man makes disposition of his estate, to take effect after his death."[32] This dictionary definition is accurate in most instances. Although wills usually dispose of property, they do not necessarily have to do this. A will might also assign an executor (if the testator was satisfied with the scheme of distribution under intestate succession), appoint a guardian for the will-maker's children, or revoke a prior will. The concern of this study is with what most people do in the will-making area; therefore, the will is here considered as an instrument largely for the

29. Mentioned in H. J. Habukkuk, "Family Structure and Economic Change in 19th Century Europe," *Journal of Economic History* 15 (1955):1.

30. Ohio Revised Code 2107.39.

31. Ohio Revised Code 2117.20.

32. *The American College Dictionary* (New York: Random House, Inc., 1956).

disposition of property. If there is no property, testacy is virtually meaningless; testacy should increase as the estate increases in size.[33]

Persons who are better educated or employed in the more prestigious occupations are familiar with legal documents and with the people who prepare them. Individuals of high social status are more apt to be sophisticated in matters of law and to understand the advantages of testacy than persons of low social status are. High social status has been shown to be related to an orientation toward the future; and through a will, it is possible to some extent to master the future.[34] Testacy, therefore, is hypothesized to be positively associated with social status.

The Cook County and Dane County studies covered the patterns of distribution chosen by testators. Both studies found that the single deviation from the intestate succession favored by the largest number of testators was the bequest of the entire estate to the spouse in circumstances where the intestate rule specifies division.[35] A probable reason for this practice is the expectation that eventually the remaining assets will be distributed to the couple's issue. It remains to be established if this deviation is a constant regardless of the size of the estate. The pattern may be more prevalent in the case of small estates, where economic maintenance of the survivor is absolutely necessary.[36]

One deviation that occurs in a relatively few cases is the willing of property to unrelated individuals or to institutions. Charitable donations during life are probably more frequent among the wealthy. The willing of property to someone other than family members who are in financial straits is generally frowned on. Either the estate must be large enough to take care of family obligations, or there must be no outstanding debts. It is inferred that the absence of responsibility coincides with the absence of immediate family.

In this study, property disposition is examined from a legal view as well as

33. Ward and Beuscher, op. cit., p. 412. Few surveys of will making among living persons have been conducted. A public opinion poll for the State Bar of California showed a definite relationship between social class and testation: 7 per cent of lower-class, 14 per cent of lower-middle-class, 25 per cent of upper-middle-class, and 46 per cent of upper-class persons were testate (cited by Jerome E. Carlin and Jan Howard, "Legal Representation and Class Justice," *UCLA Law Review* 12 [January, 1965]:387). The date of the survey, the sample size, and the definition of social class are not given. Most definitions of social class are based either upon economic status or upon indicators that correlate highly with economic status.

34. Cf. Lloyd Warner et al., *Social Class in America* (Chicago: Science Research Associates, Inc., 1949).

35. Dunham, op. cit., p. 256; Ward and Beuscher, op. cit., p. 413.

36. If the estate is large enough to be subject to federal estate taxation, conservation of the estate may dictate the disposition. The estate planner will utilize the marital deduction trust in many instances, since outright gifts to the spouse could impose double taxation upon the death of the recipient. Still it can be noted that the spouse is the primary beneficiary. Under the marital deduction trust, she would have a general testamentary power of appointment over the qualifying property. In essence, but for the tax problem, all might well be bequeathed outright to the surviving spouse.

from a sociological one. The study explores the patterns of distribution where wills are involved in comparison with the taking of the estate under intestate succession. The correlation between these two patterns of property disposition is one measure of the viability of the statute of intestate succession. Property disposition is an outcome of a complex process. Increased understanding of this process comes from analysis of structural variables and situational factors: the social characteristics of the testators and their surviving kin (the indicators mentioned earlier, that is, position in family network, marital status, sex, type of kin, and size of family).

The influence of the inheritance upon the family and upon individual family members is largely unknown. Social revolutionaries who wished to abolish inheritance possibly exaggerated the effect of inheritance upon the lives of the inheritors and the injustice perpetrated upon those who were not the recipients of inherited wealth.[37] On the other hand, some present-day sociologists are inclined to dismiss the subject of inheritance as one that applies only to a small minority of persons who receive an inheritance too late in life for it to alter their life styles significantly.[38] The authors of this study are inclined to be more sanguine and less quick to give short shrift to the importance of inheritance. In this study, the effect of inheritance upon social mobility and economic security is examined, along with the satisfaction expressed by survivors under the various forms of property disposition and the meaning of inheritance to family members. Presumably the importance of inheritance in altering the life-ways of an individual will vary according to the amount of property received in relation to resources in hand and in relation to his age. The meaning of inheritance to the receiver is associated with his position in the family network. Sufficient empirical data have been obtained to permit the post hoc formulation of hypotheses concerning the relationship of property disposition to family structure and behavior.

The economic characteristics of decedents' estates (including both assets and deductions) and contingency provisions, guardianships, conditional bequests, life estates, and trusts are also studied. The frequency with which these characteristics occur and the interrelatedness of legal and economic conditions are described.

Study Design

The examination of these issues and theoretical questions required an empirical study of a large sample of closed estates (Ohio statutes insure that all

37. Harlan Eugene Read, *The Abolition of Inheritance* (New York: The Macmillan Company, 1918). This book is representative of the genre. The third measure of the Communist *Manifesto* is "abolition of all rights of inheritance." Karl Marx and Friedrich Engels, *Manifesto of the Communist Party* (New York: International Publishers Co., Inc., 1948), p. 30.

38. Wilbert E. Moore, *Man, Time, and Society* (New York: John Wiley & Sons, Inc., 1963), pp. 80–81.

probated estates are closed) randomly selected over a prescribed time period and from a metropolitan jurisdiction. Therefore, two research procedures were employed in obtaining the data for this study. First, a 5 per cent random sample was taken of all estates closed in Cuyahoga County Probate Court between November 9, 1964, and August 8, 1965. There were 659 decedent estates in the sample. Then survivors of these decedents were interviewed during the period from February 1, 1965, to May 31, 1966. The survivor population was defined as all persons 21 years of age and over who were: (1) eligible to inherit from the decedent under the Ohio Statute of Descent and Distribution, whether or not they actually inherited, (2) legatees and devisees, and (3) those named as contingent beneficiaries. The sample of 659 decedents yielded a survivor population of 2,239, giving an average of 3.4 potential interviewees per case.

Public Records

The basic source of information was the probate docket, which provided date of death, decedent's sex and marital status, listed next of kin and beneficiaries, and their relationship to the decedent, amount of inheritance, and residence. The amount and type of property in the estate are given, as are the debts of the deceased and the costs of administration.

The probate records do not give the decedent's age, occupation, or birthplace. Ordinarily this information was obtained during the interview. If for any reason no interview was conducted, the death certificate was used to obtain this information.

Survivor Interviews

The probate record or the death certificate lacked all the information required in order to test the hypotheses of this study or to describe the probate process and its implications for family members. The educational status achieved by decedents is unobtainable on either of these two records. All property transfers at the time of death do not appear in probate; insurance to named beneficiaries is omitted; joint and survivorship deeds for real property are not probated. Although there is legislation that is intended to prevent the contents of safe-deposit boxes and joint bank accounts from being emptied by survivors, the enforcement of this statute is haphazard.[39] Gifts made in contemplation of death may alter patterns of distribution; for example, a "disinherited" relative may actually have been previously favored by a transfer of property. Thus, actual transfers of property at death may be greater than probate and tax records indicate. For these reasons, the interview was chosen as the basic instrument of this study. The interview schedule was designed to obtain

39. Prior to interviewing survivors, bank officials were questioned regarding the emptying of safe-deposit boxes and joint accounts. Their answers indicate they take the matter seriously. Several banks have employees who regularly check obituary notices.

information not reported on probate and other records and as a check on the validity of probate and death certificate data. A word of caution is necessary. Although an interview is conducted, this does not mean automatically that the missing information will be found. Persons who have not revealed assets to their lawyers or to the courts may well not divulge such information to an interviewer.

In conducting interviews with the survivors of decedents, two possible techniques could have been employed: interviewing only the key person in a case or interviewing all persons connected with the case. The latter method was chosen for a number of reasons. First, it was impossible to arrive at a consistent decision about who was the key person to interview. For instance, should it be the principal beneficiary or the executor? Random sampling within cases would not solve the problem because information about a case is not shared equally among survivors. Second, by cross-checking the views of different survivors, it was possible to obtain a measure of reliability. Lastly, because one aim of this study was to examine the effect of inheritance as it extends to family dynamics, obtaining conflicting points of view was important.

The interview, which took approximately an hour and a half, covered the following areas: (1) information and attitudes toward settlement of the decedent's estate, (2) the interviewee's personal relations with the decedent, (3) knowledge concerning the estate, including assets that were not revealed in probate court, (4) the interviewee's use of the inheritance, (5) attitudes toward testamentary freedom, and (6) the interviewee's plans for his own estate. In the last area, the information obtained was similar to that provided by probate records for the decedent, with the exception of the survivor's capital accumulation. The testator's reasons for making a will were also obtained. In general, interviewing provided the opportunity to test the consistency of the study hypotheses concerning testacy from one generation to the next. For instance, if education and age are correlated with will making, one would expect a greater proportion of testators among the better educated and older survivors of the decedents as well as among the sample of decedents.

Demographic characteristics obtained directly from the interviewee were: sex, marital status, age, birthplace, education, present occupation, usual occupation, breadwinner's occupation, income, and religion. An additional measure of social status was a rating of the interviewee's residence on a scale from 1 to 7. This was taken from a picture guide developed especially for the Cleveland area.[40] The residence rating was also obtained for those we were unable to interview.

The survivor population included the wealthy and the poor and persons

40. Marvin B. Sussman, *Rating Scale for Homes in Cuyahoga County* (Cleveland: Western Reserve University [privately published], 1960). See Appendix B for a description of the seven classes of housing.

with graduate or professional education as well as those who were illiterate. The initial population included some persons who were dead or dying and others who turned out to be incompetent. Although most of the survivors were residents of Cuyahoga County, a number of others lived in various places around the world. Table 3-1 indicates the reasons it was not possible to interview all survivors.

TABLE 3–1 REASONS FOR LOSS OF INTERVIEWS

Reasons for Loss	Number of Individuals Lost	Per Cent of Total Population ($N = 2{,}239$)
Deceased	75	3.3
Senile	42	1.9
Language barrier	13	.6
Request	77	3.4
Not located	183	8.2
Questionnaire not returned	212	9.5
Personal refusal	403	18.0
Total	1,005	44.9

The names of the survivors of a decedent are listed at the time probate proceedings are initiated; therefore, it was possible for a survivor or survivors to have died by the time an estate was settled or during the months of the interviewing. There were 75 persons in the sample listed as living on the probate records who had died by the time of case selection. In a few instances, death occurred after the initial contact but before an interview had been arranged.

Forty-two persons were senile or otherwise incompetent and therefore could not be interviewed. Some were in nursing homes or mental institutions. After unsatisfactory experiences conducting interviews in nursing homes, it was decided to exclude such cases from the sample. No attempt was made to interview patients in mental hospitals. Thirteen persons were not able to speak English, and these cases were also lost to the study.

Seventy-seven persons requested that they not be interviewed. A number of interviewees granted interviews only on the condition that a particular member of the family would not be interviewed because the experience might be emotionally upsetting. These requests were honored. The most frequent person to be so protected was the surviving aged spouse, but sons and daughters also appeared in this group. In a few cases we were asked not to interview the contingent beneficiaries because as one respondent reported, "He doesn't know he was mentioned in the will and it would only confuse the issue and might cause trouble."

Sixty-seven survivors resided in foreign countries. Questionnaires were sent to the 23 for whom addresses were available. Five returned the questionnaire.

The fact that the questionnaire was not translated into the particular survivor's native language may account for the poor response. Another reason for the poor return was the respondent's lack of knowledge regarding the estate. One woman wrote from England saying:

> I'm afraid I am unable to complete a good three-fourths of the form and wonder if you would still like me to return same. I have never seen my aunt and only corresponded with her by letter. I know nothing of her habits apart from the fact she was a very devout lady. I was unaware of any money she had and indeed was amazed to hear from a solicitor that I had inherited a third of her estate. As to who the others are I have no idea.

Of the 601 survivors living outside Cuyahoga County but within the United States, 127 returned questionnaires. When a questionnaire was not returned, a second questionnaire was sent. As a result of the first mailing, 94 questionnaires were returned completed; after the second mailing, 38 were returned. Two hundred twelve individuals did not return completed questionnaires.

As a consequence of the poor return from the mailed questionnaire, it was decided that as many respondents as possible would be interviewed among those living outside the Cleveland metropolitan region. The cost made it impossible to interview all nonresident survivors or a sample of them. Interviews were conducted where survivors were concentrated: in such locations as Florida, California, and New York. One hundred sixty interviews were obtained from survivors outside Cuyahoga County. Of this group, 42 had been sent questionnaires and had failed to return them. The response rate was lowest for those survivors residing in foreign countries and for those in Distance Zone 7, which is the area of the western mountain states (see Table 3-2). There were

TABLE 3–2 TYPE OF INSTRUMENT USED AND RESPONSE OF NONRESIDENT SURVIVORS, BY DISTANCE ZONE

Distance Zone[a]	Number of Survivors	Inter-views	Question-naires	Total Response	Response Rate (Per Cent)
2 (nonlocal Ohio)	186	83	33	116	62.4
3 (Indiana, Kentucky, etc.)	157	32	36	68	43.3
4 (Connecticut, Missouri, etc.)	83	10	22	32	38.6
5 (Florida, Minnesota, etc.)	64	18	12	30	46.9
6 (Texas, Wyoming, etc.)	17	3	3	6	35.3
7 (Montana, Arizona, etc.)	9	0	2	2	22.2
8 (Hawaii, Alaska, West Coast)	83	14	19	33	39.8
9 (Foreign)	67	0	5	5	7.5
10 (don't know)	2	0	0	0	0.0
Total	668	160	132	292	43.7

[a] Zone 1 (Cuyahoga County residents).

only nine scattered survivors in this zone; therefore, it was not economically feasible to send an interviewer to the area. Where complete reliance was placed on the mailed questionnaire, the response rate was poor. The response rate from both interviews and questionnaires was 44 per cent from those outside the metropolitan area, as compared with the over-all response rate of 55 per cent.

The probate experiences and relationships with the deceased of those survivors who lived at some distance from Cuyahoga County often differed from those of survivors who resided in the area. In a number of cases, the nonresident interviewee was the only case contact. The decision to include nonresidents in the survivor population entailed a higher rate of individual loss, but this was compensated by a lower case loss, thus improving the randomness of cases included in the study.

Failure to locate survivors accounts for 8 per cent of the individual loss. As expected, those living outside Cuyahoga County were more difficult to locate than those living within the county were: 126 nonresident survivors (19 per cent of the nonresidents) were not located; 57 persons were not located in Cuyahoga County (4 per cent of the local survivors). Of the local survivors who were not located in Cuyahoga County, some may actually have left the county, but the last address to which they were traced was within the county. Standard use was made of a crisscross telephone directory, which lists phone numbers by addresses, and the City Directory, which enumerates name, address and occupation of head of household for all residences in the county. Voter registration and credit bureau lists were also checked. Inquiries were made of other family members, neighbors at the last address, and the attorney of record. When an interviewer was sent to another area, the search process was the same, although time precluded a full search in all areas. If an interviewer was not sent to an area, the search process was necessarily reduced in scope.

The first step in arranging an interview was to send the interviewee a letter that explained the purpose of the study and the method of sampling. The letter also indicated that the person would be contacted by telephone to arrange for an appointment at his convenience. A copy of a newspaper article relating to the study, which had appeared in a Cleveland paper, was included. In some cases, this article convinced the interviewees that the study was legitimate research rather than a confidence game.[41]

Four hundred three persons refused to be interviewed. A refusal was determined when interviewers were turned away on at least two different occasions, once on the telephone and once in person. All interviewees were contacted a

41. There were many unlisted telephones among the Cleveland survivors. Later it was found that after the obituary appeared, tombstone salesmen and others had been a great nuisance; some survivors had their listing removed at this time. This may account for some of the suspicion with which our initial contact was greeted.

minimum of two times. If the interviewee made excuses or made an appointment and was not home, these did not count as refusals. Efforts persisted until either an interview was granted or a definite refusal was obtained. Some survivors were contacted over twenty times before either outcome was obtained.

The interview material was of such a nature that on occasion it aroused an emotional reaction strong enough to cause a refusal. For example, one woman who refused to be interviewed made this comment:

> After my husband died I was in the hospital. There are too many unpleasant memories. I'm just getting to the point where I'm forgetting a little.

Some survivors frankly admitted that their reason for refusing to be interviewed was that they could see no personal advantage in it. One of the most colorful of these comments was made by a wife of the deceased.

> You're not going to get any answers from me. Why am I always the patsy? I'm fed up with everything. I had to go to all that trouble and now you want the answers.

On the other hand, some survivors agreed to be interviewed because they felt we might be instrumental in getting them some money.

> What's wrong? Was there a whole bunch of money I didn't know about?

Other interviewees accepted because they felt that the subject of the study was important and that their answers might help other people either by educating the public or by changing the probate system.

> It certainly is a chance to be heard on a subject that is getting more important all the time. A lot should be done in this respect to educate people.

> At first I didn't think it was any of your business, but then I thought it over. I thought maybe information would help someone else along the way. I'm glad to see someone looking into what I consider a cumbersome system.

There were many reasons survivors refused an interview. Some persons would have refused an interview on any subject. They were too busy or not interested or felt the estate was too small.

> I appreciate your endeavor. It's very worth-while, but the estate was small and there was no property. There were no difficulties about probate, and I do not think I could advance the study.

> I'm sorry, honey; I'd like to help you. My brother Tony says you're a real nice girl. But I'm a trucker and my hours aren't my own. If I set up an appointment with you one day, I'd have to change it the next. Only Sunday I can call my own, and I do like to spend that with my family.

One very successful interviewer made some shrewd observations about why interviewees consented. She reported:

Some just wanted to air strong feelings against their relatives, lawyers, or the legal system. Some were simply lonely and seemed grateful to find someone who would listen to them. A few had a vague notion I could somehow bring justice to bear. Finally, one man let me into his office because I looked like his late wife.

There was no one reason survivors accepted or refused interviews. Although people refused because they were too busy, many other persons accepted whose schedules were already overcrowded. Some persons were unable to face the emotional trauma of an interview concerning a loved one. Others who consented broke down during the interview. Interviewing success varied with the relationship of the interviewee to the decedent (see Table 3–3). Interviews with

TABLE 3–3 RESPONSE RATE ACCORDING TO RELATIONSHIP OF SURVIVORS TO DECEDENT, IN NUMBER AND PER CENT

Relationship	Total		Respondents		Response Rate (Per Cent)
	Number	Per Cent	Number	Per Cent	
Wife	276	12.3	148	12.0	53.6
Husband	98	4.4	63	5.1	64.3
Son	537	24.0	324	26.3	60.3
Daughter	562	25.1	335	27.1	59.6
Parent	14	.6	5	.4	35.7
Grandchild	52	2.3	34	2.8	65.4
Cousin	69	3.1	34	2.8	49.3
Son- or daughter-in-law	11	.5	5	.4	45.5
Sibling	135	6.0	48	3.9	35.6
Brother- or sister-in-law	34	1.5	18	1.5	52.9
Niece or nephew	276	12.3	142	11.5	51.4
Uncle or aunt	5	.2	0	0.0	0.0
Friend	112	5.0	48	3.9	42.9
Employee	24	1.1	16	1.3	66.7
Other[a]	34	1.5	14	1.1	41.2
Total	2,239	99.9[b]	1,234	100.1[b]	55.1

[a] This category includes stepchildren, relationship unknown, and relatives of a deceased spouse taking under the half-and-half statute.

[b] In this table as well as in succeeding ones, percentages may not total 100 per cent because of rounding.

aunts, uncles, parents, siblings, and friends were least successful; and interviews with surviving spouses, children, grandchildren, and employees were most successful. For 83 per cent of the survivor population, however, the response rate by relationship corresponds within 10 per cent of the total response rate.

The social class of the survivors residing in Cuyahoga County was also used in analyzing response rates. Residence ratings were obtained for all local survivors. The residence ratings of those who were interviewed are only slightly better than the residence ratings of those who were lost to the survey. There is a small overrepresentation in residence ratings 1, 2, 3, and 4, and underrepresentation in residence ratings 5, 6, and 7. However, a comparison of those who refused and those who were interviewed reveals that these two groups are very closely matched (see Table 3–4).

TABLE 3–4 COMPARISON OF CASE LOSS WITH STUDY POPULATION IN RATED RESIDENTIAL AREAS (PERCENTAGE DISTRIBUTION)

Residence Rating	Total Population (N = 1,571)	Completed Interviews (N = 942)	Total Loss (N = 629)	Refusals: Subsample of Total Loss (N = 403)
1 or 2 (best)	5.6	5.7	5.3	5.5
3 (above average)	25.5	26.6	23.5	26.1
4 (average)	45.9	46.9	44.3	45.1
5 (below average)	17.9	15.9	21.3	19.3
6 or 7 (worst)	5.2	4.9	5.5	4.0
Total	100.1	100.0	99.9	100.0

Case Loss

The loss of cases to the study is far less than loss of individuals. In 81 per cent of the 659 cases, at least one person was interviewed. In 232 of these cases (35 per cent), all the survivors were interviewed. In the remaining 300 cases (46 per cent) where not all survivors were interviewed, the number of interviews per case ranged from one to 33.

No one was interviewed in 127 cases (19 per cent of the 659 cases). In 12 of these cases, there were no living adult survivors; in five cases, survivors in foreign countries could not be located. In six cases, the survivors could not be located in the United States, and of these six cases, the last known residence of all but one survivor was out of the state of Ohio. In seven cases, interviews were impossible because all the survivors were too ill, senile, or incompetent, or because they could not communicate in English. Thus, there was an unavoidable loss of 30 cases.

In the remaining 97 lost cases, all survivors refused to be interviewed. Often a refusal by one survivor resulted in refusals by all other possible interviewees. Survivors in a case often knew each other intimately and in several cases lived at the same address, thus increasing the possibility of total refusal. In at least one instance, the family lawyer requested that attempts to interview family members cease. He wrote:

> I represent members of the family of ________ on whom your research interviewers have made several calls recently. While I, as a lawyer, am most interested in your studies, I do respect the right of any individual to his privacy and to politely refuse to grant an interview. The members of this family would prefer not to have any interview and have so informed your interviewer, but there has been some persistence in the

efforts that have made this rather distasteful to my clients. I would appreciate it, therefore, if there would be no further efforts in the case of this particular family to conduct interviews.

The cases in which no interviews were obtained had fewer survivors per case, and the largest number of these were nonresident, as compared with those cases in which at least one interview was obtained. The average number of survivors was 2.3 for the noninterviewed group, as compared with 3.4 survivors for the total sample. Of the survivor population, 30 per cent resided outside Cuyahoga County, and the case loss of this group was 38 per cent.

For 108 of the 127 cases for which there were no interviews, death certificates were available to provide some information. In the remaining 19 cases, it is assumed that the decedent must have died out of state, since there were no records of the death in Ohio. In these cases, the only information obtainable came from probate records.

Compared with cases in the decedent sample for which there are interviews from survivors, a larger proportion of those decedents with noninterviewed survivors were intestate, and more of the decedents were male (see Table 3–5). A comparison of marital status and birthplace shows no marked differences.

Loss of cases in any study occurs for a variety of reasons; and because such loss creates bias, the researcher, therefore, attempts to keep missed cases to a minimum. Sample losses in this study are a function of the unusual sampling

TABLE 3–5 COMPARISON OF CASE LOSS SUBSAMPLE AND CASES WITH INTERVIEWS (PERCENTAGE DISTRIBUTION)

Comparison Variables	Case Loss (N = 127)	Cases with Interviews (N = 532)
Testacy		
Testate	59.8	70.9
Intestate	40.2	29.1
Sex		
Male	67.7	59.4
Female	32.3	40.6
Marital status		
Married	59.8	59.2
Not married	40.2	40.8
Birthplace[a]		
Don't know; other	1.9	.9
Ohio	38.8	38.5
United States	26.9	26.5
Western Europe	12.0	12.0
Eastern Europe	20.4	22.0

[a] Birthplace was obtained from the death certificate for the case loss decedents; hence these percentages are based on 108 cases.

procedure employed. An attempt was made to interview *all* members of a group involved in the inheritance situation. Sample loss would have been radically reduced if a procedure had been adopted that involved sampling potential interviewees in each case and then using *a single respondent* to report for the group on probate practices, family relationships, and so forth. For purposes of this study, however, it was decided that as much information as possible should be obtained about the individual's inheritance situation, and this required interviews from as many concerned parties as possible. In those cases in which interviewing completeness was achieved, the result is a rich archive of data and more bases for explaining the meaning and significance of inheritance for members of the family within the nuclear-related kinship system.

The Lawyer and the Inheritance System

The interest of this study in the decedent and his survivors—their will-making behavior, their attitudes toward one another, their experiences in dealing with the probate court and its multiple functionaries—led to the conclusion that the lawyer was a significant professional agent in the inheritance process. To ignore his role in property disposition would provide less than adequate conclusions on the issues of inheritance in American society and, moreover, would ignore one major element of explanation in the inheritance process.

For these reasons, the relationship between the lawyer and the client is examined in this study in two phases of the inheritance process: will making and estate settlement. The client's view of the lawyer is compared with the lawyer's view of the client. An attempt was made to determine how important probate practice was to the group of lawyers examined in the study. Does the lawyer's behavior satisfy his client? What activities of probate practice are most satisfying to the lawyer?

Consider the will-making process. What are the subjective reasons for making a will? What internal restraints are imposed upon testamentary freedom? Does the lawyer influence the client's pattern of distribution?[42] What are the client's expectations of the lawyer? A program of research undertaken on clients' expectations of a nonspecified "helpful" person gives the best clue.[43] The helpful

42. Most definitions of "profession" imply that the professional dictates the course of events to the client; for instance, "those occupations which involve the use of knowledge and techniques by a practitioner directly upon, or in behalf of, a client in order to maintain, or induce in, the client a culturally determined and socially approved state of well-being." Neil H. Cheek, Jr., "The Social Role of the Professional," *The Professional in the Organization,* ed. Mark Abrahannon (Chicago: Rand McNally & Co., 1967), p. 12.

43. E. J. Thomas, Norman Polansky, and Jacob Kounin, "The Expected Behavior of a Potentially Helpful Person," *Human Relations* 8 (1955):165–174; Norman Polansky and Jacob Kounin, "Clients' Reactions to Initial Interviews: A Field Study," *Human Relations* 9 (1956):239–264; Jacob Kounin et al., "Experimental Studies of Clients' Reactions to Initial Interviews," *Human Relations* 9 (1956):265–293.

person is simply one "whose profession it is to advise, counsel, and help others." This broad definition is applicable to the lawyer. More specifically, the helpful person is expected to assign importance to the problems the client has, to show willingness to maintain and broaden the range of communication, to reduce the client's discomfort, and to help him overcome decision-making difficulties.[44] Norman Polansky and Jacob Kounin conclude that

> . . . satisfactions experienced in the relationship itself seem to have much to do with the commitment to maintain a relationship. On the other hand commitment to be influenced by the helping person entails another kind of scrutiny, having to do with estimates of competence, technical skill and anticipated thoroughness.[45]

Other clues to the client's perception of the lawyer exist in studies of the public's attitudes toward and experience with the legal profession. The lawyer has had a high place in all prestige rankings since 1925, although always lower than the physician. As is the case with other professionals, his prestige is increasing.[46] It is possible, however, for public accordance of high prestige to coexist with fear, resentment, and contempt.[47] Colloquial appellations for the lawyer include such terms as "shyster," "ambulance chaser," and "mouthpiece."[48] Ambivalence if not outright hostility to the professions can be traced to colonial times. The public feared the direct impact of professional techniques, resented the professional's ability to charge fees, and believed that lawyers served the interests of the wealthy against the rest of society.[49]

The poor are less likely than the wealthy to use lawyers. Jerome E. Carlin and Jan Howard have summarized the results of five studies relating social class and the use of private lawyers. About two-thirds of those in the lower class have never employed a lawyer, as compared with one-third of those in the upper class. Various measures of social class were used in these studies: income, education, occupation, residence, and interviewer's judgment.[50] Since

44. Kounin et al., op. cit., p. 262.
45. Polansky and Kounin, op. cit., p. 293.
46. Robert W. Hodge, Paul M. Siegal, and Peter H. Rossi, "Occupational Prestige in the United States: 1925–1963," *Class, Status and Power,* ed. Reinhard Bendix and Seymour Martin Lipset, 2d ed. (New York: The Free Press, 1966), pp. 322–334.
47. For the case of the physician, see W. A. Gamson and H. Schuman, "Some Undercurrents in the Prestige of Physicians," *American Journal of Sociology* 68 (January, 1963):463–470. Goode makes the suggestion that public fear is a help rather than a hindrance to professional status. William Goode, "The Librarian: From Occupation to Profession?" *Library Quarterly* 31 (October, 1961):318.
48. The analogous terms for physicians do not seem to be as commonly used: "leech," "croaker," "sawbones."
49. Daniel H. Calhoun, *Professional Lives in America: Structure and Aspirations, 1750–1850* (Cambridge, Mass.: Harvard University Press, 1965), pp. 3–7. See also Charles Warren, *History of the American Bar* (Boston: Little, Brown and Company, 1911), p. 6.
50. Jerome E. Carlin and Jan Howard, "Legal Representative and Class Justice," *UCLA Law Review* 12 (January, 1965):382–383. Freund, in remarking upon the law-

the higher socioeconomic classes have usually had greater experience with lawyers, it is likely that there is a congruency of client's expectations and lawyer's behavior when the client is of higher social status. As a consequence, the client will be more satisfied with the relationship. Obviously, interaction does not always lead to friendly sentiments. In a survey conducted by the Missouri Bar, it was found that "among laymen who had never used a lawyer's services, 29 per cent thought that about half of the lawyers were not entirely ethical; while, of the laymen who had been to a lawyer, a slightly larger percentage held the same opinion."[51]

The experienced client's negative opinion of lawyers may be accounted for by examining sources of strain inherent in the professional-client relationship.[52] The heavy load of anxiety that the client may bring to the relationship exacerbates the strains.[53] What is a crisis for the client is routine for the professional. It is neither possible nor desirable that the professional become emotionally involved with each client's problems.[54] The dilemma for the professional is one of the proper balance between closeness and understanding, on the one hand, and objectivity and detachment, on the other.[55] The fact that the problems of the client provide the practitioner with his livelihood may lead the client to suspect the motivations of the professional.[56] There is an expectation that

yer's economic provincialism, provides this explanation: "A medical clinic for the poor is valuable for medical education. . . . In contrast a legal aid clinic is sharply limited in the scope of problems that it offers to the lawyer." Paul A. Freund, "The Legal Profession," *The Professions, Daedalus* 92 (Fall, 1963):692.

51. *Missouri Bar—Prentice-Hall Survey* (Jefferson City, Mo.: The Missouri Bar, 1963), cited in Glenn R. Winters, "Pettifoggery and Legal Delays," *Annals of the American Academy of Political and Social Science* 363 (January, 1966):54.

52. Robert K. Merton and Elinor Barber, "Sociological Ambivalence," *Sociological Theory, Values, and Sociocultural Change: Essays in Honor of Pitirim A. Sorokin*, ed. Edward Tiryakian (New York: The Free Press, 1963), pp. 91–120.

53. Ibid., pp. 107–109. The client's anxiety has been overemphasized by those less astute than Merton and Barber. For instance, this description of a patient appears in a widely known article: "quite impossible for him to perceive the precise meaning of a train of thought." L. J. Henderson, "Physician and Patient as a Social System," *New England Journal of Medicine* 212 (1935):821. At the stage of estate settlement, the lawyer often confronts the emotions of the recently bereaved. Additionally, the testator's last wishes may have a significance for the next of kin that goes beyond property values. If the deceased made no will, this too may have varied meaning and significance to survivors about the nature and quality of their relationship with the decedent. Eric Plaut, "Emotional Aspects of Probate Practice," *Practical Lawyer* 5 (1959):25.

54. Talcott Parsons, "A Sociologist Looks at the Legal Profession," *Essays in Sociological Theory*, rev. ed. (Glencoe, Ill.: The Free Press, 1954), p. 377.

55. Charles Kadushin, "Social Distance Between Client and Professional," *American Journal of Sociology* 67 (1963):517.

56. For Banton, "the most important structural problem [in the professions] is that of preventing material reward from contaminating the element of personal service in the professional role," Michael Banton, *Roles* (New York: Basic Books, Inc., Publishers, 1965), p. 162; Merton and Barber, op. cit., pp. 113–114.

professional-client relationships should be continuous, that the client should not shop around; therefore, dissatisfactions may accumulate, and yet the relationship is not broken.[57]

The professional faces and resolves conflicting loyalties. As a professional, the lawyer must satisfy three masters: the client, the court, and society.[58] Implicit in this analysis of the lawyer's interstitial position is the assumption that the lawyer may have to be an agent of frustration for the client.[59] Moreover, the lawyer and his client evaluate the former's actions differently. The lawyer must reconcile the client's wishes with legal norms and professional standards; whereas the client is concerned with accomplishing only his own aims. Lastly, the client and the professional appraise the latter's performance by different standards.[60]

The lawyer, unlike other practitioners, is constrained in his behavior by universal norms (legal statutes) in addition to those that usually govern the professional: the rules of the professional association and organizational system of which he is a member. The system of law is directed to control the behavior of all individuals; in the case of the attorney: his clients. The lawyer, at best, can interpret the law, suggest alternative courses of action to meet its demands, counsel his client about the most appropriate course, and enable the client to live within the letter of the law. The lawyer develops expertise as a definer and interpreter of the law; he solves problems created by the law or by the lawless; he does not make the law or change it as he works with it. He is constrained to work within the law, and this condition is often misunderstood by his client.

Other practitioners, such as physicians, social workers, and dentists, do not have such universal restraints. For them, meeting circumscribed professional standards is difficult enough in addition to providing the client with satisfying results. They have a wider latitude in which to use their creativity, or at least to pretend to use it, in finding new solutions to chronic problems. The client, in not making this distinction between the relatively free professional who is not a lawyer and the lawyer who is bound by norms, demands equally satisfactory results for his condition or problem. The consequences of this attitude are potentially increased ambivalence and ambiguity for the lawyer and the client in their relationship.

The handling of the lawyer's interstitial position between the client and the

57. Merton and Barber, op. cit., pp. 110–111.

58. Albert P. Blaustein and Charles O. Porter, *The American Lawyer* (Chicago: University of Chicago Press, 1954), p. 44.

59. Talcott Parsons, op. cit., p. 375.

60. Merton and Barber, op. cit., pp. 109–115. See also Eliot Freidson, "Client Control and Medical Practice," *American Journal of Sociology* 65 (1960):376. "Practice generically consists of interaction between two different conflicting sets of norms."

law and the manipulation of the court system in which disputes are adjudicated are tasks that continuously test the professionalism of the lawyer (as well as being a potentially rich ground for behavioral science research). The lawyer performs the role of a socialization agent. He educates his client in the do's and don'ts of the law and relies heavily on his skills in interpersonal relationships to satisfy his client and to make a workable court system. In order to examine these questions and theoretical considerations, it was necessary to interview lawyers.

Lawyer Sample

The lawyer sample was designed with the objective of ensuring that the lawyer would be engaged in probate practice. A simple random sample was drawn from the lawyers who were attorney of record for the sample of 659 decedents' estates.

The plan for the interview had two parts. Structured questions were designed to obtain a description of the lawyer and his practice. In the areas of estate planning and settlement, questions were designed to allow for open-ended answers. For both the planning and settlement aspects of probate practice, the following areas were central: client relationships, relationships with other occupational groups and organizational systems such as the court, fees for services, and suggestions for improving probate practices. This portion of the study followed closely the procedures employed by Hubert O'Gorman, who focused on a sample area of practice, matrimonial cases.[61]

For 60 of the 659 decedent cases, there was no attorney; most of these were release-of-assets cases. For the remaining 599 cases, 466 different attorneys were recorded. Eighty lawyers were randomly selected.

As a group, the lawyers in the sample had more experience in probate work than the lawyer population had. Of the 80 lawyers who were selected, 70 were interviewed. Of the original 80, six refused to be interviewed; one could not be located; and one had died before he could be contacted. One person listed on the probate record as the attorney was actually a layman. One attorney who practiced in another county had no knowledge of Cuyahoga County Probate Court practices, and his interview was excluded. The analysis, therefore, is based upon 70 attorneys practicing in Cuyahoga County. (A description of the lawyer sample is found in Appendix C.)

The majority of the lawyers in the sample were independent practitioners.[62]

61. Hubert J. O'Gorman, *Lawyers and Matrimonial Cases* (New York: The Free Press, 1963). Another book with focus on a particular area of practice is Arthur Lewis Wood, *Criminal Lawyer* (New Haven, Conn.: College & University Press, 1967).

62. In O'Gorman's study of lawyers who had handled matrimonial cases, 59 per cent were solo practitioners. He had no lawyers in the Other category. O'Gorman, op. cit., p. 46. Apparently probate and matrimonial cases are handled mainly by independent practitioners; but probate work, unlike matrimonial cases, can also be handled by those

Probate work does not require the resources and specialization of a large law office. The probate work of large law firms usually consists of doing such work for people who are clients in another capacity.

The persons in the Other category in Table 3–6 were not actually engaged in the practice of law (for example, a minister who had a law degree), or they were corporation lawyers or were semiretired. Their probate work was confined to favors for friends and family.

TABLE 3–6 TYPE OF LAW OFFICE, BY NUMBER AND PER CENT

Type of Law Office	Number	Per Cent
Independent	38	54.3
Small firm (2–5)	17	24.3
Medium firm (6–20)	4	5.7
Large firm (over 20)	4	5.7
Other	7	10.0
Total	70	100.0

Not all were engaged in full-time practice; some of those who maintained offices were part-time lawyers. Fifty-three lawyers (76 per cent) considered themselves to be fully engaged in the practice of law. Others held political office or were employed by government agencies; still others were in insurance, real estate, banking, and so forth.

The sample of lawyers was taken from the list of attorneys who had handled at least one of the sample probate cases. Surprisingly, two attorneys said they spent no time in probate work, and three attorneys reported no income in this area of practice. Probate work was so insignificant for these two attorneys that they could not remember their involvement, and the three reporting no income were doing gratis work for neighbors, friends, relatives, and fellow church or lodge members. However, 24 of the 70 lawyers (34 per cent) spent more than 30 per cent of their time in the wills-estates area. This contrasts with Carlin's finding that among solo practitioners in Chicago six out of 67 attorneys (9 per cent) spent 30 per cent or more of their time in the wills-estates area.[63] Thus, on the whole, the sampling method yielded lawyers who were experienced in probate work.

who are not actively engaged in law practice. Matrimonial cases require court appearance; whereas probate work can be done without the necessity of taking on the advocate's role. Criminal law is, to an even greater extent, the bailiwick of the solo practitioner. Three-quarters of the men engaged in the practice of criminal law are solo practitioners. Wood, op. cit., p. 95.

63. Jerome E. Carlin, *Lawyers on Their Own* (New Brunswick, N.J.: Rutgers University Press, 1962), p. 118.

Conclusion

In summary, the design of the Cuyahoga County study departed from the designs of its predecessors in several basic respects. First, the sample of decedent estates was drawn initially from probate documents rather than from death certificates (the procedure in the New York, Dane County, and Cook County studies).[64]

The Cuyahoga sample was a random selection of all estates closed in probate during a given time period rather than a selection of testate cases (as in Friedman's New Jersey study) or of estates of great wealth (as in the work of the two British economists, Wedgwood and Harbury) or of prominent decedents (as in Britt's study). These samples limited the authors in their generalizations. An understanding of the role of inheritance in the United States can be furthered to a greater extent by a design that does not purposely exclude "typical" decedents' estates. Since all deaths do not result in administration, any sampling from administered estates automatically overrepresents the wealthier segment of society.

With the exception of Britt and Dunham, all the authors just mentioned sampled their cases over time. They were able to discuss trends in testacy such as the relationship of the business cycle to capital accumulation and property disposition. Historical analysis is important, but because of limited resources, the sample sizes of the Britt, Friedman, Wedgwood, and Harbury studies were small. Furthermore, generalizations of historical import should be treated as hypotheses rather than as firm conclusions. The two samples in this study cover estates closed over a period of nine months. While it is not possible to speculate about changes in probate practices in the past, the plans and expectations of survivors may serve as indicators of future trends in will making and current basic orientations and perceptions of the inheritance system.

The interviews with survivors also made it possible to go beyond the ordinary treatment of decedent estates and to investigate the meaning of inheritance practices to individuals exposed to this experience. Sociologists have recognized that descriptions of norms or laws are not equivalent to descriptions of actual behavior. The divergence between ideal and real is one of the continuous and fascinating problems that can be studied. It is impossible to obtain descriptions of behavior from public records. Also, reliance upon the official picture obscures the important part inheritance plays in family relationships. The anthropological literature is rich in the meaning ascribed to inheritance by the small community and by the surviving family. Perhaps precisely because so many of these studies have been conducted in preliterate

64. The Cook County study was in part based on a random sample of estates opened in a particular year. See Dunham, op. cit., p. 241.

societies, inheritance is not treated as a purely legal and economic phenomenon.

In order to look at the social and psychological aspects of inheritance and to understand the process in terms of the relationships among decedents and survivors, an attempt was made to question all survivors. By examining whole families rather than key informants, it was hoped that a fuller picture of the inheritance process would be obtained.

Finally, in a society based upon differentiation, the perspective of the practitioner is especially important. The lawyer's task is to make the inheritance system work; he is the one who masters the legal complexities of inheritance. The lawyer's view of this aspect of his practice illumines yet another facet of the inheritance process.

Chapter 4

Testacy Versus Intestacy

THIS CHAPTER is concerned with the conditions of testacy and intestacy. There is a paucity of information on the characteristics of decedents who are either testate or intestate and on the characteristics of living persons who have or have not made wills. One purpose of this study was to determine if will makers differ significantly from nonwill makers in demographic, social, and economic characteristics. The analysis is based upon the estate practices of two groups. The *decedent sample* refers to the 659 estates that constituted the 5-per cent random sample of estates closed in Cuyahoga County Probate Court between November, 1964, and August, 1965. The *survivor population* refers to the 1,234 persons who were legal next of kin and/or beneficiaries of the decedents in the sample obtained from probate court records.[1]

Proportion of Testate Cases

Despite the advantages of making a will, large numbers of property owners die intestate. The fluctuation in the rate of testacy among jurisdictions is extreme.[2] Also, within the same jurisdiction, substantial fluctuations occur over time.

Richard Powell and Charles Looker, in a study covering the period from 1915 to 1929, found a "steady increase since 1915 in the proportion of adult decedents leaving wills which are probated, with the single exception of 1918,

1. It will be recalled from Chapter 3 that there were 19 decedents for whom even death certificate information was not available. While such information as estate size, sex, testacy, next of kin, and beneficiaries was available from the probate record, other information such as age, marital status, education, and occupation was not. Therefore, a base N of 640 for the decedent sample will sometimes be used. Otherwise, the base N will be 659. For the survivor population, there will also be two base numbers used: 1,234 represents both the survivors interviewed and those who returned mailed questionnaires; 1,102 is the number of survivors personally interviewed. The latter base will be used where information was not available from the mailed questionnaires, for example, number of next of kin.

2. Powell and Looker give the percentage testate in various jurisdictions. The range is from 25 per cent testate in Cook County, Illinois, to 64 per cent testate in Chelan County, Washington. Richard Powell and Charles Looker, "Decedents' Estates," *Columbia Law Review* 30 (November, 1930): 930.

when there was a sharp dip in the proportion."[3] This drop in will making is attributed to the large number of people who died suddenly in the 1918 influenza epidemic. The general increase in will making is attributed to trust company advertising and to the increase in the "numbers of persons who have more dollars."[4]

In Dane County, however, testate cases declined from a high of 62 per cent in 1929 to 46 per cent in 1934, and finally to a low of 39 per cent in 1944.[5] The authors could not explain this change. They had chosen these particular years in order to show the relationship of the business cycle to capital accumulation: 1929 was an example of peacetime prosperity; 1934 was chosen to show the effect of the Depression; and 1944 was thought to give evidence of the effect of a major war.[6] However, the estates of those who died in 1929 do not necessarily reflect the economic conditions of 1929.

The average age of the Dane County decedents was 69 years.[7] After age 65, the proportion of positive savers is low, and the proportion of zero and negative savers is high.[8] For some of the decedents in the Dane County sample, the years of greatest capital accumulation were past, and the process of spending capital had begun. A comprehensive and systematic study linking testacy to such factors as economic conditions, business cycles, and wars is still to be made. Undoubtedly, such relationships exist. War, for example, may accelerate or reduce the rate of testacy. But such events may have only temporary impact on the trend toward higher rates of testacy over time.

Decedent Sample

The Cuyahoga County sample of 659 decedent estates yielded 453 testate estates (69 per cent) and 206 intestate estates (31 per cent). This is the highest ratio of testate to intestate cases found in a United States study. In Table 4–1, the two most recent United States studies are compared with the Cuyahoga County sample.

The reason this study's decedent group has the highest percentage of testacy

3. Ibid., p. 926.
4. Ibid., p. 927.
5. Edward Ward and J. H. Beuscher, "The Inheritance Process in Wisconsin," *Wisconsin Law Review* (1950):412.
6. Ibid., pp. 393–394. Capital accumulation is positively related to the condition of testacy. In Dane County, 92 per cent of estates with a net worth over $50,000 were testate. Ibid., p. 412. In Cook County, 96 per cent of estates over $100,000 were testate. Allison Dunham, "The Method, Process and Frequency of Wealth Transmission," *Chicago Law Review* 30 (Winter, 1962):250.
7. Ward and Beuscher, op. cit., p. 411.
8. Janet A. Fisher, "Family Life Cycle Analysis in Research on Consumer Behavior," *Consumer Behavior,* vol. II, *The Life Cycle and Consumer Behavior,* ed. Lincoln H. Clark (New York: New York University Press, 1955), p. 35. *Zero savers* refers to persons who are not saving. *Negative savers* are those who are drawing on capital. *Dissaving* refers to either negative saving or going into debt.

TABLE 4–1 PER CENT OF TESTATE CASES IN THREE STUDIES, EITHER BY DATE OF DEATH, OR DATE PROBATE INITIATED OR CLOSED, AND BY SAMPLE SIZE

Factors	Dane County	Cook County	Cuyahoga County
Sample selected according to:			
Dates of death during year	1929, 1934, 1939, 1941, 1944	1957	None
Probate initiated	None	1953	None
Probate closed	None	None	1964–1965
Sample size	415	170	659
Per cent testate	47	58	69

cannot be completely ascertained without further research. However, experience with the Cuyahoga County project and a review of other studies suggests a number of general reasons for this variation: different methods of selecting cases, the year the study was conducted, and the location of the study population. There are other specific reasons: variations between jurisdictions in laws regarding probate, the economic conditions in the area at the time of the study, the social-class distribution of the sample studied, and the educational activities of diverse institutions such as bar associations, banks, and the mass media in matters related to testacy.

Survivor Population

The relatively high proportion of testacy among decedents in the Cuyahoga County decedent sample also exists among the survivors of these decedents. In the survivor population of 1,234, it was found that 711 (58 per cent) had already made their wills.[9] The majority of survivors of testate decedents were themselves testate (62 per cent). The majority of survivors of intestate decedents were intestate (54 per cent).

Frequency of Testacy

The association of testacy with age, location in the family network, economic class, and social status was hypothesized in both the decedent sample and the survivor population. The hypothesis was accepted if the association of the variables was statistically significant or obvious by inspection of the data for both decedents and survivors.

9. No claim can be made that these survivors or the decedents themselves were representative of the general population found in a given community. In Chapter 3, it was demonstrated in the studies cited that estate administration was initiated for a minority of adult resident decedents.

Age

The will is a declaration of intention that has no effect until death. To make a will when one is young is to prepare for an improbable event. At age 20, the average remaining life span is over 50 years. To make a will at age 70 is to prepare for an event that is most likely to take place within 12 years.[10] The hypothesis that age will be positively associated with testacy is based upon the common-sense notion that people are more likely to prepare for what is probable than for what is improbable.

The average age for the decedent sample was 67.8 years. The average age of testate decedents was 69.6 years, and that of the intestate was 63.7 years. For each additional decade of life, there was a substantial increase in the proportion who died testate (see Table 4–2). The pattern of an increase in the

TABLE 4–2 AGE GROUP OF DECEDENTS AND PER CENT TESTATE

Age Group	Number	Per Cent Testate
21–29	3	0.0
30–39	11	27.3
40–49	44	52.3
50–59	91	59.3
60–69	170	70.0
70–79	214	75.2
80–89	92	78.3
90–99	12	83.3
Total	637[a]	69.4

[a] One decedent was a minor, and age was not available for 21 decedents.

rate of testacy with an increase in age also occurred in the Cook County sample with the same variations. All the decedents age 80 and over were testate; but in the age group 70–79, only 56 per cent were testate, compared with 75 per cent in the Cuyahoga County sample.[11]

The hypothesis that age is positively associated with testacy was thus amply demonstrated. This hypothesis was based on the assumption that individuals recognize the probability of death and that the older they become, the more likely they are to make a will. This reasoning might be questioned if the wills antedated the death of the testators by many years. In that case, the objective

10. United States Department of Health, Education, and Welfare, *The Facts of Life and Death* (Washington, D.C.: Public Health Service, 1965), p. 21.

11. Dunham, op. cit., p. 248. It is difficult to understand the large increase in testacy at age 80. It is not clear whether this finding applies to the ninety-seven 1953 estates or the seventy-three 1957 estates, or both. Most likely the shift in percentage is due to the small numbers.

probability of death would have had no greater influence on testators than on the intestate individuals. A more intensive analysis of the will-making process is necessary in order to determine the nature of the age-testacy relationship.

The elapsed time between the making of the will and the death of the testator was considered as one approach to this question. A will made immediately preceding death fits the notion that the probability of dying leads the individual to put his affairs in order. There may be unusual consequences because of this act. The will may be made under the influence of the person who gives final care and may, therefore, neglect the individual who has had lifetime responsibility and affection for the decedent. The time-oriented mortmain statutes of many states are directed toward related influence factors. The purpose of these statutes, which entirely or partially invalidate charitable gifts unless the will is executed prior to a specified time before death, is to prevent the testator from being unduly influenced while under fear of approaching death and thereby deviating from the usual pattern of bequeathing to his immediate family.

On the other hand, a will made many years before death may be out of date because designated legatees are no longer living, later-born heirs are excluded, property that no longer exists is bequeathed, or because the will fails to bequeath property acquired after the will was executed.[12] The testators in the

TABLE 4–3 TIME ELAPSED BETWEEN DATE OF WILL AND DEATH, IN CUYAHOGA AND COOK COUNTY SAMPLES

	Cuyahoga County (1964–1965)		Cook County (1953)	
Time (in years)	Number	Per Cent	Number	Per Cent
Less than 1	66	14.6	35	35.7
1–3	75	16.6	17	17.3
3–5	67	14.8	16	16.3
5–10	116	25.6	21	21.4
10 or more	129	28.5	9	9.2
Total	453	100.1	98	99.9

decedent sample were early declarers of property distribution: 54 per cent had wills in force for a minimum of five years preceding death.[13] In contrast, only

12. Lapsed legacies are dealt with in Ohio Revised Code 2107.52; pretermitted heirs, in Ohio Revised Code 2107.34; alteration of property, in Ohio Revised Code 2107.36; and after-acquired property, in Ohio Revised Code 2107.50. The difficulty is not that a legal problem arises but that the legal solution might not be in accord with the testator's wishes.

13. Possible deathbed wills were infrequent; 39 wills (9 per cent) were made within six months of death; 18 (4 per cent) of the probated wills were made within three months of death.

31 per cent of the wills in the Cook County sample had been in effect five years or longer.[14]

The last will and testament is not a valid indicator of the time between will making and death because some individuals make more than one will during their lives. In 139 of the testate cases, informants reported the existence of wills prior to the one that was probated. Wills that were dated up to five years before death were more likely to have been preceded by another will than wills that were dated five years or more before death (see Table 4–4).

TABLE 4–4 TIME ELAPSED BETWEEN DATE OF WILL AND DEATH, FOR CASES WITH PREVIOUS WILLS

Time (in years)	Total Cases	Cases with Previous Wills	
		Number	Per Cent
Less than 1	66	25	37.9
1–3	75	37	49.3
3–5	67	23	34.3
5–10	116	28	24.1
10 or more	129	26	20.2
Total	453	139	30.7

It appears that the majority of testators have had wills for a relatively long period of time. As already noted, no information was available on previous wills for 76 testate decedents because it was impossible to obtain an interview with any survivor. Therefore, 139 is a minimal number of cases in which there were previous wills.

The average age of the 139 testators who had wills prior to the will probated was 73.2 years; whereas the average age of all testate decedents was 69.6 years. Thus, the older testators had made more than one will. A new will may be executed because the old one is no longer suitable to changed circumstances, or it may be made under undue influence. Whatever the reason for a second will, the important points are that individuals do not become testate in anticipation of imminent death and that sudden death does not explain intestacy. There was a six-year age difference between the testate and intestate; however, since the median age of the wills in the sample was over five years and since over 30 per cent of the probated wills were not the first will for the decedent, the age difference between testate and intestate decedents cannot account for testacy.[15]

14. Dunham, op. cit., p. 279.

15. In addition to the 139 testate cases for which there were previous wills, four intestate decedents had made out wills that were not probated. In one case, the will was not signed, although the decedent had called a solemn family convocation for the

The average age for the survivor population was 48.4 years. The average age of living testators was 52.5 years; the average of those without wills was 42.7 years. With each decade of life (except for the eighties, where the number is small), there was an increase in the percentage of persons who have made wills (see Table 4–5). If no other change in the population occurred, the greater longevity of the population would result in a larger number of testate estates. If everyone lived his three score and ten years, it is probable that over 80 per cent of the population would have made wills.

TABLE 4–5 AGE GROUP OF SURVIVORS AND PER CENT TESTATE

Age Group	Number	Per Cent Testate
21–29	104	19.2
30–39	232	41.4
40–49	349	56.4
50–59	283	67.5
60–69	153	78.4
70–79	85	82.4
80–89	16	81.3
Total	1,222[a]	57.9

[a] No age given by 8 people; no answer for testacy given by 4 people.

The survivors were asked when they first made a will. Since memory of time is not completely accurate, the responses have been placed in broad age categories (see Table 4–6).

---

reading of the will. Whether this was due to an oversight or to the machinations of the second wife was not known by the informants. In another case, a joint will had been made between husband and wife; the wife's signature was witnessed, but the husband's was not; the husband died. In two cases, the beneficiaries did not produce the wills because they felt the estates were too small. These persons were probably unaware that the penalties for concealing a will include commitment to the county jail until the will is produced, liability for damages sustained by others, and, if the will is concealed for three or more years, forfeiture of beneficial interests. See Ohio Revised Code 2107.09 and 2107.10.

It is possible that circumstances prevented people from making a will. One such circumstance could be the adjudication of incompetency and the institution of guardianship. Adjudication of insanity is not conclusive of absence of testamentary capacity. A person may be so mentally incapacitated that he is unable to take active charge of his possessions, but he may still have the mental capacity to make a will. Thomas E. Atkinson, *Wills,* 2d ed. (St. Paul, Minn.: West Publishing Co., 1953), pp. 239, 539. Twelve of the testate decedents had been under guardianship. The average age of these decedents was 73.8 years. On the average (median), their wills predated their demise by eight years. One will, written while the testator was under guardianship, was proved valid. There were six intestate decedents who had been adjudicated incompetent. Their average age was 78.8 years. It would appear that intestacy cannot be accounted for by incompetency.

TABLE 4–6 GROUPED AGE OF SURVIVORS AT TIME FIRST WILL WAS MADE

Age Group	Number	Per Cent	Cumulative Per Cent
21–30	149	21.6	21.6
31–45	310	45.0	66.6
46–60	163	23.7	90.3
Over 60	67	9.7	100.0
Total	689[a]	100.0	

[a] Age at the time of initial testation not given by 22 informants.

Although age is positively associated with testacy, it is obvious that a large number of the testate group did not wait until they were in a high-risk age category. The great age for will making was 31–45, the time of planning to meet future commitments, especially family obligations. About one-fifth of the testate group made wills when they were in their twenties, fairly soon after they were legally capable of making a will. Two-thirds of those who were testate at the time of interviewing had made their wills by age 45. By age 60, 90 per cent had made their wills. Only 10 per cent of the testate made their first wills after age 60. However, there were only 203 testate survivors over the age of 60. Of those over age 60, 67 (33 per cent) made their first wills at this relatively late age.

Location in Family Network

It is possible to name an executor for an estate without specifying to whom the property will be transferred. This largely defeats the purpose of a will, however, and all wills examined in this study named beneficiaries. In the event that no will has been made, the property is transferred according to the pattern of intestate distribution. One powerful motive for testation is the desire to choose one's own beneficiaries. What factors appear important in designating beneficiaries? One way of approaching this question is to examine the individual's marital status, sex, and type and number of surviving kin.

In the Cook County decedent sample, the divorced had the lowest rate of testacy (50 per cent); the married and the single (54 per cent) and the widowed (59 per cent) were most often testate. Dunham speculates that the widowed are more often testate because they have had previous experience with death and property disposition.[16] However, he did not control for age; and it is probable that his widowed group was older than the married, single, and divorced groups.

The widowed in both the decedent sample and the survivor population of the Cuyahoga County study had a higher proportion of testators than the sin-

16. Dunham, op. cit., p. 249.

TABLE 4–7 MARITAL STATUS OF DECEDENT SAMPLE AND SURVIVOR POPULATION, BY PER CENT TESTATE AND MEAN AGE

Marital Status	Decedent Sample			Survivor Population		
	Number	Per Cent Testate	Mean Age	Number	Per Cent Testate	Mean Age
Single	37	56.8	69.4	92	31.5	41.2
Divorced	14	57.1	59.4	36	30.6	47.1
Married	383	69.5	64.6	843	56.6	45.5
Widowed	202	72.3	74.2	258	75.2	60.6
Total	636[a]			1,229[b]		

[a] Marital status unknown for 4 decedents.
[b] Testacy unknown for 4 survivors, and marital status unknown for 1 survivor.

gle, divorced, or married individuals and were from five to twenty years older than the others (see Table 4–7).

Age alone cannot explain why the married were more often found to be testate than the single and divorced. The average age of the single decedents was higher than that of the married decedents. In the survivor population, the divorced were older than the married. Unfortunately, there were not sufficient numbers of single and divorced persons in this study to allow control for age. When age is controlled for the widowed and married, however, an interesting pattern emerges. The widowed held their advantage over the married in those age groups where widowhood was an infrequent status; but the married were found to be testate more often than the widowed in the older age groups, where there was less probability of maintaining the marriage intact. The one exception was the category of widowed decedents in the 21–49 age group, where there were too few cases for any conclusion to be reached (see Table 4–8).

The loss that the young widow (or widower) has experienced forces her (or

TABLE 4–8 MARITAL STATUS OF DECEDENT SAMPLE AND SURVIVOR POPULATION, BY AGE GROUP[a] AND PER CENT TESTATE

Marital Status	Age 21–49		Age 50–59		Age 60–69		Age 70–99	
	Number	Per Cent	Number	Per Cent	Number	Per Cent	Number	Per Cent
Decedent sample								
Married ($N = 381$)	51	49.0	70	60.0	111	73.0	149	79.2
Widowed ($N = 202$)	3	33.3	14	64.3	45	66.7	140	75.7
Survivor population								
Married ($N = 839$)	544	47.6	191	66.0	77	81.8	27	100.0
Widowed ($N = 256$)	56	64.3	69	79.7	62	75.8	69	79.7

[a] Age unknown for 2 married decedents and for 4 married and 2 widowed survivors.

him) to think of her (or his) own death as a possibility and to realize the need to make provisions for minor children. At a later age, married persons begin to see their friends and relatives losing their mates; they must confront the possibility of death breaking their own marriages. Unlike the widowed person of the same age, the married couple have responsibility for each other and therefore make wills.

Sex. A slightly larger number of females than of males were found to be testate in the decedent sample. This finding is similar to Dunham's[17] (see Table 4–9). In contrast, a slightly larger proportion of males than of females were testate in the survivor population.[18] The difference in mean age in both groups was very small. The explanation is that men are testate equally with women, and the higher proportion of testate women in the decedent sample was a result of their greater longevity rather than of a greater propensity toward will making.

TABLE 4–9 SEX AND MEAN AGE OF DECEDENT SAMPLE AND SURVIVOR POPULATION, BY PER CENT TESTATE

	Decedent Sample			Survivor Population		
Sex	Number	Per Cent Testate	Mean Age[a]	Number	Per Cent Testate	Mean Age[a]
Male	402	67.7	67.2	568	59.5	47.9
Female	257	70.4	68.7	662	56.3	48.9
Total	659			1,230[b]		

[a] Mean age calculated for 638 decedents and 1,226 survivors for whom age was known.
[b] Testacy unknown for 4 survivors.

Although the percentage of testate female decedents was slightly greater than the percentage of testate males, the number of female decedents in the probate sample was only 39 per cent. The disparity between males and females in probated estates suggests that females are disproportionately represented among those who have no property to be administered. Perhaps the longevity of the sex contributes to this condition. The findings of Ward and Beuscher on the proportion of deaths, by age, resulting in administration are relevant here.

When all years are considered as one group, there is a decline in the proportion of people who leave estates among people over the age of 90 since at this age most people have been using up past accumulations of wealth to maintain themselves.[19]

17. Fifty-three per cent of the males were testate compared with 57 per cent of the females. Dunham, op. cit., p. 246.
18. An opinion study in 1949 concluded that from the total voting-age population, three out of four men and six out of seven women had no wills; cited in Dunham, loc. cit.
19. Ward and Beuscher, op. cit., p. 397.

If the age profiles of the sexes are different, then this difference should be reflected in the admission of estates to probate court.

Type of surviving kin. It has been suggested that those who are survived by collateral kin have the most freedom in making a will. They are not subject to a forced share of any kind, and there is little social pressure to take care of kin who are remotely related. Absence of responsibility may be the reason why fewer of those with collateral kin made wills than those whose kin were more closely related. Freedom of testation apparently did not serve as an impetus to will making. Decedents whose only next of kin were their spouses were also relatively unlikely to make a will. It should be noted that in this family circumstance the intestate distribution duplicated the distribution chosen by most testators. (See Table 4–10.)

TABLE 4–10 MEAN AGE AND TYPE OF SURVIVING KIN IN DECEDENT SAMPLE AND SURVIVOR POPULATION, BY NUMBER AND PER CENT TESTATE

Surviving Kin	Decedent Sample			Survivor Population		
	Number	Per Cent Testate	Mean Age	Number	Per Cent Testate	Mean Age
Collateral kin	75	61.3	71.6	74	60.8	55.7
Spouse only	60	61.7	68.3	63	63.5	52.6
Spouse plus lineal kin	321	70.7	62.5	677	55.5	44.8
Lineal kin only	191	72.8	72.2	275	62.6	54.3
Total	647[a]			1,089[b]		

[a] There were 12 decedents who were survived by no next of kin.
[b] There were 10 survivors who were survived by no next of kin, plus 3 who refused to give the information. These figures omit the 132 questionnaire respondents, since it was difficult to obtain reliable information about legal next of kin.

Testators who were survived by spouses and lineal kin most often deviated from the statutes to bequeath the entire estate to the spouse. Decedents survived by spouses and lineal kin had a high rate of testacy despite the fact that they were from six to ten years younger than the other groups. In the survivor population, those who would be survived by spouses and lineal kin were least likely to be testate. However, they were from eight to eleven years younger than the other groups. The data in Table 4–2 showed that 70 per cent of the decedents in their sixties were testate, and the data in Table 4–5 indicated that 56 per cent of the survivors in their forties were testate.

Size of kin group. Having a large number of kin may force a person into testacy. If a decedent is intestate, the next of kin are the inheritors. Intestate division among many kin could mean excessive fragmentation of the estate. One function of the will can be to reduce the number of inheritors, although the use of contingency provisions (naming those who inherit if a primary beneficiary is deceased) allows a larger number of people, some of whom

TABLE 4–11 MEAN SIZE OF KIN GROUP, INHERITORS, AND CONTINGENTS, BY CONDITION OF TESTACY FOR DECEDENT SAMPLE AND SURVIVOR POPULATION

	Decedent Sample		Survivor Population	
Status	Testate	Intestate	Testate	Intestate
Next of kin	3.5	3.2	3.1	3.2
Inheritors	2.1	—	1.9	—
Contingents	2.1	—	1.6	—

may not be legal next of kin, to be mentioned in the will (see Table 4–11). The testators in both the decedent sample and the survivor population named fewer inheritors than their legal next of kin who would normally take of the estate under intestate distribution. Thus, the findings show that testacy is a mechanism for reducing estate fragmentation. Since the size of the kin group was nearly the same for both the testate and intestate, it must be concluded that the size of the kin group is not a predictor of testacy.

Economic Class

Although a will may accomplish many purposes, it is basically a tool for disposing of real and personal property at death. The hypothesis that economic class is positively associated with testacy is based upon this primary function of a will. The indicator of economic class for the decedent sample was size of the estate; for the survivor group, it was monthly household income.

Decedent sample. The gross median size for testate estates in this sample was $15,000; the median for intestate estates was $6,000. Net estate medians were $12,000 and $3,000 for testate and intestate, respectively.[20] The average net estate for all decedents was $27,007; for testate decedents, $35,160; and for intestate decedents, $6,694. The average gross estate for all decedents was $31,097; for testate decedents, $41,218; for the intestate group, $8,599. These means correspond with the values given in the Cook County study of $41,885 for testate estates and $7,920 for the intestate estates.[21]

Individuals who died testate had, on the average, total estates that were five times larger than the estates of those who died intestate. The chief holding of

20. The gross estate consists of all the decedent's assets as listed on the "Itemized Statement for Determination of Inheritance Tax." Included herein is a certain amount of technically nonprobate property, for example, joint and survivorship bank accounts. See Chapter 2, p. 34. The gross estate minus administrative costs, funeral expense, federal estate tax, and other debts equals the net estate. Another indication of the greater wealth of those who die testate is that federal estate tax was paid on 32 estates in the sample; all were testate.

21. Dunham, op. cit., p. 264. In the same paragraph, we learn that "in 1953 the mean testate estate was $15,000 and the mean intestate estate was $4,000. The 1957 figure was substantially higher for the testate estates where the mean figure was $22,000 compared with $5,000 for intestate estates." We believe that these latter sets of figures are

intestate decedents was real estate, most usually the place of residence; the chief holdings of testate decedents were bank savings and investments such as stocks and bonds. It is in regard to these intangibles, whether individually or jointly held, that the testate and intestate groups differ. The least difference was found in the category of tangible personal property, the most commonly listed item being the automobile (see Table 4–12).[22]

TABLE 4–12 MEAN WORTH OF TESTATE AND INTESTATE ESTATES, BY TYPE OF ASSET AND TOTAL WORTH, ACCORDING TO RATIO OF TESTATE TO INTESTATE ESTATES

Type of Asset	Testate Mean Total	Intestate Mean Total	Ratio of Testate to Intestate
Mean net worth	$35,160	$6,694	5.25:1
Mean gross worth	41,218	8,599	4.79:1
Real property	11,018	4,765	2.31:1
Tangible personal	815	450	1.81:1
Intangible personal	21,367	2,556	8.36:1
Joint and survivor	2,102	278	7.56:1
Insurance	325	268	1.21:1
Total	$35,627[a]	$8,317[a]	

[a] The totals do not equal the mean gross worth because the value of 76 powers of appointment, transfers, pensions, or miscellaneous assets were omitted from the testate type of asset; and the value of 23 pensions or miscellaneous assets were omitted from the intestate type of asset.

Since both the age of the testator and the size of the estate were found to be related to the condition of testacy, age and size of the estate were correlated. The correlation is positive but not very high.[23] The conclusion to be drawn is that age and economic class have separate and unique effects on testacy.

Survivor population. There is a tendency for will makers, more than nonwill makers, to have the highest monthly incomes among the survivor group, but this is not a straight-line correlation (see Table 4–13).

The lowest proportion of testators was found in the $401 to $600 income bracket. The survivors with household incomes of $801 to $1,000 were less likely to be testate than those with incomes of $200 or less. There was, how-

medians rather than means. The mean net worth in the Dane County study was $11,500. Ward and Beuscher, op. cit., p. 400. The Dane County figure is substantially lower than the figure in the present study. Their figure, however, is for all years going back to 1929. The Dane County study utilized inheritance tax records; whereas the Cook County values were those of the probate assets.

22. These data were derived from the probate docket and may or may not reflect the actual value of the estate. See Chapter 8, pp. 178–180, for a discussion of hidden assets such as insurance. The main point, however, is to note the large differences in the mean worth of the estates, testate and intestate. It is assumed that the proportion of hidden assets was randomly distributed among all decedent cases.

23. The Pearson r is .168 for age and gross estate, and .173 for age and net estate.

TABLE 4–13 MONTHLY HOUSEHOLD INCOME OF SURVIVORS AND PER CENT TESTATE

Monthly Household Income	Number	Per Cent Testate
$200 or less	93	60.2
$201–$400	156	55.1
$401–$600	317	43.8
$601–$800	187	55.6
$801–$1,000	157	54.8
$1,001–$1,500	129	75.2
$1,501 and over	82	89.0
Total	1,121[a]	57.2

[a] Testacy not known for 4 survivors; 109 refused to give income.

ever, an important shift in the proportion of testate survivors when the monthly income was above $1,000.

These findings can be explained partly by the income distribution according to age groups. The median income for those in their twenties was $401 to $600. The median income for those in their thirties, forties, and fifties was $601 to $800. The lowest median income was $201 to $400 and was found among those in their sixties, seventies, and eighties. When age was controlled, there was a significant positive association between income and testacy in the categories up to age 59 (see Table 4–14). A possible interpretation of this finding for the older group is that the proportion of testators at age 60 and above is so high that few readily visible differences appear between the testate and the intestate at this age.

TABLE 4–14 RELATIONSHIP BETWEEN INCOME AND TESTACY, WITH AGE CONTROLLED FOR SURVIVOR POPULATION

Age Group[a]	Number	Point Biserial Correlation	t	Significance
21–39	317	.156	2.802	.01
40–49	325	.214	3.935	.01
50–59	265	.226	3.762	.01
60–89	212	.074	1.074	n.s.[c]
Total	1,119			

[a] At both ends of the age scale, two decades were combined into a single category because of the small number of cases in these age groups. This also holds true for succeeding tables.
[b] Age unknown for 2.
[c] No significance.

While it could be argued that capital accumulation is more relevant to the condition of testacy than monthly income is, income was chosen as the indicator of economic class in the survivor population because it was thought that more people would be willing and able to divulge their income than their total assets. It cannot readily be assumed that current income is a good indicator of capital accumulation because the high point of income does not coincide with the high point of capital accumulation.[24] Given these limitations, income was shown to be a good predictor of testacy for those under 60 when age was controlled. Thus it may be said that individuals write their wills not only to dispose of their capital but also in anticipation of distributing capital they hope to accumulate from investment before death.

Social Status

The indicators of social status are occupation and education. For the decedent sample, it was necessary to use decedent's usual occupation, thereby omitting housewives. For the survivor population, it was possible to use either the interviewee's or the breadwinner's occupation. By using the breadwinner's occupation, far fewer "not employed" responses were obtained. For both groups, education applied to the particular decedent or survivor. Occupation and education were used separately in examining social status and testacy rather than in combination as an index.[25]

Decedent sample. Testacy is positively associated with professional, managerial, and administrative occupations.[26] Members of these three occupational groupings were found to be testate above the average for the entire group (see Table 4–15).

In analyzing the data by age, it was found that occupational status was associated with testacy for gainfully employed individuals. After age 60, the association between occupational status and testacy was not statistically significant (see Table 4–16). It is likely that for retired individuals the occupation before retirement is not a good indicator of social status or predictor of relevant behavior. However, nearly three-fourths of the sample decedents age 60 and over

24. Harold Lydall, "The Life Cycle in Income, Saving and Asset Ownership," *Econometrica* 23 (April, 1955): 133.

25. August B. Hollingshead, *Two-Factor Index of Social Position* (New Haven, Conn., 1957), mimeographed.

26. The Dane County study revealed no significant differences between occupational groups with respect to testacy. The occupation categories used in that study were: professional and proprietor; clerical, sales, and unskilled; skilled and semiskilled; and farmers. Ward and Beuscher, op. cit., p. 412. Perhaps both the Ward and Beuscher categories and the Hollingshead categories are ill suited to their task. A study of Columbia University and teachers college graduates in 1954 indicated that the percentages of living graduates with wills varied from 29 per cent for law to 69 per cent for pharmacy graduates. The other schools showed 47 per cent for teachers college, 51 per cent for journalism, and 45 per cent for engineering. Richard R. Powell, *Real Property*, vol. 6 (New York: Matthew Bender, 1958), p. 606, cited in Dunham, op. cit., p. 245. The high rate of testacy among pharmacists is not accounted for by relative prestige but most probably by ownership of a business.

TABLE 4–15 OCCUPATION OF DECEDENTS AND PER CENT TESTATE

Occupation	Number	Per Cent Testate
Unskilled manual	55	61.8
Semiskilled manual	76	60.5
Skilled manual	140	67.1
Clerical, sales, and technicians	92	63.0
Administrators, small business, and minor professionals	41	85.4
Managers and lesser professionals	38	78.9
Major professionals and top executives	19	89.5
Total	461[a]	68.1

[a] "No usual occupation" or "usual occupation unknown" for 198 decedents.

TABLE 4–16 RELATIONSHIP BETWEEN OCCUPATION AND TESTACY, WITH AGE CONTROLLED FOR DECEDENT SAMPLE

Age Group	Number	Point Biserial Correlation	*t*	Significance
21–49	41	.475	3.369	.01
50–59	75	.380	3.508	.01
60–69	128	.087	.979	n.s.[a]
70–79	152	.000	.000	n.s.
80–99	65	.209	1.695	n.s.
Total	461			

[a] No significance.

were testate, which adds further support to the belief that there are few apparent differences between the testate and the intestate after age 60.

The relationship of education to testacy was apparent only for the highest category, the college graduate (see Table 4–17). When the data on education and testacy were controlled for age, there was no significant positive association for any age category (see Table 4–18). For the decedent sample, occupation was a better predictor of testacy than education was. This is probably because occupation is more closely related to economic status than is education.

Survivor population. Among survivors (except those in the two lowest categories, where a reversal occurs), there is a straight-line progression between the status of the occupation and the proportion testate: the higher the occupational status, the greater the percentage of testacy (see Table 4–19).[27]

27. It will be remembered that "usual occupation" was the indicator for the decedent sample and that the indicator for the survivors was "breadwinner's occupation."

TABLE 4–17 EDUCATION OF DECEDENTS AND PER CENT TESTATE

Education	Number	Per Cent Testate
Less than 8 years	144	75.0
8 years grade school	102	70.6
Some high school	80	56.3
High school graduate	85	71.8
Some college	46	67.4
College graduate	42	83.3
Total	499[a]	70.5

[a] Education unknown for 160 decedents.

TABLE 4–18 RELATIONSHIP BETWEEN EDUCATION AND TESTACY, WITH AGE CONTROLLED FOR DECEDENT SAMPLE

Age Group	Number	Point Biserial Correlation	t	Significance
21–49	47	.118	.796	n.s.[a]
50–59	74	.080	.680	n.s.
60–69	134	.125	1.447	n.s.
70–79	164	—.013	—.164	n.s.
80–99	78	.185	1.640	n.s.
Total	497[b]			

[a] No significance.
[b] Age unknown for 2 decedents.

TABLE 4–19 OCCUPATION OF SURVIVORS AND PER CENT TESTATE

Occupation	Number	Per Cent Testate
Unskilled manual	34	38.2
Semiskilled manual	129	34.1
Skilled manual	243	48.6
Clerical, sales, and technicians	202	52.5
Administrators, small business, and minor professionals	168	57.7
Managers and lesser professionals	129	67.4
Major professionals and top executives	113	81.4
Total	1,018[a]	54.7

[a] For 4 survivors, testacy was unknown; for 9, occupation was unknown; 203 survivors were not working (widows on social security, students, and so forth).

This positive association between occupational status and testacy held for the age categories up to age 60 (see Table 4–20).

TABLE 4–20 RELATIONSHIP BETWEEN OCCUPATION AND TESTACY, WITH AGE CONTROLLED FOR SURVIVOR POPULATION

Age Group	Number	Point Biserial Correlation	t	Significance
21–39	317	.444	8.821	.01
40–49	337	.248	4.698	.01
50–59	255	.299	4.982	.01
60–89	107	– .164	– 1.702	n.s.[a]
Total	1,016[b]			

[a] No significance.
[b] Age unknown for 2 survivors.

The relationship of education and testacy for the survivor population was not as significant as the relationship of occupation and testacy (see Table 4–21). When age was controlled, however, there was a positive association between education and testacy in each age category for the survivor population (see Table 4–22). This contrasts with the finding for the decedent sample.

TABLE 4–21 EDUCATION OF SURVIVORS AND PER CENT TESTATE

Education	Number	Per Cent Testate
Less than 8 years	69	63.8
8 years grade school	86	67.4
Some high school	260	50.8
High school graduate	388	51.0
Some college	212	61.8
College graduate	206	69.4
Total	1,221[a]	57.8

[a] For 9, education was unknown; and for 4, testacy was unknown.

There was a correlation between occupation and testacy for both decedents and survivors; a correlation between education and testacy was found among survivors but not among decedents. This finding indicates that occupational status is a better predictor of testacy than education is. There is no explanation immediately apparent for the disparity between decedents and survivors regarding education and testacy. Variations in sample size and age groups may be important conditions in explaining such a difference. While similar age categories were present in both the decedent sample and the survivor population,

TABLE 4–22 RELATIONSHIP BETWEEN EDUCATION AND TESTACY, WITH AGE CONTROLLED FOR SURVIVOR POPULATION

Age Group	Number	Point Biserial Correlation	*t*	Significance
21–39	336	.330	6.377	.01
40–49	349	.219	4.178	.01
50–59	283	.185	3.166	.01
60–89	249	.132	2.092	.01
Total	1,217[a]			

[a] Age unknown for 4 survivors.

they were not numerically equivalent. The decedent sample was smaller than the survivor population, and there were far fewer persons in the age categories under 60. The average age of the decedents was 67.8 years, compared with 48.4 years for the survivors. In order to determine the impact of a less certain predictive factor such as education, a sample larger than the one presently available is required.

In order to test whether the association between occupation and testacy is a spurious one, dependent upon their common association with economic status, the survivor age group 40–49 was selected. This group had a rate of testacy similar to the rate for the entire survivor group (from 56 to 58 per cent) and was the largest age group in the survivor population. Using the 314 survivors in this age group for whom there was information on testacy, income, and occupation, an attempt was made to partial out the relative effects of income and occupation (see Table 4–23). High occupational status did have an effect independent of income, but the two variables were generally additive. The highest rate of testacy appeared when individuals were living in households with monthly incomes over $1,000 and with the breadwinners in managerial or professional occupations.

TABLE 4–23 OCCUPATION AND INCOME FOR SURVIVORS, AGE 40 TO 49, BY PER CENT TESTATE

	Monthly Household Income $1,000 and under		Monthly Household Income over $1,000	
Occupation	Number	Per Cent Testate	Number	Per Cent Testate
Blue-collar	111	43.2	10	70.0
White-collar	91	50.5	29	69.0
Professional and managerial	25	68.0	48	81.3
Total	227		87	

The age group 40–49 was again used to test whether the association between education and testacy for survivors is a result of the association of both education and testacy with income. There were 325 survivors in this age group for whom there was information on testacy, income, and education (see Table 4–24). The findings were similar to those for occupation and income: high educational status had an effect independent of income, and again the two variables were generally additive. The highest rate of testacy appeared when individuals were both college graduates and living in households where monthly incomes were over $1,000.

TABLE 4–24 EDUCATION AND INCOME FOR SURVIVORS, AGE 40 TO 49, BY PER CENT TESTATE

	Monthly Household Income $1,000 and under		Monthly Household Income over $1,000	
Education	Number	Per Cent Testate	Number	Per Cent Testate
Some high school	70	47.1	6	50.0
High school graduate	145	47.6	47	74.5
College graduate	23	60.9	34	82.4
Total	238		87	

Conclusion

Two groups, decedents and their survivors, were used to test the set of hypotheses regarding testacy. The principal finding was the importance of age in relation to testacy. For both decedents and survivors, the average age of the testate was greater than that of the intestate. With each decade of life, the proportion who were testate increased. Despite this correlation of age and testacy, the predominant age for will making was between 31 and 45 for the survivors. Exactly when the decedents made their first wills is not known. Over 50 per cent of the probated wills were written at least five years before death, the difference in average age at death between testate and intestate decedents being six years. Of probated wills drawn up within the five years preceding death, over 40 per cent superseded earlier wills.

The reasoning behind the hypothesis associating age and testacy was plausible but apparently erroneous in part. Age was taken as an indication of the probability of death and the person's recognition of this probability. Possibly this is an accurate assessment of those who make their wills late in life, but it hardly accounts for those who make their wills before age 45. The most important implication of the finding on age and testacy was that while will making was correlated with age, the imminence of death did not account for the rate of testacy in either the decedent sample or the survivor population.

Several indicators were used to depict the individual's location in the family network: sex, marital status, and number and type of surviving kin. Marital status was the only factor that had a relationship to testacy. In the younger age groups, where their status was infrequent, the widowed were most often testate. In the older age groups, where their status was less frequent, the married were most often testate.[28]

Economic class was found to operate independently of age in relation to testacy. In the decedent sample, the largest differences obtained between the testate and the intestate were for intangible assets, such as stocks and savings. But in all categories of assets, as well as gross and net estate, the testate decedents surpassed the intestate. Income was found to be a good indicator of economic class and a good predictor of testacy for survivors up to the age of 60.

Two indicators, occupation and education, were used independently to establish the social status of the decedents and survivors. For both groups, testacy was found to be associated with high occupational status for those under age 60. The relationship of education and testacy held only for the survivor population and was significant for every age category. Because it was decided that a hypothesis would be accepted only if it held true for both decedents and survivors, it cannot be positively stated, without further testing, that testacy is associated with social status. The question was asked whether the relationship in the survivor group of occupation and education to testacy might be spurious because of the relationship of both to income. In checking this possibility for a subsample of survivors age 40–49, it was found that both occupation and education had effects independent of income but that these two factors were generally additive.

28. The differential of the incentives to will making in the different periods of life was not taken into account. In Appendix D, an attempt is made to recast the data on survivors into a life-cycle framework, looking separately at the married and unmarried in each age category.

Chapter 5

Conceptions of Justice: The Testator

WHAT PATTERNS of distribution were chosen by 422 testators in the decedent sample and 620 survivors who have made their wills?[1] What were the reactions of the beneficiaries and next of kin of the decedent sample to the patterns of distribution?

The following quotations indicate the importance of making a will, and they also suggest that the value system of the will maker is exposed in the provisions of the will. Through his will, the maker identifies himself.

> Everyone should make a will for orderly dispensation of funds, to assess our relationships and responsibility. A will gives us a sense of commitment beyond ourselves. It is a step in developing a value system.[2]

> The identity he (the will maker) thereby generates for himself is perhaps the most important of a long career of identity pronouncements, for it is his last—and is unalterable.[3]

There is a related consideration: the will may be viewed as evidence of the relationship existing between the testator and his family.

> One of the primary roles . . . of a transfer and exchange is to visualize, dramatize and authenticate the existence of certain fixed relations subsisting between specific people and that this relationship has a "monetary" value.[4]

In this chapter, the testate disposition of property is compared with the distribution that would have occurred if the decedent were intestate. A comparison of the pattern of testate distribution with the equivalent intestate dis-

1. There were 453 testate decedents; but in 31 estates, the primary beneficiary was deceased and the disposition went either according to the contingency provisions or according to intestate distribution. These 31 cases are discussed in Chapter 8. There were 711 interviewees who had made wills, but 73 were questionnaire respondents whose legal next of kin were difficult to ascertain. There were also 18 interviewees who had made wills but refused information concerning their heirs.
2. Gratuitous comment from an interviewee.
3. Barry Schwartz, "The Social Psychology of the Gift," *American Journal of Sociology* 73 (July, 1967):2.
4. Paul Radin, *The World of Primitive Man* (New York: H. Schuman, 1953), p. 126.

tribution makes it possible to compare equity with equality. Intestate distribution is used as a standard of equality for two reasons: (1) The intestate succession is asserted to provide for distribution in the manner the decedent "would most likely have given effect to if he had made a will."[5] Hence, the findings may be of value for future legislation. (2) The intestate succession may be interpreted as representing society's image of a universally just distribution.[6]

What is important here is the problem of distributive justice.[7] The testator's idea of justice is inferred from his will and from the motives attributed to him by his survivors. However, a testator and his survivors may not have identical ideas about what is a just and fair distribution. Yet, since in most cases this study deals with people whose backgrounds are similar to those of the testators, it is probable that there will be a large measure of consensus.

Jean Piaget states that distributive justice can be reduced to the ideas of equality or equity.[8] Equality by degree of relationship is the key to the intestate statutes. Equity is not necessarily synonymous with equality. It can be defined as (1) "the quality of being fair or impartial; fairness, impartiality" and as (2) "that which is just and fair."[9] George Homans avoids the confusion between equality and equity by stating, "This is the problem of *distributive justice:* justice in the distribution of rewards and costs between persons."[10] The

5. Allison Dunham, "The Method, Process and Frequency of Wealth Transmission at Death," *Chicago Law Review* 30 (Winter, 1962):241.

6. Some of the intestate succession law may have other purposes than describing a just distribution. In the present chapter, the study data indicate that a testator survived by collaterals appeared to have no clear pattern of disposition. (See pp. 103–104 infra.) In this respect Allison Dunham, Professor of Law, University of Chicago, and Executive Director of the National Conference of Commissioners on Uniform State Laws, indicated in personal correspondence of 24 April 1968, "that perhaps the intestate succession rule for collaterals is an 'arbitrary' rule equivalent to a 'statutory flip of the coin' to resolve a situation where decision is essential and cannot be avoided. In other words, the rule may represent an answer which states that we cannot determine what is 'just' in collateral distribution and, therefore, we use equality of distribution as the principle, albeit arbitrary. It would be theoretically possible for an intestate succession law to be drafted with the purpose of 'inducing' wills. Society might decide that distribution by private volition is such a major value that it should do everything within its power to induce people to make a will. From such a point of view, society might well conclude that the intestate succession law should deviate from common understanding and expectation in order to induce people to do what society has assumed to be desirable."

7. Aristotle stated the concept of distributive justice in *Nicomachean Ethics,* bk. V, chaps. 3 and 4. The earliest statement in American sociology may be: Frank C. Sharp, "The Criterion of Distributive Justice," *American Journal of Sociology* 2 (September, 1896):264–273. Most recently, Blau's concept of fair exchange is "fundamentally similar" to distributive justice: Peter M. Blau, *Exchange and Power in Social Life* (New York: John Wiley & Sons, Inc., 1964), pp. 151–160.

8. Jean Piaget, "Retributive and Distributive Justice," *Moral Judgment of the Child* (New York: Harcourt, Brace & World, Inc., 1932), reprinted in *Sociological Theory,* ed. Edgar Borgatta and Henry J. Meyer (New York: Alfred A. Knopf, 1956), p. 90.

9. *American College Dictionary* (New York: Random House, 1956).

10. George Caspar Homans, *Social Behavior, Its Elementary Forms* (New York: Harcourt, Brace & World, Inc., 1961), p. 74.

equitable distribution is one in which the rewards bear a relationship to the costs. Equal costs merit equal rewards, and unequal costs merit unequal rewards. This does not mean that the rewards must equal costs, for "it is always relative deprivation that raises the question of distributive justice."[11]

The failure to recognize the importance of relative deprivation leads sociologists to ignore the element of reciprocity in property inheritance or to proclaim that inheritance involves reciprocity only in the case of the wealthy. Wilbert Moore's position is typical of the latter error.

> Property inheritance has usually been neglected by those who view the obligations between generations in terms of delayed reciprocities. For the affluent, their estate can become a *quid pro quo* for old age support by the heirs.[12]

Paralleling this study is a longitudinal project on urban family kinship systems: the network of nuclear families organized along bilateral and generational lines; it is concerned with the meaning and significance of this network for member families. The network is a voluntary system of group relationships, voluntary in the sense that it has no legal basis or strong cultural prescription and that members of nuclear units make independent decisions regarding their participation. It is voluntary in still another way, in that, like any other institutional system, this kinship system competes for users and supporters. The foundations of the network's structure and functions are exchanges of goods and services based upon uneven reciprocities. Situations, conditions, and expectations determine the uneven exchange between individuals and member families. The style of distributive justice is derived from experience and tradition. The network can persist over time only when it provides sufficient pay-off for the participants even though the exchanges are of a different order and kind.[13]

It is the contention of the present study that property inheritance is relevant to an understanding of reciprocity and distributive justice even when the amount of property transferred is so small that its value is more symbolic than real.[14] Practicing attorneys assert that heirs may be more acrimonious in small

11. Ibid., p. 243.
12. Wilbert E. Moore, "Aging and the Social System," *Aging and Social Policy,* ed. John C. McKinney and Frank T. DeVyver (New York: Appleton-Century-Crofts, 1966), p. 37.
13. Marvin B. Sussman, "Theoretical Bases for an Urban Kinship Network System," paper presented at the annual meeting of the National Council on Family Relations, October, 1966, Minneapolis, Minnesota; idem, "Relationships of Adult Children With Their Parents in the United States," *Family, Intergenerational Relationships and Social Structure,* ed. Ethel Shanas and Gordon Streib (Englewood Cliffs, N.J.: Prentice-Hall, Inc., 1965), pp. 62–92; and idem, "The Urban Kin Network in the Formulation of Family Theory," *Families in East and West: Socialization Process and Kinship Ties,* ed. Reuben Hill and René König (Paris: Mouton, 1970).
14. The distinction between reciprocity and distributive justice is this: reciprocity in-

estates; it is not unknown for the costs of a will contest to consume an entire estate.

To say that testators may reciprocate in their wills for past kindnesses does not mean that justice is paramount in the minds of all testators. One of the more famed will contests in the United States followed the admission to probate of Commodore Vanderbilt's will. To realize dynastic ambitions, the Commodore gave the bulk of his estate to one son. Although his other son and his daughters were "remembered," their anger was that of the relatively deprived.[15]

Previous studies of probate material highlighted two findings: (1) the devise and bequest of the entire estate to the spouse was the most frequent deviation from the intestate distribution, and (2) unrelated persons and institutions were infrequent beneficiaries. In this study, the pattern of giving the entire estate to the spouse was encountered more frequently in relatively small estates, and the pattern of willing to unrelated individuals and/or institutions was associated with either wealth or the absence of immediate family. The rationale is self-evident. The person with a limited estate has limited freedom. He cannot provide for his family and make bequests to others. In the case of a surviving spouse, the entire estate may be required for maintenance until death. The absence of immediate family, like the presence of wealth, is a situation of freedom for the testator. These two conditions provide the only possibility for divergence from the typical distribution.[16]

Spouse and/or Lineal Kin Survived

In this section, distribution patterns of testators who were survived by their spouse and/or kin in the direct line are discussed. This was the majority situation for both decedent and survivor testators. Of the 422 decedent testators under discussion, 382 (91 per cent) were survived by their spouses and/or lineal kin. The next of kin for 574 of the 620 survivor testators (93 per cent) were their spouses and/or lineal kin.

Spouse Was the Sole Survivor

When a person is married but has no children, grandchildren, or parents (no lineal descendants or ascendants), the intestate distribution in Ohio gives all to the surviving spouse. The majority of testators in these circumstances also will their entire estates to their spouses. In the decedent sample, there were 37

volves the exchange between two persons; distributive justice involves two or more people in their relationship with a third party.

15. For an account of the contest, see Frank Clark, "The Commodore Left Two Sons," *American Heritage* 17 (April, 1966): 4–9. See also, Wayne Andrews, *The Vanderbilt Legend* (New York: Harcourt, Brace & World, Inc., 1941); Edwin P. Hoyt, *The Vanderbilts and Their Fortunes* (New York: Doubleday & Company, Inc., 1962).

16. For the very wealthy, there is the added incentive of estate taxes. At this level, freedom is the choice between charity and the government.

cases in which the spouse was the sole surviving next of kin; in 33 of these cases, the spouse was bequeathed the entire estate.[17] In the survivor population, the corresponding figures were 39 and 34. Only a minority of decedents (11 per cent) deviated from the intestate pattern of distribution. These cases will be examined in order to describe the circumstances that led to this deviant pattern of distribution.

In two decedent sample cases, the spouse was disinherited; in two others, the spouse received only a portion of the estate.

Case 378. The decedent was an 83-year-old man whose only next of kin was his 80-year-old second wife. His will, which was written thirteen years before his death, left an estate of $4,000 to be divided equally between ten nieces and nephews. The widow elected to take against the will. We were unable to interview the widow. Our information comes from seven of the nieces and nephews. The will was drawn up after his first wife died and before he married the second. His second marriage failed in a very short time, and the couple separated. At that time, the second wife received one-half of his assets and the household furnishings that had belonged to his first wife. He did not divorce her because by not doing so, she was entitled to the wife's portion of his social security. After their separation, he lived for some years with a niece and later in a nursing home. The second wife did not attend the funeral. The nieces and nephews spoke fondly of him. They were not really bitter about the settlement, but they did voice such sentiments as, "The law should respect a man's will," and "A legal separation ought to be the same as a divorce."

Case 475. The testator, a male, left a will in which he divided his estate equally between two sisters. The will was written less than a year before his death. His widow elected to take against the will. The net estate was $23,000. This was distributed half to the widow and one-fourth to each of the two sisters. We were not able to interview anyone on the case. The death certificate was not located in Ohio.

Case 495. The decedent was a 69-year-old male who left a $30,000 estate. He left $100 to a sister in Greece and $1.00 to a brother in this country. The rest went to his wife. She said that the sister in Greece did not have much and that the money would mean something to her. The $1.00 to his brother was the lawyer's suggestion to prevent him from contesting the will. There was no bad feeling involved between the brothers. The surviving spouse has included the decedent's brother in her new will.

Case 325. The decedent was a 75-year-old woman who left an estate of $40,000 to be divided equally between her husband and her son-in-law. A sister was the contingent beneficiary for all personal property, and the son-in-law was contingent to the remainder of the property. A reading of the will gives the impression of a strong-willed woman and of a remarkable bond between her and her son-in-law. The will, written six months before her death, contained some unusual provisions: (a) no minister or priest

17. Dunham found 17 per cent of the Chicago testators (one out of six) deviated from the intestate distribution in the circumstance where the spouse was the only survivor, compared with 11 per cent in this study. Dunham, loc. cit.

was to be at her wake; (b) her burial expenses were to be $900 to $1,100 and no more; and (c) the son-in-law was to be appointed guardian of her husband if the husband became incompetent. The statement that she was "not acting under duress, menace, fraud or undue influence of any person whatsoever" appeared twice. The husband died a few days after the settlement of the estate. The son-in-law and executor, although not employed, said he was too busy to be seen. Our only information comes from the decedent's sister. She reported that the decedent's only daughter had died four years before her mother. After the daughter's death, the son-in-law had a heart attack and the decedent took care of him. He was not able to work after his heart attack, so the sister felt he needed the money and in this sense it was fair distribution. She did have suspicions about his honesty; she knew her sister wanted her to have her linens, silver, and diamonds. She wondered if she would get them. After her brother-in-law's funeral, she went to the house, and the son-in-law would not let her in the door.

There are five cases in the survivor population in which the pattern of distribution differed from an allocation of the entire estate to the spouse.

Case 330–02. A 46-year-old woman is willing her half of the house (held in tenancy in common) to her husband. In case of common disaster, the husband's children (her stepchildren) are the contingent beneficiaries. She is willing her personal things and her stocks and bonds to her brothers, sisters, nieces, and nephews. This is her third marriage; the present marriage was contracted two years ago.

At this time in this survivor's life, the attachment to her family of orientation seemed to be stronger than to the spouse of her third marriage. It would appear also in this case and others examined in this study that marriages among middle-aged and older persons were for companionship.[18] When a marriage was contracted later in life without the desire or probability of children, economic resources of the marital partners were pooled to effect satisfactory living arrangements, but at death the testator's resources, as a rule, reverted to his prior family, thereby providing intergenerational continuity and order.

Case 497–02. A 79-year-old woman who married a widower when she was 58 is willing part of her estate to her husband and part to her sister, "because I don't trust he'd bury me." She said she loved him, but they had not agreed on financial matters. When she was sick, she had to pay her hospital bill from her social security funds (pre-Medicare), while he was putting money into a joint account with his daughter.

This case illustrates the confusion surrounding these later marriages in which the financial arrangement or meaning of the marriage was ambiguous. Having contracted the marriage for companionship or "fun," the parties to it may have found that they had conflicting definitions of their responsibilities toward each other in times of crisis caused by illness, financial loss, accident, disability, and death.

18. Benjamin Barr Lindsey and Wainwright Evans, *Companionate Marriage* (New York: Boni & Liveright, 1927). See especially Chapter 1.

Spouse and/or Lineal Kin Survived

Case 257–01. A 62-year-old childless widower who had recently been married for the second time to a widow is leaving her approximately 25 per cent of the estate; the remainder is divided between both his and her relatives, with small amounts going to friends.

Case 593–01. The testator is a 59-year-old woman. She is leaving about 80 per cent of her estate to her husband. Her four cats each will receive $1,000 legacies with her husband appointed as their guardian. Specific bequests have been made to friends and to institutions. Other than her husband, her nearest relative is an elderly uncle.

Case 395–01. A 68-year-old man is willing all to his wife with the exception of bequests to various charitable and religious organizations. He said he originally made a will in order to take care of the organizations that were important to him.

In other cases, the marital situation may have been amiable, but the testator apparently felt the surviving spouse would not need all the estate, and therefore he could take care of relatives, friends, pets, and organizations.

Spouse and Lineal Kin Were the Survivors

When a person was survived by a spouse and either lineal ascendants or descendants, the intestate distribution gave a portion of the estate to the surviving spouse. This portion varied from three-quarters, when the decedent was survived by a spouse and a parent or parents, to one-third, when the decedent was survived by a spouse and two or more children. The large majority of testators altered the distribution by bequeathing all to the surviving spouse (see Table 5–1).[19]

TABLE 5–1 PATTERN OF DISTRIBUTION WHEN SPOUSE AND LINEAL KIN SURVIVE

Cases	Decedent Sample	Survivor Population
Spouse is sole heir	194	313
Per cent willing all to spouse	85.8	85.3
Total	226	367

Male and female testators differed very little in this pattern of willing the entire estate to the spouse.

It was hypothesized that the pattern of giving all to the surviving spouse would be more frequently encountered in relatively small estates. This occurred for both the decedent sample and the survivor population. In the dece-

19. In the Cook County probate study, an examination of 22 testate estates where the deceased was survived by spouse and children showed that 100 per cent left all the property to the surviving spouse contrary to intestacy laws. Dunham, op. cit., p. 252.

dent sample, the mean net estate for those who willed all to their spouses was less than half as large as the mean net estate for those with other patterns of distribution. In comparing median net estates, it was found that the difference was not as great but still significant. Those leaving all to their spouses had net estates only slightly over half the size of those who did not (see Table 5–2). In

TABLE 5–2 PATTERN OF DISTRIBUTION, BY ECONOMIC CONDITION

Economic Condition	Pattern of Distribution	
	Spouse-All	Other
Decedent sample		
Mean net estate	$17,674	$44,235
Median net estate	10,000	19,000
	(*N* = 194)	(*N* = 32)
Survivor population		
Median income (per month)	$601–$800	$1,001–$1,500
Modal income (per month)	$401–$600	$1,500 and over
	(*N* = 313)	(*N* = 54)

the survivor population, the median and modal household incomes were considerably lower for those with the spouse-all pattern than for those with other patterns of distribution.

The number of cases deviating from the spouse-all pattern (86) is too large for detailed examination. These deviations consisted of cases of complete disinheritance of the spouse, allowance to the spouse of the statutory share, and small bequests to others.

The testators who deviated from the norm of bequeathing their entire estates to their spouses generally had higher incomes or larger estates than those who followed the norm (see Table 5–2). They could afford to remember other relatives or friends in their wills. How much one can afford depends on one's style of life; an amount that is considered ample by one person may be considered a pittance by another. In large estates, tax considerations may be an important factor affecting the pattern of distribution. Consequently, the pattern of giving to charities, funds, and relatives does not necessarily indicate that a poor relationship existed between the marital pair.

In the case of a first marriage, a man may leave all to his wife with the assurance that she will leave her estate to their common children. One implication of the concept of justice is that responsibilities must be met. These responsibilities do not end with the death of the testator; the obligation of the surviving spouse to provide care for minor children may extend over a long period of her lifetime. Her need to maintain her financial independence continues well into old age, with children providing care services at the termination of life and then receiving the remains of the legacy.

Cases involving more than one marriage, with children from the prior marriage, raise a problem concerning family responsibility. If justice demands that the financial responsibilities of both marriages be met, this may be impossible unless the estate is large. Few of the decedents who remarried and who had minor estates resolved the situation to the satisfaction of family members. Remarriage created a variety of distribution patterns. In the decedent sample, there were 28 cases in which the decedents had remarried. In 16 cases, the entire estates were willed to the spouses or legatees of the last marriage; in 12 cases, the estates were divided between the legatees of the last and earlier marriages.

TABLE 5–3 COMPARISON OF REMARRIED DECEDENT TESTATORS, BY PATTERN OF DISTRIBUTION

Comparison Variables	Pattern of Distribution	
	All to Last Marriage (*N* = 16)	Divided (*N* = 12)
Duration of last marriage (in years)		
Mean	21.5	18
Median	22.5	15
Net estate		
Mean	$26,287	$31,250
Median	14,000	15,000

Testators who divided their estates between their marriages differed slightly from those who did not in two respects: (1) their estates were larger, and (2) their latest marriages were of shorter duration.

In estates where the testators divided their property between their marriages, two legal mechanisms were used: (1) the prenuptial agreement and (2) the life estate. There were four such cases.

Case 534. A 91-year-old testator left his second wife $30,000. At the time of their marriage five years before he died, they had entered into a prenuptial agreement that gave her $15,000. Two years later, in a codicil to his will, he increased the amount to $30,000. The residue of his $200,000 estate was divided equally among the three children of his first marriage. The decedent had also been the beneficiary of a trust fund set up by his first wife. With his death, the trust went to the children. In addition, the decedent had given substantial gifts during his lifetime to his children. The widow had an income from the investments of her first husband. She had no children. Her own will includes her brother, relatives of her first husband, and her second husband's children. The children had been consulted about their stepmother's portion. They expressed no objection when their father increased her share.

The settlement in this case was completely satisfactory to all concerned. Whether this amiable settlement can be attributed to communication between the concerned parties, size of estate, or the excellent financial condition of the beneficiaries cannot be easily discerned. It was discovered that prenuptial agreements, by themselves, did not circumvent later dissension.

Case 041. The decedent was a 60-year-old woman. She was survived by a second husband from a marriage contracted three years before her death and by three sons from her first marriage. At the time of their marriage, they agreed that her house, valued at $6,000 and her chief asset, should be left entirely to her three sons. The widower was the beneficiary of a $1,000 insurance policy. Litigation between the surviving spouse and the children occurred. There was disagreement concerning the ownership of certain household goods. The widower claimed that his stepchildren immediately converged on the house and began emptying dresser drawers. He had to hire an attorney to make sure they did not take what was his; he forgot to list the dryer on the inventory and had to buy it back for $50.00. The sons claimed that their mother and stepfather had a verbal agreement that the insurance policy would be used to pay for funeral expenses, but instead the widower put in a claim against the estate. This claim was allowed, but a further claim that he made for repairs to the house was disallowed. The sons were extreme in their defamation of their stepfather's character.

Despite the presence of a prenuptial agreement, the contents of which were known to all parties, the settlement of the estate involved much strife. Whether this would have been avoided by a more specific document is doubtful, since quarreling developed over relatively minor household items.

The following case illustrates the use of both the prenuptial agreement and the life estate.

Case 044. The decedent was a 73-year-old male. His will read in part, "I give, devise, and bequeath all of my real property, further known as . . . [address] to my three daughters, children of my first marriage, and to my stepdaughter, of my second marriage, share and share alike, subject however and notwithstanding to the antenuptial agreement entered into, to the life estate of my present wife [his third], who shall have full and unrestricted use of said real estate so long as she remains my widow without remarrying and thus be vested with all the rights and privileges of a life tenant and upon her remarriage her interest in the said real estate shall terminate." The life estate seemed to work to no one's advantage in this case. The widow said, "I would be better off in an apartment but I promised my husband I would stay here—he was good to me and I won't break my word, although they are waiting for me to die, but I won't die." The widow was 72 years old, and she had been married to the decedent for ten years. She was correct in her judgment that her late husband's children were waiting for her to die. The following sentiment was typical: "She may live another ten years and the house will be worth nothing by then." The house was located in a deteriorating neighborhood.

Lawrence Friedman states that, "in urban areas, the legal life estate has practically disappeared."[20] Case *044* illustrates some reasons for this decline: ownership of urban real estate has become a speculative venture, and fluctuations in

20. Lawrence Friedman, "Patterns of Testation in the 19th Century: A Study of Essex

value over a relatively short time period make it imperative that the owner has the freedom to sell at the best market price.

Case 616. The decedent was a 68-year-old woman. Her will stipulated that all real property would go to her second husband as long as he remained a widower. After his death or remarriage, the estate would go to her three children in fee simple absolute, share and share alike. Her personal property was bequeathed half to her husband and half to her children. The real property, valued at $25,000, was the chief asset in the estate. The marriage had endured for thirty years. The children felt the life estate was fair. "My stepfather has lived in that home for twenty-five years. He wouldn't just want to take up roots. If he tried anything funny or got married, he would lose his share."

An important factor in this case is that the marriage lasted long enough to be considered a "major marriage."[21] Also, the home was situated in a stable middle-class area. This may in part explain the difference in the attitudes of the children in Cases 044 and 616.

Mental anguish may be one consequence when the inheritance involves property such as a home and when there has been a remarriage.

Case 562. The decedent was a 74-year-old man. He left his house (appraised at $8,500) to a grandson (the son of a deceased son of his first marriage) and the residue of the estate, about $3,500, to his second wife. Two living children were disinherited. Eight months after probate proceedings were initiated, the wife elected to take against, rather than under, the will. Two months after that she vacated her election: "The applicant has, since said election, suffered mental disturbance and anguish, that she has been unable to have peace of mind and therefore makes this request to vacate her decision." Our only interviewee, the disinherited son, thought his father gave the house to the grandson because he wanted it to stay in the family and the grandson bore his name (the interviewee had married late and had no children). Several times during the interview, the son remarked that his stepmother should have had the house —she had lived there forty-three years. We were unable to interview the grandson-heir. On the first visit to the house, he refused at the door. On the second visit some months later, the interviewer saw a sign on the door warning against the theft of government property. The house had been purchased for a throughway. The neighbors did not know where the grandson had gone.

More than half of the remarried testators (16) willed all to their surviving spouses. In 6 of these 16 cases, the previous marriage had been dissolved by

County (New Jersey) Wills," *The American Journal of Legal History* 8 (1964):42.

21. Jessie Bernard, *Remarriage* (New York: The Dryden Press, 1956), p. 14. Bernard considers all remarriages taking place before age 25 as major and those taking place at ages 50 to 59 minor. All others are relegated to limbo. The underlying thought behind the major-minor distinction is the emotional significance of the marriage and, to a lesser degree, its duration. The Cleveland study considers duration as a better index of significance than age at remarriage. Duration reflects not only significance but investment.

divorce. This contrasted with one divorce in the 12 cases in which the testators distributed the estates between children of the first marriages and the present spouses. The divorces in these cases often resulted in alienation and isolation of the testators from their children.

Case 065. A 76-year-old man left his entire estate to his 60-year-old widow. They had been married for seventeen years. He was also survived by two children of his first marriage, a daughter whom he had not seen since she was 10 years old and a son whom he had seen twice in the past twenty years. The son came to the funeral; the daughter sent flowers. "Regardless of whether I knew him or not, we were his children," but "I didn't think I should get anything. He never contacted us; never supported us." Due to the expenses of his last illness (in a state hospital), the initially small estate dwindled to $600.

Case 159. An 86-year-old male decedent left his entire estate ($6,000) to his wife. His four children were named as contingent beneficiaries. The children differed in their views about the fairness of this disposition: "We weren't close to Father, so we didn't expect anything. We always lived with Mother." "I'm not greedy, but blood is thicker than water." "If there is just enough for her [the widow], I wouldn't want to take it." "If she [the widow] dies, it does seem like her children will get our share." The widow said her husband had wanted to leave something to his children, but she told him this was unfair and her lawyer talked him into leaving it all to her. They had been married twenty-eight years. This man also died in the state hospital.

Case 532. A 62-year-old man left his entire estate (about $200,000) to his second wife. "For reasons of my own I make no provision for any of my children." He had been divorced from his children's mother when the children were 12 and 5. Although he supported the children and had the legal right to see them, his first wife had effectively blocked his visitation rights. When his children were married, his name did not appear in the newspaper announcements. Once he was on the same plane as his daughter, and she turned her back on him. He had been married to his second wife for seventeen years. Her daughter by a previous marriage was the contingent beneficiary of the estate.

Case 202. A 72-year-old woman left her estate of $23,000 to her second husband, and a charity was named as contingent beneficiary. Five children from her first marriage were disinherited. When her first marriage was dissolved by divorce, the three oldest children went with their mother; the two youngest remained with their father. In adulthood, all the children located in the Cleveland area. Her second marriage lasted thirty-five years. The children felt it was fair that the husband received the estate: "He worked hard; they both did." The husband said, "If they had had to take care of her, it would be different. But they didn't help." Although there was a feeling of justice about the settlement, there was little love lost between the stepchildren and their mother's second husband. He was a deeply religious man, and they "picked up their wives in liquor joints."

Case 584. A 51-year-old male was survived by his second wife, two children from his first marriage, and two children from his second marriage. His wife inherited the entire estate; all four children were mentioned as contingent beneficiaries. His widow felt the settlement was fair "because when we married, he only had what he stood in; in order to get a divorce, he had to give up everything." The couple had been married eighteen years. The estate totaled nearly $50,000.

In the following case, the first marriage was ended by either divorce or desertion.

Case 290. A 61-year-old male was survived by his second wife, their son, and a son from his first marriage. Acting on the lawyer's advice, he disinherited both sons in order to avoid giving the first son any claim on the estate. According to his second wife, he "had" to marry a girl in Wales, but he never believed the son was his. He lived with her for a few months and then got a job as a seaman and came here. He never went back, and he never corresponded with her or the son. The second marriage had lasted thirty years. The estate was worth $13,000.

A number of considerations entered the remarried testator's decision to make a particular distribution between his two families. Would the surviving spouse have adequate resources? Had the spouse contributed to the accumulation of the estate? Were the children "close"? These same elements appeared to enter into the judgments of the survivors about the justice of the disposition. Few children wished to see an elderly stepparent destitute, and in most cases the stepparent's need was greater than their own. If the estate had been built up through the efforts of the partners in the second marriage, a spouse-all disposition appeared fair. If, however, the estate could be attributed in part to the efforts of a deceased parent, then generally the children did not feel it was fair that only the second spouse profited.

The probable disposition that the second spouse would make of the property was another element. If the second spouse had children of his or her own, there was the realistic fear that these children would be beneficiaries when the surviving spouse died. A life estate would seem to meet the objectives of providing the spouse with adequate resources while ensuring the preservation of the estate for the bloodline. But practically, the life estate may create as many problems as it solves.

Lineal Kin Were the Survivors

Parents or children and/or grandchildren were the only surviving next of kin for 115 decedent testators and 168 survivors. For 56 per cent of the decedents and 23 per cent of the survivors, the distribution deviated from the intestate pattern.

Parents were the sole survivors. When no family of procreation survives (that is, spouse or children), the distribution is made to surviving parent or parents under intestate statutes.

In the decedent sample, two testators were survived by their parents. In both cases, the will provided for the distribution of the estate to siblings rather than to parents. The reasons for disinheriting parents in these instances were not based on malicious forethought. Rather, this pattern of distribution was chosen because the care and protection of the parents were uppermost in the minds of the testators.

Case 560. Ninety-nine per cent of the decedent's estate was left to the sister who is now caring for the aged mother and therefore would be in greatest need of funds.

Case 296. A widowed female left all to one of her sisters, with her mother contingent. The inheriting sister commented, "The intestate distribution is not fair. Mother would squander the money. This way is better because Mary knew I'd take care of Mother." Her own will leaves her estate in trust with two other sisters for the care of the mother.

Similar concerns were expressed by ten other interviewees; the intent was not to neglect their parents, even though six deviated from the intestate pattern. In two cases, the estate was left to siblings for the specific purpose of caring for the parents. In another two cases, parents inherited 50 per cent and 75 per cent, the rest going to siblings who were close to the parents. The fifth case is interesting because of the carefully thought-out plan of a 25-year-old man.

Case 070–02. The survivor has insurance set up in a trust fund for his younger brothers and sisters, those who are living at home. His mother is the executrix. "I figured Mother would be hard pressed to get them through school. This would be a way of assuring they get to college. Anything left over goes to Mother." Excluded are any that are married and also a brother who is a priest and a sister who is a nun.

In the final atypical case, the mother is not included presumably because the survivor does not expect to predecease her. He described his relationship with his mother as very close before her stroke. He is leaving his property to siblings.

Minor children were the survivors. The "poor little orphans" are a relic from an era when the longevity of the population was considerably less than it is now. Of the entire testate decedent sample of 453, one testator left only a minor child.

Case 057. A 55-year-old widower left as his only heir his son, aged 13. He left $9,000 in trust, with his sister appointed as trustee. The will further stipulated that the sister must provide a home for the boy. After his wife died, the decedent and his son had made their home with this sister. At the time of his wife's death, he had offered his son to his wife's sister, but she refused. It was at this time that he drew up a will naming his own sister as trustee. At the time of his death, he had not been able to find steady employment. Despondent, he committed suicide. After his death, his sister-in-law instigated a custody suit and won. We interviewed the sister who was named in the will as trustee. She had surreptitiously kept tabs on the boy and found he was all right. In addition to being the beneficiary of the trust, he receives social security death benefits.

Another decedent testator was survived by both minor and adult children.

Case 201. A 58-year-old widow left four adult children from her first marriage and a minor son (aged 17) from her second marriage. Her property (about $10,000) was divided, one-half to the minor and the remaining half was distributed equally to the four surviving adult children. This distribution was in accordance with the wishes of her husband, who died about a year earlier. The division was made, not because the minor was the only child of the second marriage, but because he needed it more at his age. One of the daughters said of her stepfather, "He lost a lot of sleep trying to be fair to all of us." The widow knew she had cancer and had made her plans in collaboration with her children. She allowed her minor son to choose which of his step-siblings he would live with; she then appointed this daughter as guardian and executrix. The family had been close before the death and estate settlement; the feeling of the adult children (none of whom were "well off") was that the settlement was eminently fair.

Among the survivors, there were 48 testators who would be survived by minor children if they were to die immediately. Of the 27 survivor testators with minor children only, 26 bequeathed their entire property to their children equally. The twenty-seventh made a minor deviation.

Case 584–01. A widow with two minor children, aged 17 and 18 years, is also making a small bequest for an adult stepson. The residue will be divided equally between her own children. She did not name a guardian.

Twenty-one of the survivor testators had both minor and adult children. Twenty included both the minor and the adult children in their wills; one person disinherited the adult children.

Case 507–01. A widow with six children is making provision only for her three minor children (ages 13, 17, and 20). They will share equally in the estate. Their uncle has been named as guardian. The three adult daughters are in convents. When asked for the reason for the distribution, she said, "I love them equally, but their needs are not equal. The three younger ones would provide for their sisters if necessary."

There were four other deviations. Two survivors are leaving more of their estates to minor children than would be normally received under intestate distribution. One is giving a larger share of his business to his oldest son, who is most interested in the business. One is including small bequests to stepchildren.

Since the decedent sample contained only one case involving orphans, it appears that children are in little danger of becoming orphans. The testamentary provisions of both the survivors and the decedents further indicate that if children become orphans they will certainly not be disinherited orphans.

Adult children were the survivors. When their children were adults, more testators exercised their testamentary freedom. There were 100 decedent testators whose only surviving next of kin were their adult children.

In 47 wills, adult children were the named inheritors and inherited equally. In other words, 47 per cent of these wills duplicated the intestate pattern.

There are two major types of deviations from the intestate pattern: (1) leaving equally to children (57 per cent of the decedents left equally to their children) but also naming persons other than children as beneficiaries (for example, friends, stepchildren, parents, grandchildren, and siblings, with grandchildren most frequently named) and (2) not leaving equally to children, the most serious inequality being the disinheritance of a child. As seen in the previous section, some testators technically disinherit their children by willing their entire estate to their spouses. But this does not have the same meaning as when the children are the only next of kin and one or more of them is disinherited.

The following cases are examples of disinheritance:

Case 377. A 66-year-old divorcee left her estate equally to two adult daughters and disinherited her son. The son (now 46) had left home when he was a teen-ager. His mother had only seen him two or three times since then. She had been close to both of her daughters, living alternately with them and sharing many interests in common. The daughters felt the settlement was fair. The son was not interviewed.

Case 161. A 55-year-old widow left her entire estate to her youngest son. A daughter and two sons were disinherited, although all three were mentioned as contingent beneficiaries. The heir and his sister said this distribution was agreed upon by all family members as a fair exchange for the youngest son's taking care of his mother and promising to take care of her if she lived to be 100. The two brothers said they never had heard of such an agreement and that all the children had contributed to their mother's support. They did not feel the distribution was fair. Perhaps their brother should have gotten more, but not all.

Case 181. A 78-year-old widow made a will two months before her death leaving her entire estate (probated at $15,000) to one daughter and disinheriting the other daughter and a son. The disinherited daughter gave us the following story. Prior to her mother's last illness, the heiress had not been to her mother's home for fourteen years. All these years, the interviewee had looked after her mother. However, after her own husband became seriously ill, she had to go to work and she could not look after her mother. At this point, about a year before the death, she called her sister and asked her if she would look after the mother. Despite the previous estrangement, her sister agreed. After the death, the sister called her siblings for a reading of the will. This was the first the interviewee knew that a new will had been written. At this time the heiress said she wanted all three to share equally. Nothing came of that.

Case 363. A 76-year-old widower left about $28,000 to one of his sons and disinherited the other. We interviewed the legatee. He said that both he and his brother had helped his father accumulate what he had. "We didn't keep records, not when it's your own family. . . . It's a blood relationship, not a business relationship." He thought the settlement was fair. For the last couple of years, the father had lived in his home.

"My wife should have gotten it all. There isn't enough money in the world to repay her for her care. He had bladder trouble; all night long someone had to take him to the bathroom every hour or so. My father left everything to me because we're so close. He knew I'd see my brother got something. But my brother was never around." His brother got a ring and a watch. He is a traveling salesman; we were never able to contact him to get his reactions about the settlement. The interviewer was not convinced by the explanation given by the legatee. The will dates to the period when the deceased became ill; that is, it predates the period of his really severe incapacity.

Case 546. An 86-year-old widower divided his property (worth about $50,000) equally among four children and disinherited the fifth. The disinherited daughter is a nun. The will reads, "Daughter Joan is specifically not mentioned in my will because she has taken vows of poverty." The father's feelings on this subject are amplified by the remarks of his children: "My father said, 'I didn't work eighteen hours a day for the church; she has given her life and her services and that is enough.' " "I think his favorite was my sister who became a nun. He was heartbroken when she became a nun. He disinherited her, not because he didn't want the church to get his money, but because he said she gave up her own life." Two of the children are giving one-fifth of their inheritance to the order. A third child may do so. These three did not feel the will was fair because of the disinheritance. The fourth says, "My sister wants to give something to the order. She is a housewife. What does she know of life? I'm a businessman. If I could give the money to her personally, I would. But I won't contribute to the order." This man did not feel the will was fair because the sister who took care of their father the last few years should have received something extra. The nun refused an interview.

Case 573. A 67-year-old widow left her property ($5,000) in equal shares to her three daughters and disinherited her two sons. "I have made no provision for Carl and Frederick, since I have given them a share of my estate during my lifetime." The share referred to in the will is a share that all five received after the widow sold her home and began living with one of the daughters. At that time she gave each of her children $1,000. The sisters say their brothers were disinherited because they ignored their mother during her lifetime. One brother told us he saw his mother three to four times a week. The other brother said he visited her once or twice a week. One brother made out his army allotment to his mother; the other did the repair work on her home. Their sisters did not tell them when their mother went to the hospital; just before the end, the family doctor notified them. One of the sisters says, "Her money in the bank went lower and lower so I think she was giving it to the boys. They didn't come often, but when they did they went home with something." One of the brothers says, "My sisters used up the estate. They gave her a couple of drinks, and she'd give them $400 to $500." The probated will was the mother's second will: it was made about a year before her death. The sons' disinheritance came as a surprise except that one of them got a mysterious phone call immediately after his mother's death telling him he would not get anything. At the time of interviewing, the family was split along the lines of the inheritance. The two sides were not speaking.

Case 137. A 73-year-old widow was survived by four daughters and two sons. One son received one-third, and the other received two-thirds of an estate worth approximately $16,000. The four daughters were disinherited. The widow had made her home with the son who received the larger share. The daughters felt the division was just: "In our case, even if there hadn't been a will, we would still have given it to the boys, because they did everything for her and never asked us for a penny. Of course, I'm prejudiced for my brothers. They are just wonderful." "I wouldn't have been satisfied with the intestate distribution, because my two brothers helped mother financially whenever she needed it. When father got sick the boys were still in high school. Dad always felt he cheated them out of a college education. When he died, everything went to mother with the understanding that on her death everything went to the boys. One didn't really get more than the other, because he put money into the repair and upkeep of the house." All six siblings were satisfied. The family was close before the death and remained so after the settlement.

The preceding cases have at least one common factor: the decedent lived with one of his children.[22] In several of the cases, the aged parent was sufficiently incapacitated to require constant attention. There seemed to be consensus among the family members that a sibling who had given care to an aged parent should have received special consideration, even if the child had been living rent free. The care of a person with physical or mental incapacities was seen by all as a heavy investment that ought to be compensated.

Although final care was a factor in all the cases, it did not always account for the disinheritance. In Case 546, the disinheritance came about because the daughter went into a convent. In Case 161, the issue was not whether care of the parent should be compensated, but whether a claim based upon a commitment to care should be honored. The youngest son had promised to care for his mother, but she died before his investment greatly exceeded that of his older brothers.

It should also be noted that the giving of final care by one child results in a position of great influence. There were suspicions in a few of the cases (Case 181 and Case 573) that a sibling used his position in order to get favored treatment under the will. The statutes dealing with undue influence are rooted in medieval suspicions of clergymen with their threats of hellfire and damnation; in contemporary society, it is the children who are more apt to exercise undue influence than the representatives of "charitable purposes."[23]

22. In the United States, 28 per cent of the elderly who have at least one child live with that child. Jan Stehouwer, "Relations Between Generations and the Three Generation Household in Denmark," *Social Structure and the Family,* ed. Ethel Shanas and Gordon F. Streib (Englewood Cliffs, N.J.: Prentice-Hall, Inc., 1965), p. 147.

23. There were two decedent cases in which all children were disinherited in favor of a nonrelated person. The children were therefore treated equally. These cases are considered in the section "Nonrelated Inheritors," p. 110. There were also two cases of disinheritance of a child where children were contingent beneficiaries and the primary beneficiary (the spouse) had died. These are treated in Chapter 8 in the section "Contingency Provisions."

The only kin for 106 survivors were their adult children. Eighty-one (76 per cent) had wills identical to the intestate distribution, but the total of those leaving equally although not necessarily all the estate to their children was 96. Thus, 91 per cent of the survivors as compared with 57 per cent of the decedents subscribed to equality among children. The total survivor group was, on the average, twenty years younger than the decedent group, and they had not as yet reached the age when they require care and other special services by their children and would consequently perceive that such services should be specially rewarded.

In order to examine the motives behind unequal treatment of children, it will be helpful to look at a number of survivor cases involving disinheritance.

Case 230–02. A 62-year-old widow is leaving her entire estate to her daughter and disinheriting her son. She says she made a will because her daughter urged her to do so. She lives with her daughter. If her daughter predeceases her, the estate will go to her daughter's children. She says she feels very close to her son, but "my son can take care of himself."

Case 370–01. A 74-year-old widower is leaving everything to the daughter who lives with him and takes care of him. He is disinheriting four other children. He feels he has already given them enough.

Case 357–01. An 85-year-old widow has two sons. Her will makes bequests to charity, to her two daughters-in-law, and to her grandchildren. The residue is left to the younger son, the older one being disinherited. The widow says that the disinherited son is doing quite well, but the younger son has been involved in numerous unsuccessful business ventures and needs the money.

Case 380–02. A 67-year-old widow is leaving her entire estate to her son and disinheriting her daughter. Her son has been handicapped since birth and is not able to support himself. He lives with his mother. The daughter is appointed guardian. The widow says that her daughter will take her brother into her home and look after him.

Case 379–02. A 77-year-old widow is leaving her estate to her daughter and disinheriting her son. Her daughter lives out of state and writes every two or three weeks; her son lives in Cleveland, and she sees him every two or three months. "My daughter-in-law won't let my son bring me to his house. He is afraid I will offend her. He doesn't blame me for leaving everything to his sister."

In the first two cases, the aged parent was living with an adult child, a situation that appeared to be basic to the provisions of the will. In the third and fourth cases, the need of one child for financial support had determined the inheritance pattern. In the fifth case, the will maker was an old woman who had been virtually abandoned. She was a poor, nearly illiterate woman with two children, one married to a professional and the other a professional. Though she seemed to bear her son no malice for his wife's treatment of her, she did disinherit him.

These five were the only cases of the disinheritance of adult children by the survivor where adult children were the only next of kin. There were a few cases in which the adult children were contingent beneficiaries and one or more of them were disinherited or in which the next of kin included minor and adult children and where the minor children received favored treatment. But generally, the unequal treatment of children was not nearly so common among the survivor testators as among the decedent testators. When unequal treatment in disposition occurred among survivors or decedents, the givers were old, minor children were not involved, and the pattern of interpersonal relationships between testators and takers had been established for a long period of time. It was discovered that the five survivor testators who gave to a preferred child were similar in age to the ten decedent testators who disinherited one or more of their children. The average age of the five survivors was 73 years; the average age of the ten decedents was 72.5 years.

Children and grandchildren were the survivors. Grandchildren are next of kin only when their parent who is a lineal descendant of the testator is dead. There were 11 cases among the decedent testators where the surviving next of kin were children and/or grandchildren. Only three followed the intestate pattern.

There were three cases of disinheritance among the decedent group.

Case 545. The deceased was a 79-year-old widower. His survivors were four children and one granddaughter. The chief asset in his estate consisted of one-half of his home, which he had owned in common with his wife. When she died, she left her half of the house to a daughter who had made her home with her parents. The mother had been paralyzed for five years before she died, and this daughter had taken care of her. The widower left his half of the house to his son, who was also part of the household. The grandchild was the beneficiary of an insurance policy that the grandparents made over to her after their son (her father) died. The disinherited had no resentment over the grandchild's share, but they were resentful of their brother's good fortune.

Case 242. The legal next of kin of a 75-year-old widow were two sons, two daughters and one grandchild. The widow made equal bequests to all her thirteen grandchildren, including stepgrandchildren. The residue was divided equally between her two daughters. She had lived with one of the daughters for the six years preceding her death. Her estate was small (about $2,000), so that the daughters' inheritance was not large. She excluded her two sons because her husband had left all his property to her and his two sons. He had felt that when daughters marry they are no longer his responsibility. His widow had felt this most unfair, and she attempted to rectify the situation in her own will.

Case 310. The decedent was an 84-year-old widower who lived with his unmarried daughter. Before his wife's death, the couple had decided to leave their estate to this daughter because she was unmarried and also had had a heart condition since childhood. When the decision was communicated to her two brothers, they stopped associating with her. Three children of a deceased daughter were also disinherited. The chief asset in the estate was the house ($15,000) in which the parents and heiress lived.

When a person was survived by a spouse, lineal kin, or both, there was a pattern of distribution that was followed by 90 per cent of the testators. If a spouse was the only survivor, the testator followed the intestate distribution and bequeathed all to the spouse. If the testator was survived by spouse and lineal kin, the testator typically deviated from the intestate statute and also bequeathed all to the spouse. It was hypothesized that the pattern of giving all to the surviving spouse would be more frequently encountered in relatively small estates. Those testators who did not will all to the spouse typically left larger estates. Another exception to the spouse-all pattern occurred in the case of remarriage, where division between the progeny of an earlier marriage and the last spouse was the just solution. The remarried decedents who so divided their estates had only slightly larger estates than those who left their estates to their surviving spouses.

The patterns of distribution were more variable where the testator was survived only by lineal kin. The testators took care of their minor children and their parents, although this might have been achieved through means other than outright bequest. When the testator was survived by adult children and/or grandchildren, the intestate distribution was the pattern followed by the largest proportion of testators; but many individuals varied the amounts on the basis of emotional ties with particular family members. Very few testators disinherited their children in cases where the children were the only surviving kin. Most of these cases of disinheritance were the incidental result of the testator repaying another child for care given in old age.

Collateral Kin Were the Survivors

When a person has no spouse, no ascendants, and no descendants, his nearest relatives are collateral kin: siblings and their descendants. In rare instances, the nearest relatives, usually cousins, are descendants of his parent's family of orientation.

When the nearest kin were collateral, there was no one pattern followed by a majority of testators. The intestate pattern predominated, but it did not command the majority. There were 40 decedent testators and 41 survivor testators whose survivors were collateral kin. Seven of the decedents (18 per cent) and 16 of the interviewee testators (39 per cent) followed the intestate pattern.[24] Those who did not choose the intestate distribution chose a wide variety of patterns. Table 5–4 shows the number of testators in each category and the number choosing the intestate distribution.[25]

24. In the Chicago study, 89 per cent of those survived by siblings and 100 per cent of those survived by more distant relatives deviated from the intestate rule. Dunham, op. cit., p. 252.

25. Information obtained from 220 Kansas City adults between the ages of 50 and 80

TABLE 5–4 TESTATORS, THEIR SURVIVORS, AND FREQUENCY OF INTESTATE PATTERN

Survivors	Decedent Testators		Interviewee Testators	
	Total Number	Intestate Pattern	Total Number	Intestate Pattern
Siblings	12	3	29	13
Siblings, nieces, and nephews	14	1	4	1
Nieces and nephews	10	3	5	2
More distant relatives	4	0	3	0
Total	40	7	41	16

Estranged Families

If no single pattern was followed by a majority of testators whose nearest kin were collateral relatives, was there a "functional" family for these individuals? These relatives were estranged from the testator.

Included in the category of "estranged families" were those county residents who were disinherited, who reported contact with the decedent less often than once a month, who were "not close," and who reported no major disagreements or conflicts with the deceased.[26]

Nineteen kin members were disinherited by nine testators. Two individuals were members of the decedent's family of procreation, and 17 were related through the decedent's family of orientation. Only one of the 19 who were disinherited had knowledge of the estate or the will prior to the death of the testator, suggesting that these kin scarcely knew the decedents.

Case 629. The decedent was a 65-year-old childless widow. Her gross probate estate consisted of real estate valued at $2,500. The net estate was slightly over $1,000. The estate had been in probate for eight years. One nephew was the heir; nine nieces and nephews were disinherited. The strained relationships in the family dated back to the previous generation and an estate settlement. The decedent's mother left her entire estate to the decedent and disinherited her other children, who were the parents of the nieces and nephews. The decedent's brothers and sisters broke off their relationships with her, which meant that with one exception, the nieces and nephews had not seen

---

on their kinship revealed that solidarity with siblings was second only to that parents perceived between themselves and their own children but stronger than that which they perceived between themselves and their parents. Elaine Cumming and David Schneider, "Sibling Solidarity: A Property of American Kinship," *American Anthropologist* 63 (June, 1961):498–507, reprinted in *Kinship and the Family Organization,* ed. Bernard Farber (New York: John Wiley & Sons, Inc., 1966), pp. 143–145. The Cuyahoga County data do not support the notion of the solidarity between siblings surpassing all relationships other than that bond which parents feel toward their children.

26. Limited to county residents to equalize possibilities of contact and interaction.

their aunt since that time. The one exception was the heir, who cultivated his aunt after his own parents' death. He and his wife visited her frequently. Most of the disinherited felt the settlement was unfair. "All blood relations should get something. Even if it would be only $5.00, it would keep me in cigarettes." "The court must have cut me out because I'm the wrong religion. My cousin's wife visited her all the time; what right did she have? She is only an in-law." The heir's own brothers said he had been the shrewd one: "You can't trust him."

Although family members in Case 629 expressed sentiments about the meaning and rights of the blood relationships, they did not associate these rights with any responsibilities for providing affection and care and financial assistance to the aged aunt. A contrary position was taken by the disinherited in Case 341, where recognition was given to the services performed by a particular relative.

Case 341. The decedent was an 84-year-old spinster who left a net estate of $8,000. She made a small bequest to a former domestic employee, then gave the bulk of the estate to a second cousin, with additional bequests for the cousin's minor children. One first cousin and three second cousins were disinherited. The disinherited bore no enmity toward the decedent or heiress. The general feeling was that the decedent was perfectly right in choosing the only relative who had been close to her. The first cousin mentioned that there were other first cousins who also would have been included as next of kin, but the court was not notified of their existence.

Case 394. The decedent was an 80-year-old childless widow. She disinherited two nephews and a niece, made bequests of jewelry to a niece and a grandniece, and gave the residue (approximately $5,000) to a third niece. The legatees lived out of state and did not respond to questionnaires. One of the disinherited nephews said this about the distribution: "She visited them many times. Probably enjoyed the relatives there, and remembering those happy times she wanted to do something about it." The other nephew attributed his disinheritance to a previous inheritance situation. His mother and the deceased were sisters. He was the executor for the estate of a third sister. "I followed the will to the letter; this made her bitter. We had a verbal battle. She drew all the money out of a joint bank account with her sister. I deducted this amount from her share, and all hell broke loose. There were religious differences between us, too. I tried to be nice to her after that. When she went to the hospital I went to see her. Took her home, did shopping for her, etc., until I found out that I was out of the will."

Case 538. The decedent was an 84-year-old spinster who left a $14,000 estate to be divided equally between her brother and his son, her nephew. She left a niece some jewelry. Three nephews were disinherited. One of the disinherited nephews said he had seen the deceased four times in the last thirty-five years. Another of the disinherited had seen her about once a year until she became ill. The third had seen his aunt once or twice a year during the last ten years of her life. These men were not bitter about the distribution, but the first nephew felt that the intestate distribution would have been more fair. The decedent had for many years made her home with the brother and his son who inherited. She raised the nephew because his mother died at his birth.

Case 579. The decedent was an 84-year-old childless widow. She left a $1,000 bequest to the church. The remainder of the $4,000 estate was left to her brother and his wife, to a niece, and to a nephew of her late husband. She disinherited another brother, two nephews, and a niece. The niece who inherited had taken a great deal of responsibility for her aunt in the four years preceding her death. "I was her first niece and her favorite but she could be nasty too. The other nieces and nephews couldn't take her ways. I love family and so I could forgive her for so much. I felt a moral obligation." She felt the intestate distribution would have been less fair, with people inheriting who hadn't done anything for the deceased, but more satisfactory to her, "because there wouldn't have been any hard feelings on my side of the family. My brothers' wives resent not getting anything." She revealed that the decedent's brother had been disinherited because her aunt did not like his second wife. In our interview with him, he merely said, "She was the bossy type; we had a fight and didn't speak for several years." One of the disinherited nephews said he was on the outs not only with his aunt but with all members of the family. "When I married a Catholic they disowned me, so we kept to ourselves." About his aunt: "I knew I was in the doghouse; I snubbed her at Dad's funeral. That was the last time I saw her, ten years ago. She outlived her usefulness by about fifty years." About the inheritors: "They were brown nosers; my sister was always hovering over her."

Case 612. The decedent was a 76-year-old spinster. She left a $15,000 estate in trust for a retarded niece. Another nephew and niece were contingent beneficiaries. They are the brother and sister of the retardate. The aunt had lived in their home while they were growing up. She had been like a second mother to them. They had continued to see her as adults, and the brother had handled her personal affairs for her. She consulted them before setting up her will. Another niece who did not inherit was not dissatisfied with the settlement: "I'm completely out of touch with my father's family since he died. I only saw her at weddings and funerals. She was too right and proper for me. I never gave her anything so I didn't expect anything. The family that received had made her life pleasant."

The following case does not properly belong under the category "collateral kin were the survivors," since the decedent's mother was her only legal next of kin. However, in her will the decedent specifically disinherited 11 collateral kin.

Case 560. The decedent was a 52-year-old spinster. She left an estate of $25,000 to a sister, disinheriting her mother, seven brothers and sisters, four nephews, and one grandniece. The patriarch of the family (the decedent's father) had married twice and had two sets of children of vastly different ages. One of the half brothers said he had not known the decedent was born until she was 10 years old. Everyone understood the reason for the distribution. The decedent lived with her mother and sister. She gave to this sister in order to enable her to take care of their mother. The other family members were in no need of money. They did not know the size of the estate and were not curious either. The only complication was that the decedent had made $1.00 bequests to the disinherited. A few felt this was a slap in the face, that she should have known they would not contest the will. Others felt the small check was "cute." These people didn't cash their checks until the lawyer told them they were holding up the closing of the estate.

These cases share a number of characteristics. All involved childless women, spinsters or widows. The women were all of advanced age, with the average age being 75 years, and they all had personal idiosyncracies that made them difficult relatives. The estrangement within the family preceded the estate settlement. The blood ties between the decedents and their next of kin were fairly remote in most cases. Given these remote ties, the decedents rewarded those who had paid them some attention and ignored the others. In some cases, the next of kin accepted the justice of the distribution. Where the situation was felt to be unfair, the potential heirs were uninformed about the size of the estate.

The disinherited tended to underestimate the expenses of retirement, hospitalization, and nursing care and to overestimate the capital accumulation of the aged person. The average net estate for these women was approximately $10,000, as compared with $35,000 for the entire group of decedent testators. Some of these women had been widowed or retired for many years and had had major expenses for hospital or nursing-home care. These cases also illustrate that unhappiness over the disposition is not related to the amount involved. Case 629 involved the least amount of property, and yet there was a great deal of bitterness among potential inheritors; the estate in Case 560 was the largest, and the distribution was acceptable to those concerned.

Perhaps the most unusual aspect of these seven cases of estrangement was that the inheritance was still kept within the family. It might have been expected that under these circumstances of alienation, a friend or neighbor would have been beneficiary by default. However, with two exceptions (a bequest to a domestic servant and one to a church), the testators found individuals among their relatives to whom they could bequeath their property. Perhaps this is not so surprising. Fifty-six relatives were involved in these seven cases, an average of eight per case; 3.5 was the mean number of next of kin for all decedent testators. From this large number of distant relatives, there was a high probability of finding one who would provide care and service for an aged aunt or cousin. Sometimes, out of a sense of duty, a particular person rendered service to the aged and lonely relative. In some cases, the motive was one of possible gain. In others, the decedent may have moved into the home of a relative. In one such instance, the relative was a brother, and the decedent became "mother" to his children. Subsequently, she bequeathed to her "children" and disinherited the others.

Nonrelated Inheritors

Thirty-seven of the decedent testators (9 per cent) and 26 of the survivor testators (4 per cent) made bequests to persons who were not related to them. Only a small minority of testators went completely outside their bloodlines to select their heirs. Although such cases were few, they are of interest in this study because no revision of statutes could possibly accomplish these testators' objectives. More than any other single group of cases, they may reveal the advantages and disadvantages of testamentary freedom.

No Known Next of Kin Survived

It is axiomatic that everyone has kin; thus, the accepted phraseology is "no known next of kin," not "no next of kin." There were four testators in the decedent sample who had no known next of kin. Such persons must of necessity bequeath their property to nonrelated persons or to institutions.

In the first case the persons who benefited from the estate had done as much as would be expected of a family. The decedent had become part of a family without the bonds of either marriage or blood.

Case 617. The decedent was a 76-year-old man who left an estate of nearly $10,000. He had come from Yugoslavia as a young man and had boarded with one family for fifty-four years. After his landlady died, he lived with her two daughters who shared the home. His will made bequests of $500 to each of the landlady's sons, and the residue was divided equally between the two daughters.

The decedent in the next case willed half of the estate to his deceased wife's relatives and half to two persons who helped him when he was in desperate need.

Case 335. The decedent was a 79-year-old man whose wife predeceased him by one year. Their wills had jointly given all to each other. After his wife's death, he became ill and went for help to his neighbor (a much younger man). The neighbor called the brother of the deceased wife. The brother-in-law refused to help and refused to visit. When he was informed that the man was so ill he had crawled over to the neighbor's house in the middle of the night, his reply was, "Why don't you lock your door?" The neighbor called his own doctor, and he and his wife cared for the man by themselves until one day a former co-worker of the decedent dropped by and learned of the situation. During the last two months of life, the neighbor and the co-worker and their wives shared the daily nursing care. Eight days before death, the decedent wrote a new will, giving one-quarter each to his late wife's grandnephew and niece-in-law and one-quarter each to the two samaritans. His late wife's brother contested the will and settled out of court for $2,000 of an estate of approximately $20,000.

If the decedent had not regarded his estate as a joint one with his deceased wife, it is likely that he would have bequeathed the entire estate to the two persons who had given him care in the last months of life.

In the next case there were no such extraordinary services. The decedent was described by his closest friend as "lonely and proud."

Case 094. The decedent was a 64-year-old man; his estate consisted of a $1,000 insurance policy naming a friend as beneficiary. The insurance paid for the funeral expenses. The friend, with whom the deceased had become acquainted through business, told of their relationship and of the decedent's life. "He was old enough to be my father but I never thought of him that way. It's hard to say whether we were close friends or not. We had dinner together once in a while. I was concerned about his needs and felt responsible for him. He never married but for many years he had a lady friend who converted to his faith. She died four years before he did. After her death he sort of lost interest in life." The decedent's will named this friend as executor and as a beneficiary; the church and a nephew of the lady friend were also mentioned. The decedent had used up his savings for his lady friend's illness, but he had hoped to win a suit for personal injury; the suit was thrown out of court.

One other decedent had no known next of kin. He willed all to his son-in-law, who continued to live with him after his daughter died. In this case as in others involving bequests to in-laws and steprelatives, it is questionable whether a twofold category of related inheritors and nonrelated inheritors is sufficient. Certainly in many families the "in-law" suffix or "step-" prefix is superfluous because the person has been assimilated into the family. The justification for considering both steprelatives and in-laws as nonrelated is that ascendant and collateral in-laws never inherit under the Ohio Statute of Descent and Distribution; stepchildren inherit only after the possibilities of other relatives are exhausted; that is, distant cousins inherit before a stepchild does. It is also not unusual for a testator to leave to several types of nonrelated persons: friends, employees, and stepchildren or in-laws.

Among the survivors, five claimed they had no next of kin. One was leaving to friends and charities; two to charities only; and two to in-laws. One survivor's reason for leaving to his wife's cousin was because, "She was good to my wife and me and I want to be sure someone close to my wife will have it." The other survivor was leaving all to her deceased husband's sister, who moved in with her after her husband died.

Family of Procreation Survived

Testators who have no known next of kin are a rather unusual group. They have only the choice between allowing their estates to escheat to the state or making wills and naming their own beneficiaries. By far the largest number of those who leave to nonrelated individuals are survived by kin; some of these are survived by their family of procreation. In most cases, bequests to nonrelated persons by those who have immediate families are small.

Sixteen decedents with families of procreation made bequests to nonrelated persons. In nine cases, the nonrelated persons were either stepchildren or in-laws. The other seven decedents made bequests to friends and/or employees. In five of these cases, the amounts were small. In the remaining two cases, children were disinherited in favor of friends.

Case 471. A widower was survived by a son and daughter living in Yugoslavia whom he disinherited. The estate ($6,505) was left to a friend "for the care and help she gave me in my old age." We were unable to interview her.[27]

Case 527. The decedent was an 80-year-old widower who left each of his four children $25 "because of their complete disregard of me during my lifetime." The residue of his estate ($14,000) was given to the son of an old friend. The oldest daughter gave us this story: All the children were born in the United States, but when they were young their father shipped them and their mother back to Poland, where they lived in such poverty they had difficulty staying alive. After nine years, the father brought the children back to the United States but left their mother in Poland. The interviewee was 13 at this time. Her father cast her out of his house when she was 16. One by one he kicked the others out too. They went their separate ways, hoping they would someday be able to bring their mother to Cleveland. However, she was killed during the war. Her father refused to see the daughter's first child, his first grandchild. He was invited to his sons' weddings but refused to attend. Ten years before his death, he contacted the children and said that if they did not see him he would disinherit them. After that they saw him periodically; the interviewee saw him every three months or so. She would clean his house and listen to his complaints. The children did not realize he had a will until they began probate proceedings. When they learned his estate was to go to the son of a friend of his, they wished to drop the matter; but their lawyer insisted they were entitled to something and managed to get them $1,000 apiece ($700 after the lawyer's fees). The daughter felt that the friend who inherited was a dishonest man who had pressured her father into leaving his estate in this way. She also thought that the house, which was the largest item in the estate, was underappraised and that there possibly had been more in the joint bank account with the inheritor than appeared in the probated assets. She thought her father had disinherited them because it was easier for him to say "they ignored me" than to admit to himself that he had thrown them out.

Twelve survivors leaving to nonrelated persons had families of procreation. In eight cases, these nonrelated persons were either stepchildren or in-laws. The motives for including these persons are revealed in such statements as: "I raised her and I consider her my daughter." "I'm making a small provision for my husband's sister as a remembrance." "I promised my husband I would leave one-half to his children." In the first case, the stepdaughter had been as-

27. This woman's name also appeared as administratrix in an intestate case. In this latter case, she was also guardian of the decedent prior to and during his terminal stay at a state mental hospital. She received only the fiduciary fee, unless one is suspicious of the missing social security checks mentioned on probate records. The decedent in this case had no known relatives until they were located by a lost-heir company.

similated into the family. In the second case, the motive may come from respect for the deceased spouse. In the last case, the testator and her late husband had thought of their estate as one to which they had contributed equally and should share equally; the widow's provision for her stepchildren was the fulfillment of a verbal contract.

The four testators who had families of procreation and who were leaving to complete outsiders were leaving very small amounts, except for one case in which the relationship between the testator and his only son was strained and in which friends were major beneficiaries.

Family of Orientation Survived

Seventeen decedents and nine survivors who were leaving to nonrelated persons had no immediate family. Their nearest relatives were calculated through their family of orientation. In most cases, their closest relatives were siblings and/or nieces and nephews.

Twelve of the decedents made bequests to in-laws or stepchildren. In one case, a wealthy bachelor, whose nearest of kin was a niece, left to large numbers of distantly related kin, to in-laws, to friends, and to 12 employees. As in some other cases involving employee inheritors, duration of service was the determining factor in the disposition. The initial bequest was made on the basis of long service. In cases where more than one employee was included, the amounts were often scaled to years of service. However, with domestic employees especially, there was also the possibility that the employees had been assimilated into the family: "She had been a part of the family for thirty years." "She has been through everything with us." There was no case in which bequests to employees were resented. One relative stated, "The tremendous amount of money accumulated was not just the hard work of one man but of the many people who worked for him. They were due something."

Reciprocity was perhaps more obvious in the case of friends who inherited:

Case 033. A friend who took care of the decedent for ten years before he died inherited the bulk of the estate of $13,000. She knew about the will and the provisions. It was an agreement they had in return for his care. Small bequests were left to siblings and nieces and nephews on the advice of the lawyer to avert trouble.

The next of kin of nine survivors were relatives calculated through their family of orientation. Four of the survivors named in-laws and stepchildren in their wills. The others included friends and employees. Sometimes the motivation for leaving to friends was not only a matter of reciprocating the kindness of a friend but also a matter of positive dislike for family members.

It was hypothesized that the pattern of willing property to unrelated individuals would be associated with either wealth or the absence of immediate family.

There were at least three distinct types of unrelated inheritors: friends, employees, and the quasi-kin (stepchildren and in-laws). The circumstances differed between (and within) these three groups. They have been treated jointly here for three reasons: (1) the total number of testators bequeathing to nonrelated persons was small; (2) nonrelated inheritors were in the same position vis-à-vis the intestate statutes; and (3) some testators included all three types of nonrelated inheritors in their disposition.

For obvious reasons, the influence of wealth upon the distribution pattern was most pronounced in the case of employees inheriting. The very poor are not in a position to have employees. There were nine testators who made bequests to employees; seven of these were of above-average economic status. Despite the bias inherent in the inclusion of employee inheritors, the testators who made bequests to nonrelated persons were not as a group markedly wealthy. Only 43 per cent of the decedent testators and 39 per cent of the survivor testators were of above-average economic status (see Table 5–5).

TABLE 5–5 BEQUESTS TO NONRELATED PERSONS, BY ECONOMIC STATUS, TYPE OF FAMILY, AND MEAN AGE

	Decedent Bequests to Nonrelated Persons							
	More than 15 Per Cent of Estate (N = 19)		Less than 15 Per Cent of Estate (N = 18)		Total (N = 37)		Survivor Bequests to Nonrelated Persons (N = 26)	
Factors	Number	Per Cent	Number	Per Cent	Number	Per Cent	Number	Per Cent
Economic status above average[a]	5	26.3	11	61.1	16	43.2	10	38.5
No known next of kin	4	21.1	0	0.0	4	10.8	5	19.2
Family of procreation[b]	4	21.1	12	66.7	16	43.2	12	46.2
Family of orientation	11	57.9	6	33.3	17	46.0	9	34.6
Mean age[c]	76.0 years		75.8 years		75.9 years		61.4 years	

[a] Average decedent testate economic status was a net estate of $35,160; average survivor testate economic status was monthly income of $601 to $800.

[b] Percentage of decedent testators survived by families of procreation was 88.5; percentage of survivor testators, 90.4.

[c] Mean age of decedent testator was 69.6 years; mean age of survivor testators, 52.5 years.

Either the stepchildren and in-laws who inherit appear to have been so well assimilated into the family that the designation "step-" or "in-law" was a superfluous distinction in the testator's mind, or the bequest was made out of respect for a spouse. It should be remembered that estates are often built up through joint efforts. Therefore, justice would seem to demand that the final distribution of the estate be dependent not upon the accident of who dies first but upon the feeling that those who were important to a deceased spouse should also receive a share of the estate.

Many of the friends who inherited rendered substantial services for which the decedent reciprocated in his last will and testament. The fact that these services were rendered by friends rather than by relatives was associated with the absence of family or strained relationships with family members.

Lastly, it is important to distinguish between testators who gave only minor portions of their estates to nonrelated persons and those who made substantial bequests outside the family. Those who gave less than 15 per cent of their estates were more likely to be survived by an immediate family and also were more likely to be of above-average economic status. Again the reason is obvious. The claims of kin are so strong that bequests to nonrelated persons are likely to fragment an estate unless it is a large one. Major bequests to nonrelated persons may deprive the testator's immediate family of sustenance.

Looking at the group as a whole, it is clear that the absence of immediate family was the most important determinant of a pattern of distribution that included nonrelated persons. Even if those testators who have no known next of kin were disregarded, the proportion of testators survived by families of procreation was far less than for the entire group of testators. These testators were older than the average for the entire group of testators (see Table 5–5). Age was associated with absence of immediate family and was also associated with the need for final care. These testators, especially those who willed to friends, bore some resemblance to those testators who disinherited some children in order to repay the child who had done the most for them and also to those testators who were estranged from their families.

Bequests to Charities

Statistics on charitable giving and bequests are of limited usefulness because of the almost complete reliance on income and estate tax returns for such data. The studies available, however, indicate that philanthropy is positively associated with wealth as measured by either income[28] or estate size.[29] F. Emerson

28. Edward Jenkins, *Philanthropy in America* (New York: Association Press, 1950), p. 98; John Price Jones, *Philanthropy Today: An Interim Report* (New York: Inter River Press, 1949), p. 22.

29. F. Emerson Andrews, *Philanthropic Giving* (New York: Russell Sage Foundation, 1950), pp. 68–69. Carl Shoup, *Federal Estate and Gift Taxes* (Washington, D.C.: The Brookings Institution, 1966), p. 61: "Of the small estate returns (gross estate $300,000 or less) 86 percent of the 1957 returns reported no contributions at all . . . the 1959 percentage is similar, 87 percent. Medium estate contributors ($300,000–$1,000,000) were somewhat more numerous relatively; 74 percent (72 percent in 1959) reported no contributions. Even more surprising is the fact that in the millionaire group slightly over half the decedents reported no contributions, either during life or at death. To be sure, most of the very wealthiest were contributors; of the 52 decedents (1957 plus 1959) with over $10,000,000 gross transfers, only 5 reported making no contributions. . . . For the three groups combined, in 1957, 16 percent of the decedents

Andrews concludes that while comprehensive data on charitable giving in the case of small estates is unavailable, one should assume that these testators give very little to philanthropic institutions.[30] Probate studies have indicated the relative infrequency of charitable giving.[31]

Charitable bequests are infrequent and are only a small percentage (approximately 4 per cent) of the annual receipts of private philanthropic organizations. For some, however, such as educational institutions and hospitals, charitable bequests may be a very important source of income.[32] Large donations are more often made in the form of bequests than of gifts by living donors.[33]

Decedent Sample

Of the 422 testate estates in the decedent sample, 25 decedents (6 per cent) made a bequest to one or more charitable institutions. The total amount left to charity by these 25 decedents was over 3.5 million dollars; over 3 million dollars of this amount was left by one decedent, and the other 24 decedents left a total of $70,725.

Seven of these testators willed over 15 per cent of their estates in this way. The size of the estates varied from one valued at over a million dollars to one without enough assets to cover the bequests. All seven decedents left to more than one charity; the institutions named reflected the cultural background of the donor.

Of these seven testators, none had nuclear families of procreation surviving.[34] Two were single; one was divorced; and four were widowed. Those who had been married had never had children. Four decedents were survived by siblings or by siblings, nieces, and nephews; two were survived by nieces and nephews only; and one was survived by cousins. In none of these cases were all the relatives completely cut off.[35]

Fifty-nine persons involved in the seven cases in which more than 15 per

---

reported contributions, and the contributions were 7 percent of the total gross transfers. . . . Those who did make contributions were fairly generous, however. They gave roughly 20 to 30 percent of their gross transfers."

30. Ibid.

31. Steuart Henderson Britt, "The Significance of the Last Will and Testament," *Journal of Social Psychology* 8 (August, 1937):350. Of 191 wills, 16 (8 per cent) made some provision for charity; in only eight of these did the proportions come to a large amount, and these were all large estates. Lawrence Friedman, "Patterns of Testation in the 19th Century: A Study of Essex County (New Jersey) Wills," *The American Journal of Legal History* 8 (1964):47. In 1850, one will out of 30; in 1875, five wills out of 60; and in 1900, two out of 60.

32. Jones, op. cit., p. 41.

33. Ibid., pp. 41–42. Of 87 large ($500,000) gifts made in 1948–1949, 55 per cent were given by 37 men and women in their wills.

34. "In the sample, ten of the 15 charitable gifts appeared in estates in which brothers and sisters were the closest relatives of the deceased." Dunham, op. cit., p. 254.

35. Compare the Ward and Beuscher study, "The Inheritance Process in Wisconsin," *Wisconsin Law Review* (1950):413, where in two instances, with relatives surviving, entire estates were given to churches.

cent was left to charity were interviewed. In five of these cases, the decedent's relationship with the surviving next of kin appeared to be strained: "She was the oldest in the family. She was jealous that her brothers had children and she never had any. The whole family is jealous—begrudged each other any success." "He didn't have much respect for his family although he wasn't much of a charitable man either."

Before the death and the estate settlement, the surviving kin and legatees were almost all uninformed about the size of the decedent's estate and the provisions of his will. Over 70 per cent did not know whether the decedent had made a will. Where the estate was large, typical comments were:

I did not know if there was a will or not, but I would think a person in such circumstances would not go on without a will. How many wills nobody knows.

I was surprised and provoked, sorry she didn't go abroad for a winter in Italy. I would have urged her to, had I known she had so much money.

The attitudes of the survivors toward the testators and the charitable bequests vary.

I imagine she had a great love of charities; her first thought was a great love for people as a whole rather than as individuals.

Most of it went to charities. This is from a person who while living had not been charitable. I think the law should allow you only so much to buy your way into heaven.

Despite the fact that the next of kin would have inherited more had the decedent been intestate, only two interviewees felt the intestate distribution would have been more fair. Even in the one contested case, the plaintiff said:

Everybody is entitled to leave to whomever they want, but in more normal proportions. Everybody has the responsibility of distributing what they have. I don't approve of dying intestate.

There were 18 decedents who left less than 15 per cent of their estates to charities. Fourteen of these decedents left to religious institutions only, and seven of these bequests were for masses. In the five cases where the decedent was survived by a spouse, the amount of the bequests was less than 5 per cent of the estate; and either the bulk of the estate went to the spouse, or the spouse was adequately provided for. In another five cases where children survived, the bequests were less than 5 per cent in all but one instance, in which 8 per cent went to charity, with a residue of $90,000 going to an only daughter.

Survivor Population

Among 620 testate survivors, 22 (4 per cent) planned to leave to charities. Ten of this group included only religious institutions.[36] Three of the testators

36. Jones, op. cit., p. 84. "Religion is by far the largest single recipient of American gratitude." Ibid., p. 85. "About half of all individual giving goes to churches."

had no next of kin. Nine testators (two of whom were nuns) had no family of procreation. Seven testators had spouses; and in all but one instance, where the husband was an alcoholic, the spouses were adequately provided for. Children were the only next of kin for three testators, and the bequests to charities were small, with the bulk of the estate going to the children.

The interviewees were asked why they had made their will as they had.

I'm leaving it all to the Watchtower Bible Tract Society. That is the only hope I have in the world to do what is right.

Antiques and personal property go to my niece, the rest to the church. The estate is small and there are family conflicts. There will be no fighting this way.

I made a will because I had organizations I wanted to leave to. Church means so much to me, and all the organizations are important to me. I've set up a trust fund for my wife to prevent preying on a widow.

My husband and I were both only children with no immediate family, so a choice could be made.

Despite evidence of some personal connection, there was little evidence of reciprocity between the donor and the recipient organization.[37]

It was hypothesized that the patterns of willing property to institutions would be associated with either wealth or the absence of immediate family. The decisive factor in charitable giving appears to be the absence of immediate family (see Table 5–6).[38] None of the decedents who willed over 15 per cent of their estates to charitable purposes were survived by families of procreation. Five of the seven estates were smaller than the testate net mean for the decedent sample ($35,160). Eleven of the 18 decedents who left a small percentage (the median was 2 per cent) to charity were survived by spouses and/or children. These 11 had a mean estate size of over $79,000. The seven decedents leaving small amounts to charity who were not survived by families of procreation had a mean estate size of $126,000. Only 44 per cent of all the charitable decedents were survived by their families of procreation, as compared with 89

37. F. Emerson Andrews, *Attitudes Toward Giving* (New York: Russell Sage Foundation, 1953). On the basis of interviewing living donors about the motives for their contribution, Andrews notes the importance of a personal connection between donor and recipient organization. The donor may have benefited from the organization or had a record of volunteer service, and so forth (pp. 20, 23, 26, 120). We found no evidence of personal benefit. Our position here closely corresponds to that of Moore: "Charitable endowments, for the benefit of generations yet unborn, scarcely come within the norms of reciprocity." Wilbert E. Moore, "Economic and Professional Institutions," *Sociology,* ed. Neil Smelser (New York: John Wiley & Sons, Inc., 1967), p. 312.

38. The nuns were not included in Table 5–7 because the nature of their vocation determined the variables being tested. They of course had no families of procreation; their income, if any, was not relevant since they were part of a community; and testamentary freedom did not apply in the usual sense because they were required to make a will and often had to take vows of poverty. The two in the sample were willing their entire estates to religious communities.

TABLE 5–6 TESTATORS BEQUEATHING TO CHARITIES, BY ECONOMIC STATUS, TYPE OF FAMILY, AND MEAN AGE

	Decedent Bequests to Charities							
	More than 15 Per Cent of Estate (*N* = 7)		Less than 15 Per Cent of Estate (*N* = 18)		Total (*N* = 25)		Survivor Bequests to Charities (*N* = 20)	
Factors	Number	Per Cent	Number	Per Cent	Number	Per Cent	Number	Per Cent
Economic status above average[a]	2	28.6	10	55.6	12	48.0	8	40.0
No known next of kin	0	0.0	0	0.0	0	0.0	3	15.0
Family of procreation[b]	0	0.0	11	61.1	11	44.0	10	50.0
Family of orientation	7	100.0	7	38.9	14	56.0	7	35.0
Mean age[c]	76.9 years		79.4 years		78.7 years		62.6 years	

[a] Average decedent testate economic status was a net estate of $35,160; average survivor testate economic status was monthly income of $601 to $800.

[b] Percentage of decedent testators survived by families of procreation, 88.5; and percentage of survivor testators with families of procreation was 90.4.

[c] Mean age of decedent testator was 69.6 years; mean age of survivor testators was 52.5 years.

per cent of the testate decedents as a whole. Twelve of the 25 charitable decedents were characterized by either the presence of wealth or the absence of immediate family, and another seven were characterized by both conditions. The six charitable decedents who were characterized by neither wealth nor the absence of immediate kin gave only small religious bequests.

Eight of the 20 charitable survivors had incomes above the testate median. Within this group, 50 per cent had families of procreation, as compared with 91 per cent of the total testate survivors. Twelve of the 20 were characterized by either wealth or the absence of immediate family, and another three were characterized by both conditions. Four of the five remaining charitable survivors, characterized by neither wealth nor the absence of immediate family, were making small bequests to charities. The fifth, whose husband was an alcoholic, was leaving all to a children's home for the care of her children.

The charitable givers were similar to three previously discussed groups: those who disinherited some children in order to pay one child for care, the decedents in the "estranged families," and those who willed property to nonrelated individuals. They were old. The average age of the charitable decedent was 78.7 years, compared with the average age of the testate decedents, 69.6 years. The mean age of the charitable survivor was 62.6 years; the mean age of testate survivors was 52.2 years. It may be hypothesized that as the interviewee population ages, the proportion of those making charitable bequests will increase. It appears that aging was associated either with a weakening of kinship ties or, conversely, with heavy demands upon the existing relatives. If the demands were met by someone (a child, a niece, a friend), then the testator reciprocated in his will. If they were not met, he had the alternative of making a charitable bequest.

Conclusion

This study of property disposition and inheritance within the family and kinship systems provides the most substantial and persuasive data for establishing reciprocity as the theoretical base for intergenerational family behavior. There are several important conclusions to be drawn from these data.

First, dual patterns of serial service and reciprocity are established as existing coterminously. Transfers from one generation to the next take place in the normal course of events as evidenced by the relatively small number of gifts given to charities, friends, and distantly related family members. With the bulk of transfers occurring within generational lines, it is obvious that serial service is a dominant pattern; parents help their young children, and when these children reach maturity, they take on the responsibility and do what they can for their now aged parents. The cycle continues indefinitely over time.

Serial reciprocity complements this process of generational transfer. Specific allocations are made according to notions of distributive justice and actual exchanges of care, service, and material goods between members of the older and middle generations. Testators will their estates to designated children or other individuals according to their perception of their needs, emotional ties with them, and services exchanged among family members over the years. Serial service, the transfer of worldly goods from parents to lineal descendants that occurs in due course, exists side by side with serial reciprocity, which specifies the giver-taker relationship based on exchanges of goods and services and patterns of interaction.

A second conclusion, related to the first, is that a number of role reversals occur in which children begin to take care of their parents. These role reversals require new learning and place upon the middle generation potentially anxiety-provoking responsibilities. This generation, in addition to caring for the young, now has to care for old parents.

A third conclusion is that sibling members of the middle generation are sensitive to the problems each has in raising his own family. Therefore, they generally accept the notion that the sibling who has rendered the greatest amount of service to an aged parent should receive a major portion of the inheritance upon the death of that parent. If the sibling takes the parent into his home, other siblings expect that almost all the parent's estate should go to that child. On the other hand, if the child went to live in the parent's home during the latter's declining years, then the pay-off should be more equally distributed among the children, since the one has already profited from living in the parent's home. The data indicate general agreement that the child who performs the greatest amount of service should receive the greatest part of the estate, and where disagreements occur, they focus on differences in perception among children concerning the amount of service actually rendered by the sibling who was left the largest share of the estate.

Children feel that they should maintain intimate contact with aged parents in order to provide them with emotional support and social and recreational opportunities, and that such contact maintenance is requisite for obtaining a share of the inheritance. Exchanges may be of different orders. Children provide parents with physical care, emotional support, affection, and the niceties of social interaction in their declining years; in return, they receive financial compensation. What is suggested here is that the pattern of distribution to particular children is based upon services rendered. The child who provides the most physical and social service generally gets the largest reward.

The pattern of exchange of care for eventual financial reward does not function when the decedent does not require special attention. The normal testate pattern of distribution is for the decedent to leave his estate to the spouse if the spouse is still living. By leaving the estate to the spouse, the testator provides the widow or widower with the means to continue an independent existence or, if this is not feasible, the means with which to reward the children for their care.

The over-all conclusion from this study of patterns of property distribution within the family of procreation at the death of a testator is that service is exchanged for a financial reward at a later time, a reward that is substantially greater than one would expect to find in equal distribution of the estate or distribution under intestate conditions.

If the nearest kin is calculated in the family of orientation rather than the family of procreation, the decedent's will is much less likely to bear similarity to the pattern of intestate succession. Disinheritance and inequalities among equally related claimants become commonplace. It is also relatively more common that the decedent makes bequests to charitable organizations and unrelated individuals.

There is estrangement among some of these families. However, an examination of seven cases involving estranged families reveals that in each case, the decedent found someone, or a few persons, whose performance toward him was that of a kinsman. The decedent in turn reciprocated in his will. Although these families have within them the forces making for estrangement, they also present a great many alternatives or possibilities.

The loose integration in these families also means that the decedent has greater freedom to choose beneficiaries from outside the family. If nonrelated persons have rendered the services typically expected of relatives, they may be the recipients of the decedent's gratitude and largess. Charities may benefit from the aloneness of the decedent. No major charitable bequest was made by a decedent who was survived by his family of procreation.

Finally, it was found that it is a rare decedent who is survived by helpless orphans or parents, since the average testator outlives aged dependents and lives long enough to bring his children to their majority. The decedent may often leave a dependent spouse. Although the spouse is the most usual dependent and hence may need legal protection, there is evidence that most testators will the spouses either adequate amounts or their entire estates. The spouse's claim on the estate is widely recognized to be paramount, except in the case of remarriage.

The general conclusion is that while the location of the decedent in a family kin network does not appear to be an important factor in his decision to make a will (see Chapter 4, pp. 69–73), once the basic decision to be testate has been made, the location of the testator in the kin network is the most important factor in the pattern of distribution chosen by him.

Chapter 6

Conceptions of Justice: The Heirs

THE DECEDENT'S conception of justice is embodied in his last will and testament, in which his worldly goods are distributed among specified persons or institutions. His conception may or may not correspond to that of his heirs.[1] If it does not, the heirs may react with anger or guilt and proceed to rectify the situation.[2] In some cases, these testate successors may make a redistribution of the property of the decedent.

Society's conception of justice may be considered to be shown by the Ohio Statute of Descent and Distribution. The heirs in the intestate case may similarly react with anger or guilt if this distribution is not fair, and they may also attempt to change the distribution. In the absence of a will that would express the decedent's wishes, the heirs may redistribute the estate according to their own ideas of justice or in accordance with their interpretation of the decedent's wishes.

Conceptions of justice are revealed by verbal sentiments or the actions of the participants. In Chapter 5, justice was studied in terms of the decedent's instructions for distribution. In this chapter, the actions of the heirs are examined, either in allowing the property to be distributed in accordance with the decedent's instructions or with the statute or in redistributing the estate.[3]

1. In this chapter, the term *heirs* is used in a lay sense to indicate those who inherit either by testate or intestate succession. From the technically legal standpoint, *heir* means the person entitled to an intestate's realty and, at the most, the successor to either real or personal property via intestate succession. See Thomas E. Atkinson, *Wills,* 2d ed. (St. Paul, Minn.: West Publishing Co., 1953), p. 4.

2. Alexander and Simpson believe one of the most important contributions of Homans' work is to point out the inadequacy of hedonic explanations of human behavior: "Though borne more lightly than the burden of efforts which go unrewarded, undeserved rewards, as Homans points out, are a source of discomfort." C. Norman Alexander and Richard L. Simpson, "Balance Theory and Distributive Justice," *Sociological Inquiry* 34 (Spring, 1964):184. They go on to discuss perceived injustice: "Now when conditions of distributive justice are not met, a person tends to rectify the perceived injustice. The most interesting examples of this occur when he must incur additional costs in order to restore balance." Ibid., p. 189.

3. This chapter is based only on the cases for which there are interviews. There were 453 testate cases in the decedent sample. In 17 of these cases, there were only question-

Redistribution in the Testate Case

The number of testate cases in which the heirs redistributed the estate was small. From this, it may be inferred that the testator's disposition of the estate was satisfactory in most instances or that the heirs were unable to agree on a more satisfactory disposition.

There were only 50 cases of redistribution among the 360 testate cases for which interviews were obtained. In 21 of these cases, the redistribution involved a car; most often a spouse who was the sole beneficiary gave the car to a son or daughter. Some of these cars might almost be considered mementos, since the value ranged from $10 to $1,000, with the majority under $500, and thus equivalent in value to a piece of furniture or jewelry. The difference is that the value of a car was always noted on probate records, while furniture and jewelry were only rarely appraised, although interviewees mentioned receiving one or the other.

In 29 cases, the redistribution concerned something other than a car. In 17 of these cases, the survivors were a spouse and lineal descendants. Where the spouse was the sole beneficiary, the redistribution involved giving part or all of the estate to the children. The most interesting cases were those involving real estate.

Case 361. The decedent willed the house, which was not held jointly, to his 80-year-old wife, who then transferred it to their only son. The son and his wife lived with the parents; and the father had wanted to put the house in the son's name several years before, but the son felt at that time it would "be rushing things."

Case 391. The decedent left her estate, which consisted of half a house, to her 78-year-old husband. He has deeded the house to their daughter and also made his own bank account joint with her. The daughter, who is single, does not live with him but in another state. Another daughter is deceased. His first will left everything to his wife. He does not plan to make a new will since he has signed everything over to his daughter.

Case 256. The decedent left her half of the house to her 79-year-old husband. He sold the house and divided the money among his two sons and a deceased son's widow. Each of them has put $1,000 of the $2,500 received into a bank account to take care of the father if he should need medical care. "So far this money hasn't been touched, but he is getting old and senile and we may have to put him in a nursing home. He is getting too hard for us to handle."

Case 632. The decedent willed her half of two houses to her 69-year-old husband.

---

naires; and for 76 cases, there were neither interviews nor questionnaires. The testate section is therefore based on 360 cases. There were 206 intestate cases in the decedent sample. In eight of these cases, there were questionnaires only; and for 51 cases, there were neither interviews nor questionnaires. The intestate section is therefore based on 147 cases.

The husband has deeded the houses to their son and daughter. The children make their homes in these properties, and the widower lives with his daughter. The son commented that he and his sister signed a statement guaranteeing that they will provide for their father if this becomes necessary.

There are alternative means of paying children for the care rendered a parent in the final years. Some older persons use the method of delayed payment, and the one child who has made a home for an aged parent becomes his only heir. Other older persons prepay their care by giving to their children while they are still alive. Case 632 illustrates that this reciprocity between children and their parents may take the form of an economic exchange, although there was some doubt about the legality of the signed agreement.

Where the spouse was not the sole beneficiary, redistribution occurred with children signing over part or all of their share to the surviving spouse. In this study, there was one exception.

Case 608. The decedent was survived by his third wife and three adult children. The will followed the intestate distribution, leaving one-third to the wife and two-thirds to be divided equally among the children. One daughter mentioned that over the years her father had given each of them gifts. There was an inequity of $750 due one sister, "so we gave her that and then divided things up."

Where lineal heirs were the surviving kin, redistribution occurred in only nine cases. In three of these cases, the redistribution was of a minor nature. Three other cases involved disinheritance or a situation bordering on disinheritance.

Case 586. The decedent was a 75-year-old widow whose only property was a house worth $14,000. The will had been made thirteen years before her death, when her husband was still living. Five of the six children were contingent beneficiaries. One daughter had been disinherited because she had married a divorced man. After a period of years, there was a reconciliation, but the will was not changed. Instead, the widow called her five children together and told them to include their sister. This they did. The decedent's oldest daughter had lived with her and according to the will should have received $1,000 more than her siblings. The relationships between the siblings were so precarious, however, that this daughter felt it would be wiser to take only an equal share. "I didn't take it because I didn't want any bad feelings." Although some disapproval of her care of the mother was voiced by other members of the family, the sentiment expressed to us by several members was that she deserved the extra portion. "All the money in the world couldn't repay her care of Mother." It was also mentioned that one of the sons disapproved of sharing the estate with the disinherited daughter.

Case 611. A widowed male divided his $19,000 estate among four of his five children. To the fifth child, a son, he left $300 and notes from a $400 debt. The son had borrowed the money during the Depression to help pay college expenses. Otherwise, he had paid his own way and was the only one to go to college. He renounced his inheritance, and his legacy reverted to the residue.

In the remaining three cases, the redistribution again involved the final care of the parent.

Case 604. The bulk of the decedent's wealth was in a joint account with his daughter —$23,893. The residue was to be divided equally between the daughter and a son. This consisted of the house ($12,000), a car ($75), and $3,000 in stock. The son said, "I took the car and she kept the house, but this is as it should be. She had taken care of Dad and deserved it. She was also sole beneficiary on some insurance. After Dad retired, he couldn't make payments; my brother-in-law made them, so my sister should have been the beneficiary. Dad was probably closer to my brother-in-law than to me during the last years of his life."

Case 056. A $41,000 estate was left equally to a son and a daughter. The decedent's home accounted for $16,000 of this. The son sold his half of the home to his sister for $10. She commented that if her mother had rewritten the will, "she would have left the house to me because I've always lived here and I took care of her at the end. My brother has his own home and is doing well, and I'm divorced and don't have much."

Case 291. The decedent, a widow, survived her husband by five years. They had made mutual wills over five years prior to his death naming each other sole inheritor and their three daughters contingent beneficiaries equally. One of the daughters said that her mother was always going to change the will because she wanted the one who stayed at home to have the house, which was the bulk of the estate. The other two daughters honored their mother's verbal request and signed their shares over to their sister.

The wills in Cases 056 and 291 predated the death of the parent by sixteen years and fourteen years, respectively. The will in Case 604 was only 1½ years old. While the will did not discriminate between the two children, the decedent's arrangements in regard to his extra-probate property were discriminatory.

There were three cases of redistribution where collateral kin were the survivors and heirs.

Case 509. A second cousin of the decedent put her $14,000 inheritance in a trust fund for her daughter. She felt the decedent wanted the daughter to have the inheritance.[4]

4. There is one problem involved in describing redistribution by the beneficiaries under a will. It was sometimes difficult to distinguish between a redistribution because of some dissatisfaction with the testator's disposition and a completely independent gift by the beneficiary shortly after receiving the inheritance. We do not have a standard for distinguishing a redistribution from such a new and independent gift. Perhaps Case 509 is better placed in the latter category. It can be so considered even if the second cousin rationalized her decision to do what she did in terms of the decedent wanting the daughter to have the inheritance, for the transfer to the daughter might not be attributed to disappointment in what the decedent did.

Case 636. Ten nieces and nephews inherited. "Three of the rich relatives turned their shares over to the niece who had the least money of the living relatives."

Case 589. The decedent's two sisters were her only legatees. They gave $500 to their disinherited brother.

The last will and testament accurately depicts the disposition of the decedent's assets in the vast majority of testate cases; there was a redistribution in only 14 per cent of the cases. Where redistribution did occur, it generally reflected differential services or needs of the heirs.

Redistribution in the Intestate Case

It might be thought that a discussion of distribution in the intestate case would be unnecessary because Ohio Revised Code 2105: Statute of Descent and Distribution automatically takes care of the disposition of the intestate individual's estate. Such an omission would ignore what actually happened to the decedent's property: major redistributions occurred in over 50 per cent of the cases. Knowledge of such redistribution was obtained from interviews with the heirs. Thus, for the single purpose of knowing how the decedent's estate was actually distributed, the interviews with intestate heirs were more important than those conducted with the survivors of testate decedents. Of the total number of intestate cases (206), there were no interviews for 59 cases; this discussion is based on the 147 cases for which interviews were obtained. The case loss varied with the class of survivor (see Table 6–1).

TABLE 6–1 INTESTATE CASES, BY CLASS OF SURVIVOR AND CASES WITH INTERVIEWS

Class of Survivor	Cases in Class	Cases with Interviews	Per Cent of Cases with Interviews
Spouse	23	17	73.9
Spouse and lineal kin	94	74	78.7
Lineal kin	52	37	71.2
Collateral kin	29	16	55.2
No known next of kin	8	3	37.5
Total	206	147	71.4

Spouse Was the Only Survivor

Nearly 90 per cent of the decedent testators willed their entire estates to their spouses in those cases where the spouse was the only survivor. In the 17 intestate cases where the decedent's sole survivor was a spouse, the entire estate passed by law to the spouse. In only one instance was there a major redistribution of the property in accordance with what the spouse felt would have been the wishes of the decedent.

Case 197. The decedent was a 56-year-old woman. After the estate was settled, her husband realized $1,800. He gave $1,000 of this to the Jehovah's Witnesses, a sect to which they had both belonged. The spouse is a 75-year-old man working as a custodian.

It is scarcely to be expected that many spouses would give away a major portion of their inheritance. They would be widely regarded as having exclusive rights, not only legally, but normatively. It should be remembered that the mean net intestate estate of $6,694 was considerably smaller than the mean testate estate of $35,160. The spouses of intestate decedents were not themselves sufficiently affluent to redistribute their inheritance.

Spouse and Lineal Kin Were the Surviving Next of Kin

There were 74 cases in which the spouse and lineal descendants or ascendants survived. In 60 of these cases (81 per cent), the distribution did not follow the normal pattern of a specific division between the surviving spouse and lineal kin. In 19 of the cases the estates were so small that the spouse received all the assets. In 38 cases, the spouse received all or more than the intestate share, most often because others who had claims to the estate signed over their shares. The remaining three cases deviated because of bankruptcy, out-of-state property, or remarriage.

Why do people give up their rights in property by signing over their share to the decedent's spouse? Given a certain size estate and a number of children of a certain age, there might be a small saving in inheritance tax.[5] This may be illustrated by a hypothetical example. Assume a net estate of $21,000, with a spouse and two adult children surviving the decedent. Each of the three next of kin is entitled to one-third of the estate, or $7,000. The spouse's exemption under the Ohio Inheritance Tax Law is $10,000, and each of the adult children has a $7,000 exemption. Therefore, no inheritance tax will be paid. If the estate had been left entirely to the spouse, a 1-per cent tax would have been levied on the amount of the inheritance over $10,000 and under $25,000. The spouse would have paid a tax of $110. The Ohio Inheritance Tax is levied on the succession rights that accrue on the date of death and not on the person who by subsequent agreement actually comes into enjoyment of the property passing from the decedent.[6] Actually, no person in this sample indicated that tax savings were a factor in redistribution.

5. There would have to be a rearrangement in the nature of a transfer of the shares of the children rather than a renunciation of intestate succession rights by the children. Ohio Revised Code 2105.061 allows written renunciation of intestate succession. Any property renounced pursuant to that section is distributed as provided by law as if such competent adult had predeceased the decedent. If a child who disclaims had children of his own, the renounced inheritance would pass to them. Ohio Revised Code 2113.60 controls the disposition of property resulting from a refused legacy or bequest.
6. In re Daniel's Estate, 159 Ohio St. 109, 111 N.E. 2d 252 (1953); in re Chadwick's Estate, 167 Ohio St. 373, 149 N.E. 2d 5 (1958). On July 1, 1968, the Ohio Inheritance

A common form of property in a decedent's estate is the one-half interest in a house held by the husband and wife as tenants in common. When the children do not sign over to the surviving spouse, the ownership becomes complicated, for example, a $25,000 house where the spouse has a two-thirds interest and each of five children has a one-fifteenth interest. There were five cases in which the pattern of ownership followed the intestate distribution. In only one of these had the heirs given any thought to the problems of divided ownership. In each instance, the surviving spouse remained in the home, and the children expressed no intention of claiming the full rights of ownership. They were content with a *de facto* arrangement that corresponded to a spouse-all settlement.[7] The fact of the children's keeping their share of the property did not mean that they were hostile toward the surviving parent or particularly avaricious. It appears rather that the family was unsophisticated in legal and property matters. Since these families seemed to enjoy reasonably good relationships, it was likely that no problems were associated with their pattern of ownership. None of the interviewees who had signed over to their surviving parent mentioned the complications of divided property ownership as a reason for their decision.

The remarks of the children who had given up a share in their deceased parent's estate indicated that they made no searching analysis in reference to this decision. It was a matter-of-fact action; in their family it was the right and proper thing to do. "Why take the home away from an older parent who is still living? It is my mother's home." "Mother is more entitled to it than anyone else. She worked hard for that home." "The wife should be entitled to everything unless it's a second marriage." "Mother needs everything, she has many years ahead of her; she shouldn't have to be dependent on her children."

The parents who were the recipients of their children's generosity similarly took the action for granted for the most part. "My children wouldn't do that —not see that I have enough to live on." "The intestate pattern isn't fair. The wife should get it all. She should be able to do what she needs to do. My daughter is further ahead in her twelve years of marriage than we were much later." "If I get sick, I need the money; it is my security."

Tax was replaced by the Ohio Estate Tax. See Ohio Revised Code 5731. The tax is now levied on the transfer of the estate as a whole rather than upon the receipt of property by each beneficiary.

7. Professor Allison Dunham, in personal correspondence of 24 April 1968, indicated that he considers this "*de facto* arrangement" as more closely analogous to a will in which the spouse is given a life estate and the children the remainder interest in the home. Perhaps the answer lies in between. At any rate, as long as real estate is occupied or used by the spouse, or even by the children, there is no particular problem of fragmented ownership of a parcel of real estate. The problem arises when some of the co-owners want to sell and others do not and also when a major capital investment must be made and the question arises concerning which person or persons must make the investment.

A less charitable explanation is that in depriving the surviving spouse of home and hearth, it may be necessary for the child to assume financial and social responsibility for the parent at a time not suitable for the child's family. Thus, in providing the optimum means for independence of the surviving parent, the children postpone the day when they will have to face the situation of providing for the final care of the aging parent.

The data on the large number of redistributions where a spouse and lineal kin survive indicate that the majority of people felt that the spouse should have sole rights of inheritance. This corroborates the finding presented in Chapter 5 that the vast majority of testators willed their entire estates to their spouses.[8]

It should be remembered that children expect to inherit from their surviving parent; hence, they are not irrevocably renouncing their rights to the property. This expectation, however, is not as likely when the surviving spouse is a stepparent.

Remarriage and estate fragmentation. There were 11 intestate cases in which the decedent was survived by the most recent spouse and the children of an earlier marriage. In six of these cases, the spouse received all the property either because the estate was so small or because of the nature of the decedent's holdings. In the other five, both families profited by the death.

The following are descriptions of selected cases in which there was a division between the two families.

Case 539. A 48-year-old man was survived by his third wife (they married 2½ years before his death), his 13-month-old son by the third marriage, and a 23-year-old son by his first marriage. A boat trailer, motorcycle, truck, and car were the only assets that went through probate court, and these were valued at $610. The first marriage ended in divorce, and the son of this marriage had lived with his mother until he was 18. Thereafter, the son and father had seen each other at fairly frequent intervals. The son believed his father had made a will leaving everything to him, but the will was never found. He claims his stepmother withdrew money from bank accounts on the day of death and that she took the home by virtue of a quitclaim deed which his father had never signed. He was the beneficiary of a small insurance policy. The widow claims that the home and bank accounts had been previously transferred to her name. She was also the beneficiary of a $10,000 insurance policy.

Case 337. The decedent was a 55-year-old man who was survived by his second wife and three adult children from his first marriage. The first marriage ended in divorce,

8. It is debatable whether to consider the spouse-all pattern a matter of distributive justice, that is, investment, or only a matter of established practice. The comments of the spouses and lineal kin were not enlightening because the pattern was taken for granted. Blau criticizes Homans for using the term *investment* too broadly. Blau takes the position that established practices create expectations but that these expectations have nothing to do with investments or justice. Peter Blau, "Justice in Social Exchange," *Sociological Inquiry* 34 (Spring, 1964):2, 193–206.

and the decedent had paid alimony or support until the children had finished college. The second marriage had lasted ten years. The children were each beneficiaries of $1,000 insurance policies. They made no further claim upon the estate. The widow received approximately $13,000.

Case 635. The decedent was a 71-year-old female. She was survived by her second husband, an adult child of the second marriage, and two children of her first marriage, which ended with the death of her first husband. The second marriage lasted thirty-two years. The estate consisted of the decedent's share in a co-owned house ($7,000) and a $6,000 savings account. Initially the children were supposed to receive $133 each. Children of the first marriage protested. Their understanding with their mother had been that they were to be sole inheritors of the proceeds of their own father's estate, which was represented by the $6,000 account from the sale of the earlier home. Eventually, each of the three children received about $1,000 cash and two-ninths ownership of the home in which the widower still resided. The children of the first marriage further claimed that their stepfather withdrew money from the joint accounts. Despite the fact that they had quarreled with their stepfather over the division of the estate, they admitted he was good to their mother. She had a stroke five years before she died, and he retired in order to take care of her so that she did not need help from her children.

Case 379. A 79-year-old male decedent left $225 in traveler's checks. He was survived by his third wife, to whom he had been married for seven years, and two sons from his first marriage. The decedent had kept the rest of his funds in a bank account in one son's name. This money was used to pay for funeral expenses. There had been verbal instructions that what was left should be divided equally among the grandchildren (each son had two children), and this amounted to $150 for each grandchild. The sons thought this was just because the last marriage had been short and unhappy. The unhappiness is perhaps best revealed in the widow's comment, "He did a good thing when he died."[9]

Case 199. The decedent was a 64-year-old man who was survived by his second wife and their four minor children and an adult son from his first marriage. There is good feeling between the stepson and stepmother. The decedent's first wife ran off with another man, leaving her son with his father. The second marriage lasted fifteen years. The decedent was an accident victim, and according to his widow, they had an appointment to make a will the same week that he died. The widow was able to settle the estate almost as they had planned to in their will. In addition to the home she and her children live in, they owned rental property. The family home will be in her name, and the second house has been deeded to the five children of the deceased. The son of the first marriage was also the beneficiary of an insurance policy. The assets of the deceased totaled approximately $20,000, and the first son's share was approximately $4,000.

9. In this case, the son was the visible legal owner. However, he had secretly agreed with the decedent that he would hold the bank account in trust for the decedent's grandchildren, enjoyment by the grandchildren being postponed until his death.

In these five cases there was no instance of the children of the first marriage renouncing their claim.

In each of the following cases, the spouse received all the assets.

Case 260. The decedent was a 60-year-old man who was survived by his second wife and eight adult children of his first marriage. In addition, his second wife had five adult children of her first marriage. Two marriages have occurred between the step-siblings. Some of both sets of children live with the widow (twelve in the household); others remained in Puerto Rico. The widow received about $2,500 death benefits clear of the probate and funeral expenses, and with this money she is buying the common dwelling unit. Legally the widow has received all, but there is such a mingling of funds and families that it is difficult to say who benefited.

Case 231. The decedent was a 77-year-old man who was survived by his second wife and a son of his first marriage. The first marriage ended in divorce. The son had scarcely been on speaking terms with his father. His own mother lives with him and his wife. The son knew nothing of his father's financial affairs but was sure the estate was a small one. Only a car went through probate. (The duration of the second marriage is not known in this case.)

Case 516. The decedent was a 52-year-old man. He was survived by his second wife and three adult children from his first marriage. His car was the only property that was administered. His children alleged that his other property was previously transferred to the widow. The widow confirmed this but stated that the previously transferred property consisted of the marital home and that during the course of their fourteen-year marriage, she had made most of the payments. At one time, the decedent had promised his children they would receive one-half of his property, and he drew up a will to this effect (but never signed it). The children were exceedingly bitter toward the widow. Though she does not feel close to them, the widow is remembering the children in her own will.

Case 261. The decedent, a 54-year-old man, was survived by his second wife and an adult daughter from his first marriage. The first marriage was dissolved by divorce; but when the daughter was 6 years old, her own mother died and she went to live with her father and stepmother. This second marriage lasted twenty-five years. The only asset that went through probate was the car. The widow said everything else went in the expenses of the last illness. The daughter felt that even if there had been more, she would have had no claim. For about three months before he died, her father had stayed in her house (because it was a one-story dwelling), and her in-laws tried to persuade her to ask for reimbursement. However, she was adamant in feeling that she took care of her father because he was her father and not because she had any thought of compensation.

Case 581. The decedent was a 65-year-old male who was survived by his second wife and their two adult children and by an adult son from his first marriage, who had lived with his mother after the divorce. The second marriage lasted thirty-three years. Our only interview was with the first son, who had little knowledge of his father's finances and did not care. The only assets going through probate were the car and a savings account of less than $1,500. The deductions were greater than the assets.

Case 024. The decedent was a 51-year-old male who was survived by his second wife (the second marriage was contracted ten years before his death) and a daughter of his first marriage, which ended in divorce. The attorney was unable to locate the daughter. Only the car and a $100 savings account went through probate, although pensions and insurance meant that the widow actually received about $6,500. The widow did feel that her husband's child had a valid claim on the estate and that, if the daughter had been located, she would have offered her the car.

Some second spouses apparently believe they do not have the sole right to inherit. This is revealed by the testamentary provisions of the widow in Case 516 and by the statement of the widow in Case 024. The daughter's feelings toward her father and stepmother in Case 261 can be attributed to the fact that her stepmother reared her and that the second marriage was the major one of the decedent's life. In Cases 231, 581, and 024, the relationship between the decedent and children of the prior marriage was almost nonexistent. As a consequence, the decedent felt no obligation to provide for his children, and they did not feel they had any claim.

Special problems of spouse and surviving minor children. There were 29 cases in which a spouse and minor children survived; 14 of these included both adult and minor children. In the majority, the adult children waived their rights in favor of their surviving parent. In five cases, there was no real property involved, and other assets were minimal and released without administration.

When a decedent dies intestate and is survived by a spouse and minor children, there can be very special problems if real estate is involved because the minor children cannot sign over their share to the surviving parent. The frustration and problems were strongly stated by one interviewee who found himself in this predicament.

Case 238. "I had to come up with so much equity for my minor children. It doesn't make sense for me, although the other fellow might take off and leave the children stranded. I can see why probate court is looking after minor children, but it still doesn't make sense to me. It could have been solved if my wife had had a will, but if somebody's real sick it's hard to ask them to sign papers. I purposely neglected to do so although it would have saved me a lot of headaches and a lot of money. It doesn't seem right that a fellow has to borrow money to pay his children and still have to raise them. Also I'm under bond for my own children. At my death they'll end up owning the house I bought from them."

In another case, the husband had not intended to sell the house after his wife died and so had not filed probate documents. He remarried and then wanted to sell the house and "discovered" it had to go through administration, which involved waiting eleven months. The sale price paid off the existing mortgage on the old house, and he and his second wife purchased another house. He does not mention having to buy out the children's shares.

One husband, who did not have an attorney, complained about the length of time it took and the "emphasis placed on the fact that I had to prove I was the children's father. This is ridiculous." He felt quite competent in handling the settlement at court without an attorney since he had "friends at City Hall who steered me in the right direction." He did feel that because of the court's stringent actions to protect minor children any will he and his wife had planned would not have been worth "a hill of beans in court today" and advised getting an attorney familiar with probate law to draw up a will where minor children were involved. He had to buy out the children's shares of the house because the court wanted him to be sole owner; his home is in the path of a freeway, and the children will still be minors when the freeway is built. He complained too that the court seemed to be interested only in the children and that "all the time I had spent working was to no avail and all the money I had sunk into this place was not mine."

For one wife, the problem of owning property with a minor was resolved by her only son reaching age 21 during the period of settlement and being able to sign his share over to her. Another wife expects to buy her children's share for a token payment, although she could not explain how this would be accomplished. One wife said that she bought out her daughter's share by taking out a life insurance policy and making her daughter the beneficiary. Parents appreciated the intention of the law (that is, to protect the rights of minors) but felt the law actually made it more difficult for them to perform their own protective parental duties. The attitude might be summed up as, "It's a good law for people in general. I don't need it. I'm a good parent."

Case 348. Mrs. ________ felt children are entitled to a share of the estate but felt something should be done to avoid the complications that ensue when a minor child is part owner of a house. She had such an exasperating time in this respect that she was eager to contribute to the project in the hope that it might help others. Her husband died of leukemia. She did not bring up the subject of a will because she did not want him to know that he suffered from a fatal illness. She is presently living in the house with their 13-year-old daughter. The house is in a changing neighborhood, and she feels that if she wanted to sell the house now she could not. "I don't feel you should be tied up like this when they are underage. It's so confusing to get the house into my name. My lawyer buys it from me or something like that."

One husband, three of whose four children were minors, was more articulate but just as exasperated.

Case 520. "It seems to me the law is devious. To accomplish what you want to accomplish, you have to go to devious means to do it. To get the home in my name, the lawyer had to appoint an administrator *de bonis non,* and a paper I received indicated such administrator is selling the property to pay debts of the deceased which, as I look at it, is a big farce. It has to be done to get the house in my name, but there are no debts. The doctor and funeral expenses have been taken care of. The house is not actually being sold, and there won't be any change of funds—just a lot of rigmarole to accomplish something. I realize all this could have been avoided had we both had wills, but I didn't expect death at age 44."

It is interesting to compare these intestate decedents with those decedents who were also survived by a spouse and minor children but who made wills. Of the 57 in the latter group, all but two willed their entire estates to their spouses. They may have been better informed about the problems that could ensue with minors inheriting or were so advised by their attorneys. Not all the surviving spouses in the intestate cases were uninformed beforehand; but because they wanted to keep the knowledge of a terminal illness from the decedent, nothing was done to encourage writing a will. It appears that the law governing the inheritance of minors, although it has good intentions in trying to protect the rights of children, causes incalculable difficulties for parents in both psychic and monetary costs. The parent is caught in a maze of legal requirements that not only are expensive in time and money but also potentially threaten his relationship with the child or children.

Lineal Kin Were the Only Surviving Next of Kin

Minor children. There were two cases in which the only survivors were minors. Since only those who were 21 or over were interviewed, there are no interviews on these cases. But the information obtained from probate records is worth noting. The first case illustrates the higher cost of estate administration when the heirs are too young to supervise; it is the nearest approximation in this study to the classic poor-orphans stereotype.

Case 479. The decedent was a 42-year-old widower who was survived by five minor children. The oldest was 17, and the youngest was 11. The only asset in the estate was a $7,000 insurance policy. Court costs were $200; attorney fees, $600 (this was the only case of its size in which attorney fees were more than $500); appraiser's fees, $30; and the funeral cost, just short of $2,000 (in the entire decedent sample less than 15 per cent had funerals costing more than $1,750). The children make their home with their oldest sister, who is married.

In the following case, a sister of the decedent served as administrator, and the costs were considerably less.

Case 467. The decedent was a 38-year-old divorcee. Her survivors were two children, one 15 and the other 10. On an estate of nearly $14,000—most of it in real estate—the attorney fee was $440, the funeral expense under $1,100.

Adult and minor children. Minor children are probably well protected when they have older siblings because the older ones tend to be concerned about their younger brothers and sisters. There were only two cases involving minor and adult children as sole survivors for which interviews were obtained.

Case 369. The decedent was a 51-year-old widow who was survived by four adult children and a minor daughter, age 13. The net estate was over $8,000, the principal asset being the family residence. All the adult children decided that the entire estate should go to the minor child. One brother and a sister are paying off the mortgage. The child lives with her brother in the family residence.

Case 531. The decedent was a 53-year-old widower. Surviving him were a daughter, age 24, a son, age 23, and a son, age 18. The three children remain in the home, which was the principal asset in this estate (net value less than $7,000). Since the house has not been sold, it is more in the nature of a pooled rather than a shared inheritance.

Adult children. There were 32 cases in which adult children were the only survivors. There is less tendency for a major redistribution of the property in these cases. When major redistribution does occur, it is a result of rather unusual circumstances. Of the 32 cases, eight involved a redistribution.

In the case that follows, the redistribution may be described as a quixotic gesture, a gesture that was later regretted by one of the children.

Case 022. The decedent was a 55-year-old man whose estate was insolvent. His survivors were two daughters. The major asset was an automobile that was appraised at $1,200. One of the daughters made the final payments on this car, which was then given to the father's girlfriend. The girlfriend later married a millionaire.

The following two cases also involved a redistribution that carried out the decedents' wishes as interpreted by their children.

Case 217. The decedent was a 70-year-old widower. The only asset going through probate was a $50 car. The survivors were a son and a daughter. The deceased had actually made a will fourteen years prior to his death, but since the estate was so small, it was not probated. However, the decedent's last wishes as expressed in the will and in verbal statements later were carried out by his son, even though he had to use his own money to accomplish these wishes. In the will, the decedent had instructed his son-executor to pay the debts of his housekeeper. The son gave the housekeeper $100. In his last years, the father said he would like to do something for his grandchildren. Each of seven grandchildren was given $200, and each of two great-grandchildren received $100. The son said, "I didn't want the grandchildren to feel Gramps didn't leave them anything."

Case 254. A 79-year-old widow was survived by a son and a daughter. The son renounced his right to participate in the estate in favor of his sister. The net estate was

$1,500. The widow had always lived with her daughter; however, the daughter is not keeping the estate as recompense for the living arrangements. During World War II their father and four siblings were killed by the Germans. The widow received a pension from the German government. The daughter, with her brother's knowledge, will use the estate to buy markers for the graves in Budapest. "If Mother had left a different kind of money I might have done something else."

In the next two cases, the redistribution is based upon the children's different contributions to the decedent's welfare.

Case 312. An 80-year-old widow left her home in a deteriorating section of the city. One of her sons had lived with her, and during the last six years of her life had quit work to take care of her (she was partially paralyzed). The other two brothers contributed to the costs of the establishment, but this was considered a lesser investment. The son who took care of his mother remains in the home. One brother signed over his share to the others.

Case 607. A 74-year-old decedent was survived by six children. He left an estate of $5,700, part of which was a car. One of the daughters and her husband offered to buy the car, but her siblings agreed to give it to them. A brother commented, "My father used her husband's place of business and credit for his own business—they deserved a little more."

Rights and obligations are incurred not only in the parent-child relationship but also among the siblings, as the following case illustrates.

Case 152. The decedent was a 90-year-old widower who was survived by five children. He had no real or personal property. Administration was opened to prosecute the claim of the decedent for injuries prior to and incidental to his death. Four of the children waived their claims in favor of their oldest sister. This sister had stayed home to help raise the younger children; as a consequence, she had married late. Her siblings explicitly waived their claims because of their obligations to her. Unfortunately, the suit failed. One son paid for the funeral; he had incurred obligations toward his parents because they had helped raise his daughter when he was widowed and had made a down payment on a house for him. The final care of the decedent was managed in this family by rotating the residence of the deceased among the families of his five children.

Despite unequal involvement by children with the aging parent before death, siblings subscribed to the principle of equal distribution. This was often done even if an unequal disposition would have preserved harmony among siblings. In the following case, the decedent's wishes were carried out and overt disagreements were avoided, but some children believed that justice had not been done.

Case 140. An 86-year-old widow left a net estate of $14,000. She was survived by eight children. During her last five years, she lived with one of her daughters. This daughter commented: "Mother said, 'I had eight children and it is to be divided among eight children.' " One of her sons was a member of a religious order; he had signed a paper agreeing that any money he might inherit would revert to the estate. Instead of this, the other brothers and sisters donated his share to his school. A daughter who was a nun had asked her mother to divide her share among the others; the mother had replied, "Oh no, you are my child too." The comments of the siblings about the distribution were: "I felt the one who was taking care of her was entitled to the lion's share." "Some of my sisters gave more help than others; I would have done it differently." "There won't be any arguments with equal division." "Split equally is the best way—less disagreements."

The intestate pattern of distribution was followed in the only case where children and grandchildren were surviving next of kin.

Distributive justice was a difficult criterion to apply. If the decedent did not state his wishes, the children did the easiest thing and the estate was distributed equally to the children and per stirpes to the descendants of children.

Parents Were the Sole Surviving Next of Kin

Among the intestate decedents, there were two persons who were survived by their parents. One was a 29-year-old man who had never been married; both parents were living and shared the proceeds. The second case involved a major deviation from the intestate distribution that was accomplished without joint agreement.

Case 149. A 34-year-old divorced male was the decedent. The gross probate value of the estate was less than $2,000. The decedent's mother was the applicant and listed herself as the only next of kin. The mother was also the beneficiary of a $5,000 insurance policy. The decedent was also survived by a 13-year-old daughter who sometimes stays with her mother and sometimes with her grandmother. The decedent's mother has paid off her son's debts and is planning to use the rest of the money for her granddaughter. She says, "If he had made a will, he would have made it out to me—if he left to his daughter, her mother would get her hands on it."

Collateral Kin Survived

There were five decedents who were survived by siblings. Two of these cases followed the intestate pattern of distribution. The other three were released without administration,[10] and the disposition does not follow the Ohio Statute of Descent and Distribution.

Case 038. The decedent was a 64-year-old single woman who for ten years prior to her death had made her home with one of her three sisters. This sister was the applicant. Administration was initiated to release a $60 insurance policy that had named the decedent's deceased mother as beneficiary. In addition, the sister-applicant was the named beneficiary of a $360 insurance policy.

10. See Ohio Revised Code 2113.03.

Case 344. The decedent was a 66-year-old woman who had never married. She made her home with one of her three sisters. This sister was the applicant for a gross probate estate of slightly over $400. Additionally there was a $1,000 insurance policy, with this sister and her son named as co-beneficiaries. As in the previous case, two of the sisters received nothing.

Case 132. The decedent was a 58-year-old male who had been separated from his wife for over twenty years. The existence of this wife was not noted in probate records. The court records listed his only surviving next of kin as a brother and sister, both residents of Cleveland. Another sister not listed resided in Alabama. The sister in Cleveland waived her right to inherit. She was either unaware of what she had signed or had a change of heart because during the interview she complained that her brother had not given her half of the estate. She received $100. Net probate value was $250 out of a gross estate of $800, but in addition there were a television set and refrigerator that did not appear as probate assets.

There were three decedents who were survived by siblings, nieces, and nephews. In one case there was a redistribution of the estate.

Case 647. The decedent was a 66-year-old single woman who was survived by four siblings and six nieces and nephews. The redistribution resulted in one of the siblings receiving the entire estate. This was the sister with whom the decedent lived. The net estate was slightly over $2,000. The comments of two of the heirs who waived their rights to inherit explain the reason for the redistribution. A sibling said, "My sister deserves whatever was left after the funeral; she was up day and night with her." A niece commented, "It was only right that someone who had done something for the deceased get it."

Seven intestate decedents were survived by nieces and nephews. In each case, the intestate distribution was followed. In the following case, there was some dissatisfaction centering on reward for service to the aged aunt.

Case 651. The decedent was an 80-year-old widow. She had owned half of her house as a tenant in common with her husband and had a life estate in the other half. Her half of the house went to thirteen nieces and nephews; her deceased husband's half went to his two sisters, as stipulated in his will. The thirteen nieces and nephews were the children of six of the decedent's deceased siblings. If distribution had been per stirpes, the individual shares of the $8,000 estate would have varied from one-sixth to one-thirtieth instead of one-thirteenth each. One of the nephews who lost by this decision (his per stirpes share would have been one-sixth) said, "I think, if she had written a will, she would have done it this way." A niece whose loss was insignificant (from one-twelfth to one-thirteenth) was less satisfied: "I don't think the ones who never came to see her and never did for her should have gotten what we got." (Three of the nephews had not seen their aunt for thirty years and were difficult to locate.)

In Case 651, the adoption of a per stirpes division would have reached the same result as if deaths of the succeeding generations had occurred in their usual order, that is, at least one younger sibling outliving the decedent. The per capita division recognizes that fate frequently alters what is considered normal and that reasonable consequences should follow from facts that actually happened. Yet neither a per capita nor a per stirpes distribution would have satisfied the complaining niece; she wanted the estate divided according to the principle of distributive justice, to each according to her view of merit.

In three of the five cases in which the actual distribution did not correspond to the intestate distribution, the reason was the final care given to the decedent by one sibling.

Laughing Heirs

The term *laughing heir,* in the broad sense, signifies the "succession by one who is so loosely linked to his ancestor as to suffer no sense of bereavement at this loss."[11] David Cavers predicted over thirty years ago that ultimately the rules of succession would be revised to prevent these unintended windfalls.[12] Although some reformation has occurred, he was overly optimistic. Laughing heirs are still with us in the 1960's, but few obtain large windfalls. They receive the publicity because they have an aura of mystery and suggest, in addition, larceny in inheritance manipulating.

Several cases reported in a Cleveland daily newspaper indicate also that the locating of relatives may be a plum for the attorney. In one case involving a $22,000 estate, the attorney's fees were more than four times the suggested fee, and the administrator's were three times the suggested fee.[13] In this particular case, the attorney and administrator failed to find the heirs. Two reporters found second cousins in Iowa after checking marriage records, newspaper death notices, deeds, land sales, tax records, wills, employment records, and old city directories. About six months after they were located, the cousins were able to claim their inheritance.[14]

In another case of missing heirs, the same man acted as attorney and administrator and was awarded $7,500 in fees out of a $25,000 estate for services that included a trip to Ireland to look for heirs. The reporters first checked the estate of the decedent's mother and thereby obtained a list of the decedent's siblings. Marriage records were then used. In three days, the reporters found three grandnieces.[15]

Newspaper stories have been used for these extreme laughing-heir cases because there are relatively few such cases in which a decedent leaves no will and no known heirs. According to the newspaper, these cases average a little

11. David Cavers, "Change in the American Family and the 'Laughing Heir,'" *Iowa Law Review* 20 (1934–1935):208–209.
12. Ibid.
13. *Cleveland Plain Dealer,* 29 May 1966.
14. Ibid., 30 November 1966.
15. Ibid., 5 June 1966.

over a dozen within the county each year.[16] In the majority of 23 such cases checked by the newspaper, the attorneys were paid extraordinary fees.[17]

In other cases, professional heir hunters find the missing relatives probably through a search of public records similar to those undertaken by the reporters. These professionals usually take from one-third to one-half of the estate for their efforts.[18] A laughing heir may first be informed of his new wealth by a letter from such a tracing company. One such letter read

> We have been working on an estate matter and it appears from our investigation that you may be an heir to this estate. We should like to handle the matter for you on the following basis: in consideration of disclosing the name and location of the estate, preparing the necessary genealogical chart and obtaining necessary vital records, we are to receive an amount equal to one-third of what you recover.

In the following case, the heirs were contacted first by a firm in Boston and a few days later by one in Washington, D.C. There was no clue in the letters to the identity of the deceased or his place of residence. The heirs quickly signed contracts with the first company.[19]

Case 380. The decedent was a man of 78 years whose parents had died in his own childhood and whose wife and children had predeceased him. At the time of his death, he had accumulated about $40,000 in savings accounts. After administrative costs (including attorney and fiduciary fees of $1,500 each) and other expenses (the funeral cost nearly $3,500) had been paid, the estate was distributed to four cousins on the paternal side and thirteen cousins on the maternal side. The amounts received varied from $300 to $3,500, with the majority receiving $850. None of the cousins resided in the Cleveland metropolitan area. They were located in Ohio, West Virginia, Florida, and California. Six cousins were interviewed, and four returned questionnaires. Five did not return their questionnaires; one was seriously ill; and one died. Hence, our information is based upon the reports of ten heirs out of a total of seventeen. The four geographical areas are represented, and there were responses from both the maternal and paternal sides of the family. There is great consistency in the stories given; it is doubtful if the additional interviews would have added significantly to the case.

The term *laughing heir* (laughs all the way to the bank) appears to be a misnomer. Almost uniformly, the so-called laughing heirs were perturbed by their good fortune. None of these people were wealthy; for the most part they

16. Ibid., 4 July 1966.
17. Ibid.
18. There are at least twenty-five full-time tracing firms in the United States. Allen Rankin, "Billions of Dollars Unclaimed!" *Reader's Digest,* May, 1964, p. 78.
19. This approach can be used by disreputable firms as well as reputable ones. A California firm was branded by the Cleveland Better Business Bureau as a "get-rich-quick scheme." Their approach is to write to anyone named Davis or Nash or Perkins, or other common names, telling him of the existence of an unclaimed estate under the particular name and requesting the "marks" to send $4 to cover fees for the relevant documents. *Cleveland Press,* 10 May 1967.

were retired or the wives of retired men, living on social security and perhaps the supplement of an additional pension or small amounts of interest. The money was welcome, but they felt they did not deserve it. The following respondent did not know the deceased. She had never heard of him. She does not know anyone in the family who knew him. "The inheritance was a windfall. I needed the money and I was glad to get it. But he should have had a will so he could leave the estate to whom he wished."

According to the information gathered in this study, the next respondent was the only relative who had seen the deceased in adult life.

> I don't think things were divided up like they should be. I'm sure ——— had friends who were closer than any of the relatives who received. I was probably closest to him of all relatives, and we were not close. We really were strangers. I hadn't seen him for ten years. As a young man before I was married, he came to our house about once a year.[20]

Only one inheritor seemed to feel she had a claim to the money based upon prior services. She asked why the paternal side of the family received so much more than the maternal side. After the death of his parents, the decedent had been raised by her aunt.[21] Actually, the estate was divided equally between the two sides of the family; but as previously stated, there were many more cousins on the maternal side and therefore individual cousins received far less.

The disquieting effect of inheriting from a person one has never known is most poignantly revealed in this statement: "I would have liked to have known where he is buried, if he had a monument, what he looked like. I wish I had a photograph." A woman who last saw the deceased sixty years ago said: "It would have been better if there had been a will. The estate was so split up that no one benefited except the lawyers." In general, the heirs in this case complained about the lack of information given them by court and attorneys. An heiress said she had been promised an itemized accounting of the estate but had never received it. These complaints about high costs and lack of information are, however, tempered by the knowledge that they might easily have remained "lost" heirs.

It is not difficult to see why tracing companies take a fairly large percentage of recovered funds. Unlike the attorney and administrator, they receive nothing if their efforts are futile. In the following case, one of the relatives did not rush into a contract with the tracing firm; instead she initiated her own in-

20. "Distributive justice may of course fall in the other direction, to the man's advantage rather than his disadvantage, and then he may feel guilty rather than angry." George Homans, *Social Behavior, Its Elementary Forms* (New York: Harcourt, Brace & World, Inc., 1961), pp. 75–76.

21. She need not feel guilty over her good fortune because others less deserving were more advantaged; she was relatively deprived. Ibid., pp. 73–76.

quiry. This letter from a niece to the clerk of court is part of the probate docket of Case 480.

> About the first of July of this year, a man came to my mother's and brother's home near Galt, Sacramento County, California, and presented himself as a genealogist from a reputable firm dealing in the business of lccating unknown heirs. He stated my brother and I were among the heirs to a sum of money left by someone on my father's side of the family. He would not tell my brother who left the estate or how much it was. He also said it would take about four months to settle, and he would legally retain 40 per cent of the estate as fees. My reason for writing you is to find out, if I can, what and where the estate is, and hire my own lawyer and possibly obtain a larger percentage of the money for all the heirs.

Two months after the niece wrote the letter, an affidavit and a birth certificate were submitted by a son residing in Chicago. The affidavit stated that he was the son of the decedent, that his parents had divorced each other, and that there was no other issue of the marriage. His father had moved to Cleveland and remarried; his second wife had died; and there was no issue of the second marriage. A little over a month later, there was a declaratory judgment to determine the heirs, and the court found that the son was the sole heir. He received just under $3,000 from the estate of his 80-year-old father.

Some laughing heirs may not laugh on their way to the bank because they cash their checks at the corner grocery. In Case 385, there were twelve heirs, three of whom inherited $18.19. One heir was a nephew; the others were grandchildren of the decedent's half-siblings. Ironically, if all the unknown heirs had been found, even this amount would have been substantially reduced. The decedent had come into possession of her house when her late husband died intestate. The Ohio half-and-half statute appeared to be applicable. This statute applies when a relict (surviving marriage partner—the decedent in Case 385) of a deceased husband or wife dies intestate and without issue, possessing identical real estate or personal property that came to the marriage partner from the deceased spouse by intestate succession.[22] Under the facts of the case, the property would pass one-half to the heirs of the relict and the other half to designated relatives of the deceased spouse from whom the property had been inherited. However, relatives of the deceased spouse were unknown to the heirs of the relict. A search for these people appears to have been limited to an advertisement in the Cleveland *Daily Legal News* that ran for a total of twelve weeks. Because there was no answer, all property passed by general intestate succession to the heirs of the relict; the half-and-half statute does not apply if relatives of the deceased spouse cannot be found.

In this instance, the estate was not large. It consisted of a house with an

22. Ohio Revised Code 2105.10. This unusual and complex statute is found in its entirety in Appendix A.

unclear title in a deteriorating neighborhood; $3,700 was realized from the sale of the house. After three years, costs attendant to the administration of the estate had reduced this amount to $1,090 available for distribution. The largest single deduction was the attorney's fee of $750. Originally, the attorney asked for extraordinary fees of $1,200 for 146 hours of work, including six hours of work preparing a family tree (some of the heirs submitted family Bibles as evidence of relationship), and four hours of work researching the half-and-half statute. The requested fee was reduced to $750 after an attorney for two of the heirs objected on the grounds that such a fee represented one-third of the estate before the payment of debts. He requested that the court not allow attorney's fees in excess of $600.

Responses were obtained from five of the twelve heirs. They all had heard of the decedent or were acquainted with her, but none had expected an inheritance. "I had no claim on the estate; I don't think I deserved anything. I think people who had helped her, lived with her, helped with expenses should have received it." There was no evidence that anyone had lived with or helped the decedent; the respondent was talking hypothetically.

Not enough money involved to arouse any interest on my part . . . don't think she knew some of us were even alive.

This inheritance didn't mean anything to me; it was just a nuisance.

It would seem to be impossible to legislate out of existence the closely related laughing heir, such as a son who is entitled to inherit under intestate succession. This son may have had little or no contact with the decedent since childhood, and still he may inherit. He is an *unworthy taker*. On the other hand, something can be done to reduce the number of laughing heirs found among more distantly related kin.

The heritage of following blood kinships to any degree necessary to find a "relative" serves no purpose at all. Modern legislation cutting off inheritance if no one as close as descendants of the decedent's grandparents exists solves much of the problem, although the prospect of hilarity by inheritors remains.[23]

No Known Next of Kin Survived

There were eight intestate decedents whose next of kin were never found. In none of these cases was the estate worth the interest of reporters, professional heir hunters, or attorneys.

Case 447. A 66-year-old woman died leaving as her only asset furniture appraised at $15. A creditor for unpaid rent was the applicant and received the entire estate.

23. Personal correspondence from Professor Richard V. Wellman, University of Michigan School of Law, 17 April 1968. See also Chapter 2, p. 19.

Case 427. A 79-year-old woman died possessing a $25 insurance policy. A funeral home applied for the release. The cost of the funeral was over $700.

In two cases friends applied and received the estates.

Case 473. The decedent was a 76-year-old man whose assets did not equal his funeral expenses ($698). The applicant described herself as a friend.

Case 131. The decedent was a 55-year-old man who was shot to death by his common-law wife. None of the relatives accepted the body, so the decedent's ex-wife applied for release of his assets and arranged for the funeral. His assets ($358) were insufficient for his funeral; his ex-wife and a friend paid the balance. The decedent had three children by his ex-wife, who were, of course, the next of kin; but they were not listed in the court records.

In four cases, there were no known next of kin at the time administration was initiated; however, on the day of death, three of the decedents were survived by husbands, and in the third case a sister survived the decedent for a few weeks. In each of these cases, the decedent's estate went into the estate of the survivor.

Conclusion

The focus of this study of testate cases has been on the deviations from intestate distribution as determined by the will. In intestate cases, the deviations are the result of redistribution by the heirs. Redistribution in testate cases occurred infrequently and is a deviation from the will rather than from the statute; hence, it is not included in Table 6–2.

TABLE 6–2 CASES DEVIATING FROM INTESTATE DISTRIBUTION, BY TYPE OF SURVIVOR, IN NUMBER AND PER CENT

	Testate Cases		Intestate Cases	
Type of Survivor	Total Number	Per Cent Deviating	Total Number	Per Cent Deviating
Spouse only	37	10.8	17	5.9
Spouse plus lineal kin	226	97.8	74	81.0
Lineal kin	115	55.7	37	27.0
Collateral kin	40	82.5	16	25.0
Total	418	77.0	144	52.1

It was clear that where the spouse was the only survivor, he or she was the sole heir in the large majority of cases; only rarely did the actual disposition of the estate differ from this formula. On the other hand, in circumstances where the statute prescribed a division between spouse and lineal kin, there were a large number of deviations. In testate cases, the testator usually willed the entire estate to the spouse. In intestate cases, adult children usually signed over their shares of the estates to the surviving parents. What would have been the consequences if they had not done this? Most parents needed the entire estate; if they had been turned out of their homes, they might have become burdens on their adult children. Ohio is one of the states that has a liable-relative law; if the children do not willingly assume financial responsibility, the state may compel them to do so.

Where the children could not sign over to their surviving parents because they were not of legal age, parents may actually have been hamstrung in caring for their children. Parents were universally chagrined at the position they were in, that is, unable to sell their homes without resorting to devious means.

An exception to the spouse-all pattern occurred in the case of remarriage. In both testate and intestate cases, these estates were more likely to be divided between spouse and children than were those in which the spouse was the parent of the surviving children. Inter vivos transfers sometimes accomplished the spouse-all pattern for the remarried decedent. Sometimes the spouse received all because there was no residue after the year's allowance and exemption had been deducted from the estate.

Equality of distribution among descendants is subscribed to by more descendants than decedent testators. Among the testators, 43 per cent deviated from equality of distribution among equally related lineal kin. Nearly 75 per cent of the intestate descendants were content with equality and did not redistribute the estate. Where one child assigned his share to a sibling, it was often in payment for the final care rendered the deceased parent.

The largest divergence between the testate and intestate distribution occurred when the decedent was survived by those whose relationships were calculated through the family of orientation. The vast majority of testators deviated from the intestate rules; whereas in the intestate case, the majority of surviving heirs allowed the intestate allocation to stand and did not make a redistribution. Final care was also frequently associated with the few instances of redistribution occurring among collateral kin. The testator deviated because his affections and obligations did not follow the blood line. He was closer to some than to others; he may have been more obligated to nonrelated persons than to his own relatives. Just as some of the surviving kin may not have been close to the decedent, the survivors may not have been sufficiently close to each other to formulate and agree upon a redistribution in the intestate case.[24]

Laughing heirs have been considered unworthy takers, and they saw themselves as such. They had rendered the deceased no service of any kind; they

24. "Situations of potential injustice may be maintained with little stress if the participants accept norms which restrict or prohibit communications or which define the situation as balanced." Alexander and Simpson, op. cit., p. 191.

could not justify their windfall to themselves. Unlike Irish Sweepstakes winners, they did not even risk a shilling for their good fortune.

It would be erroneous to assume that all those persons who have not made a will want their property distributed in accordance with the statutes of intestacy. Although it is impossible to say what the intestate decedent wanted, it is possible to infer his wishes from the actions of his next of kin: (1) the married intestate did not intend that the surviving spouse share the estate with lineal kin, and (2) the intestate wanted to reciprocate for the kindness and care of the person who gave him a home. The intestate person differed from the testate in being younger and poorer.[25] However, it cannot be said that the intestate differed from the testate in their sense of justice. The life situation of the intestate, like that of the testate, may require divergences from the law of intestate succession.

25. See Chapter 4, pp. 65, 73–74.

Chapter 7

The Inheritance

WHAT WAS the meaning of inheritance to the survivors of the sample decedents? One purpose of this study was to discover the significance and meaning of inheritance to persons who inherited or who were disinherited. Did survivors believe that the distribution was fair, and did the inheritance have any effect upon the life styles of the inheritors? In this chapter, the unit of analysis is the individual survivor; whereas in Chapter 5 and 6, the unit of analysis was the case.

Fairness

All survivors under testate and intestate succession were asked whether they thought the distribution in their particular case was fair and whether distribution under intestate succession would have been fair given the conditions of their particular family situation (see Table 7–1 for the judgments of survivors

TABLE 7–1 JUDGMENT OF FAIRNESS BY SURVIVORS, IN NUMBER AND PER CENT

Judgment of Fairness	Particular Disposition		Intestate Succession	
	Number	Per Cent	Number	Per Cent
Completely fair	601	56.0	205	19.1
Indifferent	325	30.3	325	30.3
Not fair	147	13.7	543	50.6
Total	1,073[a]	100.0	1,073[a]	100.0

[a] Fairness items were omitted on the questionnaire; 29 of the interviewees did not answer these questions.

on this issue). Fifty-six per cent felt the disposition in their particular case was fair; 14 per cent, not fair. Over half of the respondents expressed the belief that intestate succession was not fair in their particular situation, and 19 per cent believed it completely fair. Thirty per cent of the survivors were indifferent and expressed ambivalence regarding the whole matter.

Approximately three-fourths of both testate and intestate decedents were survived by spouses, lineal descendants, or both. Among these survivors, there are marked disparities of opinion regarding fairness, according to whether the spouses survived and whether the decedents were testate (see Table 7–2). In testate cases, the feeling that the disposition was not fair was more likely to occur when the surviving kin were children. In intestate cases, it was more likely when the spouses and lineal descendants survived.

TABLE 7–2 JUDGMENT OF FAIRNESS OF PARTICULAR DISTRIBUTION, BY TESTACY AND TYPE OF KIN, IN NUMBER AND PER CENT

Judgment of Fairness	Testate		Intestate	
	Number	Per Cent	Number	Per Cent
Spouse and descendants				
Completely fair	301	80.7	49	37.7
Indifferent	54	14.5	29	22.3
Not fair	18	4.8	52	40.0
Total	373	100.0	130	100.0
Descendants only				
Completely fair	66	28.4	44	74.6
Indifferent	137	59.1	10	16.9
Not fair	29	12.5	5	8.5
Total	232	100.0	59	100.0

Most of the feeling of unfairness in testate cases involving spouse and children was accounted for by the problems arising out of remarriage. Fourteen of the 18 persons expressing this attitude were the survivors of remarried decedents; only 12 of the 52 survivors of intestate decedents who felt the distribution between spouse and children was unfair were the survivors of remarried decedents. In the latter group, the sense of unfairness felt by the majority cannot be accounted for by this problematic family situation. They simply objected to the intestate division. They felt that it was unfair not to themselves but to others, particularly the surviving spouse. Most of these persons felt the entire estate should go to the spouse; and in most cases, the other inheritors signed over their shares to the surviving mate. However, they were dissatisfied even though the desired result was achieved, because they felt the spouse should have the decedent's property by right and not by a series of accommodations within the family. Also, although the redistribution was usually accomplished amiably, it sometimes aroused suspicions and bitterness. A widow said, "My oldest daughter didn't want to sign over." And a daughter said, "We had bills and my husband urged me to keep it, but I signed over to my mother." In three cases, minor children shared in the estate. Therefore, there was no legal possibility of signing over to the surviving spouse.

Over half of the survivors of testate cases were indifferent regarding the fairness of the distribution when the next of kin were descendants. Where a feeling of unfairness was expressed, the primary reason was that the distribution among children was unequal where it should have been equal. An exception was a case in which two children were disinherited in favor of the decedent's sister. At the time of death, the decedent had no assets: nevertheless, the children felt the distribution was unfair. The case illustrates an important point. Since there was no money or property involved, it might be expected that the heirs would have regarded the distribution indifferently. Yet knowing that a parent has some concern and feeling is psychic income; and evidently for some survivors, this knowledge is as valuable as real property. Being in the thoughts of the decedent is often more important than the amount of money involved and the actual distribution. This issue is highlighted in a case where the testate and intestate distributions would have been identical. A survivor reported:

Case 608–03. I felt Dad made a fair and equitable distribution of his estate. I was very touched and pleased. His will and the intestate distribution are exactly the same, but since he made a will, I knew this is the way he wanted things to go. This was comforting.

Thus, the justice of the situation was not evaluated solely in terms of pecuniary gain. The receiving of money or property from the estate did not necessarily mitigate feelings of injustice about the distribution.

When descendants were the only survivors of intestate decedents, three-fourths judged the disposition completely fair because it was equal. Those who felt it was unfair were in situations that would be difficult to resolve even if the law were changed. In these cases, equality of blood did not correspond to equality in services and affection toward the decedent. The distribution was equal when it should have been unequal. The descendants wished to have the disposition made according to the criterion of reciprocity.

As discussed in Chapters 5 and 6, within the immediate family there are norms of will making that either reinforce the principle of equality among descendants or contravene the purposes of the existing inheritance law in the willing of the entire estate to the spouse. Beyond the immediate family, there are no agreed-upon norms.

Approximately 50 per cent of the collateral survivors of both testate and intestate decedents felt the disposition in their particular case was fair. But the percentage of those who felt the disposition was not fair—chiefly unfair to others rather than to themselves—was higher among the survivors of intestate decedents than among the survivors of testate decedents (see Table 7–3). Some were heirs who felt guilty because they had done nothing to earn the inheritance.

TABLE 7–3 JUDGMENT OF FAIRNESS OF DISPOSITION WHEN COLLATERAL KIN SURVIVE, BY TESTACY, IN NUMBER AND PER CENT

Judgment of Fairness	Testate		Intestate	
	Number	Per Cent	Number	Per Cent
Completely fair	61	51.7	21	48.8
Indifferent	34	28.8	8	18.6
Not fair	23	19.5	14	32.6
Total	118	100.0	43	100.0

Disinheritance

There were 139 disinherited persons (11 per cent) in the survivor population.[1] Of the 120 who answered the questions on fairness, 27 (23 per cent) felt the disposition was unfair. The proportion of those who expressed feelings of unfairness in the distribution was high among the disinherited but lower than the proportion found among the survivors of intestate decedents. The majority of the disinherited felt the disposition was completely fair or were indifferent; whereas the majority of the survivors who felt the disposition unfair were not disinherited.

In Chapter 5, cases were examined in which a child was one of a number of persons who were disinherited. In this chapter, the circumstances and reasons why these children were disinherited are examined. With the advent of mass transportation and communication, distance is no barrier to members of nuclear related families keeping in touch with one another.[2] Communication, however, is no substitute for interpersonal contact. Furthermore, there are differences in the quality and meaning of such contact, with factors such as frequency, the situation or circumstances, and the nature of the exchange being important in determining the significance of the relationship. One indication of the meaning of the relationship along generational lines is the matter of inheritance.

In Table 7–4, the percentage of disinherited children is given according to distance zone. The highest percentage of disinherited children was found among those who lived outside the United States. It should be noted that the percentage of disinherited children who lived in Cuyahoga County differed only slightly from the percentage in Zones 2, 3, 4, 7, and 8. In general, it would appear that the testators did not regard their geographically mobile sons and daughters as candidates for disinheritance.

Two variables were examined in order to determine if any relationship ex-

1. A person is disinherited if he is among the surviving next of kin and is not a legatee/devisee or contingent beneficiary or if he is specifically disinherited in the will.
2. Eugene Litwak, "Geographical Mobility and Extended Family Cohesion," *American Sociological Review* 25 (June, 1960):385–394.

TABLE 7–4 PERCENTAGE OF DISINHERITED CHILDREN OF DECEDENT TESTATOR, BY DISTANCE

Distance Zone	Total Number of Children Resident	Per Cent Disinherited
1 (local)	603	15.6
2 (nonlocal Ohio)	54	13.0
3 (Indiana, Kentucky, etc.)	48	12.5
4 (Connecticut, Missouri, etc.)	26	11.5
5 and 6 (Florida, Wyoming, etc.)	22	27.3
7 and 8 (Montana, West Coast, Hawaii, etc.)	35	14.3
9 (outside United States)	14	64.3
Total	802	16.2

isted between the quality of the child-parent relationship and inheritance: (1) the surviving child's expressed "closeness" to the deceased parent and (2) the frequency of contact between parent and child. The tests for the relationship between closeness and interaction and disinheritance were limited to children in Cuyahoga County in order to rule out the possibly confounding effects of distance upon interaction (see Appendix E, Table E–1). The results indicated that feelings of closeness and frequency of contact were unrelated to the act of disinheritance. Of those children who characterized their relationship as "close," 14 per cent were disinherited; of those who said their relationship was "not close," 13 per cent were disinherited. The likelihood of disinheritance was highest in cases where the relationship was characterized as "average"—17 per cent. The study of frequency of contact with the parent showed disinheritance of 14 per cent of those children who were in daily contact, 16 per cent of those in weekly contact, and 16 per cent of those who were in less frequent contact.

There are three caveats in interpreting this finding. The lack of a relationship between closeness to the decedent and disinheritance may be a function of biased reporting. Reports on attitudes and feelings about such issues as race relations, honesty of politicians, hippie movements, premarital sexual behavior, and legitimizing abortion are generally suspect because of wide variations in the individual's perception of the situation, historical and cultural experience, and basic orientations. Although we have healthy suspicions, we accept these reports as valid data, knowing that they are time limited and the best available for the present study. However, determining the condition of closeness, which involves the interaction and perception of two or more persons, requires some test of congruity of feeling and perceptions, a test that was impossible to conduct because the principal actors were deceased.

Frequency of contact may be at best a crude indicator of the quality of interaction among members of a kin-related nuclear network, and prescriptions of the quality and the significance of the interaction currently deduced from exchanges and interaction frequencies may be overly presumptuous as a measure.

Disinheritance is a legal condition and is reported as such in these data, without a social explanation being given to it. Consequently, a person categorized as disinherited may have received inter vivos transfers; for example, a son receiving a large sum to finance a business, education, or marriage, may have been very close to his parent and have had an understanding that upon his parent's death, distributive justice would occur. His siblings would receive the major portion of the estate, and his kindly parent would will a small trust for the grandchildren. Thus, the child who benefited materially during the lifetime of his parent and who had a congenial relationship with the decedent would be disinherited deliberately. In the record, this would be classified as a disinheritance case. The legal definition does not differentiate malice in intent from behavior based on love and concern and the sense of distributive justice.

Several empirical investigations indicate that women are more closely linked with their kin network than men are.[3] Of a total of 322 daughters, 47 (15 per cent) were disinherited. Interviews were conducted with 213 daughters, of whom 29 (14 per cent) had been disinherited, and with 179 sons, of whom 30 (17 per cent) had been disinherited. It was found that more daughters than sons were "close" to the decedent parent and that the daughters also had more frequent contact with the decedent parent than the sons had (see Appendix E, Tables E–2 and E–3). Thus, the data indicate that daughters are better integrated into the kin network than sons are. Do these data account for the somewhat more frequent disinheritance of sons? Do the relative frequencies of disinheritance reflect differential interaction and closeness? The answer to these questions is No.

Daughters who were disinherited were closer to and had more interaction with the decedent parent than sons who were heirs. Although 64 per cent of the daughters said they were close to the decedent, 40 per cent of all the daughters inherited. Only 48 per cent of the sons said they were close, and 37 per cent of all the sons inherited. As compared with 49 per cent of the daughters, 32 per cent of the sons were in daily contact. The differences in interaction and closeness favored the daughters by a large margin; whereas the differences between sons and daughters inheriting or, conversely, being disinherited were not of similar magnitude.

Since more sons than daughters would be employed and therefore perhaps

3. Sheldon Stryker, "The Adjustment of Married Offspring to Their Parents," *American Sociological Review* 20 (April, 1955):149–154; Mirra Komarovsky, "Functional Analysis of Sex Roles," *American Sociological Review* 15 (1950):508–516; Paul Wallin, "Sex Differences in Attitudes Toward In-Laws; A Test of Theory," *American Journal of Sociology* 59 (1954):466–469.

would not have the time for frequent contact, they are more likely to be excused than daughters in maintaining contact with parents. The differences in closeness may also be because of a tendency for women to sentimentalize their relationships with the deceased, thus meeting societal expectations in this instance. Men, on the other hand, are expected to be less expressive about their feelings toward parents and more instrumental in fulfilling obligations of filial responsibility.

There are still other possible explanations of these findings. The norm of equal treatment of children may have been sufficiently strong to overcome any tendency on the part of the testator to reward the daughter who saw him daily and to punish his less punctilious son. Furthermore, these are gross measures that, over a large group, mask those extreme situations of final care which give rise to some cases of disinheritance. Lastly, the testator's alternatives are not unlimited. In a situation in which all children are negligent, the testator may reward all or choose a beneficiary outside his family. The relationship of a testator with one of his children is evaluated in the context of the relationships prevailing in the family.

For children residing within Cuyahoga County, differences in the percentage of disinherited were found to be associated with social class. For the entire group of disinherited children, including those not interviewed, the percentage of disinherited is highest in the upper classes (residence ratings 1 and 2) and in the lowest classes (residence ratings 6 and 7).[4]

TABLE 7–5 PERCENTAGE OF DISINHERITED CHILDREN OF DECEDENT TESTATOR, BY RESIDENCE RATING

Area Residence Rating	Total Number of Children Resident in Area	Per Cent Disinherited
1 and 2 (best)	23	26.1
3 (above average)	164	15.2
4 (average)	287	12.2
5 (below average)	82	15.9
6 and 7 (worst)	22	36.4
Total	578[a]	15.1

[a] Residence ratings not available for 25 children.

The post hoc explanation of this "inverse normal curve" finding is that it is most common in the upper classes to skip a generation. If one's son or daughter is in no financial need, or if inter vivos transfers have been made, one may

4. Marvin B. Sussman, *Rating Scale for Homes in Cuyahoga County* (Cleveland: Western Reserve University [privately published], 1960).

leave to grandchildren directly. Thus, the testator can leave a greater estate in perpetuity over generational time by eliminating the inheritance taxes and probate costs that would be incurred at the death of his child. The children's financially secure position may, of course, also mean that the property could be willed out of the family. However, as shown in Chapter 5, it is very rare that children are disinherited in favor of outsiders. In the lowest socioeconomic group, there may be insufficient properties to leave to all children, family relationships may be more strained, or a poorly drawn will might not have provided for contingent beneficiaries in the case of a surviving spouse.

Because disinheritance may be the result of diverse situations, surprisingly little was learned from looking at individuals who were disinherited. The unit of analysis should be the family rather than the individual.

Inheritors

Data were obtained from 289 intestate heirs, 491 testate heirs, 298 contingent beneficiaries, and 139 disinherited persons.[5] Ideally, only the intestate and testate heirs would be considered as inheritors. However, some estates were so small that those designated as heirs received nothing. In some cases, heirs gave up their rights to property. Some of those designated only as contingent beneficiaries actually inherited because the primary beneficiaries had died. In this study, there were 813 persons who received something of value from decedent's estates.

Wilbert Moore has noted that inheritors are often at the stage of the life cycle where the inheritance will have little effect.[6] Other authors have maintained that the rich inherit from the rich and the poor inherit from the poor.[7] The implication of these views is that the inheritance has very little impact upon the lifeways of the inheritor.

In Tables 7–6 and 7–7, the percentage inheriting is given by age and income categories. The mean amount inherited is given for those who actually inherited. This mean amount was calculated by excluding those inheritors for whom no information was obtained concerning the value of their inheritance.

5. Seventeen persons did not fit any of these categories; they included applicants in release-of-assets cases where the estate was insolvent, beneficiaries of life insurance policies, guardians, and so forth.

6. Wilbert E. Moore, *Man, Time, and Society* (New York: John Wiley & Sons, Inc., 1963), pp. 80–81.

7. "Nor can there be any doubt that in the main those who die leave most of their money to persons of the same social class as themselves." G. D. H. Cole, "Inheritance," *Encyclopedia of the Social Sciences,* vol. 8 (New York: The Macmillan Company, 1932), p. 39. "Most of the widows of rich men have, in fact, some property of their own, and the large majority of penniless widows have practically penniless husbands from whom they will never inherit anything substantial, whatever the law on the subject." Josiah Wedgwood, *The Economics of Inheritance* (London: George Routledge and Sons, Ltd., 1929), p. 190.

TABLE 7–6 PER CENT INHERITING AND MEAN AMOUNT INHERITED, BY AGE GROUP

Age Group	Total Number	Per Cent Inheriting	Mean Amount Inherited
21–29	104	47.1	$ 5,265
30–39	232	54.3	6,048
40–49	349	67.0	7,043
50–59	284	67.3	12,131
60–69	155	81.9	10,622
70–89	102	79.4	10,580
Total	1,226[a]	65.9	

[a] Age unknown for 8 of the total survivors and 5 of the inheritors.

Most of these inheritors received something primarily of sentimental value for which it was difficult to assign a dollar value. Included in the inheritance means are extra-probate properties such as insurance.

Persons aged 60 and over were the most frequent recipients of inheritances. The largest inheritances went to persons in their fifties. Less than half of the survivors in their twenties inherited, and those who did received the smallest inheritances. Moore was correct in his assertion that most inheritors are relatively old, but whether it follows that the inheritance will have little effect is another matter. An inheritance late in life may be of vital importance to the inheritor, who is often an aged widow without adequate resources of her own.

The problem Moore posits is so conceptualized as to have us consider only those effects upon life style as a consequence of receiving a legacy at an age when personal needs and ambitions are diminishing, and a legacy that is usually not large enough to make a dent in a person's standard of living. What is overlooked in this formulation of little gain from inheritance is that, if the disposition were not forthcoming in the age periods of the fifties and sixties, there would be a serious reduction in living standards for the surviving spouse and additional responsibilities of support and care would thus be given to family members and society-wide welfare and social security systems. The effect of inheritance, therefore, is not to increase mobility, spending, status, and so forth for the largest group surviving; it is to aid the survivor, usually an aged widow, to maintain her financial independence as long as possible. Obviously, social security, pensions, and other society-wide support systems provide the largest amount of real income.

The data do not contain the variables for testing and rejecting outright the often-stated hypothesis that the rich become richer as a consequence of receiving large legacies, and that as a result, the disparity between rich and poor increases. Those who fear the concentration of wealth resulting from inheritance have selected a small percentage of those who inherit, the wealthy, in making their case. In comparison, the estates and inheritances examined in this study were modest; the sample contained very few estates over a half million dollars and very few wealthy inheritors.

Very few individuals know what their total economic worth is, since the sum of one's financial value consists of many component elements. Consequently, taking a complete economic inventory is a project of itself. Even if such a laborious undertaking had been attempted as part of this study, it is doubtful whether all the information that would have been necessary in order to assess accurately the person's financial standing could have been obtained. It is our experience and that of other researchers that individuals are willing to discuss unabashedly their family problems but become silent when questioned about their economic assets. It was necessary to rely on a single index of economic status: the individual's monthly income. This is at best a crude approximation of relative economic position because unless it is linked to expenditures, it presents a distorted picture of how well-off the individual is at his income level.

For instance, an individual aged 55, with an income of $800 a month, his home paid for, and no children at home is better off than a 30-year-old with an income of $1,200 a month, four children to support, and a mortgaged home. It was not possible to randomize the effects of such confounding variables as age, family size, and accumulated equity.

Using income as the economic indicator, it was found that the percentage of survivors who inherited did not vary greatly among the income categories (see Table 7–7). With only two exceptions, the amount of money received by inheritors did not differ significantly according to their monthly income. Only those with incomes of $200 or less and those with incomes of between $601 and $800 received substantially smaller inheritances than all others did. Those most likely to inherit were persons with the smallest monthly incomes: 74 per cent of the survivors with incomes of $200 or less inherited. The mean amount inherited was $6,592. The largest mean inheritance ($10,842) appeared for inheritors with incomes of $401 to $600; the percentage inheriting in this income category was, however, the lowest. Those survivors with incomes of over $1,000 a month received inheritances of approximately the same magnitude as those with incomes of $201 to $400 and were less likely to be inheritors.[8]

At the lower income ranges, the inheritance undoubtedly has a greater ef-

8. Less than one-fifth of a 1960 representative national sample of heads of spending units reported having received an inheritance. James N. Morgan et al., *Income and Welfare in the United States* (New York: McGraw-Hill Book Company, 1962), p. 89. A sample of a high-income group (over $10,000 annual income) yielded double that proportion of inheritors. James N. Morgan et al., unpublished manuscript, 1965.

TABLE 7–7 PER CENT INHERITING AND MEAN AMOUNT INHERITED, BY HOUSEHOLD INCOME

Income (per Month)	Total Number	Per Cent Inheriting	Mean Amount Inherited
$200 or less	93	74.2	$ 6,592
$201–$400	156	70.5	9,218
$401–$600	317	61.8	10,842
$601–$800	187	64.2	5,633
$801–$1,000	157	70.7	10,802
$1,001–$1,500	129	62.0	9,175
$1,501 and over	82	67.1	9,691
Total	1,121[a]	66.1	

[a] Income unknown for 113 of the total survivors and 72 of the inheritors.

fect. A person whose income is less than $200 a month and who inherits over $6,000 is receiving an inheritance three times the size of his annual income; whereas a person with an income of over $1,500 a month is receiving less than one-third of his annual income.

Mementos

A *memento* is defined as "something that serves as a reminder of what is past or gone."[9] For some persons, the inheritance was primarily of sentimental rather than monetary value. A memento may have market value, but more often its value lies in its association with the decedent. As a general rule, these items were not appraised among the estate assets and the interviewees seldom rendered an opinion on their worth. Their significance to the survivor may be indicated by the fact that the interviewee volunteered the information. Of the 1,102 persons interviewed, 170 mentioned that they had received something of sentimental value from the decedent's estate; for 95 persons, this was their sole inheritance.

Testamentary bequests of specific items are rare. There were only 14 decedents who made bequests of this nature. The responses to the bequests varied. One male decedent willed his neighbors his "tools, fan, heater, electric motor, and pistol." The neighbors received only the tools; they did not know what happened to the rest and they didn't care: "It would only be more junk in the garage." A daughter was very pleased: "Mother made bequests of personal effects. This gave her will the personal touch. My brother and I are going to follow suit in our own wills."

Most commonly, testamentary bequests were of jewelry, usually watches and rings. But they were not necessarily expensive pieces. A bridal set bequeathed

9. *The American College Dictionary* (New York: Random House, Inc., 1956).

to a sister-in-law was sold for $200. In one case, a diamond ring bequeathed to a granddaughter was appraised at $25. The ring was somehow lost before it could be given to the granddaughter. To rectify the situation, her parents gave her $100. Which figure more truly represented the value of the ring is not known.

In contrast with willing specific items, a fair number of decedents gave away personal items prior to death.

Some gold coins he had saved he gave us a year or two before he died.

No mementos after his death, but he gave me the family Bible and a lot of pictures at the time I left home.

I received some personal things during my aunt's lifetime—crystal, Haviland china, and a car headlight from one of the first Winton autos. My aunt's mother was the first investor in the Winton Company.

A decedent may also have designated the recipients of certain items verbally, trusting that they would be distributed according to his wishes. Most often the mementos were distributed by the surviving spouse, or if there was no surviving spouse, the heirs came to an equitable agreement about the allocation. Frequently the items received had previously been given to the decedent by the recipient.

Mother's watch was given to Doug because he bought it for her. Jack gave her a sweater that was returned to him.

He never owned any jewelry or a watch until a year before he died when I bought him a Timex. Mother gave it back to me.

I have a statue of the Blessed Virgin I had given Mom for Mother's Day years ago.

Often the heirs simply took what was of sentimental value to them.

We divided up whatever in the house we wanted. I took the old treadle sewing machine. It cost me $24 to fix it up, but it was worth it because of the sentimental value.

Family dissension sometimes occurred if one survivor took what he wanted regardless of the feelings of others who were equally entitled.

My mother had a fine set of china, a grand piano, several new appliances. My sister came over from Toledo. She went through the house like a tornado and took everything she could lay her hands on. My wife and I didn't care, we have our own things, but I felt my younger brother should have something. There were things he could have used better than she. This was the only unpleasantness in the whole thing.

Giving or saving mementos for the grandchildren of the decedent occurred frequently.

There were several mementos from the First World War, and each grandchild received one.

His pocket watch went to one of my boys and his wrist watch to my sister's boy.

I have his watch which he got for 25 years' service with the gas company. I'm saving his service buttons for the four grandchildren.

Just as some items may be passed on to still another generation, some of the mementos that were mentioned had already been in the family for years.

Mother has the family Bible, which is one hundred and fifty years old.

I now have a rocking chair that belonged to my grandmother and then my mother.

I kept mother's jewelry and watch and also her dresser which had been my grandmother's. It is my antique.

I have the family Bible, which originally belonged to my great-grandparents.

It sometimes happens that the object is so inextricably linked to the decedent that the memento is buried with him. "His lodge pins are buried with him." "We buried her with rings and rosary." "His best cuff links and tie pin were put on him in the casket."

Several norms govern the distribution of personal effects. A gift is returned to the giver. The gender of the memento is decisive in determining the recipient. In-laws may inherit mementos because they are the correct sex. Mementos are also distributed along the lines of shared occupational or leisure interests. The diploma signifying the granting of an M.D. degree and awards to the decedent of past recognitions were given to the one son who is also a doctor. Guns and hunting equipment are given to the child who shared this interest.

The survivors' attitudes toward mementos again show that the inheritance process is not simply an economic phenomenon. The distribution of the decedent's personal effects has symbolic meaning for the participants. The continuity of the relationship and of the family is represented in certain tangible objects.

Use of the Inheritance

Studies of consumption patterns of individuals on different social-class levels and at various stages of the life cycle have been undertaken, but studies of the use of inheritance are rare.[10] The studies of windfall gains are pertinent; but

10. The most famous social-class consumption study in American sociology was conducted in the Yankee City research. See W. Lloyd Warner, ed., *Yankee City*, abridged (New Haven: Yale University Press, 1963), p. 100, Table 2. Budgetary studies have a long tradition in Europe. They were an essential part of LePlay's method of social analysis. Economists and market researchers have taken the concept of life cycle from sociology, for example, Paul Glick; but sociologists have not paid much attention to the life cycle and economic variables. James N. Morgan et al. have conducted

where inheritance has been included, it is not separated from other types of windfall income.[11]

Those economists who do not consider inheritance as windfall income argue that legacies are typically expected rather than unexpected.[12] The findings of this study indicate that this was true for the majority of inheritors. In general, knowledge concerning the estate, the presence of a will, and the provisions thereof was found to be widespread among the inheritors. However, there was a considerable minority of the inheritors who were uninformed: 19 per cent did not know whether there was a will; 24 per cent of those who inherited from testate decedents did not know the provisions of the will; 35 per cent claimed they had no knowledge of the size of the estate; and 15 per cent were ignorant in all three areas.

It was hypothesized that inheritance might be treated differently from current income even if the legacy was expected by the inheritor. There were several reasons for this supposition. First, current income is usually immediately negotiable; whereas inheritance may consist of a given piece of property which has a monetary value that cannot be converted immediately into cash. Also, the form of the inheritance may influence its ultimate use. Just as the nature of mementos dictates their usage (to be kept and perhaps treasured), someone who inherits and keeps an automobile might not have spent the equivalent amount for this purpose. Secondly, earnings typically continue; whereas inheritance may be a once-in-a-lifetime phenomenon. Lastly, inheritance often has an emotional significance that is not attached to income.

There are various ways in which an inheritance may be used. The categories developed for this analysis were savings, living expenses, real estate, durable goods, bills, the education of children, and vacations.

Savings. This category represents money that will probably not be used, barring catastrophe, or if it is eventually used, the particular use was not foreseen by the inheritors. Any saving for particular expenditures is categorized under the ultimate expenditure; that is, if someone invests the inheritance to be used eventually for his children's education, this is categorized under education. If the inheritance is invested but the principal is drawn upon for living expenses, it is categorized under living expenses.

---

a study of gifts and inheritance among high-income people. About two-thirds of the receivers invested their gifts or inheritance. Morgan et al., op. cit.

11. Inheritance is included as windfall income by L. R. Klein and N. Livatan, "Significance of Income Variability on Savings Behavior," *Bulletin of Oxford Institute of Statistics* 19 (May, 1957):151–160; and by Margaret G. Reid, "Consumption, Savings and Windfall Gains," *American Economic Review* 52 (September, 1962):728–737.

12. See Ronald Bodkin, "Windfall Income and Consumption," *American Economic Review* 49 (September, 1959):604; and Roger Bird, "Consumption, Savings, and Windfall Gains; Comment," *American Economic Review* 53 (June, 1963):433.

Living expenses. The normal expenses of food, clothing, and shelter are categorized under living expenses. If real estate is all or a part of the inheritance, and the inheritor lives in the house that was a part of the estate, then that use is categorized under living expenses rather than real estate.

Real estate. This category excludes real estate that is part of the estate and is used by the inheritor as his residence, but includes paying off a mortgage on the inheritor's own property. It also includes the purchase of real estate as an investment or in the use of real estate in the decedent's estate as income-producing property, as well as the use of monies from the inheritance for the purchase of a residence or a vacation cottage, whether the inheritance represents partial or full payment. Additions or improvements to existing real estate are also included.

Durable goods. Included here are the purchase of automobiles, major appliances, furniture, and redecorating (remodeling is included under real estate). Inherited durable goods kept as such are included in this category. Most commonly, this would be a car.

Bills. These are bills for almost everything except mortgage payments, which are included under real estate, and the debts of the decedent, which are properly defined as charges against the estate rather than uses of the inheritance.

Education of children. This category is self-explanatory. For the most part, the inheritors were using or planning to use the money to pay for college education.

Vacation. All expenditures for travel and vacations are included here except the purchase of real estate for vacation use.

The inheritors were asked how they had used or planned to use the inheritance; if they indicated more than one use, they were then asked what percentage of their inheritance would be applied to the various purposes. In Table 7–8, the number and percentage of inheritors choosing a particular use are given; the use is either the one to which the entire inheritance was applied or the one for which the major portion of the inheritance was used. The ranking of uses remains the same when based upon the total number of uses.

There were distinct differences in the mean amount of the inheritance by each category of use.[13] The large inheritances were likely to be placed in sav-

13. The effect of the size of the windfall gain upon its utilization is debated. Bodkin, in studying the unexpected payments of National Service Life Insurance dividends to veterans of World War II, found a strong tendency to spend windfall income. Ronald Bodkin, op. cit., 602–614. Kreinin, using data from an Israeli survey of the behavior of recipients of lump-sum personal restitution payments from Germany, found that "marginal propensity to consume out of windfall incomes is one-fifth the marginal propensity to consume out of current income." Mordechai Kreinin, "Windfall Income

TABLE 7–8 PRIMARY USE OF INHERITANCE, BY SIZE OF INHERITANCE, AGE, EDUCATION, INCOME, AND SEX OF INHERITOR

Primary Use (N = 675)[a]	Per Cent of Inheritors	Mean Inheritance	Mean Age	Median Education	Median Monthly Income	Per Cent Female[b]
Savings	38.1	$14,179	52.3	Some college	$601–$800	56.0
Living expenses	24.7	12,509	57.4	Some high school	$401–$600	59.3
Real estate[c]	16.3	5,309	47.0	High school graduate	$401–$600	57.3
Bills	7.6	2,922	46.6	High school graduate	$401–$600	45.1
Durable goods	7.6	2,667	48.6	Some high school	$401–$600	56.9
Education	4.1	12,555	46.7	Some college	$601–$800	67.9
Vacation	1.6	2,273	55.4	High school graduate	$801–$1,000	63.6
Total	100.0					

[a] There were 22 persons who were undecided, gave no answer, or did not remember what they had done with the inheritance; 21 persons made some allocation that was not included in the categories; and 95 received only mementos. The total number who inherited something of value was 813.

[b] Of the 675 inheritors, 57 per cent were female.

[c] Over two-thirds of the inheritors whose primary use of inheritance was classified as real estate were concerned with "home ownership" as opposed to investment in income-producing property. They were either purchasing a home, paying off the mortgage, and/or making home improvements with their inheritance.

ings accounts, applied to living expenses, or used for the education of children. Those who used or planned to use the money for their children's education were the youngest of the three groups of inheritors; more of them were women; their education and income were comparable with the education and income of those who saved the inheritance; and both groups had higher incomes and were better educated than those who used the inheritance for living expenses.

The relatively young age of the "educators" was not surprising. The children of the older persons were already established. Most likely the explanation of the sex ratio is that women wanted to do something "concrete" for their children; and for many, their inheritance was the first time that they, and not their husbands, were able to bestow a significant gift upon the child. The legacy provided women with some independence and power in intrafamily relation-

and Consumption," *American Economic Review* 51 (June, 1961):388–390. Landsberger, also using Israeli data, but including restitution payments, severance pay, lottery prizes, legacies, and gifts as windfall income, finds that "the marginal propensity to consume out of windfall income decreases strongly as windfall income rises." He believes the discrepancy between Bodkin and Kreinin lies in the relaitvely small sums that served as windfall income in Bodkin's study. Michael Landsberger, "Windfall Income and Consumption: Comment," *American Economic Review* 56 (June, 1966): 534–540. On the other hand, Bodkin believes that the difference between the Israeli studies and his own lies in institutional conditions rather than size. Ronald Bodkin, "Windfall Income and Consumption: Reply," *American Economic Review* 56 (June, 1966): 540–545.

ships. The legacy was not absorbed into the family budget, as suggested by the lowest percentage of women in the use of category of "bills" (45.1 per cent). The husband was not able to command these assets.

This desire to do something personally for one's children was most clearly stated by an only daughter who was disinherited in favor of her own two children. The children's inheritance was to be used for their college education.[14] The interviewee was most dissatisfied with the disposition. She would have preferred the intestate distribution (herself as sole heiress) so that she could pay for their education. The education itself was not in question; even without the inheritance, the family had ample means for this purpose.

Those who used their inheritance for real estate had inheritances of a moderate size. They were younger than those who lived on their inheritance or saved it and approximately the same age as those who planned to use the inheritance for their children's education. They differed from the latter in having lower incomes and less education.

The average inheritance of persons using their money for a vacation, to purchase durable goods, or to pay bills averaged about $2,500. Those who took vacations received the smallest inheritances, but they were least in need of the inheritance (having a monthly income of $801 to $1,000). They were older, and more of them were women. These persons had reached an age at which they had presumably paid their bills and purchased their durable goods. More men paid bills, and equal percentages of men and women bought durable goods. It may be that men were deemed responsible for the bills the family had contracted. Paying bills was the only use category for which the percentage of women in the category was significantly lower than the percentage of men. There was also a slight difference between the two groups in age: those who paid bills were an average of two years younger than the purchasers. The median education of the payers was high school graduation; the median education of the purchasers was partial high school. Both groups had a median income of $401 to $600 a month.[15]

14. Persons under 21 were not interviewed, so that the use of the money by these child-heirs did not appear in the total list of uses. In all, 133 minors were either intestate or testate heirs. The 133 minors were the heirs in 64 cases. In 18 estates, there was nothing remaining to be distributed to the minors; either the estate was insolvent, or there was nothing left after the year's allowance and exemption had been taken. These insolvent estates involved 51 minor heirs. Forty-three minor heirs to 18 estates inherited less than $1,000. The remaining 39 minors, the heirs to 28 estates, inherited sums ranging from $1,000 to $12,752. Three of these 39 have a share in real estate that they will sign over when they are 21 years of age. An additional five have an interest in real estate; 13 minors have their inheritance invested; in two cases, the will stipulated that the inheritance should be kept intact until the heirs become 21 years old. For eight minors the inheritance is being used or will be used for their education. There was no information on the use that will be made by the remaining ten minors. These figures were based on 659 estates, including the cases for which there were no interviews.

15. The spending units in which debts are most frequent are the young married and

The influence of age upon use of inheritance may be studied by use of mean age (see Table 7–8). Those who saved their inheritance, who used it for living expenses, or who took vacations had a mean age in the fifties. Those who used the inheritance for real estate, bills, durable goods, or education had a mean age in the forties. The influence of age upon use of the inheritance may also be studied by age categories and the most common use associated with these categories (see Table 7–9).

TABLE 7–9 INHERITOR'S AGE GROUP AND MOST COMMON USES OF INHERITANCE

Age Group	Most Common Use	Next Most Common Use
21–29	Savings	Real estate
30–39	Savings	Real estate
40–49	Savings	Real estate
50–59	Savings	Living expenses
60–69	Savings	Living expenses
70–89	Living expenses	Savings

Until age 70, the majority of inheritors saved all or the largest portion of their inheritance. Up to age 50, the use of the inheritance for real estate was next in frequency.[16] After age 50, an increasing proportion of inheritors used their inheritance for living expenses; and after age 70, living expenses were the dominant use, with savings in second place.[17]

Saving the inheritance or living on it appear to represent polar extremes. It is doubtful that people used all their inheritance for ordinary expenses unless they were in need. Some inheritors were forced into this condition. Conversely, simply saving with no particular end in view implies a situation in which the inheritor had considerable freedom in allocating his resources.

Savings or living expenses were the only choice or first choice of 63 per cent of the inheritors, with savings as the first choice or only choice for 38 per cent and living expenses, for 25 per cent. The relationship between these two uses is represented by the *saving-living index.* The denominator represents

the older (over 45) married with children under 18. The single and the older couples without dependent children are relatively debt free, John B. Lansing and James N. Morgan, "Consumer Finances Over the Life Cycle," *Consumer Behavior,* vol. 2, *The Life Cycle and Consumer Behavior,* ed. Lincoln H. Clark (New York: New York University Press, 1955), p. 48. The proportion of spending units purchasing durable goods follows a similar pattern, ibid., p. 43.

16. The proportion of spending units purchasing a home in a given year is greatest among the young married. Ibid.

17. Units headed by persons 65 and over save less than any other age group. Janet Fisher, "Family Life Cycle in Research on Consumer Behavior," in Clark, op. cit., p. 35. See also Dorothy S. Brady, "Influence of Age on Savings and Spending Patterns," *Monthly Labor Review* 78 (November, 1955):1243.

the number of persons who say that all or the largest porportion of their inheritance will be used for living expenses. The numerator represents the number of persons who say that all or the largest proportion of their inheritance will be saved. The saving-living index for the entire group was 1.5. The larger the index number, the larger the number of people in the category who are saving; the smaller the index number, the larger the number of people in the category who are using the inheritance for living expenses.[18]

The largest differences were revealed when the inheritor group was categorized by the monthly income of their household (see Table 7–10). As might be expected, the lower the income, the smaller the saving-living index. The single exception to the trend was the group whose income was over $1,500 a month.

TABLE 7–10 SAVING-LIVING INDEX, BY INCOME GROUP

Income Group (per Month)	Saving-Living Index
$200 or less	.3
$201–$400	.7
$401–$600	1.3
$601–$800	2.1
$801–$1,000	5.9
$1,001–$1,500	5.6
$1,501 and over	3.5

It is difficult to explain why this highest income category saved relatively less than those with incomes between $800 and $1,500. One explanation may be the cost of furnishing children with a college education. The highest income group ($1,500 and over) was least likely to have children who were the recipients of scholarships and was therefore most likely to have borrowed money to educate the children. Since people in this income group were likely to have a considerable amount of money tied up in installment purchasing of their housing, automobiles, boats, and other upper-middle-class gadgetry, it would not be surprising that this group found it necessary to borrow money to educate their children or to use inheritances to obtain an emergency purchase of some kind that they could not handle with their regular income. In summary, it may be said that the high-status people may actually have less income because of their high standard of living and therefore may be likely to use more of their inheritance for living purposes than would be the case in other

18. The saving-living index bears superficial resemblance to the economists' conception of the marginal propensity to consume. However, the saving-living index is based on the frequency of individual behavior patterns rather than the implications of income changes on the behavior of the individual or on society as a whole.

groups.[19] However, at the other extreme, it is easy to see why few persons with household incomes of less than $400 a month save their inheritance.

The differences by age group were not nearly so striking (see Table 7–11). However, those persons who had much of their lives ahead of them were the ones who were able and willing to save. Many of the older inheritors were forced to use their inheritance for everyday living. Also, there is not much purpose in saving at an advanced age; someone else is likely to enjoy the fruits of such thrift.

TABLE 7–11 SAVING-LIVING INDEX, BY AGE GROUP

Age Group	Saving-Living Index
21–39	2.8
40–49	1.7
50–59	1.4
60–69	1.2
70–89	.7

The saving-living index by relationship to the decedent reveals that the index for all husbands and wives was nearly as low as the index for those inheritors with incomes under $200 a month and lower than the index for those aged 70 to 89 (see Table 7–12). Although the index for husbands and wives was closely comparable, the sons and daughters differed markedly, with daughters less likely to save.[20]

TABLE 7–12 SAVING-LIVING INDEX, BY RELATIONSHIP TO DECEDENT

Relationship	Saving-Living Index
Husband	.4
Wife	.5
Daughter	2.4
Son	4.1

The use by spouses of inheritance for living expenses was probably the result of several factors. First, most wives were dependent upon the husband's income. When his income died with him, the inheritance substituted for it. Dependency probably does not explain the low index for husbands. For both husband and wife, however, there was a mingling of money and property; the inheritance consisted in large part of what they had been using jointly: their home.

19. Personal correspondence from Professor Allison Dunham, 24 April 1968.
20. The four relationships constitute 71 per cent of survivor population (870 persons).

The disparity between sons and daughters cannot be explained on the basis of age or household income. They were closely matched with regard to those two factors. It may be surmised that the daughter who was dependent upon her husband for living expenses would be inclined to use her inheritance to buy extras for herself and her family. The husband, who was more likely to be the breadwinner, was less willing to put his inheritance into daily expenses because if he did so, it would indicate that he was less than an adequate provider.[21]

In summary, it was found that the objective factors associated with particular uses of the inheritance are the form and amount of the inheritance and the income, age, and sex of the inheritor.

The Meaning of the Inheritance

It was hypothesized that inherited money might be treated differently from earned income for several reasons. One of the reasons was the possible emotional significance of inheritance, a significance in part dependent upon the quality of the relationship with the decedent.

Sometimes the inheritance was used in a way that constituted a memorial to the deceased.

I used it for prayers in the Temple for Mother (the deceased). I'm going to get a grave marker for Father and my brothers and sisters in Budapest. [A daughter who inherited $1,555.]

Sometimes the use of the inheritance was a more common one, but it was motivated by a desire to remember.

Case 568–01. A daughter, who was obviously very fond of her father, will use her entire inheritance of $11,000 for a new home. If she and her husband leave the city in which they now reside, the money will be kept intact to help buy a home wherever they go. She feels this would please her father and that they will remember him in this way. Her two sons each received about $4,000. She and her husband have guardianship of the money. They could use the children's inheritance for their college education, but they choose not to because the education of their sons was something they always intended to do. Instead, she will give them their money when they reach 21. If the

21. Professor Allison Dunham, in personal correspondence of 24 April 1968, has an alternative speculation concerning married offspring. He indicates: "To me, a much more likely explanation is one rising from the practice of wives paying bills. The husband has no idea of the inadequacy of his monthly salary given the insatiable demand of consumers. The wife is more conscious of that inadequacy, because every month she wishes that she had more money to spend. I have been told that there are some studies of marriage counseling services which bear this out. One of the largest factors in marital discord appears to be finances arising from the husband's inability to understand why his wife runs close to the line every month and the wife's insatiable demand for more. This would seem to me to be a better explanation than . . . his wanting to be able to tell his friends at the club that he was able to invest his inheritance because he was an adequate provider for his wife."

two boys want to spend it for sports cars, she has no objection. The important thing is that they know their grandfather remembered them.

Of course, if the inheritance was very small, there were sometimes difficulties involved in memorializing the decedent.

We bought a vacuum cleaner and designated that it was from Grandmother. But you know how it is. You spend it twenty times over. [A granddaughter who inherited $100.]

Charitable gifts sometimes reflected fondness for the deceased.

Some charitable gifts have been made. I would have given substantial amounts anyway, but I wanted to feel part of it came from Mother's estate. [A daughter who inherited $20,000.]

I sent the money as donation to a monastery. I think this is what Aunt ——— would have wanted. [A grandnephew who inherited $80.]

On the other hand, charitable gifts sometimes reflected hostility toward the deceased.

I gave it to the Seeing Eye Dog Foundation, among other charities. I didn't want anything from Aunt ———. [A nephew who inherited $4,000.]

Some people thought of an inheritance as money that should be spent on a serious purpose; others, because they did not work for it, regarded it as something that could be spent frivolously.

We blew it on an anniversary party. Easy come—easy go. [A grandson who inherited $100.]

I bought myself an old secondhand car, a stereo, and things I wanted that were out of my reach. It was money I never expected to have, so I used it for luxuries. I have only $50 left. [A daughter who inherited $835.]

I used the money to buy a car which caught fire and burned up a few months later, so I had nothing from it. [A grandniece who inherited $250.]

For some inheritors, the inheritance did not have much significance.

My wife was in the hospital, and so I didn't care about the inheritance. I wasn't concerned about that because I was concerned about my wife and her health. I suppose I spent the money on medical expenses. [A nephew who inherited $642.]

It is entirely in savings. We had four inheritances in three years—two from my side and two from my wife's side. We didn't need it, so it went into savings. [A son who inherited $2,300.]

Case 040–28. I had no expectation of inheritance, since a second cousin is not considered a close relative by me. My husband made a $1,000 bet with me that I would receive something from the estate, while I felt I would not. So when I received $1,000, it immediately went into the bank for the education of our oldest child under the terms of the wager with my husband. Intestate distribution would not have made any difference. This was a token inheritance that was nice to receive, but I could have done without it. [A second cousin who inherited $1,000.]

It should be noted that these legacies were minor in monetary value.

Some persons obtained a measure of security that was meaningful to them, and security was likely to be provided when inheritances were sizable.

It was my mother's estate that helped buy this house. My aunt's estate paid it off. So it is free and clear. [A niece who inherited $12,680.]

It is all in the bank. I'm just going to sit and watch the interest grow. [A daughter who inherited $16,333.]

With this inheritance we can live in retirement without going into our reserves, which we had planned upon. We have not stepped up our mode of living. We may go to Europe. We really haven't done anything with our inheritance except we feel more comfortable. [A son who inherited $101,800.]

Some people needed the inheritance for survival.

I had to have it to live on. I still do. I bought a trailer. It gave me a roof over my head. Without it I would have had to move in with the children. [A widow who inherited $5,100.]

I wouldn't have known what to do without it. I had to borrow until things got cleared at probate court. Then I sold the home and paid some of those bills. [A widow who inherited $5,600.]

I used half of it for doctor bills for myself. I would have been on charity by now if it hadn't been for the inheritance. [A widow who inherited $7,255.]

One unusual result of inheritance may be the loss of freedom for the inheritor. In two cases, survivors were placed under guardianship as a direct result of the inheritance. Information concerning these guardianships came from other members of the family rather than from the ward.

Case 497. The decedent's daughter refused her inheritance of $12,000. She had not liked the decedent nor did she like courts, lawyers, and so forth. This declination was thought to be evidence of incompetence, and the heiress was placed under guardianship. The survivor's own daughter felt badly about this, yet her out-of-state residence prevented her from taking an active role. She felt the lawyer had taken the initiative about this personal and family matter.

Case 130. The decedent's widow was sole heir to his estate of approximately $15,000. She was also appointed executrix. Her reaction to her husband's sudden death was both hysterical and depressed. Her three sons, however, thought she was capable of signing the papers. They took her to their doctor who agreed that, although grief-stricken, she was still competent. It was their lawyer who insisted on the guardianship and the transfer of administration. According to the sons, the lawyer wanted to be appointed administrator and guardian; however, one son acted as administrator, and another acted as guardian. Four months later, the sons went to another lawyer and had the guardianship annulled.

For some, life became easier because of the inheritance.

Case 610–01. I'm using the interest from stock to supplement my husband's income. I repaid the loans we needed when my husband was in medical school. I bought myself a secondhand car and a dining-room set. I have a cleaning lady I couldn't have otherwise. It's been a lifesaver. [A grandniece who inherited $40,083.]

For others, the ease provided by the inheritance was only temporary.

Case 050–01. The 45-year-old childless widow appeared to have continued the style of life she had shared with her late husband. He had been a delivery-van driver, but his personal automobile was a Cadillac. They had gone to the races, dined out, and splurged on vacations. She inherited their house and car. She sold the house and spent the entire amount on clothes and travel. "I didn't care about saving. You struggle together for old age and what happens? One is gone." The $8,000 inheritance is gone, also. The widow now works in a restaurant and lives with her sister's family. The interview was conducted in a tavern because she did not feel she could invite people to her sister's home.

Inheritance did not appear to affect markedly the inheritor's chances of social mobility. Some of the money used for real estate meant a better house and therefore would be reflected in the sociologist's indicator of social class. Investments may have increased the inheritor's income and, as a consequence, may have affected his style of life. The principal may have been sufficient to cushion any future economic setbacks. The use of the money for education may have increased the chances of success in life for the next generation. In the generation of the inheritors, no one used the inheritance for his own education. A niece who inherited $1,000 used her inheritance to help put her husband through medical school.

One grandson in his mid-thirties planned to use his inheritance of $12,000 to change careers.

Case 497–01. At present the money is exactly as I received it. I'm quitting my job soon, and I plan to invest some of it in an already established restaurant business. If I do that, I would work there. Or I may use some to go into business or real estate.

A son in his early fifties used his $5,100 inheritance for the expenses of changing from insurance to a real estate business.

The indications of a dramatic change in life style or life chances were few. This was true in part because often the inheritance was small and in part because the larger inheritances fell to those who were in the middle or later years of their lives. But an inheritance may affect life before it is actually received. A person with expectations of an inheritance may borrow on the basis of those expectations and/or may have lived his life quite differently from a person without such expectations.

The inheritors were asked if their expectations had influenced their lives prior to the actual inheritance. There were fifteen persons who admitted that they had lived differently from the way they would have lived without the knowledge that ultimately they would inherit. For nine of them, it meant that they might live to the full extent of their incomes without the burden of saving. A son who inherited $110,000 said, "It enabled me to live well with no financial worries about the future." A son who inherited $96,000 said, "I was not as prudent in my savings as I might otherwise have been." A son who inherited $10,000 said, "We anticipated funds from the estate would be used for college expenses of the children (interviewee had teen-age children), so we saved less than we otherwise would have. We did some extras for this house that we might otherwise not have done. We felt a little freer this way." A nephew whose style of life was predicated upon inheriting a large sum of money from a large estate was cut off. This ever-present possibility may be the reason why so few people based their lives upon their expectations. Obviously, another reason is that in many cases the inheritance was not large; although people have expectations, they do not have great expectations.

In two cases, their expectations gave the inheritors primarily psychological security. A daughter who received $1,900, an equal share, from the distribution of the estate said, "After he brought me the $4,000 to pay off the mortgage, I learned that I was also in the will. I was so relieved because I had so many doctor bills." A sister who inherited $38,000 said, "It relieved my mind that it wasn't going to be left to Mother, who would waste the money."

In the cases of two sons, the expectation of inheritance had affected their prior living arrangements. One, who inherited $52,000, said, "I stayed in the house after marriage, knowing I was going to inherit it." The other, who inherited $12,000, said, "I wouldn't have lived here if the house were not going to come to me. Father offered to transfer the house to my name nine or ten years ago, but I thought that was rushing things."

A similar case involved a friend of the decedent who took care of him for nine years prior to death and who inherited $13,650. "I would not have been able to take care of him if I had not expected the inheritance. I could not afford the time or the money."

Finally, a wife who inherited $36,000 said, "I didn't expect to prepare myself for working despite his heart condition. I knew my husband had insurance to protect me, so I did nothing about getting training for a job. Maybe I should have. I'm thinking of selling this house and investing in a tea room or gift shop and living on the premises, because I don't know what else to do."

Conclusion

After the heirs came into possession of their inheritance, legal aspects were no longer paramount. At this juncture, economic, social, and psychological considerations assumed primary importance.

The psychological significance of inheritance was perhaps less obvious than the economic or social significance. Several findings illustrated these implications. First, survivors made judgments about the fairness of the distribution that were not economically determined. A survivor who received nothing from the estate may nevertheless have judged that the distribution was fair. Second, survivors may have been dissatisfied even though the desired economic result was achieved; for example, the spouse-all pattern achieved through redistribution among the survivors was not as satisfactory as the spouse-all pattern achieved through the testament. Third, the inheritance of mementos that by all accounts were of little monetary value was immensely satisfying to the recipients. These mementos may have been in the family for several generations, and the expressed intention of their present holders was to pass them on to the next generation; they served as personal reminders of family continuity. Lastly, some of the uses to which the inheritance was put were determined by the emotional relationship between the decedent and inheritor; the association was not a simple one; for example, charitable giving may have been based on either positive or negative attitudes toward the decedent. It was possible to identify the association between the decedent-heir relationship and the use of the inheritance, but it was not possible to show a similar association between the parent-child relationship and the probability of disinheritance. The probability of disinheritance did vary with the social class of the child, the highest probability being for children of upper- and lower-class status.

Both economic and social variables must be considered if an understanding of the inheritor's allocation of the inheritance is to be achieved. The size of the inheritance was an important factor. For instance, the mean inheritance of those who saved the inheritance, used it to educate their children, or were living on it was large (over $10,000). Variations in household income explain these different uses. Those who consumed the inheritance for living expenses had lower monthly incomes than those in the other two categories. Between those who saved the inheritance and those who employed it for the education of their children, age differentiated; those saving their inheritance were older, and presumably their children were already independent. The importance of the size of the inheritance, income, and age was also illustrated in the other use types. The educational level of the inheritors explained little that could not have been explained equally well by income and age. Less predictably, the sex of the inheritor also had some influence upon the disposition of the inheritance. Women were somewhat more likely than men to use the inheritance for a vacation or the education of their children. They were less likely than men to pay bills with the inheritance.

Nearly two-thirds of the inheritors had accurate knowledge of their inheritance prior to the death of the decedent. Very few persons admitted that their lives had been lived in a manner different from what would have been the case without this knowledge.

The vital importance of the inheritance to many of the inheritors was demonstrated by the fact that the second most important use was for living expenses. Although relatively little change occurred in life style and life chances because of the inheritance (for example, a change in a career, a move to a better neighborhood, or early retirement from gainful employment and entry into a leisure career), many takers were able to maintain their standard of living or one close to that held before the death of the breadwinner. For other inheritors, there was an actual loss in the standard of living because the inheritance was insufficient to match the loss of income as a result of the death of the breadwinner. One other reason inheritance had relatively little effect on the lives of the inheritors was that those most likely to inherit were the relatively old, regardless of economic status.

Chapter 8

Economic and Legal Aspects of Estates

THE TERM *inheritance* conjures up a perception of an estate of large size being transferred from the decedent to chosen takers. Yet in any random sample of probate cases, there is a wide range in the net worth of estates, with very few over $100,000. In most inheritance studies, the researchers do not probe for nondeclared assets such as insurance. Often, accurate accounting of debts is not made. In this study, data were obtained systematically on all economic aspects of the estate of 659 cases in the decedent sample, and these findings are presented in this chapter.

Available to any person are a number of legal devices and procedures that have been created over the centuries in order to effect a wider expression of donative intent. These devices enable the individual to plan a transfer of his assets upon death in ways that may best meet his desires and the needs of his beneficiaries. These legal means, their frequency, and use among 659 decedent estates are examined in this chapter.

Size of the Estate

There were 48 estates in which the gross estate was $60,000 or more, and therefore a federal estate tax return was required.[1] Eighty-five estates in which the gross estate was $2,000 or less were theoretically eligible for "release from administration." Finally, there were 526 estates where the gross estate was over $2,000 but under $60,000, and no special legalities were involved by virtue of size alone.

Large Estates

With the exception of two individuals, the 48 persons with gross estates of $60,000 or more had wills, 96 per cent testate as compared with 69 per cent testate in the entire decedent sample. In comparison with the entire sample, these decedents were slightly older, fewer were married at the time of death, and more of them were female. Somewhat fewer were foreign born,

1. Internal Revenue Code 6018 (a) (1).

and the median formal education was four years of high school, as compared with partial high school for the entire sample. Aside from their high rate of testacy, the most important difference was that their occupational status was considerably higher.

Although a federal tax return had to be filed for all estates with a gross of $60,000 or more, a federal estate tax was levied on only 32. For the balance, there were no taxable estates, either because of normal deductions (including the flat $60,000 exemption) or because these deductions were combined with the marital deduction that permits a decedent to pass as much as one-half of his property free of tax to a surviving spouse.[2] The gross median estate size of the federally taxed estate was $130,421, compared with $76,130 for the 16 estates not federally taxed. The amount of federal tax paid ranged from $452 to $191,267. All cases were testate.

There were 16 women, 13 of whom were widows, among the decedents whose estates were taxed: three had inherited from their own parents; one had inherited from an unmarried son; six had inherited from their husbands; and three of the women had made the money on their own.[3]

Case 263. The decedent was a widow who had only a third-grade education. Her husband had had to retire at age 35 because of heart trouble, so he kept house while she did piecework in a garment factory. Her grandson described her as "a real ball of energy with more brains than most financiers, although she could barely read and write." She died suddenly at age 87, having been to the horse races the day before. Her estate of over $200,000 was nearly all in American Telephone & Telegraph stock.

Twelve of the 16 men whose estates were federally taxed had accumulated their wealth through their own financial astuteness.

Case 610. The decedent was a retired pullman conductor who, according to a friend, had built up his initial capital by boarding dogs during the Depression. The decedent's kin had aided him through the years with gifts of secondhand clothing and were completely surprised when he died at age 90 leaving an estate of over $200,000.

Only one of the men was an example of intergenerational inheritance.[4]

Unlike the findings of Wedgwood and Harbury, there were in this study very few cases of intergenerational inheritance among these 32 decedents whose estates were assessed a federal estate tax. Whether this difference can be attributed to the fact that Wedgwood and Harbury studied wealthier decedents only or to the variations in the economic and occupational systems of the United States and Great Britain cannot be ascertained.

2. Deductions allowable to estates or residents of the United States for federal estate tax purposes are set forth in sections 2052 through 2056 of the Internal Revenue Code.
3. There was no information for three cases.
4. There was no information for three cases.

A Brookings Institution national study of federal estate taxes divided estates into three groups: small, $60,000 to $300,000; medium, $300,000 to $1,000,000; and large, $1,000,000 and over.[5] In Table 8–1, the percentage in each category is compared with the data for this study.

TABLE 8–1 COMPARISON OF NATIONAL AND CUYAHOGA COUNTY FEDERAL ESTATE TAXPAYERS

	National Study (1957 and 1959)		Cuyahoga County (1964–1965)	
Size of Estate	Number	Per Cent	Number	Per Cent
Small	31,638	82.2	28	87.5
Medium	5,752	14.9	3	9.4
Large	1,124	2.9	1	3.1
Total	38,514	100.0	32	100.0

However, even discarding the large estate category because of a single case in the Cuyahoga sample, the comparisons between the two studies are strikingly similar. This may be a chance association because the 32 estates represent 5 per cent of the Cuyahoga sample.

Small Estates

An estate with a gross value of less than $2,000 is legally considered small enough for the court to dispense with the formalities of administration. The assets are released to the applicant without formal administration, usually within a few days. In this section, those release-of-assets cases and other cases of less than $2,000 gross value that for various reasons were administered formally will be examined.

Release of assets. There were 72 estates in which the assets were released without formal administration (11 per cent of the decedent sample). These 72 decedents differed from the entire decedent sample in several respects. Virtually all (89 per cent) were intestate. Their average age was two years younger (66.0 to 67.9 years). Fewer of the release-of-assets decedents were married at the time of death; more of them were male; and their occupational status was much lower.

According to statute, the application for release from administration "shall be in writing and shall contain . . . the names, ages, and addresses of the per-

5. Carl Shoup, *Federal Estate and Gift Taxes* (Washington, D.C.: The Brookings Institution, 1966), p. 207. Table D–2, "Gross Estates by Amount in Each Bracket: All Estates, Taxable Estates, and Nontaxable Estates, Taxable Returns Filed in 1959."

sons entitled to the next estate of inheritance and their respective degrees of relationship to the decedent."[6] Considering all the safeguards built into the probate process, it is the applicant who is trusted to give the court the names of those entitled to the decedent's estate. With one exception, the only omission of the names of the next of kin was among the release-of-assets cases in which the entire estate was of little value. However, the heirs of these decedents were usually not wealthy, and therefore the estate may have been of sufficient worth for those closest to the decedent not to inform the court of other legal heirs. *Good faith* falsification, withholding from the court the names of next of kin other than those listed on the probate record supposedly to avoid legal red tape, was used by survivors in four cases.

Other small cases. There were 13 cases in which the gross value of the estate was less than $2,000 but in which the estate was formally administered with all the usual expense and delay in settlement. In six cases, probate had been initiated when the upper limit for release-of-assets was $1,000.[7] Five of these cases, though small and relatively uncomplicated, had taken over a year and hence were part of this sample. The sixth case involved the problem of unknown next of kin and was in probate for two years.

In seven other cases, the estates were given the full treatment for obvious reasons. The persons who applied to probate court did not or could not know at the time of application the extent of the estates.

Case 469. The decedent was a Hungarian who died in Hungary, "application being made apropos of foreign power of attorney under United States Consular Seal from the decedent during his life time, confirmed by his widow." The decedent's estate consisted of intangibles in the nature of litigation involving the construction of his brother's will; litigation resolved against the interest of the decedent. Other assets consisted of the liquidation value of a "specific legacy" which would not exceed $500 and might be less. The fund comprising the specific legacy due this decedent's estate is now under a blocked account under control of the United States Alien Property Custodian.

Case 558. The docket indicated: "The decedent's assets consisted of interests in two valueless pieces of real estate. It is in the best interest of the estate to abandon for tax delinquency." The executor's final statement is brief: "No money or property ever came into my possession." Since the real estate was located in Kansas and Ontario, it presumably took some time to ascertain its true worth. The case was settled in twenty months.

Case 501. The decedent's will provided for a $10,000 trust fund for a grandson. The only asset that went through probate was a car valued at $300. At the time of his

6. Ohio Revised Code 2113.03.

7. Release from administration first became possible in 1932. From 1932 to 1947, the upper limit was $500. From 1947 to 1963, the limit was $1,000. Effective September, 1963, the amount was increased to $2,000. Effective November, 1967, the amount was raised to $3,000. See Ohio Revised Code 2113.03.

second marriage, the decedent told his wife he had $40,000 in bonds. He died while visiting relatives out of state. His wife, who had remained in Cleveland, suspected that his relatives had somehow gotten the bonds. She and her attorney spent many months trying to trace this lost fortune.

In the following case, the decedent's assets were less mysterious; the case would seem to have involved a simple mistake.

Case 401. After twenty-six months in probate, the final statement of the decedent's wife and executrix reads "the sole asset in the decedent's estate was a Chevrolet automobile which was overvalued considering its condition and the balance due thereon. . . . The affiant says that she paid from her own funds all debts and funeral expenses and administration costs."

The remaining three cases involved law suits: in one case, a suit on behalf of the estate was lost; in the second, a suit was settled for $750; in the third case, a suit against the estate failed. Thus the assets, in the first two cases, and the debts, in the third case, could not be determined at the time of application for probate.

Extra-probate Assets

In an attempt to ascertain how much property is distributed at death, it is not possible to rely wholly on the material available on inheritance tax records. For most decedents, the property listed provides a comparative estimate of their assets; for a handful, however, it is virtually meaningless. Norman F. Dacey suggests several reasons probate is best avoided: it is expensive, public, and time consuming.[8]

No information is available on those who completely avoided probate; but in several cases, the decedent and his heir almost avoided it.

Case 216. From the probate information, it seemed like another case of the "poor widow." The decedent's gross estate consisted of a car valued at $1,700; the funeral expense totaled $1,200. The widow had moved from the address listed on her application for letters of administration. No doubt economies were in order. We surmised wrongly. The widow had moved into a new deluxe apartment building. In her interview, she revealed that an attorney had advised them to put everything in her name; then she made a will leaving everything to her husband. This arrangement was feasible for two reasons: (1) the couple were very close, and her husband trusted her, and (2) the probability was that he would die first; in the year preceding death, he had three major operations. In addition to the car, the decedent left $3,500 in life insurance. The widow refused to divulge the amount of property that had been transferred prior to the death. Whatever the amount, it was sufficient that her style of life was not impaired, and at the time of the interview she was not employed or seeking employment. She did state that her monthly income was between $200 and $300. Her own will names thirty-six nieces and nephews as beneficiaries; this would indicate her

8. Norman F. Dacey, *How to Avoid Probate!* (New York: Crown Publishers, Inc., 1965), p. 6.

assets are fairly substantial. Despite her reluctance to discuss her financial situation, she was open about the transfer of funds and felt she and her late husband had been well advised in their estate planning. Since the estate went through as a release-of-assets case, expense and delay were at a minimum (one could almost say non-existent). The estate attracted no publicity. The objectives of avoiding probate were admirably realized.

It is surprising that more decedents did not transfer a greater portion of their assets before death in order to save administration costs and taxes. In some cases, they may have thought they had done so but were legally unsophisticated with respect to property ownership. For example, in some cases, the family home was owned by husband and wife as tenants in common, and the assumption was made that the survivor would become the sole owner without the necessity for administration. Another rationale is that the decedents with spouses wished to protect the established power relationship between them by maintaining their assets intact, and those without spouses chose to remain independent of their children. Where transfers did occur prior to death, they were often made under conditions similar to deathbed wills. Illness and imminence of death lessened the need to maintain independent status.

Information obtained from the probate docket does not provide an accurate description of the worth of estates or the testacy status of out-of-state residents. The court does not attempt to check the veracity of reported information.

Case 225. The decedent, a resident of another state, owned Ohio property jointly with his mother after his father died intestate. His wife signed over the Ohio property to her mother-in-law. The probate docket lists the man as intestate and states that there were no assets or estate administration in California. In her interview, the mother said her son had a will and left everything to his wife and that he owned land in California.

One decedent had an estate in Ohio only because he had been injured while visiting here and had initiated a law suit. The settlement for the suit was his only asset. His residence and place of death were in Nebraska. In another case, the Ohio property of a Florida resident was administered here. This decedent also owned property in Michigan and Florida. The probate docket mentions out-of-state property without giving its value. The two survivors in this case would not divulge the financial details of the estate but intimated that there was additional property.

In addition to cases in which residents of other states owned property in Ohio, there were cases in which Ohio residents owned property elsewhere. One decedent had been under guardianship for over thirty years. The only probate asset was the proceeds from the final account of the guardian, about $1,500. Her daughter mentioned Illinois property that she and her husband succeeded in obtaining one year prior to her mother's death. This property netted them at least $12,000.

However, these are rare cases. Whether the infrequent reporting of either extra-probate assets or transfers in contemplation of death reflects actual frequency or the reluctance of survivors to admit to the interviewer facts that may have been successfully concealed from lawyer, court, and family is not known. Apart from those cases in which a survivor admitted assets not recorded at court, there was a small number of cases in which one survivor voiced suspicions of another survivor. It cannot be known whether the suspicions were well founded or not.

Insurance as an Extra-probate Asset

The major discrepancy between the actual assets of the decedent and his assets as listed in probate court resulted from nonreporting of life insurance carried at one time by the decedent. Only 55 of the 659 decedent estates (8 per cent) listed insurance. Interviews with survivors suggested that over three-fourths of the decedents carried life insurance. Information was obtained regarding insurance for 432 of the 659 decedent cases. According to their next of kin or legatees, 339 (79 per cent) of these decedents carried life insurance with an average value of $5,250. The highest figure reported was $100,000. A few carried only burial insurance.[9]

Insurance was found to be a more common type of equity among the testate decedents than among the intestate (82 per cent of testate decedents, as compared with 72 per cent of intestate decedents). Younger decedents were more likely to carry insurance than older ones, their average age being 64.9 years, as compared with 73.7 years for the uninsured. Married males were most likely to be insured (89 per cent).

For those who had insurance, the contribution that it made to the total estate was relatively greater for the smaller probated estate than for the larger probated estate.[10] For those estates with a gross probate value of $2,000 or less, the value of insurance more than doubled the estate size. The mean value of the insurance was $2,775. At the other end of the spectrum (estates over $60,000 gross probate), the average amount carried was the highest ($19,117,

9. Monies dispersed by life insurance companies as death payments shows a steady rise as does the amount of money invested in ordinary life insurance. In 1964, the average-size ordinary policy in force was $4,380; and in 1965, $4,660. Edwin Goldfield, *Statistical Abstract of the United States, 1967* (Washington, D.C.: United States Department of Commerce, 1967), pp. 472–473. *The Life Insurance Fact Book* for 1957 reported that about 70 per cent of the population owned some form of life insurance. Cited by Allison Dunham, "The Method, Process and Frequency of Wealth Transmission at Death," *Chicago Law Review* 30 (Winter, 1962):247.

10. Total estate equals gross probate estate plus insurance.

with a range from $2,000 to $100,000), but the contribution to the total gross estate was the least (under 10 per cent).

It would be possible to calculate a total estate size for estates with values of $2,000 to $60,000 by adding the approximate value of the insurance. Estimating total estate size in the cases that are at the extremes of an estate-size scale is more doubtful because any error made could be a large one. In the small estates, it might be possible to double the estate size for a decedent who had no insurance. For the large estates, the variations are significant for both the size of the probated estate and the amount of insurance.

In general, as the probate estate increases in value, the amount of insurance also increases, but the relative contribution of insurance to the total value of the estate decreases (see Table 8–2).[11]

TABLE 8–2 CALCULATIONS OF INSURANCE FOR ESTATES OF MODERATE SIZE

Probate Estate (Gross)	Insurance	Total Estate	Insurance as Per Cent of Total Estate
$4,000	$2,550	$ 6,550	38.9
$7,500	3,219	10,719	30.0
$10,000	3,150	13,150	24.0
$13,000	4,468	17,468	25.6
$18,000	4,914	22,914	21.4
$25,000	7,034	32,034	22.0
$45,000	7,500	52,500	14.3

Debts

Funeral

Probate exists in part to protect creditors. One debt incurred by almost all decedents is the expense of the funeral.[12] In most cases, the next of kin determine the style of the funeral.[13] While the personal representative and court have veto power in such matters, it is rarely used.[14] Broad guidelines are set

11. Although it is possible that Table 8–2 could be used for estimating the total value of an estate without the necessity of interviewing, it should be kept in mind that the total amount of insurance in the United States is steadily rising, so that extrapolation figures may soon be out of date. For the value of insurance held, see Edwin D. Goldfield, *Pocket Data Book USA 1967* (Washington, D.C.: United States Department of Commerce, 1967), pp. 332–333.

12. The body of one uncle in the sample was donated to a medical school; this action on the part of his heirs saved a considerable part of his small estate.

13. Two of the decedent testators used their wills to make stipulations about funerary matters. Case 325: "No minister or priest is to be at my wake; the burial expenses are to be $900 to $1,100 and no more." (The probate docket lists funeral expenses of $1,123.32.) Case 535: "My remains are to be cremated and deposited with the ashes of my wife (which are now kept in my home) in the mausoleum in ——— cemetery."

14. Six months after death, Billy Rose, the showman, reposed in a cold-storage vault.

down that the funeral should be in keeping with the decedent's station in life.[15]

However, the data in this study disclose that funeral expenses would be an uncertain indicator of the decedent's station in life. The vast majority of decedents in this sample received something like equal treatment in death, regardless of their social position. Almost three-fourths (73 per cent) of the 592 decedents whose funeral expenses were noted on probate material had funerals costing between $751 and $1,750. As David Riesman and Howard Roseborough have noted, the final expenses have not kept pace with the possibilities of conspicuous consumption of other products and services.[16] There were only 19 decedents whose burial cost more than $2,500; eight of these extravagant funerals were for decedents whose gross estates were over $60,000; but one was for a decedent who had amassed less than $6,000. At the opposite end of funereal splendor were the 21 decedents whose funerals cost $500 or less, and included in this group were two decedents whose estates were over $60,000.[17]

Today there is considerable discussion about the high cost of dying. It is not within the scope of this study to examine the question closely with the purpose of determining if burial costs are excessive or if families in time of extreme grief are being taken advantage of by unscrupulous funeral-home operators. Even among the 3 per cent (of the 592 decedents) who had funerals costing over $2,500, it is not certain if these costs were the result of the salesmanship of the funeral-home operators or ethnic or subcultural group expectations.

Allowance and Exemption

Certain preferred heirs of the decedent have a claim against the estate that must be satisfied before the property is distributed to other takers under either the will or the statute. These claims are the year's allowance to the widow and

---

His next of kin wanted a showy memorial, and his executors would not agree. The judge in the case is quoted as saying, "Burying the dead is the privilege of the next of kin, while it is the obligation of the executors to pay reasonable funeral expenses." The problem centers on what is reasonable. "Wills, The Subject is Rose's," *Time,* 19 August 1966, p. 49.

15. "The allowance for funeral expenses must be reasonable considering the amount of the estate, the station of life of the deceased and the customs of the people in the same station and if unreasonable or extravagant, the funeral shall be disallowed even as against legatees and next of kin." Frank J. Merrick and Ellis V. Rippner, *Ohio Probate Law* (Cleveland: Banks-Baldwin Law Publishing Co., 1960), p. 146, quoted in *Cleveland Plain Dealer,* 17 July 1966, under headline "Court OK's Funerals Fit for Kings."

16. "The standard of dying has hardly kept pace with the standard of living." David Riesman and Howard Roseborough, "Careers and Consumer Behavior," *Consumer Behavior,* vol. II, *The Life Cycle and Consumer Behavior,* ed. Lincoln H. Clark (New York: New York University Press, 1955), p. 14.

17. Both the Dane County and Cook County studies also noted that the financial position of the decedent did not seem to be the determining factor in the cost of the funeral. Edward Ward and J. H. Beuscher, "The Inheritance Process in Wisconsin," *Wisconsin Law Review* (1950):407. Dunham, op. cit., p. 273.

minor children and the property exempt from administration for the benefit of surviving spouse or minor children. If the estate is small and a spouse or minor children survive the decedent, the estate may be so reduced by these claims that there is nothing left for other takers.

The purpose of the allowance to the widow and minor children is to provide these persons with support for the twelve months following the husband's or father's death. In determining the amount of a widow's allowance, the appraisers and the court may consider her age, her manner of living, her physical condition, her medical expenses, the value of the estate, and the amount expended for support in the years immediately preceding the decedent's death.[18] It is difficult to say to what extent the appraisers consider and weigh these various factors. The amount of the widow's allowance bears some relationship to the size of the estate. However, over half of the allowances in this study were within a $500 range (see Table 8-3). This would lead one to believe that

TABLE 8–3 AMOUNT OF WIDOW'S ALLOWANCE, BY MEAN GROSS ESTATE

Widow's Allowance	Number	Per Cent	Mean Gross Estate
$2,000 or less	27	10.7	$ 9,444
$2,001–$2,500	20	7.9	10,700
$2,501–$3,000	146	57.9	22,664
$3,001–$4,000	30	11.9	14,333
$4,001 and over	29	11.5	83,069
Total	252[a]		

[a]There was no widow's allowance in 407 decedent estates.

the allowance is based not upon an assessment of an individual's need but upon an accepted definition of an adequate amount. The amount of the widow's allowance is in many instances immaterial, since in most cases the widow also inherits the entire estate. The property exempt from administration

> shall not exceed in value twenty per cent of the appraised value of the property . . . but in no event is the value of the property not deemed assets to be more than twenty-five hundred dollars if there is a surviving spouse, or more than one thousand dollars if there is no surviving spouse, but surviving minor children.[19]

There were 344 cases in which property was exempted from administration. In 55 per cent of the cases, the exemption was between $2,001 and $2,500. In 45 per cent of the estates, the exemption was $2,000 or less but approached the 20 per cent maximum.

18. Ohio Revised Code 2117.20.
19. Ohio Revised Code 2115.13. This code section entitled "Property exempt from administration" should not be confused with Ohio Revised Code 2113.03, "Release from administration."

Other Debts

The *other debt* category includes all obligations other than the costs of administering the estate, the funeral, and the year's allowance and the property exemption: medical expenses of the decedent, mortgages, loans, utility bills, department store due accounts, taxes (except estate and inheritance), and car payments. No debts were listed for 254 estates (39 per cent). This does not necessarily mean that the decedent had no debts at the time of his passing. Most likely his spouse or another survivor paid the lawful debts and did not bother to render an accounting.[20] It should be remembered that the vast majority of the estates in this study were small, and no tax advantage would have accrued to the heirs from careful bookkeeping and reporting. The smaller the estate size, the lower the percentage of estates with debts listed (see Table 8–4).

TABLE 8–4 PER CENT OF ESTATES WITH DEBTS LISTED, BY SIZE OF GROSS ESTATE

Size of Gross Estate	Per Cent of Estates with Debts Listed
$2,499 or less	10.3
$2,500–$6,499	54.4
$6,500–$10,499	59.4
$10,500–$15,499	59.3
$15,500–$20,499	83.6
$20,500–$60,499	87.1
$60,500 and over	91.7

Only 19 decedents' other debts exceeded $10,000. Most of the large debts were incurred by decedents who left large estates; nine of the 19 left estates over $60,000. The estates were insolvent as a result of debts in only two cases.

In 10 of the 19 estates, the proportion of other debts to gross estate exceeded 50 per cent. The average age (60.4 years) of the big debtors was

20. "There are two other possible explanations for nonlisting of debts. There is a substantial increase in what is called 'credit life insurance,' particularly in the case of installment sales and revolving credit. If the creditor has a group life plan on all of his debtors, then presentation of a copy of the death certificate to the creditor results in the debts so being paid that there is no claim to be filed by the creditor against the estate. Perhaps of equal importance is the practice of the general run 'trade creditors' not to file claims." Professor Allison Dunham, personal correspondence of 24 April 1968.

A similar comment with respect to credit life insurance was made by Professor Richard V. Wellman in personal correspondence of 17 April 1968. Professor Wellman indicated that there are many nonprobate devices for securing payment of a decedent's debts. Creditors do not have to concern themselves with probate devices for obtaining payment if the debt is secured, or if, as the project data show, the survivors usually assume that they should pay the decedent's bills and do so without regard to legal technicalities.

younger than the average age for the entire decedent sample (67.9 years); and the percentage of females was higher (47 per cent) than it was for the entire decedent sample (39 per cent).

These differences in age and sex warrant further study. The earlier age at death of the big debtors and the higher percentage of women indicate that more obligations would be expected if death occurred during the active work career of the decedent than if death occurred after the decedent had retired; that it is possible women are more extravagant than men or less experienced in handling funds, or that surviving women may never have had sufficient time to pay off completely the debts incurred by their deceased husbands.

Insolvency results from too few assets rather than too many debts. There were 54 insolvent estates, 47 of which were release-of-assets cases; in three others, the gross estate was under $2,000. In the remaining four, other debts made a substantial contribution to the insolvency.

The debts do not have to be large to cause delay in the settlement of an estate and trouble for survivors. One decedent's son, who was executor, said that his own credit had been threatened by the decedent's debts. The estate had a gross probate vaue of nearly $28,000. The troublesome debt was submitted by a department store for approximately $600. At issue was whether the store had filed its claim within the four-month period.[21] The attorney for the company alleged that the executor tried to evade payment and was "sneaky." The executor's attorney said the store's efforts to contact the executor were "sloppy" and inefficient. The account was eventually settled for $200, and the estate was closed after a period of twenty months, a distinctly longer period of time than was usual for this sample of decedent estates (see Chapter 10).

In general, however, debts did not constitute a significant problem in the settlement of an estate. First, the debts usually constituted a small proportion of the gross estate. Second, the survivors of the decedent usually made provision for payment without the necessity of court proceedings.

Will Contests and Personal Claims: Settlement Aspects

There were will contests in six (1 per cent) of the 453 testate cases. In five of these, there was a jury verdict, and the will was upheld. In each of these five cases, however, an out-of-court settlement was also involved. The other case was settled out of court without a jury verdict. The net size of the estates ranged from $8,500 to $3,811,000; and the size of the settlements ranged from $400 to $150,000. In some cases, the information regarding the out-of-court settlement was available at court; in other cases, information was obtained from the survivors.

21. See Ohio Revised Code 2117.06.

Debts

Case 345. The decedent, a 76-year-old widow, was survived by two sons and a daughter. She left one son $5,000, a grandson $100, the daughter one-fourth of the residue, and the other son three-fourths. The bulk of her estate (gross $75,000) had been inherited from a deceased son. The son who later inherited the largest share gained power of attorney because he was living at home. The daughter's husband died, and she moved in with her mother and brother. There had been an earlier will leaving equally to the decedent's children. The second will was contested on the grounds that it had been improperly executed. The plaintiffs were the son and grandson who inherited a minor share of the estate. In a jury verdict, the final will was upheld. However, the contesting son received $10,000 instead of $5,000 in a settlement out of court. There had been dissension in the family prior to the settlement; and since the settlement, the sons have not spoken to one another, despite the attempts of the grandson and his wife to mend the rift.

Case 535. The decedent, aged 79, died a year after his wife's death. He was survived by no known next of kin. The decedent and his wife had had mutual wills leaving all to each other, but her will was not probated at the time of her death. Eight days before he died, the decedent made a new will naming two of his wife's relatives, a neighbor, and a friend as equal inheritors. A contest was instituted by other relatives of the wife on the basis of the half-and-half statute. The will was upheld, but there was an out-of-court settlement of $1,900.

Case 627. The decedent, an 80-year-old widow, had made two wills. The first was made in 1946, leaving all to her husband, who was then living, and naming as contingent the sister or sisters who survived her, and specifically disinheriting her nieces and nephews. By 1960, her husband and also all her sisters had died, and she was persuaded to make a new will by one of the nephews. This will read, "to the nieces and nephews of full blood living at the time of my decease, share and share alike, but not any of their children." On the day of her death, less than three months later, both wills were presented at probate court, the earlier will by a grandnephew who was unaware of the second will and the second will by a niece, the sister of the nephew who had persuaded the decedent to make it. Since the second will revoked the prior one, the grandnephew contested on the ground that the executor had failed to name all the legal heirs. The unnamed heir was a niece of the decedent, but she had been adopted by a stepfather and was therefore excluded from inheriting from or through her natural father, a deceased brother of the decedent. Therefore, the 1960 will was upheld by a jury verdict, but again there was a settlement out of court. The grandnephew claimed he got less than $1,000, but another survivor said it was settled for $3,000, which was $1,000 less than the nieces and nephews received.

Case 262. The decedent, a single male in his eighties, was survived by nieces and nephews. The gross estate was $800,000. One nephew, the only one who bore the family name, was not included in the will that was presented at probate court. He contested on the ground that this was not the last will and testament of the deceased. During the interview, he said he had known there was a will but not the one read at death. He also said there were many discrepancies in the second will, such as names spelled incorrectly, and he is convinced there was fraudulent collusion. A jury verdict upheld the will. There was an out-of-court settlement for $7,500, of which the attorney received 40 per cent by prearrangement. There were other claims against the estate that were also settled out of court, one by a grandnephew with whom the decedent lived prior to his death. The grandnephew was not an inheritor and based his claim on the fact that he had paid his uncle's room and board. He settled for $3,000, although he had claimed $6,000. The other plaintiff was a niece who was an inheritor. In addition to her inheritance of $7,000, she claimed the decedent signed a written memo to his attorney directing him to pay her $10,000 when and if she purchased a new home. The executors, who were the defendants in this case, said the claim was made too late (after nine months from their appointment) and that the decedent only signified his intention to give a gift in the future. In order for a gift to be valid, delivery must be completed. The plaintiff countered by saying the gift was contingent on her purchase of a home, which occurred over a year after the executors were appointed. The plaintiff added that, although the decedent passed away, the instructions to his attorney were not withdrawn. This claim was settled for $5,000.

Case 040. The decedent, a 79-year-old male who had never married, left a small portion of his sizable estate to a niece who would have been the sole heir had he died intestate. Her inheritance was not only relatively small but was also left in trust with the stipulation that she would have the use of the income from the trust but that upon her death it would revert to the estate. The niece contested on the grounds that the decedent was not of sound mind at the time the will was executed. The will was upheld, but an out-of-court settlement gave her an additional $150,000. The bulk of the estate went to charities.

Case 135. The decedent, an 85-year-old male, left his entire estate (net $8,524) to his 70-year-old second wife, who died before the estate was settled. Contingent beneficiaries were her two children, his stepchildren. The decedent was also survived by five children from his first marriage, whom he disinherited. Four of them live in Hungary, and one lives in Canada. The daughter in Canada claimed the 1945 will that was probated was not her father's last will and testament. This case did not come before a jury. Instead there was an agreed settlement between the parties, and the plaintiff received $400.

Six cases involved claims against the decedents' estates. In each of them, there was some kind of settlement, most often out of court.

Case 041. A 58-year-old decedent was survived by a second husband and three adult children. There was a prenuptial agreement in which the husband waived all rights to inherit. The decedent left her entire estate (net $3,706) to her three children. The husband put in a claim for repairs to the house and funeral expenses. It was settled out of court for $1,600.

Case 111. The decedent, a 64-year-old widowed male, died intestate. He was survived by two adult children and two grandchildren, the children of a deceased daughter. He left a net estate of $15,298. Five years prior to his death, he became bedridden and was persuaded by his housekeeper to sell his home and move in with her. When he died and probate proceedings were begun, she put in a claim against the estate for $23,725 for services rendered plus the rent of part of her home. Her petition stated that, "I never received any payment from him at any time although he constantly and continuously promised me he would reimburse me for the services I rendered. He never paid me anything." She died three months after the decedent and ten days after initiating the claim. Her daughter, who was executor for her estate, continued to press the claim. It was finally settled out of court for $1,000. The son who was administrator for his father's estate felt the claim was the daughter's idea. He and his sister agreed the housekeeper deserved something, although not the amount of the claim. This case was in probate court for four years; and in addition to the claim, the defendants paid $4,000 in attorney fees.

Case 022. The decedent, a 61-year-old widowed male, died intestate. He was survived by two daughters. The deductions exceeded his gross estate of $1,408, and consequently he was insolvent. Three months prior to his death, the decedent's car collided with a rubbish truck, fatally injuring a man. The man's common-law wife put in a wrongful death claim against the estate for $50,000. Her claim was based upon loss of his support. In testimony it was revealed that she was gainfully employed and had not lived with her common-law husband for eight years. This case was settled out of court by the insurance company. The amount was not noted in the court records. According to the decedent's daughters, the man had jumped from the garbage truck into the path of her father's car. "The police exonerated Dad right away. Two months later he got sick—thought it was asthma but discovered he had cancer. Dad lost the will to live. He felt it was an 'eye for an eye,' since he had killed a man. He died less than two months later."

Case 583. The decedent was testate. He left his estate to his brother and also appointed his brother as executor. Prior to his death, his niece, the daughter of his brother, served as guardian (the decedent had cancer of the brain). Two months before his death, the niece withdrew money from her uncle's bank accounts to be used for hospital expenses. This was done on the advice of her attorney, who was also the attorney for the estate. These accounts were payable on death to the decedent's mistress. After death, the mistress filed suit for recovery of the bank accounts. She won, and the guardian's home was attached until payment was made. At this time the estate was already in the hands of the brother, but since he was also the guardian's father he made good.

Case 609. The decedent, an 82-year-old widowed female with no children, died intestate. Since her estate consisted of property identical to that of her deceased spouse, the half-and-half statute applied, half of the estate going to his relatives and half to hers. A petition was filed by relatives of the decedent to the effect that the "appraisers appointed in the estate of the decedent's husband set off the sum of $1,370 as her exemption and the further sum of $3,000 for her year's allowance . . . that the executrix of the estate did not pay the above to the decedent and that the estate of the decedent has a good and valid claim and lien against the estate of her husband." They won their claim, with the result that the decedent's side received $10,000 to be divided among the heirs, and her husband's side, $2,000.

People who instituted claims or contests had a very good chance of getting something, but the amount was less than they asked. In general, it appears that the conflicting claims and principles involved in a will contest are resolved through compromise.

Inferences with Regard to Economic Aspects

The amount that is actually distributed to the takers under either the will or the statute is dependent upon the decedent's gross estate and upon the deductions made. Contests and claims may also affect the amount shared by inheritors.

Forty-eight estates were valued at over $60,000, and a federal estate tax return was required; however, for 16 of these estates, the deductions reduced the estate to the point where a tax was not actually levied. All 32 decedents whose estates were taxed were testate. At the other extreme, nearly 90 per cent of the 72 decedents whose estates were released without administration were intestate.

Funeral expenses and other debts may drastically reduce the amount of the estate available to those with succession rights. Fifty-four estates were actually insolvent because these debts equaled or exceeded the gross estates. These were almost all extremely small gross estates. The frequency and amounts of other debts increased as the gross estates increased, but the debts were usually within the ability of the estates to pay. Thus debts bear a positive relationship to the size of the estate. On the other hand, the study indicated that funeral expenses bear little relationship to the size of the estates; the very wealthy and the poor may have equivalent funeral expenses.

Interviews with survivors were necessary in order to ascertain the value of the decedents' insurance. Such information was usually not reported on the probate forms. The interviews also revealed minor deficiencies in the listing of next of kin in release-of-assets cases and in some cases that involved nonresident decedents. Finally, out-of-court settlements were usually made with those who contested the wills or made claims against the estates.

Testamentary Devices of Control

It was stated in Chapter 3 that a possible motive for testation is the desire to master or control the future. This possibility exists with any will; the testator chooses his beneficiaries, his executor, and so forth, but usually the testator's control extends no further than this and is ended when the estate is distributed and the executor renders his final account. Testators may, however, control the distribution of the estate for many years and impose conditions upon the beneficiaries through the use of a number of devices: trusts, guardianships, life estates, conditional bequests, and contingency provisions. With the exception of contingency provisions, it was found that these devices were used by a minority of decedent testators.

Trusts

The mere presence of a trust is not sufficient proof that the testator's desire was to control his heirs, but it is obvious that control is a latent consequence of the creation of a trust. It is also important to distinguish in this regard between trusts set up for the welfare of beneficiaries of normal capacity and legal age and those set up for the aged, minors, and others who are incompetent. Barring adjudicated incompetents and minors, the degree of capacity for handling financial matters is relative.

The provisions of tax laws in the United States serve as an important impetus to the formation of inheritance trusts where the estate is large enough to incur federal estate taxation. Where a spouse survives the decedent, the marital deduction trust has proven to be especially advantageous.[22] It was difficult in this study to determine what role the tax laws did play in the decedent's decision to set up a trust. Many testators with large estates provided for outright distribution. Despite the undetermined role of taxation in the setting up of trusts in large estates, it is clear that in small estates, tax laws play no role.

There were trusts in seven estates that were large enough to incur federal estate taxation. In five of these, a spouse survived the decedent and was the principal beneficiary of the trust. For example, the trust device may be used to care for an incapacitated spouse.

Case 006. The decedent was an 82-year-old retired engineer whose estate totaled over $440,000. Most of the assets were in a living trust. The beneficiary of the trust was his widow, who at the time of the survey was in a home for the aged. The trustee was directed to pay the income from Trust A at least quarterly and was empowered to use the principal as needed for the widow's comfort and welfare. In the event of the widow's incapacity, the trustee was directed to distribute only so much of the income as was deemed necessary for support and maintenance. Upon the widow's demise, there were provisions for both Trusts A and B to be distributed to seven relatives (siblings, nieces, and nephews) of both the decedent and his spouse, a friend, and a charity. The widow was given a power of appointment over Trust A.[23] In this case, the wife expressed resentment regarding the provisions established by her late husband through two trusts.

Case 311. The decedent was a 70-year-old man who was survived by his wife, son, and daughter. He had been a retail jeweler. The gross estate was over $196,000. This estate was divided into Trusts A and B, with the income from Trust A to be paid to the wife quarterly. If the income proved insufficient, the trustee was directed to convert trust income into productive property. Following her demise, provisions were made for

22. Cases 006 and 311 involved the marital deduction trust. The terminology of "Trust A" and "Trust B" used therein is one developed by the tax lawyer for the marital deduction trust procedure. Such terminology in the will is meaningless from the standpoint of trust law. Its presence indicates that the will was part of a comprehensive estate plan.
23. A power of appointment can be considered the right given by one person to another to control the ultimate disposition of property.

the son to receive $150 a month for life and for the daughter to receive the residue outright. The widow was given a power of appointment over Trust A. The widow felt her husband had done her a grave injustice. She was resentful of the remarks made by a trust official on her living arrangements ("Even millionaires don't live like this") and felt helpless because her powers were so limited. After her husband's death she was forced to borrow from her son-in-law for even the funeral expenses. "It is one thing to have your husband tell you, but I don't see where the bank carries the right." The widow felt her husband had planned the estate in this fashion to prevent her from being extravagant and to prevent the son from throwing the money away. The son, a college graduate, worked as an unskilled laborer when he worked, but at the time of the interview was living on social security disability payments in a men's boarding house. The daughter's comment on her father and his will was, "He thought he could control us through money. He never realized it didn't matter to us."

In the sixth case, a trust was set up for the benefit of the decedent's parents and daughter. In the seventh, trusts were created for the benefit of charities and distant relatives.

The trustees in five of these seven large estates were banks. Trust advertising proclaims that a very important aspect of having a bank as trustee is continuity over time. The corporation continues in perpetuity. One of the two decedents who did not choose a bank as trustee appointed an 82-year-old man.

There were nine testamentary trusts so small in assets that avoidance of federal estate taxation could not have been the reason for the testator's decision. Two of the nine were set up for the benefit of the decedents' widows. Four trusts were to provide for the support, protection, or education of minor children or grandchildren. In three of these, the trusts were not actually set up, either because the "minors" were already over 21 years of age at the time of the testator's demise or because the decedent's estate was insufficient for the trust he had planned. In only one instance in four cases was the trust actually operative.

Two trusts were set up for the benefit of incompetent relatives. An incompetent niece was the beneficiary of one trust. In the other case, the beneficiary was an incompetent brother.

Case 628. The decedent was a 72-year-old retired machinist. He left his entire estate of nearly $37,000 in trust for an invalid brother. The beneficiary was one of seven surviving siblings. The bank, as trustee, had used some of the principal to repair the beneficiary's roof; the siblings would like the principal protected because after their brother's demise, the trust will be distributed to them.

Since the siblings objected to any expenditure of the principal, it is probable that the testator felt that someone who had no vested interests in the conservation of the estate would look after his brother better than the family members would.

Case 352 shows a unique use of the trust.

Case 352. The decedent was a 71-year-old divorced man. His legal next of kin were four adult children. His will directed that his estate ($28,000) be held in trust until six months after the death of his former wife (the divorced wife was 47 at the time of the divorce, 51 at the time the decedent wrote his will, 60 at his death, and 67 at the time interviews were conducted). Six months after her death, the proceeds are to be distributed equally to the children. If before that time a grandchild should become orphaned and have no means of support, the trustee is authorized to furnish the necessary funds. Otherwise, no provision has been made for distribution of principal or income during the term of the trust. The oldest son was appointed trustee. One of the daughters said this about her father's will: "I hope his mind is in the minority. . . . This bitter revenge my father had for my mother. . . . Whatever my father left is not worth the love and respect I have for my mother. . . . If this thing could be terminated by other means than my father's vicious wish, I'm sure our family could speak to one another and be human beings." Another daughter said, "They shouldn't allow wills that reach out from the grave to affect the living. If mother knew what was in the will she would be heartbroken. . . . It would kill her. She would think she was standing in our way to get the money."

In four of the nine cases, the trustees were professional. These were the cases where the beneficiaries were wives and incompetent relatives. In the other five cases, the testator chose a member of his family. In the case of smaller estates, the employment of a professional trustee is not so common as it is in the case of large estates.

Guardianship

A person may inherit not only rights to property but also the duties of the decedent.[24] Four decedent testators made provisions for guardianship in their wills. Three of these decedents left minor children. One decedent appointed his wife guardian of their 18-year-old son. He divided his property equally between wife and son. A widow appointed her 24-year-old daughter the guardian of a 17-year-old son. She was survived by three other adult children, but the boy himself had selected this sister as the one with whom he would like to live. A widower appointed his sister the guardian of his 13-year-old son. The widower and his son had made their home with this sister.

In all the preceding cases, the ward was not legally competent by virtue of age. The provision for guardianship in another case was unusual. At the time the will was made, the ward was not legally incompetent. The decedent appointed her son-in-law the guardian of her husband in the event that her husband should become incompetent. Since her husband survived her by only four days, this provision did not take effect.

24. In discussing Roman law, Maine says: "Inheritance was a universal succession occurring at a death. The universal successor was Haeres or Heir. He stepped at once into all the rights and all the duties of the dead man. He was instantly clothed with his entire legal person." Henry Sumner Maine, *Ancient Law* (Boston: Beacon Press, 1963), p. 175.

Life Estates

Two life estates in real estate were discussed in regard to remarriage in Chapter 5. In the case of remarriage, the decedent was able to make a compromise that ostensibly took care of the claims of both spouse and children.

There were six other decedents who made use of the legal life estate. There was no tax incentive in any of these cases because they failed to qualify for the marital deduction.[25] The incentive appears to have been simply the preservation of the estate for those who would inherit after the death of the person who was vested with the life estate. There was also a strong element of social control. Most of the life estates were to be terminated not only at death but also upon some other condition, such as remarriage.[26]

Case 302. "I give, devise, and bequeath to my beloved husband, ———, a life estate in and to all my real and personal property which I have or may have an interest in at the time of my death, provided he does not remarry. In the event of the remarriage of my beloved husband, then this life estate shall immediately terminate upon happening of the said event. Subject to the life estate which I have provided for my beloved husband herein as to my real and personal property, I give all the rest, residue and remainder of all my estate and property, whether real, personal or mixed whatsoever to my three children, ———, ———, ———, in fee simple, absolutely and forever." The 64-year-old widower explained that he had once gone on a gambling spree, so at that time the house was put in his wife's name. She had promised to leave him the house in her will; he was surprised that she had not. He resented the situation sufficiently to ask the lawyer about breaking the life estate. "I worked for this house; now I'm retired and I have nothing."

It is difficult not to be sympathetic with his plight. His eldest son, the only child resident in the county, also felt that an outright devise would have been best. According to both their stories, the marriage was a long and happy one; the gambling, a mere episode. The widower blamed the law rather than his late wife.

In the next two cases, the survivor did not resent the fact that the estate was not left in fee simple.

Case 596. An 80-year-old woman left her spouse a life estate conditional upon his remarriage, with their five children as remaindermen. She was described as a woman fanatically devoted to her children and to the Roman Catholic Church. The widower

25. The so-called terminable interest rule is the principal barrier to qualification of property interests for the marital deduction. See Internal Revenue Code 2056 (b) (1) (A) and (B).

26. "An exception to the illegality of total restraints on marriage is the case of second marriages. Where the condition restrains remarriage, it is held valid by the vast weight of authority. . . . In spite of the illogical basis for this exception to the general rule, it continues to be reaffirmed in the infrequent cases where the situation arises." John J. Murphy and James S. Parkhill, Jr., "Conditional Bequests and Devises," *Boston University Law Review* 42 (Fall, 1962): 543.

had been a heavy drinker all his life; forty years ago he had been so negligent in his support of wife and children that a court order for support had been obtained.

In the other case, the husband and wife had mutual wills, and each had left the other an unconditional life estate in the real property with their two children as the remaindermen. The 64-year-old widow and the children were satisfied with the disposition. Another case involving a spouse was that of a 53-year-old widow who received a life tenancy on condition that if she remarried, the property would go to two minor children. The widow refused an interview.

In the remaining two cases, the decedent was widowed. In one, the decedent's legal next of kin was his son. He willed approximately $4,000 in savings to his sister and also left her a life estate in his home, with the grandchildren being the remaindermen. The property was disposed of in this manner because the decedent and his son did not get along and, more importantly, because his death was preceded by a half-dozen years of failing health. At some personal sacrifice, his sister had moved into his home in order to take care of him. In the other case, the life estate was vested in one of three children.

Case 324. The decedent was an 85-year-old widow who left her home to one daughter. Her other two children were named as remaindermen. If, however, they should die first, the daughter would then own the home in fee simple. The daughter who received the life estate had moved back home after a divorce and at the time of her mother's death had lived in the home for nearly forty years. The reason for the life estate appears to be the fact that after so long a period of residence, the mother felt her daughter should not be forced to move. The will predated the decedent's final illness by many years, and the actual nursing care during this illness was provided by the other daughter. The two sisters agreed that the disposition was fair and satisfactory. Their brother, however, felt his mother was pressured into making her will in this fashion. He said that the children had signed over their rights to the property when their father died intestate. The son had signed over in the belief that his mother would leave it equally to the three of them. This time he did not sign the waiver of notice until the lawyer threatened him. (The property was appraised at less than $4,000.)

Altogether, there were eight life estates in a decedent sample of 453 testate cases.[27] A life estate appeared to be a legal device that had great potential for family discord in these cases. The testator apparently wanted to accomplish too much with too little.

Conditional Bequests

"A condition in a will is a clause describing a particular event or occurrence the happening or non-happening of which operates to suspend, revoke or modify the devise or bequest."[28] A *precedent* condition limits the acquisition of the

27. The life estate appeared in 2 per cent of the wills. In the Cook County study, there was one life estate in 98 wills, or 1 per cent. Dunham, op. cit., p. 284.
28. Murphy and Parkhill, op. cit., p. 521.

devise or bequest. A *subsequent* condition limits the retention of the devise or bequest.[29]

The most common subsequent condition is life tenancy terminable upon remarriage. Enforcement of a subsequent condition depends upon the possibility of use without consumption.[30] Thus it would appear that the feasible means of enforcing this condition are to devise a determinable legal life estate in real estate or a life estate in trust. Relatively few estates in this study were large enough to allow the beneficiary to live solely on the income from a trust. Those few decedents who bequeathed to their spouses life estates in trust did not impose conditions upon this bequest. All but one of the decedents who left their spouses life estates in real estate imposed the condition of remarriage. It was also possible to impose a condition upon a bequest of personal property, but this was most likely to be a condition precedent.

Case 331. The decedent was survived by his wife, two minor children, and two adult children. The two minor children were to receive legacies of $5,000 apiece if they were unmarried at the time. The legacies were never paid because there were insufficient funds. The deceased owned real estate in a deteriorating section of the city, and his widow filed for bankruptcy.

The next case is an example of a quite different restraint on marriage. The decedent willed all to his spouse, with their five children contingent equally. The contingent bequest to one of the daughters was only to be made, however, "providing she is no longer residing with her husband." The widow had written the same condition into her will. She stated, "My husband's hard-earned money is not going to that drunk."

The conditional contingent bequest in another case was similar. One of four children was to share equally only if "he is no longer a member of a religious order." By the time the estate was settled, the son had left the order.

In the final example, the decedent made two conditions: (1) the principal heir was to take the real estate if he paid the bequests, and (2) "If anyone opposes the will, they forfeit their share."[31]

29. Ibid., p. 526.

30. Life estates may be created by bequests of personal property including sums of money; but it has been held that such estates are not favored, and the testator will not be held to have so intended unless such condition is clearly and unequivocally expressed. *Corpus Juris Secundum*, vol. 96, *Wills* (Brooklyn: The American Law Book Co., 1957), sec. 894. Further, it has been held that if it sufficiently appears that the bequest cannot be enjoyed except by its consumption, it will be held that it was the intention to give the absolute title to the beneficiary. Ibid. These rules would apply where money is given on the condition that it will revert if the beneficiary remarries. The beneficiary, in the absence of contrary condition, would be able to spend the money before remarriage.

31. There have been many arguments advanced concerning the validity of such provisions. The principal objection appears to be on the grounds of public policy. If the

Case 258. The decedent was an 83-year-old woman who was survived by nine children. She left her real estate (a three-family house) to a son who made his home with her. She also bequeathed $1,000 to seven of her children and $1,200 to the eighth. One daughter received $200 more for nursing care given after a minor operation some years before death. Another daughter had rented an apartment in her mother's building for eighteen years and had helped her mother at that time. She moved out when her mother raised the rent. About the disposition, she said, "I'm thrilled my sister got $200 more; they all thought I was the one out to get the money."

Reciprocity in this family seemed to be closer to economic than to social exchange. There was good reason for the no-contest provision.

Contingency Provisions

One advantage of a will is the possibility of naming contingent beneficiaries: those who will inherit in the event (or contingency) that the first-named inheritor predeceases the testator, dies with the testator in a common disaster, and/or does not survive the testator for a stipulated period of time. The testator in effect formulates a priority of inheritors: first this person; if not this person, then these. It is possible, furthermore, to think of contingency provisions not only in their strict legal application but also as an expression of the desire of the testator, which it may be incumbent on the first beneficiary to respect. The testator may be saying, "Ultimately I would like my estate to be distributed to these people." Although this is merely an expressed wish without the legal effect of a life estate, it is possible that the wish will be honored.

Devises or bequests that would lapse without the benefit of contingency

---

provisions are sustained generally, without regard to good faith, a weapon is provided for encouragement of fraud and undue influence, which may deter honest contestants. In contrast, the chief arguments in favor of the provision are that the public is not interested in whether or not the testator's heirs received their property and, further, such provisions tend to reduce litigation and suppress family dissensions. Of course, another argument in favor would be that testator's intent, as manifested by the provision, should be carried out. See generally, *American Jurisprudence,* vol. 57, *Wills* (Rochester, N.Y.: The Lawyers Co-operative Publishing Co., 1948), sec. 1513. In many jurisdictions, the doctrine is advanced that a beneficiary does not lose his share under a no-contest provision, where he brings an action contesting the will in good faith and for probable cause. The justification would be that the provision does not apply to a contest so initiated. This view has not been universally accepted, there being a respectable body of authority indicating a no-contest provision is valid even with respect to a proceeding begun in good faith and for probable cause. Ibid.

The Ohio view with regard to "good faith proceedings," is, at best, ambiguous. In Bender v. Bateman, 33 Ohio App. 66, 168 N. E. 574 (1929), the court held that there was no such exception to the validity of a no-contest provision, concluding that to recognize the exception would be to depart from the testator's intent. But, in Maskowitz v. Federman, 72 Ohio App. 149, 51 N. E. 2d 48 (1943), the court stated that the modern doctrine with respect to these provisions is that public policy, probable cause, good faith, and a variety of other matters should be considered, and that hard and fast rules cannot be pronounced and be made applicable to all cases.

provisions; that is, fail because the beneficiary died before the testator, are often saved by an anti-lapse statute. Anti-lapse statutes are classified under three categories: (1) those having the most limited coverage, where the predeceased inheritor is a lineal descendant of the testator; (2) an intermediate type, where the beneficiary must be a relative of the testator; and (3) the most flexible type, where the legislation applies to any person who predeceases the testator.

Ohio and the majority of jurisdictions have the intermediate statute. Ohio Revised Code 2107.52 reads as follows:

> When a devise of real or personal estate is made to a relative of a testator and such relative was dead at the time the will was made, or dies thereafter, leaving issue surviving the testator, such issue shall take the estate devised as the devisee would have done if he had survived the testator. If the testator devised a residuary estate or the entire estate after debts, other legacies and devises, general or specific, or an interest less than a fee or absolute ownership to such devisee and relatives of the testator and such devisee leaves no issue, the estate devised shall vest in such other devisees surviving the testator in such proportions as the testamentary share of each devisee in the devised property bears to the total of the shares of all of the surviving devisees, unless a different disposition is made or required by the will.[32]

It is important to note that the Ohio anti-lapse statute saves the gift only if the beneficiary-relative has left issue who survive the testator. Also, "relative" means relative by blood, not by affinity. Consequently, a predeceased spouse is not within the scope of this legislation.

Frequency of contingent provisions. A little more than half (52 per cent) of the decedents' wills included contingency provisions.[33] The testators who were most likely to designate contingent beneficiaries were those who at the time of testation were survived by a spouse and lineal kin; nearly three-fourths did so. Those least likely to include provisions for contingent beneficiaries were the testators who were survived by lineal or collateral kin; in each case, more than three-fourths failed to do this (see Table 8–5).

It is clear that contingent provisions were most frequent when the testator was survived by spouse and lineal kin. In the event of the spouse's death, there were other near kin, that is, children whom the testator would have liked to benefit. His contingent beneficiaries were obvious to him. In a sense, he followed the intestate pattern but in two stages, leaving first to his spouse and then to his children; whereas the intestate pattern would have given to the spouse

32. Under the common law, a lapsed share of the residue would pass by intestacy. In Ohio, surviving residuary beneficiaries would prevail even in cases not fitting within the anti-lapse statute. See Commerce National Bank of Toledo v. Browning, 158 Ohio St. 54, 107 N.E. 2d 120 (1952).

33. Fifty-five per cent of the wills in the Cook County study had substitution clauses. Dunham, op. cit., p. 282.

TABLE 8–5 CONTINGENCY PROVISIONS, BY TYPE OF KIN SURVIVING AT THE TIME OF TESTATION

			Contingents Named			
	No Contingents Named		Related Only		Other[a]	
Type of Kin	Number	Per Cent	Number	Per Cent	Number	Per Cent
Spouse only ($N = 41$)	20	48.8	8	19.5	13	31.7
Spouse plus lineal ($N = 251$)	65	25.9	171	68.1	15	6.0
Lineal ($N = 115$)	98	85.2	11	9.6	6	5.2
Collateral ($N = 42$)	33	78.6	7	16.7	2	4.8
No known next of kin ($N = 4$)	2	50.0	0	0.0	2	50.0
Total 453	218	48.1	197	43.5	38	8.4

[a] "Other" is nonrelated and charities or a combination including relatives plus nonrelated and/or charities.

and children. Over 70 per cent of the testators who were survived by spouse and lineal kin and who made contingency provisions designated their children as equal beneficiaries.

Where only lineal kin survived, the lack of contingency provisions may have been based on the assumption that the testator would not outlive his descendants or certainly not all of them. In the cases where collateral kin survived, perhaps the circle of those whom he would have liked to benefit had been exhausted in the naming of primary beneficiaries.

Those least likely to confine their contingent inheritors to relatives were those whose only next of kin were their spouses; however, five of the 13 who named nonrelated persons included their in-laws as contingent beneficiaries. Given the distance of their own kin, they were apt to choose their spouses' kin in place of, or in addition to, their own. The decedent may, of course, have positively disliked his nearest kin. This appears to have been the case in one of the examples of a contingent charitable bequest.

Case 279. "I make the above bequests with full awareness of the fact that I have brothers and other relatives living, but it is my intention that no part of my estate shall go to my family in the event that I am not survived by my wife."

Effect of contingent provisions. How often do contingent beneficiaries actually inherit? In the sample of 453 decedent estates, there were 21 cases (5 per cent) in which the contingent beneficiaries inherited. The primary beneficiary in all these cases was a spouse who predeceased the testator. There were no cases of common disaster. The remaining next of kin for 18 of these decedents were adult children. In 12 of these 18 cases, the children were to share equally. In another four cases, adult children were contingent equally, but grandchildren were also named. In the remaining two cases, one child was disinherited in the contingency provisions. In one of these cases, the children redistributed the estate so that in reality there was no disinheritance.

Case 563. The decedent was a 69-year-old widower. He died one year after his wife and had not revised his will. He was survived by four adult children. Three children who resided in Cleveland were named as contingent beneficiaries. A daughter living in Czechoslovakia was disinherited. The Cleveland interviewees said that when the family came to the United States, their sister chose to remain behind. At that time, she had received the family farm in Czechoslovakia. They felt it would have been unfair if she had received a share of the property here.

Siblings were the remaining next of kin in two cases. Had the testator not named contingent beneficiaries, the siblings would have inherited equally. In neither case was this the wish of the testator.

Case 403. A widowed female named two sisters and a niece as contingents. However, the sister with whom she had lived was contingent for the bulk of the estate. The other sister and niece received small bequests.

Case 270. The decedent was a male whose wife predeceased him by seven days. He had named his stepson contingent, thus disinheriting his three sisters who, according to the stepson, never paid much attention to him.

The twenty-first case was an unusual one. Unfortunately, it was impossible to interview anyone connected with the case; so the reasons for this strange will are unknown, and it is not clear why it was not revised.

Case 618. The decedent made a will in 1960 leaving all to his wife Joan. By the time the decedent died in 1964, Joan had predeceased him, and he had remarried. His son had been named executor and his daughter-in-law contingent for the entire estate. No mention was made of the children of a deceased daughter. Settlement proceedings were commenced under the impression that the decedent was a resident of Cuyahoga County, and the widow concurred and also renounced any interest in the estate, although she could have claimed a one-third interest. Later she changed her mind and started proceedings in Florida, which is where the decedent died and is also her place of residence. The final entry in probate court here noted that all assets of the estate are being administered in Florida, and the only funds that came into the executor's hands were in a joint account he had with his father for $1,074.

In another six cases, the primary beneficiary died after the testator in the decedent sample but before the settlement of his estate. Technically, the estate of the decedent in the sample went into the estate of the primary beneficiary, who in each of these cases was the spouse.[34] Where the husband and wife had joint or mutual wills, it made little difference who died first. The contingent beneficiaries were the same in both wills, and they inherited. This was true in four cases. The other two cases were complicated for different reasons.

34. Ohio Revised Code 2105.21 (presumption of order of death) had no effect in these cases.

Case 653. The decedent left all to his wife, with their children named contingent equally. The wife died six months later, but within that time she had a disagreement with the oldest daughter and made a new will leaving $500 to her, 30 per cent of the residue to two other daughters, and 40 per cent to the only son because of his "traditional status as eldest son." But after the mother died the children agreed to divide the estate equally.

Case 657. The decedent and her husband, who died shortly after, were survived by two sons and a daughter. One son was contingent for all on the advice of the other son, who felt his brother had done the most for the parents. Not long after the parents' deaths, the son was killed in an accident. Legally his wife would then inherit the entire estate. However, she intends to share the estate equally with the surviving son and daughter.

There were also four cases in which the only inheritor was deceased, but no contingent beneficiaries were named, or if named, were also deceased. In two cases, adult children were the remaining survivors, and they inherited. In another, two single sisters died within two days of each other. Each will left all to the other without naming contingents. Their nieces and nephews inherited. The fourth case also involved two single sisters, but the distribution was different.

Case 484. The estate of the decedent consisted of a one-fourth interest in a home that she had shared for many years with her two single sisters and the widow and son of a deceased brother. At the time of her death, the household had dwindled to one sister and the nephew. The sister was named beneficiary of her estate, and there were no contingents. Before the estate was settled, the sister died, leaving her estate, which included the share from the sample decedent, to the nephew. There were eight nieces and nephews in all. We interviewed five, all of whom felt it was eminently fair that the one nephew should receive the house. "The one who took care of them deserves it all. Nobody knows how much he had to do for them—moneywise, care and all."

The intent of the testator in the majority of cases was carried out because contingents had been named. Of course it would have been possible to have made a new will; 20 of these wills were over five years old. One reason for not making a new will may have been the influence of the dead beyond the grave, especially because in all but two cases the decedent was a husband or wife. If the estates are considered to be the result of joint effort on the part of spouses, then reciprocity and distributive justice were served in all but a minority of cases.

Inferences with Regard to Testamentary Devices of Control

With the exception of contingency provisions, the testamentary devices described in this section (trusts, guardianships, life estates, and conditional bequests) were used by a minority of testators. Thirty-two wills (7 per cent of the 453 testate estates) had provisions of this nature. Not all these provisions took effect because the ward attained adulthood or the estate was insufficient for the testator's intentions to be carried out. Slightly more than half of the decedent's wills included contingency provisions. These provisions actually took effect in only 21 cases (5 per cent of the 453 testate estates). In terms of actual consequences, all these testamentary devices were a minority phenomenon.

Conclusion

Although the previous focus was upon the extreme estates, the large and the small, it should be recalled that nearly 80 per cent of the estates (526) were valued at over $2,000 but under $60,000. About 80 per cent of the decedents with estates in this middle range carried insurance that on the average may have represented between 14 per cent and 39 per cent of the total value of the estate. Deductions from the gross estate are: funeral expenses for nearly 90 per cent of the estates, "other debts" for 62 per cent, exempt property for 52 per cent, and finally, the year's allowance for 38 per cent.

In contrast with this general picture, it was found that testamentary control devices were infrequently used (with the exception of contingency provisions) and that will contests and personal claims against the estate were also rare. The rareness of these items can perhaps be attributed in part to the fact that the vast majority of estates in the study were of an intermediate size. Unless there is a feeling of gross injustice, contesting the will simply may not be worth the effort and expense. Nor is the average estate large enough to make trust provisions useful. The life estate in real estate, which could be thought of as the poor man's trust, seems to create more problems than it solves.

Guardianships and conditional bequests, other than determinable life estates, were probably rare for reasons not related to the size of the estates. It has been noted that few decedents leave minor orphans; hence, the need for guardianship is minimal. Conditional bequests appear to be flagrant examples of social control. However, if the testator truly disapproves of his daughter's husband or his son's occupation, he has an alternative: he can disinherit his offending next of kin. There are other probable reasons why social control devices were uncommon. It is likely that most persons approach will making with the intention of being just and that lawyers try to prevent gross unfairness.

Chapter 9

Will Making

A WILL IS a legal instrument usually drafted by a lawyer in consultation with his client. The actual interaction between client and lawyer is not accessible, but an examination of the attitudes of clients and lawyers may illuminate the transaction. Why does a person make a will? How free should he be in decisions about the distribution of his worldly belongings? What is the lawyer's definition of his role in will making? Is he properly rewarded for his work? What is his image of the client in this area of practice?

Client

Chapter 4 was devoted to an analysis of the social and demographic characteristics of both testate and intestate decedents and survivors in order to determine which characteristics were associated with the condition of testacy. From this analysis, a rough sketch of the lawyer's will-making client emerged. The typical will maker is likely to be a married man in early middle age, and although he is more affluent than the general population, he is not wealthy.[1]

The data in this section are based upon the responses of 1,230 survivors.[2] Of these persons, 58 per cent (711) had already made a will; 35 per cent (427) said they planned to make a will; and only 8 per cent (92) had no plans to make a will. There is, of course, no way of knowing how many of the survivors will carry out their intentions.

1. In the survivor population, males were more likely to be testate than females (60 per cent as compared with 56 per cent). In the decedent sample, this condition was reversed; 70 per cent of the females and 68 per cent of the males were testate. Females, however, constituted a minority of the decedent sample, approximately 40 per cent. In the 5 per cent random probate sample, there were 272 male testate decedents and 181 female testate decedents. The predominance of male testators over female testators in the probate sample was 1.5 times. As shall be seen, the lawyer is not merely interested in drafting wills but also in administering estates. If the practices of will drafting and estate administration are combined, the lawyer has two female clients for every three male clients. Although testacy was more frequent among the widowed than among the married, there were more married persons among his clientele. The mean net estate for testate decedents was $35,160; the median household income for testate survivors was between $601 and $800 per month.
2. Four survivors refused to answer the question of testacy.

Reasons for Testacy

The client seeks the assistance of a lawyer because he has a problem which he believes requires expertise that he does not possess. Will drafting requires knowledge of the law and some experience with the problems of family relationships. In seeking the help of the lawyer, the client is willing to reveal confidential information in order to obtain counsel and appropriate action in matters of serious import to him.

In this study, the initial approach to the study of the client-practitioner relationship was to investigate the reasons individuals make or do not make wills. The testate survivors were asked why they had made their first wills. Those who did not have wills but who planned to make them were asked for their reasons. Those who indicated no intentions to be testate were also queried.

Of the 92 who planned to remain intestate, 52 (57 per cent) stated that they did not have enough property. Eighteen were satisfied with the intestate distribution. There were 22 additional idiosyncratic reasons. The finding that a lack of property was the major reason for intestacy proved to be consistent with the datum of a positive association between property and testacy.

In spite of the over-all finding that persons with higher equity were more likely to be testate, the notion of having "enough" property to make a will varied considerably according to the individual. One elderly woman who planned to make a will gave as her reason, "I have a new winter coat. It cost $75. I want to leave it to someone who will appreciate it." A serious consideration of motivations for testacy must account for these highly subjective and individualistic perceptions of worth.

The reasons for making a will fall into two categories: (1) personal circumstances or change in them and (2) the perceived capabilities of a will. These reasons are interrelated, but the degree of connectedness depends upon the individual's situation at any given time. It cannot be said that a change in personal circumstances automatically produces a condition whereby intestacy is unsatisfactory and that a will remedies the situation. Some changes in personal circumstances would not be relevant to testacy. For instance, the fact that a man changed jobs would not in itself be relevant. However, if the new job entailed more dangerous work, or if it paid more, such differences could provide the motivation for testacy. The capabilities of a will may be directly relevant to personal circumstances. For example, a testator who is alienated and angry because his children have "let him down" by converting to another religious faith may use the testamentary device of the conditional bequest with the expectation that the children will recant and come back into the fold rather than lose their inheritance.

Table 9–1 gives the reasons for will making for the two groups of survivors: those who have already made a will and those who intend to make one. These groups differ in their reasons for will making. In this analysis, personal circumstances are considered as factors that "push" into will making, and the advantages or capabilities of a will are factors that "pull." An inspection of Table 9–1 reveals that those who were already testate had felt some push into their action. Those who intended to make wills admitted the advantages of testacy, but at the time these advantages were not so salient to their own personal circumstances. Personal circumstances were mentioned far more frequently by the testate than by the planners.

TABLE 9–1 MOTIVES GIVEN FOR TESTACY BY TESTATE SURVIVORS AND SURVIVORS INTENDING TO MAKE WILLS

Motives Given for Testacy	Testate Survivors		Survivors Intending to Make Wills	
	Number	Per Cent[a]	Number	Per Cent[a]
Personal circumstances				
Marriage, children	128	18.0	68	15.9
Aging, illness, trip	81	11.4	7	1.6
Acquired property	57	8.0	25	5.9
Compulsion, suggestion	50	7.0	1	.2
Decedent's death	29	4.1	11	2.6
Advantages of will				
Alter distribution	165	23.2	158	37.0
Faster, cheaper	157	22.1	130	30.4
Guardianship	170	23.9	68	15.9
Executor, taxes	13	1.8	7	1.6

[a] The percentages are based on 711 survivors with wills and 427 survivors intending to make wills. Some persons gave more than one reason.

The "compulsion, suggestion" category contains those responses which indicate special circumstances that pushed the individual toward testacy and those responses which specify the influence on the individual of a role model, superior, or salesman in the will-making decision. Will makers gave reasons that belonged in this category fifty times; whereas only one planner was so classified. Almost half of the reasons listed in this category have to do with military service. The possibility of death while in military service is evident. It is strongly recommended to the recruit that he make provisions for his family in case of his death. A typical response from a former serviceman was, "I was in the Air Force; someone came around and said it was a good idea. It didn't cost anything."

Individuals can be influenced to make a will by the suggestion of a friend, a relative, a lawyer, an insurance agent, or some other influential person. One planner reported, "The lawyer suggested it. He said he'd do it. I don't really think there is any advantage." Testators had also received advice from their lawyers and from their insurance agents. The data indicate that the insurance salesman was as important in this respect as the attorney. Whether the insurance men advised their clients out of personal conviction or because they had been instructed to do so as part of comprehensive estate planning is not known. One survivor, who was himself an attorney, said, "I was required to make a will by my instructor in a course on wills." Several testators were compelled to make wills when they entered religious life. Other suggestions emanated from testators: "My wife's father is an attorney; she felt it was necessary." "My sister made me do it. She said it was important even though I don't have savings." "Friends and neighbors advised us."

The possibility of death because of old age, serious illness, or while making an extended trip were motives given far more frequently by the testators than by the planners. Either the experiences of the two groups differ (the testate group is older) or their reactions to similar experiences are different. An impending trip may be the impetus for will making, but only if it is associated with the possibility or heightened probability of death. This association is evident in the following statement: "We were traveling to California. Well, you know, accidents can happen." The notion of imminent death was given relatively infrequently even by the testate group; 11 per cent of the testators offered responses that fell into this category. This response is not surprising, since most individuals express an invincibility regarding their own death.

Economic wealth was positively associated with testacy for both the decedent sample and survivor population, but the acquisition of property was mentioned by a small minority of both the testators and those who intended to be testate, 8 and 6 per cent, respectively. The absence of property operated to deter people from making a will, but the presence of property was not paramount in the decision for testacy. Property was a necessary but not sufficient condition for will making.

This group of survivors had recent probate experience and may consequently differ from the general population in their motives for making wills. Their experience may have impressed upon the survivors the importance of having a will. One hundred forty-three testators had actually made their first wills immediately after the deaths of the decedents for whom they were beneficiaries or next of kin. Twenty-nine of these gave the decedent's passing as their principal reason. Eleven of those intending to make a will also mentioned the death as their reason for planning a will. Of the approximately 20 per cent of the testators who made their wills after the death of the decedent, the percentage was three times as high for the survivors of intestate decedents as it was for the survivors of testate decedents: 43 per cent to 15 per cent.

The situations that were by far the most salient to will making were getting married and having children. The subjective responses of both testators and planners showed the importance given to family responsibilities in making a will. One hundred twenty-eight of the testators (18 per cent) and 68 of the planners (16 per cent) gave one or both of these reasons as their motivation for testacy.

Related to this emphasis upon familial responsibility was the desire to alter the intestate distribution. One hundred sixty-five of the testators (23 per cent) and 158 of the planners (37 per cent) said they made or would make wills because they preferred not to have their property distributed in strict accordance with the intestate statutes.

A sizable number of respondents had the mistaken notion that having a will solves all the cumbersome problems of property distribution and many survivors were surprised at the delays encountered with probate procedures. One hundred fifty-seven (22 per cent) of the testators and 130 (30 per cent) of the will planners felt that having a will saves time, money, or both. But there are other popular misconceptions about the advantages of a will. One widow remarked, "What good did my husband's will do? I still had to go to court. You shouldn't have to go to court if there is a will." Others, although they did not hold the mistaken belief that the presence of a will obviates the need for all court procedures, did believe that a will makes things go more quickly or that having a will means that the estate settlement costs less. They did not have in mind anything so specific as the saving of estate taxes or dispensing with the administrator's bond. Taxes and the appointment of an executor were categorized separately, and they were mentioned by only 13 testators and seven planners. The client was inclined to put little emphasis on those facets of the will that could challenge the attorney's skill; the client was seldom interested in tax savings except as he or she misconceived the advantages of testacy. The client had given little thought to the selection of an executor; he may have realized the position is one of trust, but he usually knew little or nothing of the executor's specific duties.

The naming of a guardian of the person and estate of minors was the most important motive for making a will among the testators (24 per cent).[3] The choice of a guardian may be of utmost importance to the client; but the qualities required of a guardian are not defined by law except at a minimum level, nor are they necessarily within the lawyer's competence. Among the planners, guardianship ranked equally with marriage and children (both 16 per cent) but was far less important than other reasons, such as altering the intestate distribution (37 per cent) and saving money or time (30 per cent).

The reason given most frequently by survivors (323) for making a will was altering the intestate distribution. The most frequent modification was to will the estate to the spouse with the objective of maintaining family continuity.

3. Guardians were rarely named by the decedent testators (see Chapter 8). Perhaps this was because the probated will was usually written after the children had achieved their majority. Or perhaps custom is changing in regard to the testamentary appointment of guardians.

This concern for altering the distribution in order to meet the individual's perception of what is an equitable distribution raises the basic question of testamentary freedom: How much freedom should the testator be allowed?

Testamentary Freedom

A Nebraska survey of 860 adults demonstrated the popularity of sentiments in favor of restricting testamentary freedom. A majority felt the law should not permit parents to disinherit their children nor to discriminate among them.[4] The majority disagreed with the present law that allows both disinheritance and discrimination.[5]

The issue of testamentary freedom and concomitant notions of family responsibility in the modern period of history has been a source of much discussion and debate. Concern with this question led to an investigation of the study respondents' feelings about testamentary freedom. A Likert-type testamentary freedom scale was devised, consisting of five statements with five degrees of agreement-disagreement.[6] The scale had possible scores from 5 to 25. Low scores indicated a preference for restriction; high scores, a preference for freedom. The statements were as follows:

1. When a person makes a will, he or she should be required by law to leave money or property to his or her minor children.
2. When a man makes a will, he should be required by law to leave money or property to his wife.
3. When a woman makes a will, she should be required by law to leave money or property to her husband.
4. When a person makes a will, he should be required by law to leave money or property to adult children.
5. When a person makes a will, he should be required by law to leave the same amount to all children.[7]

4. Julius Cohen et al., *Parental Authority: The Community and the Law* (New Brunswick, N.J.: Rutgers University Press, 1958), p. 77.
5. In the Cuyahoga County study, excluding those cases where children were disinherited in favor of a surviving spouse, where children survived, a significant minority of the decedent testators disinherited or discriminated among their children.
6. A discussion of Likert-type scales is found in many methodology texts, for example, Claire Selltiz et al., *Research Methods in Social Relations* (New York: Henry Holt and Company, Inc., 1959), pp. 366–369.
7. A determination of the discriminating power of the questions was made on a subsample of 95.

Question Number	First Quartile	Fourth Quartile	Difference
1	1.892	3.285	1.393
2	1.750	3.178	1.328
3	1.714	3.357	1.543
4	2.250	4.035	1.785
5	2.464	3.964	1.500

Questions 2 and 3, which concern the requirement to leave money to spouses, do not go beyond the present legal situation.[8] There is no legal requirement to leave money to minor children; in fact, wills are often written precisely to avoid the complications of property falling into the hands of minors. Neither are there requirements to leave money to adult children or to leave the same amount to all children.

It was hypothesized that a preference for testamentary freedom would be positively related to higher socioeconomic status, specifically to higher education, higher income, and more prestigious occupations. Education is the only measure that pertains strictly to the survivor himself. The two measures of socioeconomic status refer to the family. "Income" is monthly household income, and "occupation" is the major breadwinner's occupation whether or not he is the survivor. Education and occupation are coded according to the Hollingshead categories.[9]

The mean scores on testamentary freedom for the survivor population, by education, income, and occupation, are given in Tables 9–2, 9–3, and 9–4.

Although differences were small, categories of persons who were better educated, wealthier, and in "higher" occupations did favor a greater degree of testamentary freedoom. This preference may be interpreted as based on the desire to make the best allocation for the whole family, thus meeting the norm of familial responsibility. These respondents were perhaps better able to understand the distinction between a moral obligation and legal compulsion. They valued freedom and opposed legal restraints that may not have been in consonance with the realities of their particular situations.[10]

All survivors were given the following statement and were asked to indicate whether or not it was true: "When a person makes a will, he should be

8. A person need not leave any part of his or her estate to the surviving spouse, but if the deceased died testate, most states give the surviving spouse an option to renounce the will and take a forced share. A widow has this option in all states except the Dakotas. In 1962 the widower lacked the right in eleven states. (See Chapter 2, p. 25.)

Professor Allison Dunham, in personal correspondence of 24 April 1968, indicated: "In the recent attempt at revision of probate law undertaken by the National Conference, we have discovered in talking with lawyers about the 'non-barrable' share of the surviving spouse that the lawyers are prepared to admit that a client who is determined to 'disinherit' his spouse may easily do so by a series of lifetime conveyances and the lawyers are also prepared to admit . . . that very few testators in fact attempt to disinherit the surviving spouse. They then argue that a major function of the 'non-barrable share' is to permit them, as custodian of the general cultural mores as to what is proper at death, to inform a client by an appeal to third party authority that 'you should not' attempt to disinherit the spouse."

9. August B. Hollingshead, *Two-Factor Index of Social Position*, mimeographed (New Haven, Conn., 1957).

10. Samuel Stouffer, *Communism, Conformity and Civil Liberties* (Garden City, N.Y.: Doubleday & Company, Inc., 1955). Stouffer believes the tolerance of the educated to be based upon their exposure to different values.

TABLE 9–2 SURVIVORS' TESTAMENTARY FREEDOM SCORE, BY EDUCATION

Education	Mean Score[a]	Number
Graduate school	16.23	98
College graduate	16.00	108
Some college	14.86	212
High school graduate	14.49	388
Some high school	13.43	261
8 years grade school	12.47	87
Less than 8 years	12.44	69
Total	14.34	1,223[b]

[a] Scores range from 5 to 25; the higher the score, the greater the preference for freedom.
[b] Education unknown for 11 survivors.

TABLE 9–3 SURVIVORS' TESTAMENTARY FREEDOM SCORE, BY INCOME

Monthly Household Income	Mean Score[a]	Number
$1,501 and over	16.26	82
$1,001–$1,500	15.46	129
$801–$1,000	14.75	157
$601–$800	14.39	187
$401–$600	14.09	317
$201–$400	13.31	156
$200 or less	13.27	93
Total	14.37	1,121[b]

[a] Scores range from 5 to 25; the higher the score, the greater the preference for freedom.
[b] Income unknown for 113 survivors.

TABLE 9–4 SURVIVORS' TESTAMENTARY FREEDOM SCORE, BY OCCUPATION OF BREADWINNER

Breadwinner's Occupation	Mean Score[a]	Number
Major professionals and top executives	16.37	113
Managers and lesser professionals	15.25	129
Administrators, small business, and minor professionals	14.79	168
Clerical, sales, and technicians	14.10	203
Skilled manual	13.97	244
Semiskilled manual	13.98	129
Unskilled manual	13.44	34
Total	14.54	1,020[b]

[a] Scores range from 5 to 25; the higher the score, the greater the preference for freedom.
[b] Not employed, 204; occupation unknown, 10.

allowed to leave his money or property to whomsoever he pleases." Altogether, 900 persons (73 per cent) agreed with the statement. But 724 (80 per cent) of these same 900 persons had previously agreed with one or more of the restrictive statements. The majority of survivors were caught in a logical inconsistency. For example, they agreed that the law ought to require people to leave money to adult children, which is in sharp contrast with the position that a person should be allowed to leave his money to whomever he wished. A total of 87 persons who agreed with all five restrictive statements took the contrary position that a person should have unrestricted testamentary freedom. The ambiguous posture of most respondents suggests that the majority want it both ways. Perhaps they feel that there is considerable merit in the existing statute if the individual does not abuse his right to testamentary freedom. On the other hand, they may believe in testamentary freedom as a privilege in a free society, and with this privilege comes responsibility. The law acts as a monitor and permits the exercise of testamentary freedom in a responsible manner.

There were 176 persons (14 per cent of the survivor group) who took a position of absolute testamentary freedom. These individuals differed from the entire survivor population in that they were slightly better educated, had higher incomes, and were employed in more prestigious occupations. For the survivor population, the median educational level was high school graduation; occupational category was lower-white-collar; and income ranged from $401 to $600 a month. For the "freedom" group, the median educational level was some college; occupational level was upper-white-collar; and income ranged from $601 to $800 a month. The mean age was 48.4 years for the survivor population but 45 years for the freedom group. There was virtually no difference regarding the condition of testacy; 58 per cent of the survivors were testate, as compared with 57 per cent of the freedom group.

Legal sophistication of will makers. Making a will provides some socialization into testamentary options. The individual learns the available legal devices and which one is most appropriate to his situation. Such learning does not necessarily imply mastery of the intricate processes and mechanisms of probate law. Few are able to achieve this type of knowledge. Furthermore, this capability is more to be expected of the lawyer than of the client.

Will makers and intestate individuals had similar testamentary freedom scores: 14.44 for the testate and 14.36 for the intestate. There were, however, differences between the two groups in examining individual statements on increasing or restricting testamentary freedom. This supports the hypothesis that the testate are slightly more sophisticated than the intestate about inheritance law. An examination of each of these statements helps to clarify the differences between the two groups. The first two statements have some basis in law and restrict testamentary freedom.

"1. When a man makes a will, he should be required by law to leave money or property to his wife." Although the law is not stated this way, the effect is

the same, since a widow may elect to take a statutory share of the estate if the testator wills her nothing or a smaller portion than the statutory share; 74 per cent of the testate survivors, as compared with 70 per cent intestate, agreed with this statement.

"2. *When a woman makes a will, she should be required by law to leave money or property to her husband.*" According to Ohio law and the majority of jurisdictions, the widower's rights are the same as the widow's; 68 per cent of the testators agreed with this statement, as compared with 64 per cent of the intestate.

The following three statements restrict testamentary freedom and have no legal basis.

"3. *When a person makes a will, he or she should be required by law to leave money or property to his or her minor children.*" In this case, 57 per cent of the testate, as compared with 62 per cent of the intestate, agreed with the statement.

"4. *When a person makes a will, he or she should be required by law to leave money or property to adult children.*" Among the testate, 25 per cent agreed; among the intestate, 28 per cent agreed.

"5. *When a person makes a will, he or she should be required by law to leave the same amount to all children.*" In this case, 33 per cent of the testate, as compared with 39 per cent of the intestate, concurred.

These differences between the testate and the intestate, although small, are in a direction that is consistent with the hypothesis that the former are better informed than the latter about the laws of property disposition. More of the testate appear to know what the law provides. However, it was not determined whether testators possessed a higher level of knowledge than the intestate prior to their will making or whether it is a consequence of their encounters with lawyers and the legal system.

Qualifications of freedom. The survivors were asked to indicate the conditions under which they would limit or allow full testamentary freedom. Those who agreed that a person should be able to leave his estate to whomever he pleases were asked, "Can you think of any circumstances in which this freedom ought *not to be* allowed?" The survivor who took the opposing position (that testamentary freedom should be restricted) was asked, "Can you think of any circumstance in which this freedom ought to *be* allowed?"

Nearly one-fourth of the survivors expressed the view that no conditions or circumstances would persuade them to qualify their stance (see Table 9–5).

The largest number (35 per cent) would restrict individual freedom for the interests of the family. Some confined themselves to the nuclear family, but others favored restricted freedom in the interests of the extended kin. Typical responses were: "not in the event that he has blood kinfolk" and "only if there is enough after minor children and the spouse are provided for." The ob-

TABLE 9–5 SURVIVORS' QUALIFICATIONS OF TESTAMENTARY FREEDOM

Qualification	Number	Per Cent
No qualifications	300	24.3
Family obligations	437	35.4
Competency of testator	197	16.0
Characteristic of beneficiary	130	10.5
Combination	149	12.1
Other	21	1.7
Total	1,234	100.0

ligation to look after the widow was mentioned many more times than the obligation toward the widower; in fact, the widower or husband was never mentioned specifically, but only included in the more general term "spouse." A few persons felt the obligations to kin should be restricted for inherited property but not for property that was the result of lifetime earnings. Others distinguished between those with large estates and those with the more modest ones. Those who are less wealthy should be restricted; those who are more wealthy should be free to leave part of their fortune to nonrelated persons and philanthropic institutions. Testamentary freedom was considered to be justifiable when there was a surplus equity and the testator could take care of his family and still afford to exercise his freedom.

The respondents expressed concern over the competency of the testator and the influence of unscrupulous persons upon the testator, and they would support restrictive measures in such instances. Current laws that disqualify those of unsound mind from writing a will or invalidate the testament of such a person were supported. A person was not considered competent if he was unduly influenced. The elderly were supposed to be especially subject to undue influence. They were thought to be looking for companionship and therefore to be susceptible to flattery by fortune hunters and confidence men. Addiction to drugs was also thought to be a sign of incompetence. One respondent believed persons confined to Veterans Administration hospitals were particularly apt to be subjected to undue influence, and he recommended that there should be tighter controls on the VA.

Statements concerning the characteristics of the beneficiary were more diverse. Some felt that the testator should be obligated to provide for the needy members of his kinship group. Some persons felt that an incapacitated relative should be taken care of first and then other family members; automatic claims on the testator's bounty were not accepted. Some of this sentiment for the needy was based on a verbalized concern for the community: "the handicapped would otherwise be a burden on the community" or "a child with a chronic illness or a senile spouse must be taken care of or they will be a public burden." In contrast with the obligation to take care of the deserving needy, the testator should be prevented from giving to the unworthy. Cats and dogs were most frequently mentioned among the unworthy. The Communist party, Ku Klux Klan, a golfing association, subversive organizations in or out of the country, and any other "un-American causes" were mentioned as unworthy. Unrestricted bequests should not be permitted to the following types of individuals: alcoholics, dope addicts, subversives, paramours, the mentally ill, the mentally retarded, gamblers, and criminals.[11]

Although a large number of persons would restrict individual freedom in favor of family welfare, there were others who felt that the welfare of the family and/or testator required testamentary freedom. Their comments were in line with Jeremy Bentham's observations that the power of making a will encourages family virtue, represses vice, assures the testator against ingratitude, and generally keeps the family house in order.[12] Some of the situations in which respondents felt the testator should be free to disinherit kin and bestow his goods upon others were:

If you were a Catholic and couldn't divorce your wife, but you wanted to, then you shouldn't have to leave her your money.

You may be treated better by strangers than by your own family, or your child may be a wastrel and throw the money away.

If you had a second wife and she was no damn good. . . .

If the kids are juvenile delinquents and disown you. . . .

Members of his own family may have nothing in common, may not even be friendly. A friend might have stood by.

Thus, both restriction and freedom were justified in terms of moral principles. Freedom was justified in terms of reciprocity; restriction was justified by absolute standards.

Analysis and Implications of Client Attitudes Toward Will Making

Only a small number of the survivor population deliberately intended to remain intestate. Whether those who planned to make a will actually did so, however, is a moot question. In part it may depend upon the extent to which these persons eventually experience the circumstances that pushed those who were already testate. To see the advantages of a will is not sufficient; those

11. These persons are considered beyond the pale. Schwartz reminds us that, "the gift is a way of dramatizing group boundaries." Barry Schwartz, "The Social Psychology of the Gift," *American Journal of Sociology* 73 (July, 1967):10.
12. Jeremy Bentham, "Utilitarian Basis of Succession," *The Rational Basis of Legal Institutions,* ed. John H. Wigmore (New York: The Macmillan Company, 1923), pp. 420–421.

advantages must be relevant to one's own situation. It should be remembered that most of the intestate were already middle-aged. The majority of those who made a will did so before age 45. Some of the testators made their wills when they served in the military or entered a religious community. The planner will probably not experience this particular kind of change in personal circumstances. The planner will, however, be increasingly subject to the pressures of old age and illness.

The most important push into testacy for both testators and planners was a change in family circumstances: getting married and having children. The weight of responsibility for family members was not borne lightly. The vast majority of the survivors believed in testamentary freedom, but they also believed that a will maker should be required to leave money to his spouse and to his minor children. The majority thus did not believe in absolute testamentary freedom, but rather in a qualified freedom. It was felt that the testator should be free to dispose of his property as he wished if he had no family or after he had provided for his family.

As hypothesized, those who were better educated, employed in more prestigious occupations, and who earned higher incomes were more likely to take the stance of freedom. The results were consistent in the hypothesized direction.

Testators and planners had similar scores on the testamentary freedom scale, although they differed slightly in their answers to individual questions. Those who were already testate were most likely to restrict freedom where the law was itself restrictive, for example, in reference to spouses. Also, they were more likely to express a preference for freedom where the law allowed freedom, for example, with respect to children. The differences between testators and planners in an item analysis were consistent with the hypothesis that the testate are more sophisticated in matters of law, but again the differences between the two groups were not extreme.

The preceding analysis has implications for the lawyer-client relationship. It appears that the lawyer not only has to write a will that disposes of the client's property to his chosen successors but also in some cases may be called upon to influence the client's choice of successors. For example, he can point out the disadvantages of leaving property to minor children. The client in most instances is concerned with the welfare of his family and kinship group, but he may be ignorant of the means to achieve his goals. Where the client perceives the immediacy of death, it may be important for the attorney to determine if the client's plans are well considered and satisfactory for potential inheritors in the foreseeable future. The attorney may also find it necessary to educate the client concerning the duties of the executor so that this position will not simply be given as an unwelcome honor to a favored family member. In many cases, it might also be helpful if the lawyer explained that having a will does not mean probate proceedings are avoided. Undoubtedly some of the misconceptions of the testator are shared by his family and contribute to their later dissatisfaction.

Lawyer

Estate planning is preventive law, and will making, as one facet of estate planning, is usually done with legal assistance. The role of the attorney in the estate-planning phase of the inheritance process will be examined in this section. The approach of the study was an investigation of the lawyer's self-definition of his role in this area—an area in which the average lawyer in the sample had had much experience.[13]

The lawyer-client relationship is voluntary. With minor exceptions, for example, in cases where testators are compelled to make a will by religious authorities, the client makes the decision to be testate and chooses his attorney. The lawyer-client relationship is also fiduciary; at this stage in the inheritance process, the lawyer may be the only person, other than the testator himself, who is aware of the testator's aims and desires. The size and composition of the estate may be unknown to the testator's family and closest friends; the natural objects of the testator's bounty may be uninformed of their status in his last will and testament.

The lawyer's compensation for drafting the will is on a fee-for-service basis. Complexity of will provisions, income of client, and possible future business are the basic criteria in assessing the fee. Although this relationship conforms to the professional model, a missing element is the professional monopoly in an area of competence; such a monopoly is scarcely found in the field of estate planning, where banks, estate planners, and insurance agents encroach upon the legal profession's domain.

Image of the Client

The lawyer's view of his client was elicited in two ways. The lawyer was asked, "Could you describe the ideal client in the wills area?" Indirectly, the lawyer's image of his client was reconstructed from the answers to several questions dealing with the difficulties lawyers said they faced in this area of practice.

The lawyer has the license to obtain, and the client is required to make known, information concerning matters of a private nature.[14] The client may

13. Forty per cent of the lawyers said they drafted over fifty wills a year; only five lawyers drafted fewer than ten a year. Over 80 per cent of the lawyers had been in practice over ten years. Thus, through the years, most of these lawyers had drawn up hundreds of wills.

14. Everett Hughes, *Men and Their Work* (New York: The Free Press, 1958), p. 81. See also Robert Merton and Elinor Barber, "Sociological Ambivalence," *Sociological Theory, Values and Sociocultural Change: Essays in Honor of Pitirim A. Sorokin*, ed. Edward Tiryakian (New York: The Free Press, 1963), p. 112.

hold back essential information if he does not have sufficient confidence in the attorney. Understandably the lawyer appreciates clients who trust him.

A client who realizes the need for a will and for basic estate planning, who is willing to completely confide in his attorney, who is able to consider problems raised by the attorney in an objective manner, and who will finally make decisions in carrying out his basic desires as to disposition which will be in accordance with the legal advice of his counsel is the ideal client.

The ideal client is one who tells you everything, who doesn't hold back anything even if it means bringing out family skeletons, because sometimes skeletons can make a difference.

A client may trust his lawyer and yet be unable to provide the necessary information, as illustrated in the following examples of lawyers' difficulties with their clients.

They frequently wish to have a will drawn because of some pending trip and fail to have at their fingertips all the necessary information to do a proper job of estate planning.

I have a great number of clients with vast real estate holdings and with personal distribution of these holdings among the family without keeping adequate records. Small parcels of property, but a lot of them. They are not exactly sure what is in their estate.

Trust is part of the Boy Scout image held by attorneys in the sample regarding the ideal client. One attorney stated it succinctly: "The ideal client is a good, honest individual—truthful and sincere."

A will is an important document, and the lawyers do not care to draft wills for clients who have not given the matter serious thought. Nor do they wish to aid and abet the person who wants to use his will as an instrument of vengeance. Attorneys do not see themselves as psychologists or psychiatrists. They would like a client who has previously determined his beneficiaries according to a "normal" or "fair" pattern and who does not change his mind thereafter. They desire a normal business transaction. But if will making became too routine and perfunctory, there would be a corresponding loss of creativity in providing personal service in an area charged with strong emotional feelings; in essence, there would be a loss of one dimension of the professional role.

One problem is dealing with psychoneurotics who when in emotional upheavals consult a lawyer, people who on impulse want to disinherit some members of the family and include strangers. Then twenty-four hours later they want to change it.

I recall many instances when I made a will where the party went home and tore it up because he was so confused he didn't know what to do. You have a problem with people who are emotionally unbalanced and want to change their will every other week or month. This type of will would be the simplest thing in the world to break.

Some clients have vacillating minds. They are overzealous to have certain members of the family have the estate, due to recent kindnesses, and forget what has happened in the years before.

Remarriage is one family problem singled out by lawyers as being most troublesome whether the second marriage has actually occurred or is anticipated. Hence, the remarried client is less than ideal.

Second marriages are always a big problem, especially in the absence of an antenuptial agreement to provide that all children are somehow going to receive a fair share from their parent; and it is not a question of luck as to which will die first. Or in the first marriage one spouse will hesitate to give it to the surviving one because he or she might remarry.

Most common is that a large percentage of husbands and wives are apprehensive as to what the survivor will do with money that comes into their hands. They frequently fear remarriage and that the estate they have worked together to accumulate will be placed in the hands of someone who put forth no effort in its accumulation.

Clients wish to restrict the use of their property after death in a fashion that normally isn't justified. Example: A husband or wife desiring to have the surviving spouse have the benefit of the estate but subject to a restriction such as remarriage. And then there are complications in second marriage situations with children of each spouse. These can be prevented by antenuptial agreement, but that doesn't happen as often as I think it should.

The lawyer in a remarriage case is dealing with a highly charged, affective interpersonal situation about which there is considerable folklore and which has its roots in history. The belief that marriages made in this world are permanent and even continue in the hereafter is a general conception steeped in religious and cultural traditions. The thought of remarriage of one's spouse arouses less than a charitable response. It is an option a spouse can take, but "I will be damned if they will dance on my grave; I did not work myself into the grave for that!" The attorney is aware of the problems of remarriage, but he is less informed of the reasons for them. Since he dislikes the role of family counselor, he ignores the problem and stereotypes the client as a difficult one.

A minority of attorneys were found to associate wealth with their picture of the ideal client. For a few, the ideal client is not only wealthy but also has his wealth in the form that poses few complications: "Lots of money in stock and bonds—or cash, no real estate." "One who has a large estate, all or most of the assets in the state of Ohio." One lawyer preferred complications as a challenge to his legal acumen and for the probability of a higher pay-off.

Getting into a fantasy, aren't you? I like the client with unlimited money and unlimited legal and tax problems that will necessitate a tremendous amount of legal work; one with previous experience with legal charges.

Another lawyer was more realistic.

How many millions should he have? That's awfully difficult. Actually he would be one who had an estate in the area of $250,000 to $500,000 and who would take the time to prepare the intelligent will covering all the contingencies; who would let tax considerations be secondary to actual disposition of property. The millionaire has a million advisers before he gets to the attorney.

Attorneys hope not only to draw up the will but also to administer the estate. Fees for estate settlements are determined not on the basis of time but on the size of the estate. Given this method of compensation, it is to be expected that the lawyers would prefer wealthy clients.

Various elements compose the lawyer's view of the ideal client in the area of will making. He likes the client who has sufficient equity to make the preparation of the will challenging to his skills and which, because of its size and complexity, can provide adequate compensation. He appreciates the stable, well-informed client who has unsullied personal traits and characteristics. As the lawyers described their basic job in drafting the will and their method of counseling the client, it seemed that their view of their own role was predicated upon the client being close to their ideal.

Drafting the Will

The extent to which lawyers influence their clients at the will-making stage was of particular interest in this study. Over 85 per cent of the lawyers applied the concept of testamentary freedom in counseling their clients. Attorneys urged their clients to make their own decisions regarding the disposition of their property. Although this practice suggests that the attorney is liberated from the cultural restraints on testamentary freedom, it is impossible to overlook the fact that the lawyer, like his client, is a product of our culture and that in subtle and unobtrusive ways he influences his client to make the right decision. This decision is generally in consonance with maximizing the well-being and stability of the family over generational time.

Of the 70 attorneys, 60 were characterized as having a nondirective approach to counseling their clients. They were first and foremost concerned with getting the facts. Given this knowledge, the attorney's role is to interpret correctly the intent of the client and not to impose his ideas upon the client.

Ten of the lawyers routinely advised the client concerning who should be the legatees. Two of these attorneys suggested that clients consider the differential needs of family members and charitable giving.

I try to find out were they ever helped by an organization. If they were, I feel they ought to leave something to such an organization. Also if they have kids and one is in a better position than the other, I suggest it might make life a little easier to give one a little extra.

I usually ask how he would like his estate to go. If he is better off than average means after making provisions for the family, I go into the question of charities and bequests to favorite organizations. I usually try to have them consider churches, schools, and hospitals for benefits. Whenever indicated by the composition of the estate and the desire of the testator, I discuss trusts.

The remaining eight lawyers were concerned with the testator's family and gave specific advice.

I ask what the client has in mind, a simple or complex will. If whatever he has is the result of marriage, I feel that everything should be left to the surviving spouse in the first instance and then to the children. Generally the client will always indicate that this is what he had in mind in the first place. I would attempt to discourage any disinheritance of the spouse or children.

I just talk to them and ask them what they want to do; what their wishes are. Then I usually try to give them my opinion as to the needs of the children and surviving spouse. I always try to point out that a woman needs as much education as a man. Then we just talk it out and whatever they want goes into the will. Usually they go along with my suggestions.

Another facet of the lawyer's will-making role is the attorney's relationship with family members other than the testator. Eighty per cent of the sample indicated that they never consulted with other family members, such as the spouse or children. This finding suggests that lawyers perceive the relationship with the client to be a fiduciary one and that under ordinary circumstances consultation with other family members would be unprofessional behavior. No attorney consulted with family members routinely or without the permission of the client.

Attorneys may not consult with family members, but they do consult extensively with their law colleagues and other professionals attached to financial institutions. A little over 60 per cent reported consultation with other specialists (see Table 9–6).

Some attorneys will use consultants if their clients request it.

TABLE 9–6 CONSULTATION BEHAVIOR OF LAWYERS REGARDING WILL DRAFTING

Consultation Behavior	Number	Per Cent
Never consults	27	38.6
Consults with bank representatives	17	24.3
Consults with other attorneys	15	21.4
Consults with others[a]	11	15.7
Total	70	100.0

[a] This includes insurance agents, accountants, and so forth.

Lawyer

I consult only if the testator requests it. It's a confidential thing, but sometimes they request it. A lawyer is only allowed to discuss a confidential matter if the client requests it. In the majority of cases it is a family matter between husband and wife. I only talk with bankers or insurance agents when the client requests it. However, with the estate plan you recommend that others be involved because the client does not know all that is involved. I bring in a banker, insurance agent, accountant and have a little seminar on it—but only with his permission.

Consultation is likely to occur if the estate is large or if the property is legally complicated. By and large, consultation is not routine. When it occurs it is usually with associates, partners, or office-space sharers. Only one attorney indicated that family problems were a significant reason for consulting with other professionals—this despite the variety of problems reported, such as disagreement among family members, mental incapacity, second marriages, and minor children.

Slightly less than 40 per cent of the sample were generalists. These attorneys believed that they have the competence to handle whatever legal complexities may arise. The following statements are typical of the attitude of the non-consulting group: "I don't have to consult with anyone, for I draw up simple wills." "They consult me because of my experience. I have never had occasion to consult with anybody else."

For some of these simple wills, a standard form suffices. Thirty-eight lawyers said they used a standard will form for routine cases, either one they devised or adapted from a book form.

I use a standard form extensively—in every simple case. There may be some variations from it, but it is generally routine and repetitious.

We use them to the extent that they fit in with the client's wishes. We adapt them to situations not covered.

I use my own form, a form that includes the best provisions that I am able to find from other sources—Cuyahoga County records, form books, and suggested provisions in legal publications.

Twenty-six attorneys (37 per cent) indicated that all wills were written individually.

This division over the use of standard forms was reflected also in satisfaction with the compensation for drafting a will. Those who had routinized the drafting of wills tended to be well satisfied with their compensation; they viewed their participation as minimal and gave full credit to their legal secretaries. In routine cases, will making was viewed more as an ordinary business transaction than as a professional task. Here are two typical responses:

In 90 per cent of the cases, most wills are pretty much form. The ordinary will is very routine. Of course, we have a wonderful secretary, and I just say, "draw up a will."

The girls have been here seven and sixteen years and have made so many simple wills that I can give them the names of the testator and beneficiaries and let them draw up the will.

The drafting of a will was often not thought of as a distinct activity with a fair price agreed upon by members of the bar. There was a minimum scale recommended by a local bar association, but only 16 attorneys said they determined their fees accordingly. The majority of attorneys felt that while drafting a will resulted in minimal financial reward, it was very good public relations. It was considered by these attorneys to be a community service resulting in good will and familiarity between the public and the law profession. Public service and good will were related to long-range economic gains. Will making was seen as the initial step to more lucrative estate administration. Here is how several attorneys put it:

Drawing up the will creates a close contact with the client. It creates a climate of their thinking of you as their family lawyer. They'll use you in the future and generally at death.

I do many wills for free. I urge people to make wills, and I let them know if they can't pay, I'll do it free. Of course, if I were maintaining a full-time office, I'd have to cover overhead. [This was a part-time lawyer holding political office.]

If I had to, I'd do it for nothing. Often this is the first time people have come to an attorney. I tend to set the fee on the low side, because we don't want to scare people away.

You charge for a will with the expectation you will eventually get the estate—and then compensation will be received.

In general, fees charged ranged from $15 to $35 for an uncomplicated individual will and from $25 to $50 for reciprocal (husband-wife) wills. A minority of attorneys object to will drafting as a method of public relations or as a speculation on future estate business.

I'm paid adequately because I won't do it for less. Will drafting has got to pay a reasonable going wage, based on a reasonable hourly rate . . . none of this "loss leader" stuff. That's crazy in my book.

In this office, we charge for estate planning. We don't plan to make it up in probate.

There were several reasons some lawyers felt they could not charge an adequate fee. First, they thought the public was unwilling to compensate them for the work involved. Attorneys who believed the compensation to be inadequate expressed feelings that they were working for charity without receiving the ennobling benedictions for such efforts. They felt strongly that clients did not understand the time involved in drawing up an adequate will and were unwilling to pay a professional fee for rendered services.

Because people don't know what's involved or I don't tell them or something—I suppose because we attempt to charge what people expect to pay and it's not adequate. I draw wills for next to nothing and expect to get a return from handling the estate. People don't expect to pay for the time it takes. I try to guess what I think the client would like to pay.

I am undercompensated. If done properly, it requires more time than the public realizes in terms of a proper estate plan. The general public has a notion that it should be no more than a $25 job.

You can't charge people what it's worth to prepare their will. If you could charge a millionaire proportionately, it would even out, but you can't because most wealthy people got that way by squeezing pennies.

Also, attorneys tend to undercut one another, a practice that lowers the cost of will making. This competition makes it difficult for an attorney to charge for actual time in preparing the document. Two attorneys complained:

People shop for the cheapest one. Some attorneys will do it for $5, but I'd never go below $25.

I'd like to charge the bar association's recommended fee—if everyone else did—but some lawyers charge nothing.

A self-proclaimed rate buster said:

I have been severely criticized by other attorneys for ruining the profession. I should charge a lot more; they are absolutely right.

There was an indication of competition from lay individuals or entities, especially banks. The attorneys were faced with the basic problem of their inability to control an area of practice that historically belongs to them but in the modern period is equally claimed by banks, insurance companies, and other institutional systems.

In essence, in the will-drafting stage it appears that the public has cornered the legal profession. Charges for what can be considered routine wills are low. From the time standpoint, the attorney is not adequately compensated if he puts in any time at all. The will has to be considered as "an accommodation for people you hope to get business from." Perhaps the attorneys' approach toward will drafting can best be summed up with the words of one sample member: "If you wanted to make your living drawing up wills, you'd be a hungry boy."

Encroachment

The lawyers in this study resented the banks for engaging in wills-estates work. This unhappiness reflected differences over scarce pecuniary rewards more than professional postures and practices regarding estate work. Seventy per cent of the lawyers thought competition with banks was a major problem in the will-making area. There is obviously a breakdown in communications between financial institutions and the average member of the bar. It appears to be a battle of David against Goliath. The following outspoken expressions indicate the meaning of this competition for the lawyer:

Competition? Yeah—because they are able to advertise their trust services and they get paid for the administration of a trust. As a consequence, in order to bring in trust money they will render a great deal of advice. What's worse is that the most incompetent attorney can have the bank do the whole thing for him. The bank is like his ghost writer. That being the case, the lawyers who know what they are doing can't really be paid for their time because the client can get it wholesale—either from the bank directly or from the attorney who doesn't know what he is doing, so has the bank write the will and doesn't have to charge much. All of this is extremely detrimental to the client's welfare.

I believe banks and insurance companies should be kept out of the wills-estates area. I find insurance companies are prone to give much misinformation for purposes of selling insurance by rather poorly trained salesmen and giving poor tax advice. Banks, primarily in drawing up suggested wills, are more interested in obtaining trusteeships or executorships than they are with true consideration of testators' problems. However, if the estate is large, work done by some attorneys is not especially knowledgeable.

There is competition not with insurance companies so much as with banks. Banks advertise their trust departments and with that the testamentary trust. My experience is that they advertise, which cuts into our business. They have no compunction in drawing wills and doing legal work. If I can't advertise to get business, their legal department should not be able to do so. I have an abhorrence of the unauthorized practice of law. I will not, if I can help it, recommend a bank as trustee. On the other hand, I find that their trust departments do a good job. They know their business. I am opposed to the size of the fees and the fact that they are lay people.

A few attorneys intimated that a conspiracy existed between the banks and large law firms. In answer to the competition question, one lawyer stated:

There is no doubt about it, particularly with trust companies and with big law firms who have a peculiar method of soliciting business. Larger firms frequently employ the son of a wealthy man in order to get the business of his father's estate.

In the words of another lawyer in the sample:

Banks, where they don't handle it themselves, direct legal work to firms with whom they have a close connection; so they control a great deal of estate work in that manner.

Those who perceived no competition had established a symbiotic relationship with trust departments of banks. A successful practice in any profession is usually achieved with assistance.[15] In the wills-estates area, the bank's referral of a client may be worth more than a dozen "through the door" clients or referrals from other lawyers. The bank-referred client is likely to be wealthier than the average; in addition, the bank assists the lawyer by helping with the preparation of the requisite documents. An attorney who works in conjunction with the banks receives valuable assistance and ample financial rewards for a minimum effort.

The hostility of our attorneys toward banks because of the latter's involvement in estate work reflected unhappiness over competition for economic gain as well as priorities of professional practice. Banks are legally entitled to act as executors and trustees. Accordingly, they are able to solicit business in this respect. It would appear that their advertising concerning the value of estate planning is of social benefit. It makes people think about what will happen to their progeny and other kin when they die.

Banks have frequently been faced with the problem of how far they can advise clients on wills-estates matters without being accused of the unauthorized practice of law. The drafting of wills, trusts, and like instruments coupled with responsibility for the estate plan is a function for the attorney and not the bank. Some attorneys were concerned that their colleagues might be inclined to shift this responsibility to the banks in a *de facto* manner by merely signing the instruments and thus losing control over this professional area of practice. Ordinarily trust departments prepare drafts of instruments for the attorney. These drafts are so expertly done that they may turn out to be final documents. The attorney is in the middle between the bank and the client, and the bank is close to the practice of law. Yet the lawyer ultimately has the decision-making function. If he can control the bank, he maintains his autonomy in this area of practice. In the Cleveland area, he has enhanced his prospects of autonomy by the formulation of a code of conduct for banks that is intended to regulate respective spheres of influence (see Appendix F).

Generalizations Regarding Lawyers and the Will-making Process

The attorney engaged in will making voices a philosophy of being client-oriented and adhering vigorously to his confidential relationship with the testator. He is nondirective in eliciting the wishes of the client but is guided by legal and cultural norms that he has internalized as his own. These norms become operative when he confronts a client whose desires for distribution offend his sensibilities.

The attorneys are general practitioners rather than estate planners. The

15. For the analogous situation among physicians, see Oswald Hall, "The Stages of a Medical Career," *American Journal of Sociology* 53 (1948): 327–336.

mode of activity suggests meeting the exigencies of the situation rather than the conditions of long-range planning. According to James F. Farr:

> Estate planning is not susceptible of precise definition; it is as broad as the human imagination. It involves the use and arrangement of property for and among the members of a family group under a planned design affording the greatest enjoyment to the whole group commensurate with sufficient conservation.[16]

The lawyers resent the intrusion of banks in the estate-planning area and covet the banks' more lucrative clientele. The propensity of the lawyers to "go it alone" is related to their notions that small estates require simple wills. A frequent expression was, "I draw simple wills." They state that small estates do not necessitate the drafting of trusts. Fifty-four per cent of the lawyers utilized some type of standard form in drafting wills. The implication is that they harmonize the type of will with the testator's financial worth. This is done even if it is recognized that persons with small estates have as many affective relationships and family problems as individuals with large estates, making estate planning a difficult task irrespective of the assets involved.

Some attorneys find this area of law practice exciting and capable of tapping their most creative impulses. The challenge is to meet the expectations of a client, maximizing the client's expression of testamentary freedom within the constraints imposed by law and culture. Simultaneously, there must be a consideration of the needs of the survivors, who are potential clients of the attorney. The development of an attorney's practice over client generational time (father to son, the older generational family to the younger one) is a natural characteristic of estate planning. The lawyer who can approach will making as a creative task and think through, with his client, the implications of the will for the next generation is guaranteeing for himself a legacy as important as that received by the inheritors.

The possibility that the lawyer will provide for his own retirement on fees from administration of estates is no conjecture. It is expected and achieved by lawyers with a heavy estate-planning practice in which will making alone would be a profitless task. This is an excellent illustration of deferred gratification in which will making is the first step of a process that will provide ample returns in the later years of the lawyer's practice. Will making, with its fiduciary relationship, provides the attorney with the opportunity to establish a relationship with the family that will place him in a favorable position to get the estate business that can logically follow.

Partial substantiation of the study hypotheses concerning intergenerational practice, deferred gratification, and retirement security for lawyers from estate administration came from data analyzed by the age of the attorney in

16. James F. Farr, *An Estate Planner's Handbook*, 3d ed. (Boston: Little, Brown and Company, 1966), p. 3.

TABLE 9–7 MEAN NUMBER OF WILLS AND ESTATES YEARLY AND RATIO OF WILLS TO ESTATES, BY AGE GROUP OF ATTORNEY

Age Group of Attorney	Mean Number of Wills	Mean Number of Estates	Ratio of Wills to Estates
20–29	25	10	2.5
30–39	55	15	3.7
40–49	35	15	2.3
50–59	25	15	1.7
60–69	20	20	1.0

relation to the number of wills drafted and estates managed in a given year (see Table 9–7). Lawyers in their sixties achieved a balance between the number of wills drafted and the number of estates opened in a year. Up to that age, the lawyers drafted far more wills than opened new estate cases. In the twenties, the ratio appears nearly as favorable as in the forties; but attorneys in their twenties did not have so large a volume of wills and estates as the older attorneys did. The data are based on a cross section of attorneys at one point in time and do not reflect the change in practice for a given attorney over time. Nevertheless, within the limitations imposed by the data and the assumptions regarding change in estate-planning practice during a particular career, there is some indication that estate administration, with its greater psychic and financial rewards and professional autonomy for the lawyer, comes in the later years of life.

Conclusion

The main reason why individuals made wills was their desire to protect the well-being of members of their immediate families, namely, their spouses and children. The will maker was usually in the childbearing or childrearing stage of the family life cycle and was under the age of 45.

Testamentary freedom, the right of an individual to dispose of his property as he wishes, was viewed in a very special way by the survivors in this study. They stated that an individual should have testamentary freedom but they also felt strongly that a will maker should, and if necessary should be legally required to, leave his property to his spouse and to his minor children. In probing this apparent contradictory position, it was discovered that the survivors felt strongly that the testator should be free to give his equity to whom he pleases, provided he has no immediate family to care for or after he has taken care of their needs. Essentially, they believed that the wealthier individual could and should exercise testamentary freedom because he has sufficient resources to be able to afford this privilege.

This overriding concern expressed by the testators and planners that members of their families be taken care of at the cost of absolute testamentary freedom has implications for the lawyer-client relationship. The desire to provide for kin is so strong that there is a danger that the individual who is faced with the possibility of imminent death may make hasty and short-sighted decisions regarding the provisions of his will. In his desire to provide for his minor children, a client may name them in a will and be unaware of the disadvantages of such an action. The task and responsibility for the lawyer is to educate the client to avoid legal pitfalls and potentially strained intrafamily relationships, which can result from the too hasty naming of legatees, guardians, and executors.

Attorneys did not perceive will making as a highly professional task except for that aspect which involves a fiduciary relationship with the client. Will making was regarded as the entry point into a process that leads to estate administration, the latter providing substantial financial reward and work satisfaction because it permits the greatest exercise of autonomy. (The professional aspects of estate administration will be discussed in subsequent chapters.)

Lawyers were very concerned about the competition in the will-making area from banks, insurance firms, and other economic, religious, and social institutions. The strongest reactions were against banks; the chief reason was competition over scarce financial rewards, as well as professional postures and practices regarding estate work.

The majority of lawyers in this sample were generalists, undertaking by themselves the simplest to the most complex tasks and procedures of will making. The range of complexity varied from using a standard will form to holding a series of meetings with the client and even going as far as involving members of the family who were potential legatees. If necessary, the lawyer employed consultants as specialists, just as generalists in medicine do. The posture assumed by the lawyer was dependent upon his own experience and motivation and that of the client, with the potential size of the estate as an added variable.

Will making was felt to be a possible lead into a family-practitioner relationship that may provide continuous pay-offs in estate administration and other legal business. Estate administration, especially, may provide a regular maintenance income in the later years of the attorney's career, thus reducing his need to seek additional practice.

Chapter 10

Estate Settlement: Purpose and Function of Probate Court

THE PROCESSES of probate and estate administration are discussed in this chapter. Essentially, this means an examination of the purpose and function of the probate court. Although laymen may believe that they know who will take their property at their death, few people have any real understanding of how the transfer is to be effectuated. The objective of this chapter is to describe what happens to an individual's estate when he dies.

The discussion is limited to testate and intestate succession. There are also, of course, the so-called will substitutes (discussed in Chapter 2). Such property arrangements or transfers are mentioned here only as a reminder of their significance as mechanisms for transmitting wealth and property in our society. The important concerns here are probate court assets and such questions as: What happens to a person's estate when he dies? Why is such a procedure necessary? How long does it take? How much does it cost?

Estate settlement is to a great extent both technical and detailed because of statutory control. Insofar as possible, the discussion will be kept general. Where it is necessary to use specific references, Ohio law will be utilized. Therefore the reader should keep in mind the fact that the statutes of his state may not always be in accord with the Ohio Revised Code.

A person's estate must generally be administered whether he dies with or without a will. Although the administration process is basically the same in both testate and intestate succession, the intestate decedent has given up a fundamental right: testamentary freedom, the ability to choose his successors and the manner of their succession. His estate will not necessarily be distributed according to his desires.

Probating the Will

A person may die believing that he has left a will, and yet his estate may pass by intestate succession. The court may reject the will when it is offered for probate; although it is likely that in 99 per cent of the cases, the will is valid.[1] When a will is submitted for probate, the following events occur more

1. See Chapter 8, p. 184.

or less in sequential order. First, the will must be found; probable locations are the testator's home, safe-deposit box, and the office of the attorney who drafted the will. In Ohio and many other states, it may be left for safekeeping with the probate court in the county in which the testator lived.[2] What must be located is the executed will, not an unexecuted carbon copy. Although lost or destroyed wills may be probated if they are unrevoked, the procedure is difficult, and presumptions exist against the validity of such wills.

The will usually names a person or corporation as executor. There are no special requirements for an individual to be an executor. He is likely to be a member of the testator's family, for example, a spouse or a child, or he might be a friend, a business associate, or the attorney who drafted the will. In large estates, where trusts are common, the executor is often a trust company or a bank having trust powers. It is quite common, in such large estates, to have coexecutors, one an individual and the other a bank.

Although it is not necessary for a person to name an executor in his will, it is advantageous for him to do so. Even without an executor, the will would nonetheless be probated and the estate administered, but the court would appoint an administrator to take charge of the estate. Both the executor and administrator are the personal representatives of the estate and act in a fiduciary capacity. The administrator would have to give bond; whereas such a requirement for the executor could be waived by the testator in the will. The administrator appointed might be someone held in low esteem by the decedent during his lifetime, a person he would never have chosen to handle the distribution of his estate. By using an executor, who, if he is a near relative, may not wish compensation for his services, the testator will likely avoid red tape and save time and expense.

The executor is the logical person to petition for the probate of the will, although any other interested person may offer the will for probate if the executor does not.[3] It should be noted that someone must offer the will for probate because ordinarily the court will not do so on its own motion.

In actuality, the executor will hire an attorney to advise him and to handle the legal work that is involved. Technically, there is no such office as attorney for the estate, although the term is sometimes used to indicate the attorney for the executor or administrator. Some probate courts have adopted rules requiring the designation of counsel for the personal representative. For example, in 1966, the Probate Court of Summit County, Ohio, adopted a rule that requires a personal representative to name the attorney who will represent

2. See Ohio Revised Code 2107.07.

3. Although the interested person is generally one who benefits under the will, it is usually not necessary that the proponent so benefit. He may merely desire to start the proceeding for settlement along proper lines, which is the case where the proponent is a creditor of the deceased.

him in carrying out his duties. This rule further requires that all papers filed by the personal representative either be prepared by the designated attorney or carry a certificate that the attorney has examined the papers and finds them correct and proper.[4]

Even probate courts that do not have such written rules attempt to discourage executors who do not have attorneys. There is much logic behind this approach. Although a person may represent himself in court, a layman attempting to represent another layman is engaged in the unauthorized practice of law. The executor who is not also the sole beneficiary is representing the interests of others, as well as his own interests.[5] Also, in general, legislation prohibits judges or nonlawyer probate court staff members from giving legal advice concerning the administration of estates. Employees of the court, even if they are lawyers by training, are limited to administration of the law. They are not permitted to advise or assist individual litigants.

Thus, the legal work is entrusted by the executor to his attorney, who sees that the will is submitted to the proper court. Such courts, incidentally, may have different names in different states, for example, Probate, Surrogate, or Orphan's Court.

To probate the will means "to prove" the will. *Verifying* relates to matters of external validity. This means that the court's decree will adjudge matters of genuineness, proper execution, and testamentary capacity and also establish that the instrument offered for probate has not been revoked.

On the first visit to probate court, the executor, through his attorney, files the last will and makes application to probate it. In fact, if the witnesses have met with the lawyer and given testimony, and if all persons entitled to notice have waived this right, the will can be probated at once. This is the approach followed in Ohio, and the aforementioned facts indicate a rather informal hearing. If the attorney is unable to obtain waivers from all next of kin, the probate of the will must be set for hearing and notice must be given to designated persons: the surviving spouse and/or next of kin who are residents of Ohio and have not waived. If waiver is not secured from all necessary parties, probate will then proceed in a formal hearing. Although Ohio, like most jurisdictions, has no statutory period within which a will must be established, this study found that most wills were offered for probate within a relatively short time after death. The time between death and application for probate is shown in Table 10–1.

It should be noted that in approximately two-thirds of the testate cases and slightly over half of the intestate cases, application for probate of the will or for letters of administration was made less than one month after death. It is

4. Rule No. 23, Probate Court, Summit County, Ohio (see Appendix G for text).

5. A leading decision in this respect is a Wisconsin case: State ex. rel. Baker v. County Court, 29 Wis. 2d 1, 138 N.W. 2d 162 (1965).

TABLE 10–1 TIME BETWEEN DEATH AND BEGINNING OF PROBATE COURT PROCEEDINGS, BY CONDITION OF TESTACY

Time	Testate		Intestate		Total	
	Number	Per Cent	Number	Per Cent	Number	Per Cent
Unknown	2	.4	1	.5	3	.5
1 week or less	79	17.4	29	14.1	108	16.4
More than 1 week–1 month	221	48.8	78	37.9	299	45.4
More than 1 month–3 months	90	19.9	58	28.2	148	22.5
More than 3 months–6 months	33	7.3	16	7.8	49	7.4
More than 6 months–1 year	15	3.3	9	4.4	24	3.6
More than 1 year–2 years	10	2.2	6	2.9	16	2.4
Over 2 years	3	.7	9	4.4	12	1.8
Total	453	100.0	206	100.2	659	100.0

likely that the lower percentage of intestate probate cases commenced within this period may be explained by the fact that the logical person to start court machinery is the executor named in a will. In cases where there is no will, there is uncertainty about what to do and who should do it.

Not everyone may be satisfied with the prospect of the will being probated. One of the next of kin, who would take by intestate succession but who is excluded from the will, may desire to contest. The procedure for will contests varies from state to state. It is possible that the will may be contested within a specified time in the probate court, upon appeal from the order establishing the will or rejecting it from probate, or in a separate action in a court of general jurisdiction. The third approach is followed in Ohio. The will contest comes after the will has been probated and takes place in the court of common pleas.[6]

In Ohio, the procedure for probating, or proving, the will is not adversary in nature. In fact, those opposed to the will cannot call any witnesses; they are limited to the cross-examination of the proponent's witnesses.[7] The will is admitted to probate if the proponent makes what in an ordinary lawsuit would be considered a prima-facie case. This means that the will is admitted to probate if, taking all the evidence and construing it in a light most favorable to the proponent, reasonable men could disagree about whether or not the will is valid. The will is rejected if reasonable men could come to only one conclusion: that the instrument offered is invalid. In fact, before the will is rejected, there will be a further hearing. Those in favor of the will are then given a second chance to probate it, and it is only if they fail at that time that the will is denied probate.[8] If the will is denied probate, the proponents may appeal

6. Ohio Revised Code 2741.
7. Ohio Revised Code 2107.14.
8. Ohio Revised Code 2107.181.

this decision to an intermediate appellate court and ultimately to the Ohio Supreme Court.[9]

If the will is admitted to probate, those opposed are not permitted to appeal but they can contest the will. This procedure is strictly adversary, with both sides being able to present witnesses and a jury rendering the decision. The question is still the same as it was in the probate court: Is this piece of paper the will of the decedent? The losing party in the contest may then utilize appellate procedure to determine the validity of the instrument.

Once the will has been determined to be valid, it is not subject to collateral attack on such grounds as forgery, improper execution, lack of testamentary capacity, or revocation. It is conceivable that a more recent will might subsequently be discovered. This later will could be probated and would have priority over the earlier one.[10]

When these preliminaries are completed, the provisions of the will are ready to be construed and the estate is ready to be administered. Yet, the following question may be asked: The law says that a will has to be probated, but why is it necessary to prove a will? The answer to the question is quite simple. Those claiming under a will establish their rights and interests by having its validity determined. Probate proves the authenticity of the document, insuring that it is a valid statement of intentions. Although takers might establish rights without probate, probate is the most certain and the easiest method of proving rights and of preserving the evidence of that proof.

Administering the Estate

Whether or not there is a will, the administration procedure will vary only slightly. The personal representative, either executor or administrator, has as his job the winding up of the decedent's financial affairs, culminating in the distribution of the estate property. His attorney will assist him in this endeavor. The purposes of administration are: to collect the assets of the estate, to pay the lawful claims against the estate, and to distribute the balance to the takers (legatees and devisees under the will or heirs and next of kin by intestate succession).

Many states, however, release from administration what are considered to be "small" estates, whether testate or intestate. This practice is followed in Ohio. Its code during the period of the field work for this study set forth procedures for releasing from administration an estate having a value of $2,000 or less in assets. The situation is usually one where there is no will. If there is a will, it is

9. Ibid.

10. Ohio Revised Code 2107.22. However, persons who are bona fide purchasers from takers under the first will are generally protected. See Ohio Revised Code 2107.47.

admitted to probate but an application is not made for the appointment of a personal representative. Once the will is admitted to probate, the same procedure is followed as in the case of intestate succession release cases.[11]

Family Member as Personal Representative

The individual most likely to be chosen to be executor in testate cases or administrator in intestate cases is a family member (see Table 10–2).[12]

TABLE 10–2 RELATIONSHIP OF EXECUTOR-ADMINISTRATOR TO DECEASED, BY CONDITION OF TESTACY

Relationship	Testate		Intestate		Total	
	Number	Per Cent	Number	Per Cent	Number	Per Cent
Spouse	216	47.7	58	28.2	274	41.6
Child, child-in-law	144	31.8	36	17.5	180	27.3
Other relative	35	7.7	18	8.7	53	8.0
Lawyer	30	6.6	19	9.2	49	7.4
Other nonrelative	15	3.3	11	5.3	26	3.9
Bank	8	1.8	0	0.0	8	1.2
Combination	5	1.1	0	0.0	5	.8
No one	0	0.0	64	31.1	64	9.7
Total	453	100.0	206	100.0	659	99.9

In 80 per cent of the testate cases, the executor was a spouse, child, or child-in-law. The percentage for administrator in intestate cases appears to have been considerably lower—only 46 per cent. A comparison of percentages is not fair without considering that 31 per cent of the intestate cases had no administrator, that is, they were release-of-assets cases. If these release-of-assets cases are dispensed with, a figure of 66 per cent is obtained.[13] On this basis, only 20 per cent of the testate cases and 34 per cent of the intestate cases were not handled by a personal representative who was close to the deceased.

It is important to note that the administration process is a legal means that is provided for the protection not only of the estate beneficiaries but also of the estate creditors and those who are indebted to the estate.[14] Protection relates to people within as well as across these classes. The reason for the per-

11. See Ohio Revised Code 2113.03.

12. For testator cases the personal representative is called *executor;* in intestate cases the individual is called *administrator*. In the 343 cases where a spouse survived and an executor was named or an administrator was appointed, the spouse was named or appointed in 80 per cent of the cases.

13. Since a spouse or child is often appointed administrator, one reason for appointing an executor is likely to be the saving of a bond.

14. Estate administration is not absolutely necessary for creditor protection. See Chapter 8, p. 183.

sonal representative is that it has been deemed legally advantageous for such a person or entity (in the case of a bank) to handle the collection, payment, and distribution of outstanding assets and debts.

Lawyer as Personal Representative

There were 49 cases in which a lawyer served as the executor or administrator; 19 of these estates were intestate, and 30 were testate.

The Ohio Revised Code gives priority for the appointment of an administrator to the decedent's spouse or next of kin if resident in the state.[15]

Of the 19 intestate cases, there were four in which the decedent was survived by a spouse. In one case, the spouse was a resident of Cuyahoga County. She had been born in the Ukraine and spoke English with some difficulty, although she did manage to run a small business.[16] In the other three cases, the spouses were residents of California, Hungary, and Pennsylvania.

There were six estates in which the deceased was survived by children. In four of these estates, the children lived outside the state. In three of these four cases, the lawyers who acted as both administrators and attorneys for the estates had been known by the families before the deaths. Two decedents were survived by children who lived in Cuyahoga County. In one case, the son felt that "one should go to a specialist these days." In the other, Old Age Assistance had a lien on the decedent's real property, and the attorney for Old Age Assistance administered the estate. There were seven cases in which the decedents were survived by kin calculated through the families of orientation. In three of these, at least one of the kin resided within the state, but the eligible next of kin were unable (mentally ill) or unwilling to serve. There were two cases in which the sole survivors of the decedents themselves died before initiation of probate. The attorney for the survivors' estates also administered the estates of the sample decedents.

In none of the 19 intestate estates in which the court appointed an attorney were there next of kin qualified and willing to take the position. The median time of settlement for these 19 cases was between fifteen and eighteen months, although only one-fifth of all intestate cases took this long. Lawyers were ap-

15. According to Ohio Revised Code 2113.06:

Administration of the estate of an intestate shall be granted to persons mentioned in this section, in the following order:

(A) To the surviving spouse of the deceased, if resident of the state;

(B) To one of the next of kin of the deceased, resident of the county;

(C) To one of the next of kin of the deceased, resident of the state;

If there are no persons entitled to administration, or if they are for any reason unsuitable for the discharge of the trust, or if without sufficient cause they neglect to apply within reasonable time for the administration of the estate, their right to priority shall be lost and the court shall commit the administration to some suitable person who is a resident of the county.

16. Rule 31, Probate Court of Cuyahoga County, states that: "No person shall be appointed a fiduciary who cannot read, write and speak the English language, unless the Court for good cause shown directs otherwise."

pointed as fiduciaries in cases similar in size to all intestate cases; that is, they were small. The deductions were not markedly different from the deductions for the entire intestate group of cases. The low margin of difference in the percentage of the gross estate that was lost is especially remarkable in view of the fact that where a member of the family served as administrator, fiduciary fees were customarily foregone (see Table 10–3).[17] Included in the entire in-

TABLE 10–3 COMPARISON OF LAWYER-ADMINISTRATOR INTESTATE CASES WITH ENTIRE INTESTATE SAMPLE

Cases	Gross Estate	Net Estate	Deductions as Per Cent of Gross
Lawyer-administrator	$8,158	$5,579	31.6
Entire intestate sample	$8,599	$6,383	25.8

testate sample are the 64 intestate release-of-assets cases, in which all fees were minimal. There were no release-of-assets cases among the 19 intestate cases for which lawyers served, since such cases were not administered.

The lawyer in the intestate case serves as personal representative when the court appoints him in the absence of legally qualified and willing kin. In the testate case, the decedent makes the judgment concerning the qualifications of his kin. The testator weighs the qualifications of his relatives against the complexities of his estate.

There were 30 testate estates for which the lawyer served as executor. Ten decedents were survived by spouses. All these decedents were men. None of the surviving spouses were disqualified by virtue of residency requirements; all resided within Cuyahoga County. However, for six of these women, the settlement of a simple estate might have been too much to handle alone. Four were aged and sick, and two were foreign born and spoke English with difficulty. The remaining four estates presented more than the usual complexity.

Ten decedents were survived by their lineal descendants. In seven cases, all the next of kin resided outside the state of Ohio. In another case, the decedent was survived by one child who resided in the state but outside Cuyahoga County. The principal asset of this estate was a partnership interest. Probate assets were over $100,000. In two other cases, the decedent chose an attorney for executor because he was an outsider.

17. In some jurisdictions, an attorney who also acts as executor or administrator may not take compensation for both positions because "the representative's personal interest in the charges conflicts with his official duty to scrutinize the amount of the attorney's bill." Thomas E. Atkinson, *Wills,* 2d ed. (St. Paul, Minn.: West Publishing Co., 1953), p. 656. The attorney is allowed compensation for both roles in Ohio. In re Estate of Cramer, 46 Ohio Law Abs. 521, 69 N.E. 2d 204 (1946).

Case 546. The comments of four of five children showed unanimous approval of an attorney-executor. "Father figured an outsider would be more impartial than any of us. He was afraid one of us would show partiality." "I like the idea of an outside executor like father wanted. It saves hard feelings." "It's necessary to have a lawyer when there is a disagreement among the heirs like in this case." "Good idea instead of one of the family. It's not so personal."

Case 316. The gross estate was $6,000, but tax problems were involved and the decedent's business had to be sold. The comments of two of four daughters indicated that complexity was not the reason for the choice of an attorney-executor. "It was probably necessary. In our case there were four daughters, and without an attorney there probably would have been many issues to be haggled over. Mother felt that with four girls the only answer was to appoint an attorney." "There were four women involved. We needed a bystander to say 'Now wait.' "

Nine decedents were survived by more distant relatives, ranging from siblings to cousins. In five cases, these next of kin, who were also the legatees, lived outside the state. The choice of an attorney as executor was made in another three cases because there was dissension within the kin groups. In another case, the attorney named as executor was a close personal friend. In the final case, the decedent had no known next of kin.

There appear to be several reasons for the choice of a lawyer as executor. Nearly half of the decedents were survived by next of kin who were disqualified by virtue of residency requirements. In the cases in which spouses survived the decedents, the complexities of the cases may have been too great for the capacities of the widows. Thirdly, a few of the decedents were survived by warring relatives; in two cases, these disputes reached the stage of will contests. Lastly, some decedents chose attorneys because they were actually closer than anyone else.

Taken as a whole, these lawyer-executor cases involved considerably less wealth than the average testate case. The attorney was not cheating the estate. The deductions compared favorably with the testate sample as a whole (see Table 10–4). The median time for settlement of these cases was one year to fifteen months; 75 per cent of all testate cases were settled within fifteen months.

TABLE 10–4 COMPARISON OF LAWYER-EXECUTOR TESTATE CASES WITH ENTIRE TESTATE SAMPLE

Cases	Gross Estate	Net Estate	Deductions as Per Cent of Gross
Lawyer-executor	$27,533	$22,466	18.4
Entire testate sample	$41,218	$34,538	16.2

Corporation as Executor

There were eight testate cases in which banks served as fiduciaries. These estates had a mean gross of $707,125 and ranged in size from $32,000 to nearly $4,000,000. Attorneys have little need to worry about competition from banks for the average case. The banks do not have a large volume of the estate trade, but they do get the larger estates. The mean deduction for these estates was $94,375, and the median settlement time was between two and three years.

In four cases, the estates involved trusts, with the bank serving as trustee and executor. In the other four cases, the estate was distributed outright; however, in one of these cases, the decedent was the beneficiary of a trust that was dissolved upon his death. In the remaining three cases, there was the need for an outsider to serve either because the next of kin did not reside in the state or because the relatives were fractious.

Elements of Estate Administration

The first step taken by the executor or administrator in the administration of the estate is to ascertain what assets comprise the estate. He must take inventory and have the estate appraised. He must see to it that the surviving spouse or minor children get any property exempt from administration to which they are entitled[18] and must have set off sufficient funds for the widow's allowance.[19] Making an inventory is not a simple act; it involves locating and identifying all the decedent's belongings.

The attorney ascertains that the personal representative files appropriate preliminary tax notices, obtains tax releases, and opens an estate bank account. This estate bank account is established for the purpose of paying the estate's debts. Available cash will be transferred to it. Sufficient funds must be placed in this account to meet the present debts and expenses of the estate, especially those liabilities involved by the last illness and the funeral.

For legatees and heirs, the next steps of the administrative process give rise to ambiguity and uncertainty over current happenings and impending events, and some inheritors express fears and suspicions regarding their attorneys and officials of the probate court. Subsequent to the inventory and appraisement, some property such as stocks and bonds may have to be sold in order to facilitate the payment of debts and ultimately for distribution purposes. A decision might have to be made whether a decedent-owned business should be continued, liquidated, or sold. In Ohio, this problem may not be overpowering where the will gives the executor power to sell assets and specifically to continue or dispose of the testator's business. The time to consummate these decisions

18. Ohio Revised Code 2115.13.
19. Ohio Revised Code 2117.20.

varies. Statutory formalities must be substantially complied with in cases of intestate succession, and this also takes a long time and may be costly as well. The possible assets to be found in an estate are limitless, from ordinary jewelry or antiques to the family home or oil rights. During this phase of the administration process, the assets of the estate must be managed; the executor or administrator becomes a type of housekeeper. Continuing expenses have to be met. Court authority for acts to be done must be obtained in many cases, especially where there is no will.

A good example of the complexities encountered in the management stage, from the standpoint of Ohio law, would be the management of real estate. Unless the will has provided otherwise, it is necessary for the personal representative to make application to the probate court to manage real estate.[20] There will be a hearing and notice, and the application will be approved if deemed in the best interest of the heirs or devisees.[21] If bond has been previously given, additional bond may be required.[22] The fiduciary has the obligation to collect rents and from these rents to pay taxes, insurance, repair costs, and other expenses; but the fiduciary is not to advance money without court order.[23] The property can be rented only on a month-to-month basis, unless the court approves rental for a period up to a year.[24] The personal representative has to account periodically for receipts and disbursements and may at intervals not to exceed one year pay heirs and devisees their shares of the net rents.[25]

In brief, there are many matters to be considered prior to reaching the distribution stage of estate administration. Required procedures must be followed where the sale of personalty or realty is involved. Unless authorized by will, such sales can only be by court order. The executor or administrator determines whether the sale is public or private. Notice has to be given to interested parties. It is hoped that the executor or administrator is in a position to know what and when to sell and how to get a good price for what is sold. During this time, the management of the estate continues, a process that could last perhaps only a few weeks or months in a small estate or that could stretch into years in more complicated cases.

Time Involved in Estate Administration

It is possible in Ohio for an estate to be completely administered within nine months. Ohio Revised Code 2113.25 states:

20. Ohio Revised Code 2113.311.
21. Ibid.
22. Ibid.
23. Ibid.
24. Ibid.
25. Ibid.

So far as he is able, the executor or administrator of an estate shall collect the assets and complete the administration of such estate within nine months after the date of his appointment.

For larger-than-average estates (that is, those of more than $60,000), tax consequences would usually require more than the nine-month period for completion of administration.[26] The federal estate tax return must be filed within fifteen months of date of death,[27] and assets are valued as of the date of death[28] or one year from date of death.[29] This optional valuation date causes many personal representatives to wait as long as possible to exercise the option. Of necessity, if the election is made to value one year after death, the estate cannot be closed in the suggested time. There is no requirement, however, that a person must wait nor that the estate tax return must be filed at the very end of the fifteen-month period. Furthermore, meeting the nine-months-or-less timetable to an extent requires that there be no complications. For example, although creditors must have their claims filed in Ohio generally within four months after appointment of the fiduciary and in no case longer than nine months, if the claim is not allowed, a lawsuit may result and the administration time in such cases may be extended beyond nine months.[30]

How much time was spent in probate court for the settlement of the cases involved in this study? Did they approximate the ideal suggested in the statute? How many closed within nine months or a reasonable time thereafter? (See Tables 10–5 and 10–6.)

TABLE 10–5 TIME IN PROBATE COURT, BY CONDITION OF TESTACY

	Testate		Intestate		Total	
Time in Probate	Number	Per Cent	Number	Per Cent	Number	Per Cent
9 months or less	107	23.6	103	50.0	210	31.9
9 months–15 months	231	51.0	59	28.6	290	44.0
15 months and over	115	25.4	44	21.4	159	24.1
Total	453	100.0	206	100.0	659	100.0

Approximately three-fourths of the testate and intestate cases were completely administered within fifteen months. More intestate than testate actions

26. Internal Revenue Code 6018 (a) (1) requires a federal estate tax return where the gross estate exceeds $60,000.
27. Internal Revenue Code 6075 (a).
28. Internal Revenue Code 2031 (a).
29. Internal Revenue Code 2032.
30. See Ohio Revised Code 2117.12, which concerns actions on claims rejected by the executor or administrator. The action based on a rejected claim will be brought in a trial court of general jurisdiction, and this could delay estate settlement for two to three years.

TABLE 10–6 MEDIAN TIME CATEGORY IN PROBATE COURT, BY SIZE OF ESTATE

Size of Estate	Number	Median Time Category
$11,499 or less	309	9 months–1 year
$11,500–$20,499	186	9 months–1 year
$20,500–$60,000	116	9 months–1 year
Over $60,000	48	18 months–2 years
Total	659	

were closed in the time recommended in the Ohio Revised Code, and this was because 64 of these intestate cases were estates of $2,000 or less and thus required no formal administration. Extremely large estates took more time to settle. A federal estate tax return must be filed for estates in excess of $60,000. As a rule, such estates vary in types of assets and their location.

For estates subject to federal estate taxation, the time after the filing of the return during which the Internal Revenue Service is examining the return is quite important. The personal representative wants to be assured that he is not personally liable for a mistake in the tax return. Consequently, he is likely to refuse to distribute the estate, even after the estate tax return has been filed, until the time has expired before which he cannot obtain an official closing from the Treasury. This explains the data in Table 10–6, which indicates that estate tax return cases took three to nine months longer than the maximum fifteen-month filing period. Theoretically, the estate could have been closed on the day the return was filed, whether it was the maximum fifteen months or the time suggested by state law (such as Ohio Revised Code 2113.25).

There were six intestate and nine testate cases that deviated from the norm by being in the administration process for more than five years. In the testate cases, the delay had one of two causes: (1) various legal entanglements arising out of lawsuits or will contests (five cases) or (2) apparently gross incompetence on the part of the personal representative or his attorney (four cases).

In two of the six intestate cases in which the settlement time exceeded five years, the obstacles to settlement were remarkably small.

Case 050. The decedent was a 44-year-old male who was survived by his widow and his father. His father was entitled to one-quarter of the estate. But the estate took nearly six years to settle, and the father received nothing because he died in the interim. The item holding up the estate settlement was the failure of the administratrix to pay court costs of $19.85. The bondholders complained bitterly to the attorney that he had furnished them with two incorrect addresses for his client. Eventually they paid, stating: "Although primary responsibility for payment of court costs rests upon Mrs. ________, she has departed for parts unknown." (It was later found that Mrs. ________ had used her inheritance to travel.)

Case 075. The decedent was a 63-year-old widow whose survivors were a son and daughter. Her assets were inadequate for funeral expenses. Between the time of her death and the time that the savings were withdrawn, the bank issued one share of stock. They caught their error about six years later. And so probate was not finally closed until the share ($50) was released.

In three cases, the obstacles to settlement were wrongful death suits that were initiated either against the estates or on behalf of the estates. The obstacle in the sixth case appeared to be a problem of locating numerous heirs.

Considering the cases as a whole and the multiplicity of problems potentially involved, it can be said that the Cuyahoga County Probate Court functions within the recommended time limitations set forth in the statute. Certainly, the intestate cases that took over five years were not delayed through the fault of the court.

Expenses of Estate Administration

The cost of estate administration is of vital concern to actual and potential heirs and legatees. The data relating to probate court expenses may be broken down into four areas: (1) court fees and costs, (2) appraisers' fees, (3) personal representatives' fees, and (4) attorneys' fees. A word of explanation is necessary with respect to each of these areas. The state of Ohio does not utilize the fee system as a means of compensation for county court officials.[31] All personnel are salaried. Fees and costs of the probate court are code regulated and appear to be moderate assessments.[32] Ohio Revised Code 2101.16 enumerates 78 possible fees. Of these 78 only one, petition for sale of real estate, is $15. Thirteen fee categories are at the $10 level. The remaining 64 are less than $10.

TABLE 10–7 COURT FEES AND COSTS, BY CONDITION OF TESTACY

	Testate		Intestate	
Court Fees and Costs	Number	Per Cent	Number	Per Cent
$50 or less	113	24.9	138	67.0
$51–$100	297	65.6	56	27.2
$101–$200	32	7.1	11	5.3
Over $200	11	2.4	1	.5
Total	453	100.0	206	100.0

Court fees and costs were analyzed according to the condition of testacy (see Table 10–7). Approximately 90 per cent of all testate cases and 94 per cent of

31. See Ohio Revised Code 325.02.

32. Although other isolated code sections may be involved periodically, the basic statute sections controlling probate court fees are Ohio Revised Code 2101.16–21.

all intestate cases had court fees and costs of $100 or less. Only 2 per cent of the testate cases and less than 1 per cent of the intestate cases had fees and costs in excess of $200. Judgment of the cost of estate administration as high or low was facilitated by examining fees and costs in relation to the size of the estate (see Table 10–8). Of the total testate and intestate cases under $60,000, only two had court fees and costs in excess of $200. Even for those estates over $60,000, only one had fees and costs exceeding $500. Actually court costs and fees in 98 per cent of the 659 cases were $200 or less.

TABLE 10–8 COURT FEES AND COSTS, BY SIZE OF ESTATE

Size of Estate	Number	Median Fee and Cost Category	Per Cent Above Median Fee and Cost Category
$2,499 or less	97	$50 or less	5.2
$2,500–$20,499	398	$51–$100	5.3
$20,500–$60,000	116	$51–$100	10.3
Over $60,000	48	$51–$100	43.8
Total	659		

The appraisers' fees are another expense of estate administration. This was the charge most often disliked by attorneys and survivors, and some questioned its relevance for the probate process. (It is discussed in detail in Chapters 11 and 12.) Fees paid to appraisers were controlled by statute, with the amounts paid for services normally fixed by local rule of court.[33] Three suitable disinterested persons were appointed by the court to make the appraisement. In Cuyahoga County, Rule 11 of the probate court governs fees (see Appendix G).

For the sample, appraisers' fees were $100 or less in nearly 90 per cent of all cases with fees listed (see Table 10–9). Of the testate cases with appraisers' fees in excess of $100, 35 were less than $250, and eight were between $251 and $500. Fees for one case were in the $500-to-$1,000 category; and for one additional case, fees exceeded $1,000. No intestate case had appraisers' fees beyond the $101-to-$250 range. Table 10–10 shows all cases broken down by dollar valuation of the estate. In estates with a value up to $20,499, the median category of appraisers' fees was $50 or less; and of those above the median, only one exceeded $100. In estates valued between $20,500 and $60,000, the median fee category was from $51 to $100. Of those cases for which fees were above the median fee category, none exceeded $250. Only in cases valued in excess of $60,000 was there a significant relationship between dollar valuation

33. See Ohio Revised Code 2115.06, which states in part: "Each appraiser shall be paid two dollars per day or such amount as the probate judge may allow for his services."

TABLE 10–9 APPRAISERS' FEES, BY CONDITION OF TESTACY

Fees	Testate		Intestate	
	Number	Per Cent	Number	Per Cent
None listed[a]	103	22.7	118	57.3
$50 or less	238	52.5	69	33.5
$51–$100	67	14.8	17	8.3
Over $100	45	9.9	2	1.0
Total	453	99.9	206	100.1

[a] No fee was listed on probate records.

TABLE 10–10 MEDIAN FEE OF APPRAISERS, BY SIZE OF ESTATE

Size of Estate	Number	Per Cent No Fees Listed[a]	Median Fee Category[b]	Per Cent Above Median Fee Category[b]
$2,499 or less	97	94.8	$50 or less	0.0
$2,500–$20,499	398	24.9	$50 or less	9.4
$20,500–$60,000	116	15.5	$51–$100	15.3
Over $60,000	48	25.0	$101 and over	[c]
Total	659			

[a] No fee was listed on probate records.
[b] Median fee categories included only those estates where there were appraisers' fees.
[c] Maximum fee category analyzed was $101 and over.

and appraisers' fees. Here, approximately 65 per cent of the fees were greater than $100, but only ten of these exceeded $250 (as previously noted).

It would appear then that complaints levied against appraisers were not directly related to the expense involved. Actual expenses attributable to appraisers' fees were relatively low. Yet if an appraiser was doing nothing or was perceived as being paid for negligible services, criticism occurred. What was being questioned was the whole appraisal system—its current structure and function.

Personal representatives' and attorneys' fees were significant expenses in estate administration. The fiduciary fee will be considered first. There are statutory provisions relating to compensation for executors and administrators. Ohio Revised Code 2113.35 allows commissions to these parties. It is percentage based (see Appendix A). Section 2113.36 of the Code provides for additional allowances for an executor or administrator. These are allowances that the probate court considers just and reasonable. They may be for actual and necessary expenses and/or for extraordinary services not required of an executor or administrator in the common course of his duty (see Appendix A).

For the estates in this sample, no personal representative's fee was listed in 60 per cent of the testate cases and three-fourths of the intestate cases (see Table 10–11). Often no fee was taken because the executor or administrator

TABLE 10–11 PERSONAL REPRESENTATIVE'S FEE, BY CONDITION OF TESTACY

Fee	Testate		Intestate	
	Number	Per Cent	Number	Per Cent
None listed[a]	271	59.8	156	75.7
$100 or less	11	2.4	8	3.9
$101–$300	62	13.7	22	10.7
$301–$500	39	8.6	12	5.8
Over $500	70	15.5	8	3.9
Total	453	100.0	206	100.0

[a] No fee was listed on probate records.

was a very close family member or else because the estate had been relieved from administration. Listed fees exceeded $300 in less than one-fourth of all testate cases and in less than 10 per cent of all intestate cases. Table 10–12 shows the relationship of personal representatives' fees to the size of the estate. Fiduciary fees were listed in only six cases in which the estates were under $2,500. In four cases, fees were $100 or less. Since the median fee category was calculated only for those estates that listed a fee, the 33 per cent that were

TABLE 10–12 MEDIAN FEE OF PERSONAL REPRESENTATIVE, BY SIZE OF ESTATE

Size of Estate	Number	Per Cent No Fee Listed[a]	Median Fee Category[b]	Per Cent Above Median Fee Category[b]
$2,499 or less	97	93.8	$100 or less	33.3
$2,500–$20,499	398	68.1	$101–$300	11.6
$20,500–$60,000	116	40.5	$501 and over	[c]
Over $60,000	48	37.5	$501 and over	[c]
Total	659			

[a] No fee was listed on probate records.
[b] Median fee categories included only those estates where there was a fiduciary fee listed.
[c] Maximum fee category analyzed was $501 and over.

above the median fee category represented two estates where the fee was between $101 and $300. For the estates valued between $2,500 and $20,499, the median fee category was from $101 to $300, and only 12 exceeded $500. Personal representatives' fees did not seem to be a significant expense except for estates valued at more than $20,500. Although the percentage of cases with no fee listed decreased as estate size increased, there were still close to 40 per cent in the category of estates valued in excess of $60,000.

The attorneys' fees are in part determined by Ohio Revised Code 2113.36. An attorney who has been employed in the administration of the estate is entitled to reasonable attorney's fees to be paid by the executor or administrator in the common course of his duty. Local court rules will determine the extent of these fees. Rule 26 of the Cuyahoga County Probate Court sets forth a guide for attorneys' fees (see Appendix G). Lawyers' fees for estates in this sample are presented in Table 10–13 by condition of testacy. Without question,

TABLE 10–13 ATTORNEY'S FEE, BY CONDITION OF TESTACY

Fee	Testate		Intestate	
	Number	Per Cent	Number	Per Cent
None listed[a]	62	13.7	91	44.2
$100 or less	6	1.3	6	2.9
$101–$300	178	39.3	48	23.3
$301–$500	77	17.0	28	13.6
$501–$1,000	62	13.7	25	12.1
$1,001–$5,000	58	12.8	8	3.9
Over $5,000	10	2.2	0	0.0
Total	453	100.0	206	100.0

[a] No fee was listed on probate records. For 60 of the 659 decedent cases, there were no attorneys; most of these were release-from-administration cases.

the most significant expense in the estate-administration process was the attorney's fee. Ten cases had fees in excess of $5,000, and 66 cases had fees between $1,001 and $5,000. Yet over two-thirds of the cases with fees listed had fees of $500 or less. It should be noted that the percentages allowed the attorneys by Rule 26 for counsel fees are higher than the percentages for fiduciary commissions.

There was a direct correlation between the attorney's fee and the size of the estate: the larger the size of the estate, the larger the fee (see Table 10–14). For the majority of estates valued from $2,500 to $20,499, the median fee category was from $101 to $300. Of the 40 per cent of these estates with fees above the median fee category, only three exceeded $1,000. For estates valued between $20,500 and $60,000, the median fee category was from $501 to $1,000, and in no case was the fee over $5,000. For those estates over $60,000, the median fee category was from $1,001 to $5,000, with ten estates having fees of $5,001 and over.

TABLE 10–14 MEDIAN FEE OF ATTORNEY, BY SIZE OF ESTATE

Size of Estate	Number	Per Cent No Fee Listed[a]	Median Fee Category[b]	Per Cent Above Median Fee Category[b]
$2,499 or less	97	86.6	$101–$300	25.0
$2,500–$20,499	398	14.6	$101–$300	40.0
$20,500–$60,000	116	6.0	$501–$1,000	27.5
Over $60,000	48	6.3	$1,001–$5,000	22.2
Total	659			

[a] No fee was listed on probate records.
[b] Median fee categories included only those estates where there was an attorney's fee listed.

The trend in attorneys' fees approximated the trend in personal representatives' fees. The large fees were found for estates valued at more than $20,500. The following is a comparison of the percentages allowed attorneys, executors, and administrators:

Attorneys		*Executors and Administrators*	
6 per cent on first	$ 2,000	6 per cent on first	$1,000
4 per cent on next	$13,000	4 per cent on next	$4,000
3 per cent on next	$15,000	2 per cent on balance	
2 per cent on balance			
Minimum fee $150			

The comparison is relevant for personal property.[34] The executor or administrator receives no commission on real estate passing directly to the decedent's successors. Formerly, attorneys' fees were based upon varied percentages where real estate was involved. Attorneys' fees are now controlled by a revised Probate Court Rule 26. This rule became effective on November 1, 1965, after the project data from probate records were gathered (see Appendix G). Under this revised rule, the percentage allowed for attorneys' fees is uniform for personal and real property. Based on the above-mentioned percentages, the suggested compensation by size of the estate (100 per cent personalty) is shown in Table 10–15. Compensation for special services is not included in these figures.

Conclusion

The objective of this chapter was to describe the estate settlement practices of the probate court within the legislation that guides such practices. Estate settlements involve property transfers at the death of an individual under testate

34. Compare Ohio Revised Code 2113.35 with 2113.36 and with Cuyahoga County Probate Court Rule 26.

TABLE 10–15 SUGGESTED ATTORNEY AND PERSONAL REPRESENTATIVE FEES, BY SIZE OF ESTATE (100-PER CENT PERSONALTY)

Size of Estate	Attorney Fees	Personal Representative Fees
$3,000	$160	$140
$7,000	$320	$260
$11,000	$480	$340
$16,000	$670	$440
$21,000	$820	$540
$61,000	$1,710	$1,340

or intestate conditions. Examined are the procedures of estate administration including the selection and functions of the personal representative, his relation to the lawyer, and the use of the family member or lawyer as personal representative.

Corporations such as banks are used as executors where the estates are high in financial worth and equities are from a number of sources. Where estates consist of numerous sources of value such as real estate, stocks, bonds, bank deposits, and the like, there is an extended time period before the transfer is made to heirs and beneficiaries; and the uncertainness of this period causes a sense of ambiguity for potential inheritors.

There appears to be a correlation between the size of the estate and the condition of testacy with the time and cost for its settlement. The larger the estate the longer it takes to close it and the higher the court, lawyer, and appraiser fees are. Because intestate cases are likely to involve estates smaller in size than testate ones, the time to close such cases is less than those which are testate. Considering state and federal legislation affecting estate settlement, the cases in the sample indicated that estates were administered within a reasonable time period in the Probate Court of Cuyahoga County. Court fees and costs were small in dollar and percentage amounts. Appraisers' fees were not a considerable expense. (Whether the fees paid to the appraisers were earned is not at issue here.) The personal representatives' fees were in line with the commissions that were considered ordinary compensation in Section 2113.35 of the Ohio Revised Code, and the attorneys' fees did not indicate overcharging on the part of the lawyer.

Chapter 11

Estate Settlement: Client Attitudes Toward the Probate Process

ESTATE SETTLEMENT is technical. The decedents' survivors can scarcely be expected to understand the process in detail. However, all the survivors were interested parties in the settlement, and they had their own opinions of the probate process. Critics of the probate court singled out administrative costs and the time involved in settlement as especially bad features of the system. Time and cost were also matters of concern to the interested survivors. The most important functionaries in the system from the point of view of the survivors were the court personnel, the lawyer, and the appraisers.

The survivors were asked questions dealing with the activities, including fees charged, of the court, lawyer, and appraisers.[1] Information concerning the activities of the court and others in relation to the estate is available as part of the public record; nevertheless all the survivors did not use such information resources. They either were uninformed of the availability of these resources or were disinterested. A substantial proportion of the survivors claimed not to have sufficient information upon which to base an opinion. The response of incompetence to judge ranged widely, from 24 per cent for the question on the lawyer's handling of the probate case to 63 per cent for the question on the appropriateness of the charge made by the appraisers (see Table 11–1).

TABLE 11–1 AREAS OF NO INFORMATION[a]

	Handling		Fees	
Functionary	Number	Per Cent	Number	Per Cent
Court	319	25.9	558	45.2
Lawyer	294	23.8	465	37.7
Appraiser	719	58.3	773	62.6

[a] Percentages were based upon 1,234 survivors.

The lawyer was the best-known person, slightly more than three-fourths of the survivors had some judgment on his competence to handle the case, and 62

1. Court fees included any related court costs.

per cent expressed some judgment on the fee he charged. He was considered the most significant professional in estate settlement.

Of the survivors who indicated they had sufficient knowledge to make a judgment, more expressed satisfaction than dissatisfaction with the work of the court, the lawyer, and the appraisers. However, they were not equally satisfied with all three. Their opinion of the appraisers was the least favorable (see Table 11–2).

TABLE 11–2 SURVIVORS' OPINIONS REGARDING HANDLING OF FEES BY PROBATE SYSTEM AND FUNCTIONARIES (PERCENTAGE DISTRIBUTION)

System or Functionary	Favorable	Neutral	Unfavorable	Total	
				Number	Per Cent
Court					
Handling	56.7	21.6	21.6	915	99.9
Fees	62.0	14.3	23.7	676	100.0
Lawyers					
Handling	71.0	11.1	17.9	940	100.0
Fees	61.2	8.6	30.2	769	100.0
Appraisers					
Handling	49.7	22.5	27.8	515	100.0
Fees	51.2	15.8	33.0	461	100.0

It was also clear that for each functionary, the handling of the estate received fewer unfavorable responses than the fees attendant to that handling. For instance, only 18 per cent were dissatisfied with the lawyer's handling of the case, but 30 per cent felt the lawyer's fees were unreasonable.

Further examination of opinions about estate settlement was confined to those survivors who held either favorable or unfavorable opinions. As a measure of the relative satisfaction with the various functionaries, a comparison was made between the number of survivors satisfied with both handling and fees and the number dissatisfied with both.

The survivors' experiences with estate settlement formed the bases for their judgments. In recounting their experiences, the survivors revealed their standards of evaluation. Although positive judgments were more frequent, the negative comments were usually more informative; therefore, more negative statements will be quoted in the following discussion. These statements describe expected behavior and do not indicate the frequency of a specified one.

The Probate Court

Only a minority of those who were knowledgeable about the estate settlement expressed themselves as being dissatisfied with the probate court's handling of the case and the fees charged (see Table 11–3). Judgments concerning handling and fees were relatively independent of each other. One hundred

TABLE 11–3 SURVIVORS' SATISFACTION WITH PROBATE COURT[a]

	Handling		Fees		Handling and Fees	
Condition	Number	Per Cent	Number	Per Cent	Number	Per Cent
Satisfied	519	42.1	419	34.0	286	23.2
Dissatisfied	198	16.0	160	13.0	59	4.8

[a] Percentages were based on the total survivor population of 1,234. There were 517 survivors who either were neutral or had no information regarding handling and 655 who were neutral or had no information regarding fees.

ninety-eight survivors were dissatisfied with the handling of the estate, and 160 survivors were dissatisfied with the fees. But only 59 persons were dissatisfied with both the court's handling of the estate and the fees charged by the court. Nearly five times as many people were satisfied with court involvement and fees as were dissatisfied with both.

On what basis did persons make their judgments? What experiences inclined them toward favorable or unfavorable judgments about the court? It was observed that people who were dissatisfied were not always concerned about the fees. One of the more important factors seemed to be how survivors were treated by the personnel employed by probate court.

Case 323–02. The clerks in probate court are very rude and downright insulting. They brush you off as though you were something dirty. It seems to be beneath their dignity to answer any questions. It makes me burn when I know we peasants are paying their salaries.

Case 372–02. The people in probate court are not even qualified. I've worked in offices and I know good office procedures. One "stupid broad" there had to use the "hunt and peck" system to type a simple form—and she erased three times. Besides she was so rude to us. It took her forever, and she stopped to puff on her cigarette while making out a single card. Don't these people know that they are there to serve the public? No business office would put up with this kind of sloppiness.

Case 648–03. I think the public becomes accustomed to services provided by the state, and you expect to be treated a little less than human—I wasn't disappointed. There were a little lack of helpfulness and a little lack of feeling on their part. If it weren't for the lawyer, we'd have been very confused.

In some cases, this feeling that the court personnel were less than adequate civil servants was combined with the feeling that it was all part of their effort to make the person get a lawyer to take care of the matter.

Case 217–01. I was just bluntly told to "go over there." The clerks were abrupt and indifferent. They gave the impression that if you want satisfaction at all, you had better have an attorney.

Some of the dissatisfaction is a consequence of the layman's misconception of what court personnel are permitted to do according to law. Court personnel are not permitted to practice law or advise persons concerning legal matters, yet many laymen want such information in order to handle the estate in probate court without the aid of an attorney. When they cannot receive advice and counsel, they are disgruntled with the court personnel.

Case 374–01. The layman is intelligent enough to handle the probate process without a lawyer when simple wills and estates are involved. The layman should be able to get enough information from probate court to handle the situation himself. The people at probate court should function as an information bureau.

Survivors who felt that the court should have provided more information were not concerned with changing the probate process. They made a positive suggestion that by being informed on the various steps of estate administration, the court could reduce the anxiety engendered in a new and unfamiliar situation.

Case 341–04. Is it true that each estate is completely different, or are there certain categories? Could they write leaflets on the general procedures so you could read it and understand what needs to be done?

More people were satisfied than were dissatisfied with probate court in their particular cases, and many stated the importance of a probate court system.

Case 109–02. Our courts do a very excellent job. They do protect people, which is very important. Their fees were reasonable; after all they have expenses too.

Case 113–01. People in court here are very pleasant and answered all my questions once I explained the case to them. The court requires beneficiaries and their representatives to go through an elaborate accounting of funds to protect beneficiaries from the small per cent of dishonest executors. They force the majority of people to go to extreme lengths to protect these few.

Seventy-six survivors (6 per cent) indicated that there was no need for the probate court in simple cases or that it was an infringement on personal liberty for the government, through its court system, to distribute a person's private estate.

Case 359–02. I don't feel that any government authority has any business investigating, taxing, or distributing any man's personal estate. . . . It's just not right. No one has any business interfering. Federal tax people are the biggest robbers of all. The lowest form of human being is the grave robber, and that's what this amounts to.

Others were less adamant about the court's right to become involved but were nonetheless concerned about it. It is interesting that in both Cases 502–01 and 309–02, the respondents, although questioning court involvement, were generally satisfied with the way the court handled their cases.

Case 502–01. I was very satisfied with what the court did. But I don't see why the courts have to come into it. Why do we have to bother? This was mine to begin with. We built this house together—every nail and every board. Why do the courts have to interfere?

Case 309–02. We pay taxes for the probate court—it should do the work for us. I have no complaints about the process however. The whole thing costs about what it should. But why couldn't I just get my own bank account and my own house?

The survivors had few if any yardsticks with which to measure the fairness of the fees charged. In these circumstances, over twice as many persons expressed satisfaction as expressed dissatisfaction with the fees. Most of those who were satisfied believed that the absolute amount charged was not exorbitant; whereas the responses of the dissatisfied reflected more varied bases of opinion.

Some of the people who objected to the fees charged by probate court did so on the grounds that this service should be paid for by tax money. Others found the total amount unreasonable and felt they were being exploited.

Case 342–01. The fees are ridiculous—they are out to get every dime they can. When someone dies, they soak you.

Case 042–02. It seems that everything at court costs money. I thought the courts were for the people, but they are for themselves.

There were people who accepted the fee system but complained either about the size of the bill or the number of bills that probate court sent them. Most of these people were irritated by the inconvenience that this caused them.

Case 328–02. Court fees were terrible. Every time someone had to sign his name there was a fee. My father was "25-dollared" to death by the court, although I do feel that there had to be legal involvement to protect the heirs. There had to be some jurisdiction.

Case 343–02. I can't really remember what the fees were for probate court, because there were so many small bills I just paid them—what could I do? There is nothing you can do except pay them.

The constant stream of poorly explained bills from probate court coupled with little or no business knowledge or experience was devastating for some.

Case 587–03. It seemed like I was putting out $35 and then $35 again. Every time I turned around there was another $35 gone. I don't even know what it was for. I had to sell my house to live. I never handled the business end of things while my husband was alive.

The attitude toward fees charged was bound up in the person's views of the work and functions of the court. The people who felt that the court did not do anything in their cases objected to the fees that the court charged.

Case 047–01. The court did not do much. They checked out everything they could, but too much of the load is on the executor. They didn't give me too much cooperation. Ycu do everything, and then you have to pay a lawyer and probate court—for what?

An examination of all the responses regarding treatment by court employees and fees charged for services leads to the conclusion that the general opinion of survivors toward the probate court was one of satisfied indifference. Because very few of the survivors got directly involved in probate court activities, they therefore assumed that everything was going smoothly.

Case 525–01. All we did was wait a year after his death and just changed the names on the deeds. There was no court involvement to speak of.

Although satisfied indifference was by far the most prevalent posture assumed by survivors, it is impossible to ignore those individuals who ran into a number of problems in the probate process. To some of them, such as an aged widow, these problems were formidable and came at a time of high anxiety and, often, severe financial loss. These special hardship cases illustrate the need for simplified procedures easily communicated and understood by the average person.

The Lawyer

With respect to attorneys, the ratio of satisfied to dissatisfied survivors was about 4 to 1, somewhat less than the corresponding ratio for the probate court (see Table 11–4).

TABLE 11–4 SURVIVORS' SATISFACTION WITH LAWYER[a]

Condition	Handling		Fees		Handling and Fees	
	Number	Per Cent	Number	Per Cent	Number	Per Cent
Satisfied	667	54.1	471	38.2	430	34.8
Dissatisfied	169	13.7	232	18.8	102	8.3

[a] Percentages were based on the total survivor population of 1,234. There were 398 survivors who either were neutral or had no information regarding handling and 531 who were neutral or had no information regarding fees.

In addition to the questions on handling and fees, the survivors were asked whether or not they thought a lawyer was necessary. A majority did (see Table 11–5).

In most instances, the decedent's survivors did not have to search for a lawyer. In 346 (74 per cent) of the 470 decedent cases for which information was available, the lawyer for the estate settlement was already known to the decedent's survivors.[2] Either he had done legal work for the decedent or executor or the survivors knew him personally.

2. In 21 cases, the survivors interviewed did not know how the lawyers were chosen. In the remaining cases, either there were no lawyers or no interviews had been obtained.

In 124 cases, the survivors sought out an attorney for the settlement. In 29 of these cases, the lawyer was recommended by a relative; in 43 cases, by a friend; and in 52 cases, the recommendation came from a variety of sources. This indicates the relatively minor role that quasi-official agencies of the bar played in the selection of a lawyer and the way in which informal contacts were used in the selection of a lawyer. Only two persons sought the advice of a legal reference bureau. One lawyer was recommended to the family by the owner of a restaurant they patronized. One person sought the advice of her baby-sitter; another, her landlord; a third, her lodger. A public utility gave one family a list of a half-dozen lawyers to choose from. Others asked those with whom they had some financial dealings. Three attorneys were recommended by insurance agents; three, by accountants; and six, by banks. Funeral directors recommended the lawyers in seven cases.

TABLE 11–5 NECESSITY OF LAWYER

Survivors' Opinions	Number	Per Cent
No opinion	89	7.2
Not necessary	189	15.3
Somewhat necessary	198	16.0
Absolutely necessary	758	61.4
Total	1,234	100.0

The fact that most persons employed lawyers who were previously known to the families may have a bearing on the satisfaction that was generally expressed by the survivors. The beneficiaries were likely to feel more at ease and to trust someone they knew. There are large numbers of foreign-born persons in Cuyahoga County.[3] The ability to communicate in the survivor's language may have been an important factor in selecting an attorney and in producing a comfortable lawyer-client relationship.

Case 525–01. The lawyer contacted us. He was Polish, and he put Mother at ease. He didn't throw the jargon around.

The selection of a lawyer on the basis of ethnicity was sometimes questioned by the second generation.

Case 588–01. My parents chose their lawyer because he spoke Lithuanian. In foreign neighborhoods, lawyers take advantage of their clients' ignorance.

In some cases, friendship with the attorney coexisted with a generally negative attitude toward the legal profession.

3. Thirty-four per cent of the decedents were foreign born; 16 per cent of the lawyers were foreign born.

Case 654–01. Since he was a personal friend, feelings are very good. He seemed to handle it smoothly. In general, all that attorneys are looking out for is self-aggrandizement. They are not out to serve humanity at all.

In cases where the lawyer was both a friend and competent, the situation was particularly easy.

Case 030–01. Anything I asked, I got a good explanation on; in many instances I didn't even have to ask. He had been the lawyer for my wife's family for years and years. It probably makes a difference if you have a lawyer you can put complete trust in, and this is the way it had to be. Also his fees were very reasonable. They were about 1½ per cent of the estate.

Case 091–01. I don't know what I'd have done without him. He guided me every step of the way. He was a very good friend. He earned his fee.

Although the majority of cases in which friends acted as attorneys were satisfactorily handled, there were a few exceptions. In some cases, the beneficiaries felt that the lawyers took advantage of their friendship. This prompted one survivor to make the following comment:

Case 659–01. The lawyer was a family friend, and he let me down. It was a very difficult situation, and so I depended on him because I knew nothing about such things—he overcharged me exceedingly.

In another case, the so-called friendship was a ruse. The survivor had to pay $200 to be released from a lawyer who had offered to make the couple's will as a gift. At the time of the husband's death, the widow found a clause in the will which said that the attorney who had made the will would have to be the one to settle the estate. She felt she had been tricked by someone who had posed as a friend.

In another case in which the lawyer had inserted the clause that he would be the attorney for the estate settlement, the survivors did not attempt to get a release and were dissatisfied with the results.

Case 577–02. The lawyer knew Dad through the coin club. Dad put it in his will that he was to be the lawyer. I felt there was some involvement on the part of the attorney in the coin collection. He had the same hobby and expressed undue interest in that part of the estate. He wanted the coin collection, but Mom refused to sell. I would have liked to drop him, but he had done so much already.

One criterion used by the survivors to measure the lawyer's performance was the degree to which he kept them informed. If there was a will, the survivors wanted to have it read to them. There was some confusion concerning whether the court, lawyer, or executor should be held responsible, but usually the reading of the will was felt to be the responsibility of the lawyer.

Case 393–07. I think the rest of the family is entitled to know how the estate was settled. To the best of my knowledge, only three or four out of a family of ten had any knowledge. I am the oldest of the family, and I never saw or heard the will.

Case 044–05. The lawyer sure had peculiar actions. He didn't want to bother reading the will. My husband made him read it.

Case 161–04. I would have liked to have known just exactly what was in the will. I thought when the will was read everyone should be there, but this is something I don't talk about to the rest of family.

Case 105–02. I wasn't satisfied about his not reading the will. You should be able to know what is in a will. The attorney should read the will to the whole family—not just to one person.

It is difficult to ascertain where the survivors got the idea that reading the will is customary procedure. Possibly they have been influenced by the mass media. A formal reading of the will was not practiced in the estates in the decedent sample.

A further difficulty was that the lawyer considers himself the executor's attorney; the survivors, however, consider him the attorney for the heirs or next of kin. They expect more than minimal contact with him.

If the lawyer-client relationship is clarified, and if the meaning and circumstances of will reading are established, then many of these disparities in the expectations of survivors can be eliminated. The difficulty lies in a set of differential expectations.

The failure to communicate information regarding the conditions and steps involved in settling the estate was especially trying for those who did not live in Cuyahoga County. Most of these persons were outside the circle of family gossip; they could not easily go to probate court or communicate with the lawyer. In one case, an heiress residing in England was dissatisfied with the lawyer:

Case 304–01. I do feel an explanatory letter should have been dispatched to me instead of one just informing me of my aunt's death and that I was an heir to her estate. Once I was informed that I was an heir, I heard nothing for six months. If I had been in the United States, I would have gone to see the lawyer. A conversation is always more enlightening than a dictated letter.

Other out-of-state residents complained that they received insufficient information and poor cooperation from the lawyer.

Case 376–01. He didn't keep me informed. There were problems with selling the real estate. His correspondence wasn't good; when I called him I got little response.

Case 566–01. He gave scanty information or wrong information. I kept calling long-distance for information. For two months his secretary told me he was out of town, but she never told me how long he would be out of town. Some of his advice was wrong, so I finally had to get a lawyer here to straighten things out.

On the other hand, if the attorney kept his out-of-town clients well informed, they were extremely likely to have a favorable opinion of him.

Case 566–02. I would recommend this man to anyone. He explained how long it would take and why. He explained the basis of his fees. I am just very satisfied.

Another criterion used to judge the lawyer was competence in probate matters and whether the attorney took over the detail work involved in the administration of the estate.

Case 207–01. He was a good lawyer. He took over for me. I never had to take time off from work. The lawyer did an awful lot of running arcund.

Dissatisfaction with the lawyer resulted if the executor was inconvenienced.

Case 126–01. I could have done just as well without an attorney. I've done more running around than the lawyer did. I arranged for the transfer of the title to the car.

Some of the dissatisfaction with the lawyer resulted from a lack of understanding regarding the complementary but distinct roles of the lawyer and the executor. It is the executor's responsibility to locate the decedent's assets, but one respondent believed it was the lawyer's job and therefore was unhappy with the lawyer's performance.

Case 204–02. I don't believe he did a full-time job on this case. He doesn't have a law office. He was very casual—part-time lawyer and part-time realtor. He hasn't tried to locate the bank account that we think Dad had nor a safe-deposit box.

The clients were also concerned about the honesty of their lawyers, and there were a few complaints about unethical practices or unscrupulous lawyers. It was difficult to determine if these feelings arose because the lawyer was unethical or because clients were not well informed about the lawyer's work.

Case 392–02. I'm just sick over the whole thing. Attorneys force you to do things you know are wrong. I would never want to involve an attorney in a court case like that. Attorneys are nothing but legal thieves, and there's nothing you can do about it. I just finally signed the papers and let it go at that. Fees? He [attorney] wrote himself a check for $600. I went to the judge, and he finally reduced the fees. So I fired the attorney and got another one, who did the same sort of things. I finally signed all the papers to get rid of the case.

Case 553–01. By prolonging the case, the lawyer sees to it that the estate is slowly eaten away. They drag the case out to make more money. The lawyer doesn't give a damn about the pecple involved. Lawyers take advantage of you at the time you are most shocked by the death of a relative.

One source of dissatisfaction with the lawyer's fee was that the clients were not informed of the cost before the services were performed; or if they were informed, the estimate was less than the actual charges. It appears that these survivors approached the probate work as though it were an everyday contractual business transaction rather than a professional task in which it is difficult to designate beforehand a price for services rendered. Although this problem is beyond the scope of the present study, it is important to point out that variations in role expectations were a continuous source of tension and dissatisfaction in client-practitioner relationships.

Case 589–03. The lawyer quoted me $150 and actually charged $403.03. I thought hiring a lawyer would save money, and I thought the lawyer should pay the court fees.

Another survivor was thoroughly satisfied with the lawyer except for his fee.

Case 239–04. I could ask the lawyer anything, and he'd tell me. He never tried to cover anything up, and he would give his advice without waiting for me to ask for it each time. I thought the fee was rather high, although I don't have anything to compare it with. I object to the fact that they wait until it's all over before they tell you what it will cost.

Relevant factors in the calculation of the fee were variously seen by survivors to be the lawyer's time and professional knowledge and the size and complexity of the estate. The client, although questioning the value of these elements and the services related to them, was nevertheless gratified to have someone do the difficult and time-consuming work involved in settling the estate.

Case 028–02. The time the lawyer spends is impossible to figure out, because lawyers are inconsistent. On the one hand they say we are paying them for their skill and professional training. On the other hand they bill you for every trip to court and every phone call as though you were paying them hourly wages. They can't have it both ways. They get you coming and going.

Case 339–01. The settling of bills can become too complicated in an emotional time such as the death of a dear one. His fee was reasonable, and he is entitled to it by virtue of the vast knowledge necessary to do a good job.

Case 109–01. He took care of it real well. He let us know what was necessary; he gave us all the details; and he called us—we didn't have to call him. Considering the time spent, it was money well spent. I wouldn't have known where to start.

A few persons judged the fee on the basis of what they thought lawyers should earn; perhaps they were thinking of the style of life appropriate to a professional man.[4]

Case 241–03. I was very satisfied with the lawyer. I didn't have to do anything outside of provide him with facts. I think he saved me money by knowing his way around

4. Adam Smith said, "We trust our health to the physician, our fortune and sometimes our life and reputation to the lawyer and attorney. Such confidence could not safely be reposed in people of a very mean or low condition. Their reward must be such, therefore, as may give them that rank in the society which so important a trust requires." Cited by T. H. Marshall, *Class, Citizenship and Social Development* (Garden City, N.Y.: Doubleday & Company, Inc., Anchor Books, 1965), p. 159.

and checking things that I would have overlooked. They more than earn their fee. This appears to be the most logical argument for having a lawyer. Based on time involved and knowing what lawyers should earn, I'm sure that the fee was reasonable.

Case 133–01. He did things the way I wanted them to be done. His fee was fair enough because you can't get a lawyer for a small fee. Most honest ones will charge in line with circumstances.

The ideal lawyer, according to the survivors' conception, was one who informed all interested parties of the contents of the will and the details of the process of estate administration. The ideal lawyer also informed the survivors in advance of the fee for his services. Easy communication between the client and attorney was desired by the survivor, and this was facilitated when the survivors and attorney have been acquainted prior to the estate settlement. The ideal lawyer also took over the more onerous and inconvenient tasks of the executor. Finally, he was fair and honest.

Appraisers

The ratio of those who were satisfied with the appraisers' handling and fees to those who were dissatisfied was less than 2 to 1, far lower than the ratio of satisfaction with the probate court and lawyers (see Table 11–6). On this basis, it can be said that the estate-appraisal system was the least satisfactory of the three aspects examined.

TABLE 11–6 SURVIVORS' SATISFACTION WITH THE APPRAISERS[a]

Condition	Handling		Fees		Handling and Fees	
	Number	Per Cent	Number	Per Cent	Number	Percent
Satisfied	256	20.7	236	19.1	155	12.6
Dissatisfied	143	11.6	152	12.3	86	7.0

[a] Percentages were based on the total survivor population of 1,234. There were 835 survivors who either were neutral or had no information regarding handling and 846 who were neutral or had no information regarding fees.

Dissatisfaction with the appraisal system was expressed concerning the procedure for appointing the appraiser; his qualifications; the belief that appraising the estate was unnecessary or, if it had to be done, that not more than one appraiser should have been used; and the belief that the estate was overcharged for the work performed.

Case 012–03. Why three appraisers—each charging $25? One of the appraisers listed was a lawyer in this same lawyer's office, and he never came out. When the bank sends an appraiser out for loan purposes, they charge $10 and check inside as well as out.

Case 029–01. A big joke! For one thing I never saw the appraisers—don't know how they did it. Somebody was home all the time, and nobody ever came to the door. Any fee you get for not doing a job is exorbitant.

Case 182–04. Why do we need appraisers? Tax value gives the true appraisal. They think we're simple-minded; that's what gets me. We know what a house will go for—by common sense.

Case 105–02. They valued the house very high. I had my own appraiser come from the bank. He valued the house at $5,000 less than the court appraiser. The court put a high value on the house so they could get more money.

Case 659–01. Just a political plum! If it's going to be a plum, I'd rather choose who's going to get it.

Survivors who were satisfied with appraisers indicated that the estate estimate was an accurate reflection of its market value. The person who was satisfied with the fee charged was either looking at the fee as a percentage of a total investment that is similar to a brokerage or real estate fee or as a relatively small absolute amount. The difference between those with favorable opinions and those with unfavorable opinions was a matter of perspective: fees relative to services performed versus absolute amount of fees, the accuracy of appraisement versus its necessity.

The Executor or Administrator

The executor or administrator has an important role in estate settlement, and his position is quite different from that of the lawyer or the appraiser. First, the executor or administrator is usually a member of the family. Second, he is frequently a beneficiary and very often the principal beneficiary. Third, if he is not a lawyer or banker, he is usually inexperienced in the responsibilities of his position.

Those survivors (excluding those who served as executors or administrators) who made a judgment were overwhelmingly satisfied with the executor or administrator (see Table 11–7). The ratio of those who were satisfied with

TABLE 11–7 SURVIVORS' SATISFACTION WITH EXECUTOR OR ADMINISTRATOR[a]

	Handling		Fees		Handling and Fees	
Condition	Number	Per Cent	Number	Per Cent	Number	Per Cent
Satisfied	501	40.6	349	28.3	305	24.7
Dissatisfied	103	8.3	52	4.2	27	2.2

[a] Percentages were based on the total survivor population of 1,234. In 630 cases the question was not applicable, there was no information, or the respondent gave neutral answers regarding handling of the estate. In 833 cases regarding fees, similar conditions existed.

both the handling and the fees of the executor or administrator to those who were dissatisfied with both was better than 11 to 1.

The comments of these satisfied persons were of the order, "She did fine, she is my mother." Thus they provided a general measure of satisfaction but no specific clues about the expectations survivors hold concerning the role of the executor or administrator in estate settlement.

Among the dissatisfied, there was seldom only one single reason given for dissatisfaction. Instead, there was much overlapping of three major complaints: lack of information, dishonesty or collusion, and incompetence. Where there was a lack of information, suspicions were easily aroused concerning the honesty or competence of the executor or administrator. In a few cases, the survivors felt the conduct of the executor or administrator had resulted in a personal loss.

Case 541–01. She never notified me when furniture was to be sold, and I wanted to buy several pieces. She and the lawyer worked together. Would you call this collusion? He called her "honey-pie," and she is married!

Case 273–04. The house could have sold for more if it had been cleaned and fixed up.

In families where there was already friction, the settling of the estate reinforced old antagonisms or brought to the surface hostile feelings that had not been openly expressed before. In a few previously close families, the settlement caused a rift in family relationships. Among the survivors in these families, there was widespread sentiment for the choice of an outside executor or administrator.

Outside executors or administrators, however, were not free from criticism. Survivors were dissatisfied with a high proportion of the professional fiduciaries. The 103 survivors dissatisfied with the handling of the case represented 67 cases; in 17 of these cases, a bank or an attorney served as personal representative. In the total decedent sample of 659 estates, there were 57 cases with professional fiduciaries.

It appears that the executor or administrator may become the focal point of general dissatisfaction with the estate settlement or that the general dissatisfaction may include the attorney and courts as well. It is only fair to mention in conclusion that survivors who served as executors and administrators often spoke of their task as a thankless one.

Time Taken for Estate Settlement

The time a case takes to be settled may be the "fault" of the statutes or errors, inefficiences, or negligence by the lawyer, the court, or the executor. The sample survivors openly and bluntly expressed their dissatisfaction with the time it took to close an estate. The majority felt that the time to settle was unreasonably long. Among the survivors, 733 persons (59 per cent) felt the settlement time was unreasonable; 208 (17 per cent) thought the settlement time was reasonable; 193 (16 per cent) were indifferent; and 100 (8 per cent) had no information about the settlement time. The survivors not only held unfavorable opinions concerning time for settlement but also were better informed about this aspect than about the specifics of fees and the work of various functionaries.

In general, if the lawyer had informed the survivors about the statutory limits, they were less impatient. However, even with some knowledge of the law, the client was sometimes resentful.

Case 576–02. The six-month waiting period is ridiculous if a will has been left transferring everything to the wife. You shouldn't even need probate court for this.

The waiting period was sometimes a source of antagonism between lawyer and client.

Case 659–01. The nine-month waiting period gets you anxious. The lawyer said he couldn't hurry it along because of the date. Nothing could be submitted before nine months. Once it got going, it went fast.

When cases were actually in probate court for an extraordinarily long time, it may have been the lawyer's fault.

Case 251–01. We changed lawyers twice because it was taking too long [in probate twenty-one months]. Our main thing is this: after a certain amount of time, probate court should step in. It seemed like the delay was deliberate. This cost the principal heir quite a lot of money.

Occasionally, a survivor remarked that while the time had not been important to him, it could be a source of grievance to others.

Case 030–01. To me it didn't matter very much. I was in no hurry to move. But it did take over a year, and this was a simple estate. Why should it take so long? I think this is partly because of the relaxed atmosphere in courts, which do not really function on a full-day basis. Small estates such as my wife's involve no hardship; but if the situation had been reversed, it would have been a hardship for my wife.

A few people thought that it should take longer to settle an estate.

Case 306–01. Why does everything have to be hurried, especially when you feel so miserable and there's so much to be done?

Thus, it appears that the lawyer received an undue share of criticism regarding the length of time it took to close an estate, a matter for which he is not primarily at fault or responsible. The time involved in the probate process from initiation to settlement is determined by law. Even when clients were informed of this, there was the tendency to disbelieve and to use the lawyer as a scapegoat for the expression of their frustrations, sorrows, and hostilities.

Attitudes Toward Estate Settlement in General and Fees in Particular

The respondents' attitudes toward estate settlement and fees were assessed by the use of two Likert-type scales. The first scale of general attitudes consisted of five questions.

General Attitude Scale

1. What is your opinion or feeling regarding court involvement in the estate?
2. What is your opinion or feeling regarding fees charged by probate court?
3. What is your opinion or feeling regarding the time involved in settling the estate?
4. What is your opinion or feeling concerning the lawyer's handling of the case?
5. What is your opinion or feeling regarding the lawyer's fees?

The total score on the General Attitude Scale may range from 5 (most favorable) to 15 (least favorable). All these items were scored: favorable = 1; no knowledge or indifferent = 2; and unfavorable = 3. "No knowledge" was scored with "indifferent" because all the survivors were involved in the case (they were heirs or next of kin) and could have had access to the information if they had wanted it. Two additional items, appraisers' handling and appraisers' fees, were omitted because they did not discriminate sufficiently on attitudes.[5] Also, personal representatives' handling and fees were excluded because, in the majority of cases, family members served and therefore no fees were charged.

The general attitude expressed by over half the survivors was indifference or ambivalence. For the remaining approximately 45 per cent of the survivors, over twice as many were favorable toward the settlement as were unfavorable (see Table 11–8).

5. Discriminatory power of items was analyzed by comparing mean scores for first and fourth quartiles. See Claire Sellitz et al., *Research Methods in Social Relations*, rev. ed. (New York: Rinehart & Winston, Inc., 1965), pp. 184–185. On this basis, the items on appraisers' handling and appraisers' fees were dropped because the discriminatory power was less than one. The results were as follows:

Questions	First Quartile Score	Fourth Quartile Score	Discriminatory Power
Court handling	1.086	2.160	1.074
Court fees	1.173	2.240	1.067
Time	1.217	2.653	1.436
Lawyers' handling	1.043	2.384	1.341
Lawyers' fees	1.173	2.500	1.327
Appraisers' handling	1.478	2.192	.714
Appraisers' fees	2.521	2.153	.378

TABLE 11–8 GENERAL ATTITUDE TOWARD SETTLEMENT

Attitude	Number	Per Cent
Favorable (5–7)	392	31.8
Somewhat favorable (8–9)	321	26.0
Somewhat unfavorable (10–11)	353	28.6
Unfavorable (12–15)	168	13.6
Total	1,234	100.0

Fee Attitude Scale

The second scale, the Fee Attitude Scale, was specifically developed to measure attitudes toward fees. This scale utilized two questions from the general scale: the question on court costs (question 2) and the question regarding lawyer's fee (question 5). A third question was: "What is your opinion or feeling regarding appraisers' fees?" This question was included on the Fee Attitude Scale in the interests of completeness, despite its discriminatory weakness.

Although nearly half the survivors were indifferent or ambivalent toward the fees, of the remaining survivors, as many were unfavorable as were favorable (see Table 11–9).

TABLE 11–9 ATTITUDE TOWARD FEES

Attitude	Number	Per Cent
Favorable (3–4)	318	25.8
Marginal (5–6)	594	48.1
Unfavorable (7–9)	322	26.1
Total	1,234	100.0

Determinants of Attitudes Toward Settlement

It was hypothesized that satisfaction and dissatisfaction would be related to socioeconomic variables and to the experience of the settlement of the estate. The expectation that the higher the individual ranked on socioeconomic variables, the more satisfied he would be with the lawyer, was based on the presumed greater experience that persons of higher socioeconomic status have with professional practitioners.

The data confirmed the hypothesis concerning client attitudes toward the lawyer in one respect: those who ranked higher in education, occupation, and income were more likely to believe that a lawyer was necessary in estate settlement. On the other hand, they were not as likely to have been satisfied with their lawyers as those of lesser education and income and occupational status were (see Appendix E, Table E–5). Those who were more highly placed as indicated by socioeconomic variables were more likely to be the survivors of decedents with larger and more complex estates. Therefore, they felt a lawyer was needed, but they were less likely to be satisfied with him because the lawyer's competence was tested against a more difficult task; or since the survivors were better educated, they were likely to judge him according to more exacting standards.

Are the survivors' attitudes toward estate settlement in general and fees in particular conditioned by socioeconomic variables? Using the General Attitude Scale and the Fee Attitude Scale, scores were found not to be associated with the indicators of socioeconomic class. In an effort to introduce a control on the experience of estate settlement, the tests were rerun with the survivors of release-of-assets estates omitted from the population. With these survivors omitted, there was still no relationship between attitudes toward the probate process and indicators of socioeconomic status. It must be concluded that socioeconomic status does not differentiate the attitudes of survivors toward estate settlement.

The available data concerning the settlement of decedent estates were examined: (1) the time between initiation of probate and the closing of an estate and (2) the various fees charged against the estate, including court costs, lawyers' fees, and appraisers' fees. If the fees were high and the settlement time was long, then would the survivors have negative feelings about the settlement and fees? Conversely, if the estate was settled with a minimum of time and expense, would the expressions be favorable?

The survivors' satisfaction regarding the settlement of the estate was found to be associated with the time the estate was in the probate process. In cases where estates were settled in less than one year, survivors expressed greater satisfaction than survivors in cases where the estates were in probate court more than two years (see Appendix E, Table E–6).

It was found that the higher the costs, the more negative the feelings toward the settlement of the estate. This was especially notable when costs exceeded $100 (see Appendix E, Table E–7). If the lawyer's fee was over $200, there were fewer expressions of satisfaction and correspondingly more expressions of dissatisfaction than when the fee was $200 or less (see Appendix E, Table E–8).

Control over the actual administration process was introduced by omitting the survivors in release-of-assets cases from the analysis. The association between feelings of satisfaction and the time and cost variables remained.

Attitudes toward fees were also found to be associated with time in probate court, court costs, and lawyers' fees. The longer the time and the greater the expense, the more negative the attitude.[6]

The relationship between attitude and time and expense were statistically

6. Although the question regarding attitude toward appraisers' fees was included in the scoring of the Fee Attitude Scale, the association between this scale and the actual

significant and not attributable to chance on both scales, with one exception. This was the lawyers' fees on the Fee Attitude Scale, where the level of probability was .10 (see Appendix E, Tables E–9, E–10, and E–11). The omitting of survivors of decedents whose estates were released without administration did not change the nature of the relationship.

Time in probate court would appear to be the single best indicator of attitude toward the settlement in general and fees in particular, since the relationship between time and attitudes was strongest, as indicated by gamma values (see Table 11–10).[7]

TABLE 11–10 GAMMA VALUES FOR RELATIONSHIP BETWEEN ATTITUDE AND EXPERIENCE VARIABLES

Variables	General Attitude	Attitude Toward Fees
Time	.25	.28
Court costs	.12	.13
Lawyer's fee	.16	.11

Conclusion

This chapter has discussed two related topics: (1) the survivors' evaluation of the various professionals and nonprofessionals involved in estate settlement and (2) the objective determinants of these attitudes. A large number of survivors were uninformed about these functionaries. As might be expected, the survivors were better informed about the activities of the lawyer than about those of the court and appraisers.

Of the survivors who felt they had sufficient knowledge on which to base an opinion regarding the settlement of the estate, favorable responses outnumbered unfavorable responses by a large majority. However, the ratio of satisfaction to dissatisfaction varied according to the specific probate element or procedure. Nearly five times as many were satisfied with the court's handling of the case and the fees charged as were dissatisfied; less than twice as many were satisfied with the appraisers' handling and fees as were dissatisfied.

Negative sentiments about the court were to a large extent attributed to the alleged rudeness of clerical personnel. Another source of discontent stemmed from a dislike of outside interference. Some of the interviewees believed estate settlement should be a personal and family matter.[8] Objections to court fees

appraisers' fees was not analyzed because there was insufficient variation in such fees for analytic purposes.

7. William L. Hays, *Statistics for Psychologists* (New York: Holt, Rinehart & Winston, Inc., 1963), pp. 655–656.

8. As in much research, hindsight is the best vision. We regret not having specific

were based upon the method of billing that produced a flow of small charges during the course of probate as well as the absolute amount charged.

If the lawyer was judged honest and kept the survivors informed of progress in the case, they generally felt that he was doing a good job. They apparently could not evaluate his competence, but they expected that he would take a sufficiently active role in the case in order to reduce their involvement to a minimum. Most likely, many highly regarded lawyers assumed some of the burdens of administration and in this way performed services to the families beyond the requirements of their professional role for a single fee.

The appraisal system came under attack for various reasons. Some survivors believed that the appraisers were chosen on the basis of political patronage and were not especially equipped to make property evaluations. Others felt that the work of the appraiser was unnecessary and if "one has to live with the system" then no more than one appraiser should be used. The appraisers' fees were generally a small part of administrative costs, but they were objected to on the basis that little work or needless work was performed.

The executor was usually not a stranger to the respondents, as other probate functionaries usually were. He was most often a family member and quite often the principal beneficiary. Thus it was difficult for many people to separate their evaluation of the person from their evaluation of his performance in the role of executor. If the executor was an outsider (a lawyer or a bank), the likelihood of dissatisfaction was high. Balanced against this finding were the statements of survivors who said that the executor should be an outsider. Many family members who served as executors felt the same way. As with the attorney, one of the chief complaints against an executor was that he failed to keep other family members informed.

A chief source of dissatisfaction for the survivors was what they considered an unreasonably long time to settle the case. The questions concerning the various aspects of settlement were combined to make two scales: the General Attitude Scale and the Fee Attitude Scale. Only the General Attitude Scale included the question on time, yet actual time in probate court was highly associated with attitude on both scales. If the estate was settled in less than one year, the interviewee's attitude toward the various functionaries and their fees was favorable. If the estate was not settled within two years, the attitude of the interviewees was apt to be unfavorable.

Finally, it should be remembered that most cases were settled in less than two years and that, on the whole, the probate system was regarded favorably or ambivalently by the survivor population.

---

questions regarding the necessity of a probate court and also attitudes toward estate and inheritance taxation. From the negative sentiments voluntarily expressed concerning these topics, it is likely that many persons would favor abolishing both courts and estate taxes.

Chapter 12

Estate Settlement: Lawyer Attitudes Toward the Probate Process

ESTATE SETTLEMENT differs from estate planning, and these differences have consequences for the relationship between the lawyer and his client. The employment of an attorney in the settlement of an estate by the executor or administrator is imperative in most cases.[1] Clients cannot decide to do it themselves or disregard the need for a settlement, as it is possible for them to do in regard to will making by deciding to be intestate. The legal profession has a virtual monopoly of estate settlement. Banks may serve as executors and as trustees, but they cannot serve as attorneys; and probate and administration are court procedures requiring the services of lawyers as officers of the court. This monopoly, however, may be theoretical where the bank is executor. In such cases, it is likely that the bank will control the actions of the attorney hired as its counsel.

Once hired, the lawyer's fee will be enforced by the court; the attorney is generally paid before the assets are distributed so that he has a guaranteed income. In these respects, estate settlement is an excellent area of practice for the lawyer, providing him not only with a steady income but also with a large degree of professional autonomy.

In other respects, estate settlement is a complicated area of practice. Although the lawyer technically represents the executor or administrator, in actual fact, the survivors may also consider him their attorney. In estate planning, the fiduciary relationship between lawyer and client can be maintained because all necessary interaction takes place in a dyad. In the estate settlement phase, little occurs that is not a matter of public record. In fact, in the estate settlement, the court's procedures dominate the process, in large measure determining when the case will be closed.

Estate administration occurs over a long period of time. Many separate acts are required by statute, and the length of time in which it is possible to close an estate is determined by requisites of the probate-law structure. Even though these acts of the settlement process are recorded at court and are known to

1. Attorneys were employed in over 90 per cent of the decedents' estates; those estates without an attorney were generally very small.

those who seek them out, the lawyer is still in a position to control the situation. He has a fund of knowledge and expertise in the intricacies of the process, and few clients can evaluate the actual amount of time the lawyer consumes in estate administration or the skill required to carry out successfully the will of the testator or the terms of the intestate succession statutes. The lawyer in estate administration has a greater degree of autonomy over the work situation in using his professional skills; he can charge fees more to his liking and consequently is more satisfied in this phase of inheritance work than with any other phase.

The Ideal Client

A group of 17 attorneys was asked to describe the ideal client. They considered a number of characteristics and situations such as the financial characteristics of the estate, the complexity of the family situation, the client's appreciation of the services performed by the attorney, and the personality traits of the client. The following are some typical responses of these attorneys regarding the ideal client:

> The client who brings it in, says: "The assets are thus and so. Here's the will. You prepare the papers, and then we'll pay the bill," is ideal.

> Ninety per cent of my clients are ideal in this area. A person who understands a little bit about probate but not enough to accomplish it on his own, so will go along with you, co-operating in any way to finish it up, is what you want.

> A reasonable man who will accept the decision of a good lawyer is the kind of client I want.

The ideal client accepts the expertise of the lawyer, has faith in him, generally is easy to communicate with, and interacts with the attorney and his staff with a minimum of friction and hostility. This counselor's view of the ideal client is understandable, since achievement of a closed case depends on having a model client, one who permits the attorney to control the interaction situation. Moreover, the lawyer is constrained by legal statutes and cultural prescriptions in matters of will making and estate administration. He can perform best with a client who accepts these limitations, asks few questions, provides information readily, is receptive to the advice and counsel of the expert, and has few expectations beyond those provided by the attorney.

Estate settlement is largely an economic activity. The will or intestate succession has determined the pattern of property distribution. Consequently, the attorney is more approving of the "accountant type" of person who can keep accurate records than of the "financially disordered, unpaid-bill" type.

> Someone who is very orderly in keeping records of his property relating to investments, insurance, titles to real property, etc.

If he has records all assembled for you, it cuts down substantially the amount of time it takes to handle all the items of the estate.

Normally an accountant who usually will keep very good records. They generally can grasp what their duties really are.

Somebody who had a close working knowledge of the deceased's life, business, etc.—who doesn't call the attorney, is patient, and who quickly compiles any necessary data. Especially one who doesn't bother you with the standard question, "What's new?"

One with a million-dollar estate! That's not true. One who is intelligent enough to understand the processes involved in probating an estate.

Two words, "intelligent" and "organized," best summarize these desired client traits. It is now too late for the will maker to be fair. Whether he was or not, the settlement of the estate must take place. Decision making is routine. The probate and administration process largely involves the filing of the right paper at the right time. Since the attorney for the executor or administrator will be preparing the necessary forms, he must have the available data. Thus, there is an overwhelming emphasis on "good records."

Estate Settlement Problems

It is technically the personal representative's job to proceed with the completion of estate settlement in the shortest practicable time. The attorney should have ready access to necessary data in order to facilitate the process. However, there are times and conditions when estate settlements are difficult to effect in a reasonable amount of time. The sample attorneys listed a number of conditions or events in their practices that created such problems (see Table 12–1).

TABLE 12–1 MAJOR CONDITIONS OR EVENTS THAT PRESENT DIFFICULTIES IN ESTATE SETTLEMENT

Difficulties	Number	Per Cent[a]
Family disagreement (among selves)	27	38.6
Idiosyncratic character traits or behavior	19	27.1
Uncooperative with lawyer	14	20.0
Lack of money to pay debts or legacies	3	4.3
Nondisclosure of deceased's assets in possession of family	3	4.3
Complicated family situation	2	2.9
Locating heirs and legatees	2	2.9
None	8	11.4
Total	78	111.5

[a] Percentages were based on 70 attorneys. Total exceeds 100 per cent because some attorneys gave more than one answer.

Some attorneys expressed no difficulties at all. One lawyer reported, "Normally they don't do anything that makes it difficult. The probate laws supersede anything they could possibly do."

Certain areas of difficulty received little emphasis and to a large extent were procedural in nature: (1) lack of money to pay debts or legacies, (2) nondisclosure of the deceased's assets in possession of family members, and (3) locating heirs and legatees. The locating of heirs and legatees has become a popular business, and difficulties in locating them have been related to the time and costs of settling an estate. Yet only two of 70 lawyers considered this to be a major problem.

The two cases involving complicated family situations concerned a remarriage and a common-law marriage. One attorney mentioned that "most problems arise with a second or third marriage." The second stated, "Not much really that the survivor can do. Of course there is the problem of the so-called common-law wife." The case involved a woman claiming to be the spouse of the decedent in a common-law marriage. Common-law marriage may present problems because a person who enters such a marriage often believes he can leave it in the same way. However, a formal divorce decree is necessary despite the lack of wedding formalities; and the claimant (the alleged subsequent spouse), though in good faith, may be nothing more than a mate in illicit cohabitation. Yet the responses of the sample attorneys indicate that common-law marriage is not a major problem in estate settlement.

Two major problems are the noncooperative heir or legatee and conflict within the family. The lawyer engaged in estate settlement requires the confidence of the decedent's successors. This he cannot automatically achieve. If he is the will-making lawyer, his attorney-client relationship has been with the decedent and not with the potentially contesting survivors. His relationship is now with the personal representative. Yet in a sense, the successors are quasi-clients, and the degree to which they will cooperate with a lawyer depends on their perceptions of how well the attorney is representing their vital interests. Conflict and misunderstanding result from the confrontation between completing the job without delay according to legal precepts and the uncertainty of potential takers regarding procedures of settlement and regarding the fact that the lawyer represents their interests.

They question every procedural step. This is not true of the less educated and those of foreign extraction. They depend on you and trust you. The more educated are likely to question everything.

In a number of cases the person made fiduciary may come into possession as fiduciary of a large amount of money and begin to feel that the money belongs to him and spend it as though it is his. So I ask for joint control with the bonding company so no checks can be issued without my signature.

Quite often clients are wives who have heard all types of rumors as to what the law is.

They can think of everything. For example, they are dissatisfied with the will, won't take money, want more money, want less money, want to gear it around to suit themselves; and they don't see why you should worry about courts.

They listen to what the neighbors say and get advice from everyone but an attorney.

Conflict among family members over the inheritance is another source of difficulty for the attorney. Contrary to his wishes, the attorney is frequently drawn into such conflicts. He is viewed by heirs and legatees as an advocate-judge representing their interests alone. Since he is more accustomed to the role of advocate than he is to the role of Solomon, he is bound to take sides, to champion the "right" individual or group, and to attempt a settlement within a reasonable amount of time. The lawyer has preconceived ideas about the causes of family quarrels.

Greed is the sole cause of problems in settling an estate, and blood is of no moment. This is part of human nature. Parents may deny themselves to accumulate an estate; then fighting devisees create untold expense in litigation, and the estate goes down the drain. While it creates business for me, it is a vicious indictment of human practice.

Wherever you have a situation involving money, it seems that people invariably get to haggling and lose their sense of equilibrium, build up more legal expense, and in a sense turn it over to an attorney who takes it all up in fees. Some kind of strange emotionalism prevails in our society where the thought of having money raises all kinds of conflicts not based on reason or logic.

Fight! They all think they ought to get more. But that usually takes place where an older person dies without children. Then I'd say you earn your money—every dime!

While family feuds present difficulties to attorneys in the settlement of estates, apparently those who suffer the most in the long run are the family members. If litigation is involved, the expenses and costs will cut into the estate assets. Attorneys receive more money in such cases but dislike the labeling of such fees as "blood money" by disgruntled clients, and most would have preferred to have administered the estate without litigation and to have received the usual compensation.

Sometimes a lawyer has the combination of a quarreling family and uncooperative survivors in one case. His deceased client was a good man to work with, but the survivors are creating all kinds of trouble. Lawyers might consider choosing their clients more carefully in the will-making and estates area. Since estate planning and settlement involve two generational families and occur over time and with stages requiring the lawyer to interact with different family members, this suggestion is not so outlandish. The best estate-planning client may or may not have relatives or family members who are as pleasant or as cooperative as he is. Disagreeable and uncooperative potential takers could hinder final disposition through lawsuits, and the lawyer's hands would be tied.

They fight among themselves or wait until the last minute to give you information.

They get sick, get old, get senile, and unreasonable—mostly—or get into arguments with relatives.

They refuse to come into the office or refuse to abide by the lawyer's request to come in and sign papers. There is interference by in-laws in property settlement. Ninety per cent of trouble in the estates area is created by in-laws.

People become bitter enemies upon the death of the testator as a result of distribution of the estate. Money changes people! I have had few cases where there wasn't some bitterness if the estate wasn't equally divided, and people will even begrudge the few dollars the executor will get for administering the estate. They complain about any costs connected with the administration of an estate.

Fourteen attorneys stressed idiosyncratic personality characteristics or behavior of clients as major sources of difficulties.

They draw their own wills. When they do it, it's improper. The will is no good, and the property has to go through intestacy.

They don't pay the bills as fast as they should: funeral bills, court costs, appraisers' fees, and attorneys' fees.

The executor or administrator who pays debts without obtaining adequate receipts is a problem.

They are always in a hurry to get their share. This ties in with the socioeconomic status of clients who are in financial need. I get repeated telephone calls in this respect.

I just had a problem with an estate where the executrix was appointed without bond. Unknown to us, she had an alcohol problem and expended a substantial portion of the estate. There were no funds when time came to pay the inheritance tax. Her parents came up with the money due the heirs and for tax estimation and attorneys' fees.

The responses of two attorneys offer a particularly clear description of the ideal client from the standpoint of will making and estate settlement. Regarding will making, the first attorney felt the ideal client was "one who is aware of the nature and extent of his property and knows how he wishes to dispose of it." To the second attorney, the ideal client was "one who has given sufficient thought to the extent of his estate and the provisions he wants to make for those left behind." The first attorney's opinion of the ideal client regarding estate settlement was "a person of reasonable intelligence who recognizes that administration is not an overnight thing. People who are inheriting money generally feel they should get it yesterday, and it's not a 'yesterday' proposition. In a situation where there is room for argument about creditors, charges, or compromise of conflicting claims, a reasonable person does not demand everything legally possible. Clients, like lawyers, should be reasonable." In the opinion of the second attorney, the ideal client in the estate field is "an executor who will follow our instructions and not try to project himself into legal work. One who will let us tell him what steps must be followed and not concern himself with minor unimportant details."

There is some contrast between the concept of the model client in the areas of will making and estate settlement. Although the client must place his trust and confidence in the attorney and should be intelligent and orderly, he should be somewhat vigorous and energetic in the estate-planning phase. He must know his own mind. He must know the extent of his property and must make decisions concerning the disposition of the estate. The decision-making process on the part of the client is crucial in will making. He must think. The lawyer is merely an instrument, phrasing in a legal manner the testator's expressed wishes. However, in the estate settlement or administration process, the more passive the executor, the better things are. Although technically he may be legally responsible for decision making, in actuality, the executor becomes the conduit. He should furnish the necessary information and sign required papers. But here, decision making is the function of the lawyer, even though his decisions are controlled by rigid statutory material with which the lay person is unfamiliar. In essence, the client and the lawyer enjoy a reciprocal relationship in will making; but in estate settlement, the lawyer attempts to control the client with the aid of statutory provisions.

Ambiguity and tension between survivors and the attorney may appear during the process of estate settlement if the decedent's attorney becomes the counsel for the estate representative. Survivors generally have not had a close relationship with this attorney. He was engaged by the testator and is expected to effectuate the wishes of the testator through probate and administration. The testator's objectives concerning property disposition may not be in consonance with the objectives of the successors. The attorney uses a business model in estate settlement. He is for efficiency and suggests a no-nonsense economic formula that, if followed, will close the case as quickly as the law permits. He tends to disregard the latent or manifest emotional problems of the inheritors. Because he considers thinking and planning to be part of the will-making phase, he cannot see the need for them among the survivors and generally does not communicate the reasons for his role shift, or perhaps he does not communicate it well enough to satisfy the successors. Rather, he views estate settlement as an outcome of a previously initiated process. These different views of the stages of the process cause tension and ambiguity in the lawyer-client relationship at the time of estate settlement.

The Lawyer's Compensation

The attorney is entitled to receive a fee for drafting a will and settling an estate. Initial compensation is received for his services in the will-making stage. Considerable advice may be given by the lawyer at this time. He may plan the disposition of a complicated estate or serve as a scrivener in the preparation of a simple will which takes only a few minutes. The majority of cases handled by the sample attorneys fell in the latter category. The attorney who drafts the will may also be the counsel for the executor or administrator upon the death of the deceased. In such a case, he will receive a second fee. It is also possible that the attorney who makes the will may not be the attorney of record for estate administration. The tasks involved in drawing up a will and in settling an estate are very different, especially in terms of the time involved. Yet attorneys viewed this as one continuous process. Most engaged in will drafting, which was not especially lucrative, because of the possibility that they would subsequently administer the estate of the decedent. They had the inside track because survivors were likely to rely on them initially. This presents the possibility of a case-building practice over generational time.

The attitudes of the attorneys toward compensation for estate settlement showed a different pattern from their attitudes toward will drafting. Ninety per cent of the lawyers thought that compensation received for estate settlement was adequate. Only seven lawyers believed compensation to be inadequate; five of these indicated that they were not compensated for the time spent. Why were lawyers, with very few exceptions, satisfied with the fees they received? The answers are best found in their own words.

> Because most of the time I do not file an application for fees. I work it out with the client and heirs. I don't have to file when I can make my agreement with heirs and all those interested.

Such a procedure is allowed by Rule 26 of the Cuyahoga County Probate Court, which reads in part: "Where all the interested parties have consented in writing to the amount of the allowance of compensation or fees, no application need be made for the allowance thereof, provided such consent is endorsed on the account or evidenced by separate instrument filed therewith." This provision facilitates the collection of fees, and the court is merely an observer. The percentages suggested in Rule 26 still function as guidelines in the setting of fees.

> It amounts to adequate compensation on a time basis.

> Basically the ultimate terms constitute reimbursement to this office of $35 to $50 an hour, sometimes more.

> It is adequate for me because I usually go out and get the estate case, take down the facts regarding the decedent, and so forth, and then give the case to my associate,

who takes care of it. Then I collect the fee. I do this because I find I can make better use of my time with cases that come into the office.

This is the one area of my practice where I can say that compensation is adequate.

I'm satisfied. When I'm not, I ask for more fees. I have one right now where the scheduled fees were $600 and I got $1,500 extra.

The last statement demonstrates that the probate court is flexible in fee allowances; the percentages suggested in Rule 26 serve as guides rather than as minimum or maximum fees to be charged. The attorney may receive a higher fee where he can justify it.

One lawyer believed attorneys were overcompensated. The rules of the Probate Court of Cuyahoga County were amended as of November 1, 1965. The new rule includes all real property as well as personal property in the basic percentages. The attorney who indicated compensation to be overadequate stated:

As far as real estate is concerned, I have nothing to do but file a certificate for transfer of title. What business do I have charging my client a large per cent just to transfer a title? This is especially true in cases of large amounts of real estate.

He thought the former fee schedule was adequate. (See Appendix G for the old and new versions of Cuyahoga County Probate Court Rule 26.) Another attorney analyzed the situation in the following words:

It is only in the probate field that many attorneys can pick up slack in fees for other areas. This is why attorneys will write a will for practically nothing. Without wills you don't get estates. Without estates you couldn't practice law.

Five of the seven attorneys who considered compensation for estate settlement to be inadequate were time oriented.

The compensation is inadequate. Administration of an estate takes more time than the average lawyer realizes. Most don't keep accurate records of their time, and if they did they would be shocked to learn they are getting less than $20 per hour. Moreover, if you have litigation, you can't possibly collect for time involved. You might wake up in the night mulling over problems. How can you charge for that? In a will contest you practically have to live with the people involved for periods of months. You get to be a part of the family.

This attorney appeared to be thinking of whether or not the compensation was adequate for attorneys in general. In his own case, it may well have been adequate, since he said, "I use the time that I put in as a basis for the charge in every case. I keep a daily record on clients' folders up to date till yesterday." Another attorney stated that the compensation was adequate in the case of large estates, but inadequate in the case of small and medium-sized estates. In these latter estates, he submitted that the time required was worth more than the allowable fees under the probate schedule.

The other two attorneys who felt the compensation was inadequate were thinking specifically of their own situations. They said that if they charged regular fees in accordance with the schedule, they would be adequately compensated; but because their clients were poor, they charged lower fees.

> I would be properly compensated if I charged regular fees, which I don't. Most of my work in estates is from people around here who can ill afford to pay. Estates which come through my hands are mainly aged widows or widowers whose only assets are property they live in, so I gauge my fees to meet their pocketbooks.

This individual was a salaried attorney. His private practice was part time. His clients in estate matters were employees or the immediate family of employees of the organization for which he was attorney, basically a service organization.

Over-all, attorneys were satisfied with the compensation received in estate settlement. The probate schedule brought a return that most lawyers consider to be the equivalent of a satisfactory hourly rate. Although the attorneys may be cornered by the public with respect to will drafting, the public has little to say about fees for services rendered by the lawyer in the area of estate settlement.

The finding that lawyers were satisfied with fees received for estate settlement and dissatisfied with fees received for will making warrants further discussion. As mentioned previously, in will making the lawyer has competition from functionaries of other institutional systems such as banks, and in addition, the mass media have communicated the notion that making a will is a simple matter. More important, making a will is a one-time operation. It may take as little as half an hour or at most three or four hours to complete the will. Even if a lawyer has a number of consultations with his client, the time seldom extends beyond a few weeks. In this instance, what the lawyer does is highly visible and enables the public to place a value on the services rendered, much to the chagrin of at least half the lawyers in this sample. In contrast, estate administration occurs over a fairly long period of time; there are many separate acts involved, and as a result the client cannot effectively evaluate (as he can in the case of will making) the actual amount of time and skill required to settle an estate. The lawyer's remuneration is higher, and therefore he is generally satisfied.

The Probate System

The attorneys were asked questions concerning the functioning of the probate court. These questions related to the delegation of duties by probate judges to referees, the number of judges needed in Cuyahoga County, and needed changes in the probate law or procedures.

Attorneys believed that the judge-referee system was working rather well in

Cuyahoga County, with 63 per cent stating that the present system needed no change (see Table 12–2).

TABLE 12–2 ATTORNEY SATISFACTION WITH EXTENT OF DELEGATION OF DUTIES TO REFEREES

Extent of Delegation Found Satisfactory	Number	Per Cent
No delegation	1	1.4
Less than now	16	22.9
Same as now	44	62.9
More than now	0	0.0
No opinion or unknown	9	12.9
Total	70	100.1

The single attorney who held the opinion that the probate judge should delegate nothing to referees said, "That's why we have probate judges to take care of these matters." In further questioning, he was asked if he was opposed to the use of referees. He told the interviewer, "Yes, ma'am. And I like the referees down there, too. But I'm opposed to having the matter referred to a referee when it's a court matter."

This view was in disagreement with the statutory authorization for probate court referees as found in the Ohio Revised Code.[2] The probate court referee is a deputy clerk who is an attorney at law admitted to practice in the state of Ohio. He serves in his capacity as referee at the pleasure of the judge and receives no other salary than that as deputy clerk. In the Cuyahoga County Probate Court, there were seventeen referees assisting the two probate judges in all areas of their jurisdiction. The function of the referee is broader than that of a fact finder. He can also make legal decisions. Section 2315.31 of the Ohio Revised Code reads as follows:

> Referees must state the facts found and conclusions of law separately. Their decision must be given, and may be excepted to and reviewed, as in a trial by the court. Their report upon the whole issue shall stand as the decision of the court, and judgment may be entered thereon as if the court had tried the action.

Thus the referee has the authority to decide factual and legal questions. A reference may be assigned to any case where the parties consent; or it may be directed by the court without the consent of the parties if the situation involved is one in which the parties are not entitled to a trial by jury. As a matter of fact, if the proceeding so referred is uncontested, the court may receive the report of the referee without requiring that the facts found and the conclusions of law be stated separately.[3]

2. Ohio Revised Code 2315.37.
3. Loc. cit.

The data in this study suggest that the 23 per cent of the attorneys who desired less delegation to referees were probably generally opposed to the referee system established by the state legislature. This referee system is not in any way limited to the probate court. Statutory authorization for referees is found for the courts of common pleas,[4] municipal courts,[5] and juvenile courts.[6] Referees are also frequently utilized by the courts of appeals and the Ohio Supreme Court. Although there are no statutory provisions authorizing such references, they are considered to be either within the courts' inherent authority or a necessary adjunct to the statutes pertaining to their jurisdiction.

One attorney believed that judges were likely to be more impartial in decision making.

Obviously they've got to delegate something. Frankly, I don't think they should delegate as much as they do, because we sometimes find that the referee is bound not by legalities but by modes of behavior and patterns he has followed for the past forty years. If there is anything to be gained from elected judgeship, he should bring fresh insight to problems that are presented to him. A judge is more apt to look at the problem with a degree of impartiality.

Another attorney favored allowing delegation on all "minor" affairs, questions of law as well as fact, but would have "delicate" affairs handled by a judge. Yet how does one draw the line between what is "minor" and what is "delicate"? Such terms are too vague and indefinite to furnish guidelines. On the other hand, a line can be drawn between factual and legal issues.

The basic concern of some members of the bar was that the probate judge would rely too much on the opinion of the referee, that is, that he would merely rubber-stamp the referee's opinion. This feeling was expressed by the attorneys wanting less delegation either for fact finding or conclusions of law in routine cases.

I am concerned that the judge will not scrutinize the report of the referee but just sign it. That is my objection to the system.

In my opinion, where there are issues that are controversial, I think there is an overindulgence on the part of the judge in delegating duties. I know he has to sign all matters, but I think he should give closer scrutiny. In view of the number of administrative assets, I think the tendency to let a referee handle all details seems to be gilding the lily. I don't think that they have so much judicial work that they need to delegate so much in controverted issues.

The majority opinion was favorable to delegation.

By and large, the job of referee has been very well discharged. They are very capable and are in a better position to recommend a ruling than the court is, and I would say

4. Ohio Revised Code 2311.04, 2315.26 et seq.
5. Ohio Revised Code 1901.13 (A).
6. Ohio Revised Code 2151.16.

that without referees we would be so swamped that the backlog would be great and administration of estates would be hampered considerably.

I see nothing wrong with the present system. Most of the referees are as good if not better than the judges, and I can have informal conferences at which I can accomplish more than in judicial conferences or trial. I like the system—it's informal. They help you as much as you help them.

At the time of this study, there were two probate judges in Cuyahoga County. No attorney said he would be satisfied with a lesser number, and two-thirds were satisfied with the *status quo* (see Table 12–3).

TABLE 12–3 NUMBER OF PROBATE JUDGES DESIRED BY ATTORNEYS

Number Desired	Number	Per Cent
No response	8	11.4
Fewer than now	0	0.0
Same as now	46	65.7
More than now	16	22.9
Total	70	100.0

A cross-tabulation of the 44 lawyers who were satisfied with the present pattern of delegation with the 46 attorneys who expressed satisfaction with the current number of probate judges showed that 82 per cent of those approving the referee system were also satisfied with the present number of judges. This indicated that lawyers who could accept the use of referees for probate work did not see any great need for additional judges on the probate bench. Of the eight attorneys who did not fall into this category, four had given no thought to the number of judges, and four felt there should be more judges but did not relate this desire to the referee system.

It is obvious that if the referees were less involved in the functioning of the probate court, as was desired by 16 attorneys (23 per cent), then the judges would have to be more involved. The percentage of attorneys wanting more probate judges was identical with the percentage who wanted less delegation to referees (as shown in Tables 12–2 and 12–3). Yet only seven of the 16 who wanted to reduce the activities of the referees felt the need for more judges. Of the remaining nine lawyers who wanted to increase the number of judges while maintaining the referee system, five felt the present judges were overworked; two felt that in the future, the population explosion and the lowering of the death rate would lead to more older people and the problems of incompetency; one wanted four judges for the balance of political power; and the other sought the extra judge as a substitute in case illness should temporarily incapacitate one of the judges.

It should be stressed that over 65 per cent of the attorneys interviewed were satisfied with the present number of judges and that this was largely the group satisfied with the delegation of duties to referees in the probate court. There was, furthermore, consensus that a backlog of cases in probate court did not occur, as it did in the other courts. The probate court was deemed most efficient, with judges available and no difficulties involved in getting hearings within a short period of time.

I have never been delayed in anything. The two probate judges are serving adequately —using the referee system. I have no complaints at all. Mechanically, the presiding judge is running a good outfit and doing a good job.

Despite this general approval, the attorneys had some proposals regarding possible changes in the probate laws and administrative procedures. Each lawyer was asked to place himself in the position of chairman of a hypothetical bar association section responsible for suggesting new legislation or practices in the probate area. Changes mentioned were categorized in several basic areas: professional responsibility (such as the unauthorized practice of law), laws concerning wills and intestate succession, taxation laws, and probate procedure of an administrative nature (see Table 12–4).

TABLE 12–4 CHANGES IN THE LAW OR PROBATE PRACTICES SUGGESTED BY ATTORNEYS

Area of Change	Number	Per Cent[a]
No changes	21	30.0
Probate procedure of an administrative nature	26	37.1
Wills and intestacy	25	35.7
Professional responsibility	7	10.0
Taxation	4	5.7
Total	83	118.5

[a] Percentages were based on 70 attorneys. Total exceeds 100 per cent because some attorneys gave more than one answer.

No changes were proposed by 30 per cent of the attorneys. In some cases, they were satisfied with the present situation. In others, the attorneys had not given any thought to the problem until they were faced by the question. The answers of those who responded "off the top of the head" represented the concerns of lawyers regarding changes in the probate process. Approximately the same number who desired substantive changes in wills and intestate succession law also desired procedural changes.

Five individuals were concerned with keeping the banks from engaging in the practice of law. One attorney went further:

We need greater control by the bar association of sources of advice given in connection with estate planning to more effectively limit the role of insurance counselors, accountants, and banks so that they perform nonlegal functions.

One lawyer was concerned with the part-time attorney.

I think a man should be fully engaged in the practice of law before he is permitted to do this type of work, rather than someone who is in another type of work and is doing this for supplemental income. The probate schedule is such that it allows anyone to do this on the side. They don't get enough experience to do a good job.

The appraising process received the most attention from the attorneys whose responses were coded "probate procedure of an administrative nature." One-half of these attorneys suggested changes. Legislation is very explicit regarding the employment of appraisers in probate. It states, in part:

The real estate and personal property comprised in the inventory required by section 2115.02 of the Revised Code, unless an appraisement thereof has been dispensed with by an order of the probate court, shall be appraised by three suitable disinterested persons appointed by the court, and sworn to a faithful discharge of their trust. The court may appoint separate appraisers of property located in any other county.[7]

If the decedent has no surviving spouse or minor children and the probable value of the personal property is less than $500 or consists entirely of money, deposits, stocks, bonds, or other securities, the court may dispense with the appraisement and direct that only an inventory be filed.[8] However, there is no statutory authority for the probate court to dispense with an appraisement when the value of the personal property is more than $500.

The attorneys' attitudes are best left in their own words:

We should review the probate code to do away with a lot of laws that are just not of very practical value and yet impede efficient settlement of estates. An illustration is the appointment of appraisers where the court appoints two and the lawyer one, whereas in reality the appraisal is brought in at the lawyer's figure. In small estates, appraisal could be handled by the lawyer himself with the right of other heirs to object if they are not satisfied with it.

We should dispense with the appointment of appraisers in most cases where they really don't serve any function, that is, where property is involved that doesn't require any real work to evaluate.

There should be some sort of control of appraisers, since many of them are interested only in the fee. It is a problem of political appointment.

I would allow the executor or surviving spouse in small estates to appoint all appraisers.

7. Ohio Revised Code 2115.06.
8. Ohio Revised Code 2115.02.

Appraisers are nothing but rubber stamps, willing to agree to anything you [the attorney] want.

We need some way to waive this extra expense that is needless, especially in the case of a widow receiving one-half interest in a house.

Let's have at least two of the three men be experienced in appraising.

I think the procedure in connection with inventory and appraisal could be revised, with a view toward expanding circumstances under which appraisal could be dispensed with.

It is interesting that these views are similar to those held by the survivors, who were usually persons without legal training and with limited knowledge of the probate process. The appraiser was the most disliked functionary and the most verbally abused even though appraisal fees were a relatively minor cost of probate when compared with attorney fees.[9] The basis for this universal rejection of the appraiser was the feeling that these men frequently lacked experience, did nothing of importance, and yet openly reaped rewards or obtained economic sustenance through institutionalization of a role based on political means rather than competence and performance of a needed service. The lawyer engaged in probate work was somewhat defensive regarding the fees he charged, no doubt because the probate system has been widely attacked and its nonconforming cases have been highlighted in the press. Although the lawyer performs a service, the appraiser may not. The public dislikes a system that benefits individuals who fail to earn their way. The appraiser is part of such a system and therefore receives society's disapproval.

Some attorneys likened appraisers to parasites feeding upon the estate; many wanted to see the laws and regulations concerning appraisal of estates put on a more realistic basis. One attorney suggested that the law be changed so that the probate court would have a staff of professional, well-paid appraisers, which would tend to cut down the amount of fees paid by the estate. A somewhat analogous arrangement not relating directly to appraisement was mentioned by another attorney, who wanted to see highly skilled, certified auditors on the court staff, with their sole job being the audit of estates.

A number of the attorneys were concerned with jurisdictional variations in estate settlement procedures. Two wanted uniform practice before the probate courts in different counties. An example of regional differences is the probate court of neighboring Summit County, which recently adopted a new rule requiring a personal representative to name the attorney who will represent him in carrying out his duties.[10] No such rule exists in Cuyahoga County.

Another attorney suggested a review of probate court forms in order to

9. See Chapter 11, pp. 258–259.
10. See Chapter 10, pp. 228–229.

eliminate duplication. Another questioned the value of the preliminary notice required by the state inheritance tax department because at the time it is filed, the true estate worth is frequently an unknown factor. He felt it would be more appropriate for an attorney to file all the papers involved in estate settlement at one time, rather than at periodic intervals.

Section 2107.07 of the Ohio Revised Code permits the testator to deposit his will, for safekeeping, in the office of the judge of the probate court in the county where he lives. One attorney wished to amend this provision, making it mandatory for wills to be deposited with probate court. He believed that this would ensure the testamentary disposition, eliminating the problem of lost, spoliated, or destroyed wills.

The attorneys expressed the hope that the estate settlement process could be simplified. Land sale proceedings were of particular concern, especially in the case of the small estate. The normal probate process was questioned in cases where decedents left only a one-half interest in their homes to beneficiaries. In cases where there were no debts, the lawyers felt that the probate time schedule could be fixed by setting bond and closing the estates in days rather than months. In such cases, the heirs or legatees would take the inheritance under the bond for the duration of the time schedule for closing the estates. All papers could be filed at once. If the procedure could not be simplified in all cases where there were no debts, it could at least be done where the sole taker was the surviving spouse, or the spouse and children. According to one attorney, the bond requirements were unfair.[11] In a case where there was a widow with no children, and where the deceased was intestate and the widow was the only person to inherit and was also serving as administratrix, requiring her to post bond was deemed senseless.

The attorneys had further suggestions concerning changes that were substantive as opposed to procedural in nature. For example, dissatisfaction with the existing state of the law in the matter of small estates was mentioned frequently. They hoped that a way could be found to get through the red tape involved when there is virtually nothing in the estate. The attorneys felt that there should be an increase in the dollar amount of an estate that could be relieved from administration. The amount most often mentioned by the lawyers as a proper limitation was $5,000. In a related sense, changes were suggested concerning guardianship in the case of small estates. As Ohio law presently stands, guardianship may be dispensed with only where the estate of the ward does not exceed $1,000 in value.[12] It was suggested that this limitation also be increased. With respect to guardians for minors, one attorney felt that the law should be revised so that in cases where guardianship is necessary, an

11. See Ohio Revised Code 2109.04–.20.
12. See Ohio Revised Code 2111.05.

office could be established to perform the functions that are required to protect the interests of minor heirs or legatees.

Two other matters that received considerable attention were the limitation of laughing heirs[13] and the abolition of the half-and-half statute.[14] The accomplishment of such changes would streamline the law of intestate succession in Ohio.

The attorneys favored lowering the age of competency for will making at the time of the interviews for this study the age level was 21. Legislation effective in 1965 lowered the age requirement to 18.[15]

Possibly the most unique suggestion was made by one attorney who thought there should be a procedure for proving a will while the testator was still alive. He indicated that the will maker should be permitted to appear in court with the witnesses. All would sign affidavits verifying the fact of the execution of the will, and there would be no verification problem after death.

Conclusion

The majority of lawyers in this sample considered estate settlement a personally satisfying and financially rewarding area of law practice. Chapter 11 indicated that the majority of the survivors were well satisfied with the lawyers' handling of the decedents' estates. They were somewhat less satisfied with the lawyers' fees, usually the largest single expense of estate administration. This general satisfaction on the part of both parties does not mean the lawyer-client relationship was free of tension.

There were two areas in which tension was likely to arise. First, the survivors were eager for information about their particular cases and about the administrative process in general. The lawyers were reluctant to spend their time giving lengthy explanations and resented repeated requests for information. Second, the majority of estates were settled about as fast as allowed by law; the lawyer was understandably irritated by the heir who felt he should "get it yesterday." On the other hand, the majority of survivors felt that the time involved in settling the estate was unduly long. When this time was actually longer than average, they were likely to become dissatisfied with the entire process. The lawyer and client held different time perspectives; a matter of urgency for the survivors was a matter of routine for the professional.

One area of agreement between lawyer and client was the appraisement system. Both groups felt that the present system was of little value in estate settlement and that appraisers could be dispensed with or that qualified appraisers would be an improvement upon the present practice of patronage.

A minority of survivors considered estate settlement a strictly personal and

13. See Ohio Revised Code 2105.06.
14. See Ohio Revised Code 2105.10.
15. See Ohio Revised Code 2107.02.

family matter. They felt that the court and attorneys were intruders and parasites, a view not shared by the attorneys. However, the lawyers were sensitive to this view and made suggestions that would drastically reduce both time and cost factors for small, uncomplicated estates. Some attorneys would virtually do away with the probate process in the situation where a spouse was the sole taker.

In general, the interests of attorney and client were similar. Neither gained when the proceedings were complicated by litigation or by human error. In such cases, the lawyer earned a higher fee, and he often felt the burden of the "blood money" charge. In the end, the fee had to be balanced against his investment of time and of himself.

The lawyer in probate work exhibited a strong preference for the predictable case, one that had few or no technical and human relations problems. An executor who used simple accounting procedures in recording estate receipts and expenditures was a great asset to the lawyer. Since the vast majority of executors were chosen on bases other than their business acumen, the lawyer rarely found the ideal client-executor. Failing to have the ideal executor as a partner in settlement, the lawyer directed the willing executor and even took over some of the more menial tasks. Legally the executor-lawyer-judge relationship was viewed as a system of checks and balances against the possible exploitation of the estate by any one functionary. In actuality, although no charge was made regarding use of excessive influence or exploitation by the lawyer in settling the estate, the lawyer's role was the dominant one.

The lawyer's dominance means greater freedom for him to exercise autonomy in estate administration. He can employ his expertise and skills and control his work situation, thus fulfilling one component of his professional role.

Chapter

13

Findings, Implications, and Analysis

THE TASK of a researcher is to examine his data and to select those findings that are most relevant to substantiating or negating his hypotheses or that succinctly answer the questions he poses. A further obligation of the researcher is to examine these findings for their relevance in providing explanations of individual and group behavior and to determine how such data might be used by those in practice or in administrative positions within society. To do either of these two things requires some interpretation of research findings, and in this the investigator has to call upon his experience, knowledge, and expertise. He has to take intellectual risks because he may be exceedingly right or wrong in his analyses of the data. Here, we take such risks and realize that we may have misinterpreted the inheritance patterns of the group we studied and the relationships of inheritance to law and to the family.

Findings

We shall not atttempt to summarize in great detail all the findings of this study. Rather we have selected those findings that reinforce commonplace expectations, as well as other findings that are unexpected according to commonsense observation. The objective is to present the reader with a set of facts that has potentiality either for corroborating what is already known or for challenging current stereotypes regarding the effect of inheritance on the family, the perceived faults of the probate system, the role and tasks of the lawyer in matters of estate planning and administration, and the client's view of the probate structure and its multiple functionaries.

After a review of previous studies and the relevant literature, the probate case was chosen as the unit of analysis, with the court documents as the initial source of information. The most important technique was the subsequent interviewing of available successors and survivors of the decedents together with a subsample of lawyers selected from those who were the attorneys of record in the cases. The significance of the conclusions rests on whether relevant questions were asked initially and whether appropriate methods were then employed in studying them.

Prerequisites for Comprehensive Inheritance Study

A completely comprehensive study of the inheritance process would require a national probability sample drawn from all jurisdictions in the United States and would involve the use of probate records and extensive interviews with heirs and legatees and functionaries of the probate and law-related social systems. A study of one jurisdiction does, however, provide a prototype of what is likely to be found elsewhere. Cleveland is a reasonably typical metropolitan area, and Ohio probate law is similar to the probate law in the majority of states, the major exception being the community property states. Even the variations detailed in Chapter 2 are characteristic of the kinds of modifications existing in other states.

Obtaining at minimal cost a relatively comprehensive description of the inheritance process and its meaning and consequence for the family, legal profession, and society in general necessitates use of probate documents rather than death certificates in drawing cases and of a random sampling of all estates closed in probate rather than a selection of testate cases or large estates. Beginning the study with death certificates may result in more comprehensive coverage of the inheritance process as well as higher costs. The procedure requires waiting for probate to be completed (in a few cases it may take ten years) and then interviewing the next of kin.

An understanding of the interrelated social, psychological, and legal aspects of the inheritance process requires extensive interviewing. The significance of inheritance to family members can be more comprehensively ascertained by interviewing as many survivors as possible than by relying on a single informant or by using a mailed questionnaire or probate material only. In order to obtain insights into the process, it is necessary to interview survivors and practicing attorneys to find out how they feel, perceive, and act with respect to such tasks as will making and estate administration.

The importance of interviewing must be stressed because probate records do not have the necessary information for a comprehensive understanding of inheritance in American society. Information concerning property transfers —gifts inter vivos, insurance to named beneficiaries, "emptying" of the contents of safe-deposit boxes, and jointly owned real estate with right of survivorship—that can avoid the probating of real property are unavailable from probate records. Through interviews such transfers can be accounted for; and in addition, a description of the redistribution among the heirs (a condition not usually noted in probate records) can be provided. Excluded also from the probate record are demographic and social characteristics that are necessary in order for meaningful sociological analyses of the data to be made.

Testacy and Its Attributes

The condition of testacy was examined in two groups. The first consisted of 659 decedents randomly selected from all estates closed in Cuyahoga County Probate Court during the period from November 9, 1964, to August 8, 1965. This group was referred to as the decedent sample. The survivor population consisted of 1,234 individuals over the age of 21 who were interviewed and were from the group of 2,239 who were eligible to inherit from the decedents under the Ohio Statute of Descent and Distribution or who were legatees and devisees or were named as contingent beneficiaries.

For both the decedent sample and the survivor population, the principal finding was that testacy was associated with age. With each decade of life, the proportion of individuals who were testate increased. However, in examining this relationship carefully, it was discovered that the life period during which most survivors made wills was between 31 and 45 years of age. Also, the imminence of death did not account for the rate of testacy in the study populations. In the decedent sample, over half of the probated wills were written at least five years before death; and over 40 per cent of those wills executed within the five years preceding death superseded earlier wills.

Economic class was found to be a good predictor of testacy: the higher the economic class of the decedent or survivor, the greater the probability that these individuals would be testate. Comparison of the gross and net estates of individuals who were testate or intestate indicated that testate decedents surpassed the intestate in all categories of assets and that the largest differences between the two were intangible assets such as stocks, bonds, and savings.

Occupation was correlated with testacy for the decedent sample and the survivor population up to age 60 (about the time of retirement). The higher the individual's position on the occupational scale, the more likely he was to be testate. With the onset of retirement after age 60, the correlation did not hold. Other factors such as getting one's affairs in order became more important in determining will making in the later rather than in the early years of life.

Education was correlated with testacy only for the survivors and not for the decedents. For the survivors who had made their wills, the higher their educational attainment, the more likely they were to be testate. This factor deserves further examination for its predictive capabilities.

There was a lineal progression from low to high rates of testacy as both the married and unmarried survivors progressed through the various stages of the family life cycle. The concept of family life cycle is based on the assumption that the individual over his life span is in a developmental process. Within each stage of the cycle (beginning families, childbearing families, families with preschool children, with school children, with teen-agers, and so forth), the individual member and the family as a unit have different needs and tasks that must be performed in order to meet these needs. The growth in awareness of needs and the individual's acquisition of skills to handle these tasks are incremented with age. In matters of testacy, it was found that individuals in their twenties, the period when death has a low probability and the individual has a strong sense of mastery, gave little thought to making a will. Those who made wills during this period were beginning to feel some burden of responsibility. During the age period 20–29, three times as many of the married as of the unmarried were testate. In the 30–39 life stage, 43 per cent of the married were testate, compared with 26 per cent of the unmarried. During the thirties, the number of dependent children in the family is greatest and income is increasing, so that the incentive for making a will is a combination of family responsibility and the handling of either accumulated capital or anticipated capital gains.

In the age period 40–49, over half of both the married and the unmarried were testate, but three-fifths of the unmarried will makers were widowed. Among those in their fifties, 75 per cent of the unmarried were testate (over three-fourths were widowed) compared with 66 per cent of the married. Among those in their sixties and seventies, the percentage of the married who were testate increased dramatically: 100 per cent of the married over age 70 were testate. For the unmarried, after age 50 the percentage who were testate remained virtually the same. In the later years, family responsibilities for minor children are almost absent. The married person's obligation is then toward his living spouse; and provisions, if not already completed, are made for the orderly transfer of assets. In this old age group, the overriding factor that contributed to the increased percentages of testacy for the married was undoubtedly the probability of death.[1]

Patterns of Distribution

The pattern of inheritance distribution observed in this study suggested that generational linkages were based on both serial service and reciprocity.[2] It was likely that if lineal kin survived, they eventually inherited under testate or intestate succession, thus substantiating the notion that serial service is a normal and expected phenomenon.

There was one major detour to this intergenerational transfer. If the testator was survived by a spouse and lineal kin, the overwhelming majority named the spouse the sole heir. By doing so, the testator provided the widow or widower with assets in order to make it possible for the spouse to continue an independent existence and to have a legacy to use in bargaining for services

1. The life cycle data are in Appendix D.
2. Wilbert E. Moore has developed this notion of serial service, the unilateral "passing on" of goods and services from one generation to the next. See *Order and Change* (New York: John Wiley & Sons, Inc., 1967), pp. 245–249.

from children and other relatives later on. This transfer of the entire estate to the spouse deviated from the intestate division between spouse and issue. In intestate cases, deviation occurred when adult children signed over their shares of the estate to the surviving parent. Children made this transfer because of filial responsibility, a realistic appraisal of their parent's financial condition, and a sense of justice that the surviving parent had earned the legacy. Thus they accepted what is basically an economic transfer from the older to the younger generation as a two-step process: first to the surviving spouse and then to the children.

Exceptions to the spouse-all pattern were found among the larger estates or where remarriage had occurred. In cases of large estates, bequests were often made to charities and other individuals after the spouses had been adequately provided for. In cases of remarriage, estates were more likely to be divided in testate cases, and to remain divided in intestate cases, between the spouse and the children than in those cases where the remaining spouse was the biological parent of the surviving children.

When only adult children survived, decedent testators divided their entire estates equally among children in slightly fewer than half the cases. Approximately three-fourths of survivor testators planned to divide equally if their spouses predeceased them. In those cases where surviving children did not share the entire estate equally, there were usually other takers, most often grandchildren. These other takers were usually given an equal share with children.

When adult children were the only survivors of intestate decedents, nearly three-fourths were content with equal shares and did not redistribute the estates. In those instances where a redistribution occurred, it was most often in payment for special care given to the decedent.

Reciprocity was expressed through the distribution to particular children for services rendered to parents. Children who took care of their elders (for example, providing them with a home, attending them when they were ill, giving emotional support, or supplying financial and other kinds of aid) generally received the largest share of the parent's property or the only share if the estate was very small. In addition to this act of reciprocation by appreciative parents, siblings who had not provided services of any kind, or very little in comparison with that given by their brothers and sisters, recognized this reciprocity by signing over their shares of inheritances or portions of their shares to the siblings who attended the parents. This most often took place under intestate succession, where the equality principle would normally be invoked.

Another indicator of reciprocity was the expectation by survivors that children or other kin should share alike in the inheritance when the parent did not require or receive preferred care and attention from any of the potential heirs or legatees. It was generally expected that if children were to be justifiable takers they should maintain some contact with their parents. However, parent-child interaction by itself, most often related to the propinquity of respective households, did not give one child a preferred status over another child as a potential taker in cases where the parent was competently independent. If the surviving parent had lived in a household apart from the children and had not required any special attention, then the pattern of distribution most often followed the principle of equal distribution.

When no spouse or lineal kin survived and the decedent's next of kin were calculated through the family of orientation (the family in which the decedent was reared), there were a variety of distribution patterns, few of which followed the intestate pattern. It was among these decedents that nonrelated individuals and charities were most often named in the will. Again reciprocity for services rendered was the motivation for choosing among more distant relatives or nonrelated persons. The absence of immediate family was the primary factor in making charitable bequests.

Meanings and Uses of Inheritance

In most discussions of inheritance, the social and psychological meanings associated with such transfers have been largely neglected. For example, the actual amount of resources a person received via succession often was unrelated to the survivor's satisfaction regarding the particular distribution. There were cases in which the survivor received no economic return and still judged the distribution to be fair. Most respondents agreed that the spouse-all pattern was the proper one. It enabled the testator's spouse, in most instances the respondent's aged mother, to maintain independence for a longer period of time while still physically able and mentally alert. It is interesting to note that the survivors of testate decedents were far more satisfied with the spouse-all pattern than survivors of intestate decedents were, even though members of the latter group brought about the spouse-all pattern by signing over their shares. They expressed discontent that the decedent had not made a will providing for the spouse, an act that symbolized to them the intimacy and emotional quality of family relationships.

Another illustration of the psychological meaning of inheritance came from the data on the distribution of mementos. Items such as watches, rings, or furniture, although of relatively low monetary value, were highly prized by survivors because they memorialized what had once been a close and confidential relationship. The uses made by some survivors of their inheritance expressed the affective characteristic of the interaction at one time with decedents. In some instances, the inheritor donated to charity or provided for the education of a child. In others, he distributed to other kin because of his belief that the testator had intended or would be pleased by this use of the equity.

Survivors reported that they used their inheritances for three major purposes: (1) savings and investments, (2) current living expenses, and (3) real estate. As might be expected, heirs and legatees with higher monthly incomes were generally more likely to save their inheritances than the individuals with lower incomes were.

Women used their inheritances differently from men. They were more likely to use the equity for extra things such as vacations. They gave a higher priority to using their acquisitions for the education of children, than for the payment of regular bills. Women considered the inheritances theirs to do with as they saw fit. Property passed on to them from their side of the family was regarded as not belonging to the husband and therefore not properly a part of the family's general account. Although reserving this "right to use" and independence, these women nevertheless were likely to use these new resources in what they perceived to be the best interests of their families.

Almost all elderly survivors used their inheritances for living expenses, medical care, and the normal amenities of life, except where other resources were available. Those who were better off financially left such legacies intact in savings, property, and stock investments for eventual transfer to children and grandchildren.

There appeared to be no dramatic change in the life styles of the sample survivors as a result of inheritance. The majority received their inheritances too late for major changes. They were in their middle or later years, and the few who inherited major sums had already established their styles of living. The majority had to use their inheritances for living expenses. This suggests that for most of the inheritors (who were widows), there was a gradual decline in their standard of living and very few occasions to invest the inheritance in order to make money.

Economic and Legal Factors in Estate Settlement

There were 85 estates in which the gross estate was $2,000 or under, and the majority of these were intestate. Of the 48 estates over $60,000, all but two were testate. The large majority of estates (80 per cent) were between $2,000 and $60,000.

The major reason probate records do not provide a complete accounting of a decedent's assets is that insurance to a named beneficiary is usually not listed. Insurance is a major equity item for the majority of decedents. In interviews with survivors, it was reported that over three-fourths of the decedents for whom information was available had insurance worth $5,250 on the average. As estates increase in size, the amount of insurance also increases but the relative contribution insurance makes to the value of the estate decreases.

The elaborateness of a funeral for a decedent is determined more by personal considerations and patterns for burying the dead established by the funeral industry than by the size of the estate. For most decedents, funeral costs ranged between $751 and $1,570.

More than one-third of the administered estates reported no outstanding financial obligations other than the costs of administration and the funeral. There was an inverse relationship between the size of the gross estate and the percentage of estates with no debts.

Testamentary control devices such as trusts, guardianships, life estates, and conditional bequests were rarely employed. One exception was the use of contingency provisions where the intent of the testator was less to control his legatees after death than to transfer to secondary beneficiaries in the event that primary beneficiaries predeceased him. The small size of most of the estates was the main reason that there were so few trusts. Conditional bequests are modes of social control not in consonance with current values. Life estates in real estate usually create problems for beneficiaries; for example, in selling the property or a share of it, and, therefore, are not recommended by most lawyers. Finally, few decedents left minor orphans; hence, the need for guardianship was minimal.

Will-making Practices and Attitudes Among Survivors

Will making was found to be a common practice or intended action among the overwhelming majority of survivors in this study. Of the 1,234 survivors, over half had wills of their own; a third reported that they planned to make a will; and only a small minority did not plan to make one.

Testators and planners (those individuals intending to make a will) differed in their reasons and the circumstances for will making. Both groups cited the advantage of altering intestate distribution by making a will, and they stressed family responsibilities as a reason for will making. However, testators specified personal circumstances that pushed them to making a will, for example, military service, the pleadings of insurance counselors and lawyers, the debilitating concomitants of aging, extended illness, and the need to "place things in order" before an impending trip, usually one far from home. Planners either had had little experience with or were less influenced by the potential push of these factors.

A preference for testamentary freedom (the ability to leave property to whomever a person pleases) was expressed by nearly three-fourths of the survivors; this was juxtaposed with the finding that 83 per cent of this same group felt that a person should be required by law to leave money or property to his spouse and children. Freedom and responsibility were the mix: a person should have the freedom but should act according to societal and community expectations. The responsible family member should not be coerced by legal restrictions to take care of his family; he ought to have the privilege of doing it of his own volition.

Lawyers and Probate Work

Probate work is a continuing process that begins with planning the estate; this is followed by making the will and then by settlement of the decedent's estate. In the will-making phase, the lawyer must develop and maintain a close relationship with his client and maximize the expression of testamentary freedom within constraints imposed by the law and culture. In administering the estate, the lawyer has a greater opportunity to exercise autonomy, namely, employing his skill and using his knowledge with a minimum of supervision. There are few criteria to judge his competence because the lawyer operates in an area of client ignorance.

Will making was not perceived as a highly professional task by the sample lawyers because of the competition from nonprofessionals, and in many instances it was a one-time relationship in which a standard form was used. In more complicated estates, however, there was a condition for a fiduciary relationship with the client. Over-all, will making was viewed as a necessary activity in order for the lawyer to gain entrance into the more lucrative area of estate administration.

Lawyers were very concerned about the competition they encountered from banks and to a lesser degree from insurance firms and other economic, religious, and social institutions involved in will making. This expressed anxiety and irritability referred more to a potential reduction in the number of administrable estates than to the professional competence of these competing organizational systems and their functionaries.

The will-making–estate-administration continuum is an excellent example of deferred gratification both in relation to financial pay-off and professional behavior. In the later years of his career, the lawyer will receive a steady income and use his expertise maximally from work in estate administration. In this sample, the incidence of will making by lawyers decreased with age while the incidence of estate-administration cases increased. The fiduciary relationship with the testator begins with will making and provides the lawyer with an initial advantage in becoming knowledgeable about the activities of family members. Subsequently, he may be chosen as lawyer for the personal representative. His knowledge of the will, the testator's wishes, the family members' needs and wishes, and the probate process gives him an entree with the legatees and the financially rewarding estate business. In estate administration, the lawyer finds a situation for the expression of autonomy. He can use his skill and knowledge unmonitored and optimally, and this is highly satisfying to him.

The sample lawyers' ideal client in will making and estate administration was one who is willing to enter into a fiduciary relationship and place his trust in the lawyer's capabilities and intentions to serve the best interests of the client. The clients' image of the model lawyer was one who is responsible, "honest," responsive, communicates effectively, settles the estate quickly, and is a "friend of the family."

Probate practice may generate tension in the lawyer-client relationship for two reasons. The first centers on a communication breakdown, a consequence of misconceptions of what the information linkage between the attorney and the client should be. Survivors were eager for progress reports on the settlement of the estates and sought information from the personal representatives. Many heirs or legatees believed that the attorney for the executor or administrator (personal representative) was also their lawyer and therefore sought information directly from him. The lawyer, on the other hand, was reluctant to spend large amounts of time or effort giving lengthy explanations or responding to repeated requests for news for which he was not likely to be compensated.

The second reason is the time factor. The settlement of estates simply takes time, the length of which appears to be inordinately long to the client. The attorney has no control over this time period. It is structurally determined by administrative rules and court procedures. The survivor had had no anticipatory socialization for handling this event. He had assumed that once the probate process was begun, the ensuing steps toward closure would occur rapidly depending upon the expertise of the lawyer. The attorney was aware of this institutionalized system of procedures over time and of the reasons for them. His efforts to explain the process; for example, why it is necessary to protect the claims of creditors against the estate by providing a reasonable amount of time in which they can file liens, were futile. The client rejected the explanation as a lawyer's device to prolong the liquidation of the estate in order to milk it. Because of these different communication and time perspectives, tension and conflict were likely to occur between the attorney and his client. However, the client who had trust and confidence in the lawyer's knowledge and abilities to handle the estate matter, who in effect surrendered himself to the lawyer and believed in him, was likely to accept the attorney's explanation of the process and to be reasonably patient regarding the time it took to close the estate.

Estate Administration: Factors and Attitudes

In approximately two-thirds of the testate cases, petitions to probate the will were made less than one month after death. In half of the intestate cases, letters of administration were applied for in the same time period. The actual beginning of probate court proceedings was less than three months for more than four-fifths of both testate and intestate cases.

The time in probate court varied according to whether the case was testate or intestate. Testate estates as a group were larger in size than intestate estates and, therefore, had more diversified forms of equity to be accounted for and distributed. Half of the testate cases were in probate court between nine and fifteen months; approximately one-fourth took under nine months; and one-fourth, over fifteen months. Half of the intestate cases were settled within nine months.

Family members were executors for the great majority of the testate cases and administrators for two-thirds of the intestate cases. Friends, lawyers, banks, or a combination served in the remaining cases. There were very few reported abuses attributed to attorneys in this fiduciary role. This finding varies from the commonly held stereotype communicated through the mass media that lawyers are in control of large numbers of estates and milk those in which they are fiduciaries.

Time and cost were significantly related to the survivor's attitude toward the probate process. The shorter the time in court and the lower the costs, the more positive the attitude toward the system, with time being the single best indicator.

A large number of survivors exhibited ignorance or ambivalence toward the activities of the probate court. Lawyers had firmer opinions, as might be expected. Most believed that the system of delegation of duties to referees was adequate, although nearly a quarter of the sample lawyers thought that there should be less delegation. Approximately two-thirds believed that the two probate judges then serving were sufficient to handle the work load, with about a quarter suggesting that additional judges should be appointed.

The probate court (with its component institutional and occupational subsystems), although in need of modernization and improvement, was still regarded by most lawyers and survivors who felt qualified to express an opinion as workable, operating adequately within the constraints imposed by existing probate laws. Although the complaints concerning the courts' implementing activities were few, this does not mean that the suggestions of lawyers and clients for improving estate administration should be ignored.

The Implications of the Study Findings for Initiating Changes in Legislation and Public and Legal Education in Probate Work

Initially, we were reluctant to make specific recommendations for changes in the statutes, the probate system, or legal education in reference to probate. This reticence stemmed from the view that although the study was one of the more comprehensive empirical ones ever undertaken, it was by no means exhaustive. Also, it was not one of the original objectives to find out how to reform probate. However, at a time when a number of studies on probate reform are already underway, others are proposed, and a recent best-seller is titled *How to Avoid Probate!*,[3] we cannot ignore the implications of the data for initiating or influencing changes in legislation, probate policy and practice, and legal and public education. The moral philosophy and ethos undergirding the value systems of legal institutions and systems, and the expressed rhetoric, which to-

3. Norman F. Dacey, *How To Avoid Probate!* (New York: Crown Publishers, Inc., 1965).

gether provide the rationale for their existence, are that the welfare of the individual and the family is paramount. We share the concern of others in wishing to make these systems less cumbersome and more responsive to the needs of families and their members, and, therefore, we make our recommendations.

Another reason for our initial hesitation to propose specific changes in probate law, policy, and practice is that such recommendations might possibly be outdated by the time this book was published or within a few years afterward. For example, during the course of the study, the law was changed so that the ceiling of $2,000 for release of assets without administration was raised to $3,000 and the age at which a person can make a will was lowered from 21 to 18 years. Despite such possibilities, if changes do occur tomorrow or next year that coincide with our suggestions or are similar to them, we would have more confidence that our recommendations are well founded and should be adopted.

It is legitimate to question the general applicability of data from the study of a single jurisdiction. Should such data be used in recommending changes in current probate practices in all jurisdictions in the United States? An answer that would satisfy all readers is obviously an impossibility. Ohio inheritance law and probate procedure are similar to those found in other jurisdictions except the community-property states. While uniformity in statutes and practice is not the most salient characteristic of the field of law, a tendency toward standardization of procedures, institutional forms, and mechanisms is discernible. There is more commonality of probate law and practice among the states than there is divergency. Slowly over time, individual states have introduced legal changes and adopted new processes; often these are measures that have been successful in other states. This borrowing has occurred without benefit of a comprehensive national study of the needs of the probate system. The conclusion is that state probate systems are very similar to each other and that therefore the Ohio system is representative.

There is little reason to doubt that if researches were conducted in other jurisdictions using a similar conceptualization and design, the results would be more analogous than they would be divergent from those of the Cuyahoga County study. While this argument may be perceived as conjectural, the prospects of comparative studies being undertaken very soon are small, and we cannot afford to wait until such studies are undertaken and completed before recommendations are made. In this instance, the study data will have to suffice as a basis for proposing changes in probate law and in public and legal education regarding the probate process, even if this means risking the disapproval of colleagues and practitioners in the field.

Legislative Reform

There can be no doubt that the probate process as it now exists is cumbersome. With the present exception of estates under $3,000, all estates in Ohio must go through the same time-consuming, red-tape procedure, whether they are small or large, simple or complex, and without regard to who the survivors are or whether they are amiable or contentious. The legislation that has accrued over the years was designed to protect interested parties whether they were the legal next of kin or creditors. Although few can quarrel with this aim, the resulting effect seems to reverse the normal legal stance in this country—that one is innocent until proven guilty. The majority of estates in the sample were small and uncomplicated, and the survivors were on good terms with one another. With due regard for the need for protective legislation for the minority of difficult estates, it is necessary, considering the majority of average cases, to make the process more flexible and to shorten the time of probate. *We recommend* investigation of the possibilities of adapting one of the existing computer systems to the flow and processing of probate decisions. Given the steps of the probate process and the associated investigative procedures, can a system be developed that will be sufficiently comprehensive and thorough to cover statutory requirements and the needs of clients and attorneys and that will still reduce the complaints over the length of time in probate and the complexities of the procedures?

The single major deviation from intestate succession was effected by married testators with children. The overwhelming majority of these testators, by willing their entire estates to their spouses, exercised their testamentary freedom for the purpose of providing for the surviving spouse, a finding consistent with the findings of previous studies. Under intestate conditions in Ohio and other noncommunity property states, the estate is divided between the spouse and children. Through interviews with the survivors in such intestate circumstances, it was found that the majority of children signed over their share of the inheritance to the surviving parent. Children responded to the financial needs of the surviving parent with a sense of justice that the parent had earned the legacy, part of which they might receive in the future. Also, they were responding with sentiments of filial responsibility. This was buttressed with the knowledge that if they did not sign over their share, they would have to take on the burden of financial responsibility for an aging parent. The economic transfer over generational time is a two-step process. The first step is actually a delay in completing the generational transfer whereby the estate is given to the surviving spouse, and the second step is the final transfer to the children.

Because of the predominance of the spouse-all pattern, *we recommend* a review of current laws regarding intestate succession. Considering the sentiments of the decedents and the survivors if there is a surviving spouse, it is logical to transfer the major share of the estate automatically to the surviving spouse. The exact amount of such a transfer should be related to such factors as the size of the estate and the standard of living of the surviving spouse. The co-ownership of property such as the family residence provides an excellent test situation in which to experiment with changes in the statute and associated processes that would effect a spouse-all pattern with a minimum of discomfort for those involved, especially the spouse.

Major complaints were voiced by surviving spouses and largely shared by next of kin about the difficulties and delays in receiving the decedent's interest in the property. There was also a widely held misconception that property which is co-owned by husband and wife automatically succeeds, upon the death of one, to the survivor. Some surviving spouses felt for the first time that they "did not own the house" which they thought of as theirs and that they were simply boarding in it, dependent upon the action of the court and the willingness of the children to sign over their interests in the property. Others who had limited resources (often the house was the only equity) found that they were unable to meet their current financial obligations and yet could not sell the house until the estate was settled.

We recommend a change in the statutes giving all or a larger share to the spouse in those instances when a spouse and minor children survive the intestate decedent. Because minor children cannot sign over their share to their surviving parent, the parent is handicapped in functioning responsibly. He must clear every financial action involving the use of the child's inheritance with the court. The court in this instance functions as a third party to what is normally a close and fiduciary parent-child relationship with its own norms and techniques regarding the socialization of the child.

A major variation of the spouse-all pattern occurs in cases where there has been remarriage. In intestate cases, the estate often is divided between the spouse and the biological issue of the decedent and is likely to remain divided. There is considerable resentment among the surviving children of the decedent if the spouse of a second marriage receives all or a large portion of the estate. Any change, therefore, in legislation regarding intestate succession should be principally concerned with first marriages. Regarding remarriage, *we recommend* an investigation of the current use and effectiveness of antenuptial agreements in relation to inheritance distribution and of whether new legislation is required to effect transfers that are based on distributive justice as perceived by surviving children.

Seventy-two of the study cases in which the gross estate was $2,000 or under were released to the applicant without formal administration. Lawyers and judges have advocated raising the ceiling to $5,000, with the expectation that the number of cases going through probate would be cut drastically. *We support this recommendation.* In a survey conducted in Cuyahoga County by one of the probate judges, it was found that raising the ceiling from $2,000 to $5,000 and providing for immediate transfer of the decedent's interest in a co-owned home to the surviving spouse would result in approximately 45 per cent of the cases being probated with minimal expense and within a few weeks after filing. If these provisions had been applied to the study sample, the proportions would have been about the same. This suggests a fourfold increase in the number of cases that could be handled quickly and with a minimum of cost.

One procedure that could be used to determine the dollar ceiling for release of assets without formal administration is a formula similar to the cost-of-living index that is used to determine wage levels in a large number of basic industries. The formula would contain such elements as the economic status of the survivors; the number and amount of outstanding debts; the needs of the survivors for medical care, financial assistance, and education; and the income-producing capability of survivors. A scale would then be used to determine when there should be a release of assets without administration. Regardless of how the ceiling is determined, *we support* its rise in order to reduce the number of formally administered estates.

The unhappiness expressed both by a large number of survivors and by lawyers over the appraisal system suggests that consideration be given to changes in this part of the probate process. The major complaints concerned the way in which appraisers were appointed, their qualifications for the job, the number of appraisers required, and the size of fees in relation to the actual work. *We recommend* that appraisers become part of the civil service systems of their respective jurisdictions and that programs be developed in order to train individuals for the occupational specialty of appraiser. A change in this system has implications for the organizational structure of the court and political relationships in the community.

Public Education

One of the results of interviewing survivors was the discovery of a number of commonly held misconceptions. For example, many interviewees believed that if a person dies intestate it takes more time to settle the estate and that the state takes all or a larger portion of the estate than if there had been a will. In contrast to this, some people believed that with a will the estate does not have to be administered. A large number of survivors confused co-owned property with jointly held property having survivorship rights. And finally, many people were under the impression that the functionaries at probate court should provide the necessary legal information so that the survivors could settle the estate without an attorney.

We recommend a full-scale program of public education sponsored by the American Bar Association in conjunction with state bar associations that would not only clear up these misconceptions but would also provide information about the probate process. The result may be an informed public whose support is necessary for legislative change.

Education regarding will making should be another component of the suggested program. The finding of a lineal progression of increased rates of testacy for both married and unmarried individuals along the stages of the life cycle suggests the advisability of public education in order to increase the proportion of individuals who make wills during their early years. In the 40–49 age group, a time when married persons have major family responsibilities and when both married and unmarried persons are likely to be accumulating capital, over half of both decedents and survivors had wills. With the earlier age of marriage and the concomitant assumption of family responsibilities, placing one's "legal house" in order is a laudable objective.

Another reason for encouraging an education program on early will making is to counteract the impact of present legislation regarding guardianship when a parent dies leaving a spouse and minor children. In the event of early death, present legislation that is aimed at protecting the child actually causes hardships for the surviving parent. The dominance of the spouse-all pattern in both testate and intestate succession has already been established. Under current statutes governing guardianship, the surviving parent must continuously establish the validity of his claim to supervise the child and must prove to the court that he is not taking advantage of his child. This situation appears incongruous with common practices of providing for the spouse, with the implicit understanding that while there are minor children the spouse will care for them. Until the present laws are changed, *we recommend* strongly, as part of a public educational program, that the need for the newly married to make a will in order to handle the problem of unexpected death be stressed.

In this study, the unmarried as a group, particularly those without lineal descendants, had wills with great variations in provisions. The majority did not follow the intestate pattern nor did any one pattern emerge, as was the case with married testators, where the spouse-all pattern dominated. Only through a will can individuals accomplish a distribution in consonance with their obligations or feelings toward relatives, friends, and institutions.

The need for a public educational program encouraging will making is further supported by the finding that although the majority of survivors of intestate married decedents redistributed the estates in order to achieve the spouse-all pattern, they did so with some feelings of discomfort. They would have preferred that the decedent had had a will in which he effected the spouse-all pattern while at the same time indicating through contingency provisions his emotional ties with his children and his concern over the eventual transfer of the estate to the children. Here, the argument supporting an educational program to increase will making among the general population is that inheritance is not simply the acquisition of economic assets and the need for orderly passing on of property. In addition, inheritance transfers express past affective states and emotional ties that have meaning and that survive long after the death of the family member. A will in which the testator provides adequately for his surviving spouse not only fulfills the testator's primary familial obligation but also avoids potential ambiguity among the survivors. Furthermore, in naming children as contingent beneficiaries, he expresses his regard for them and implicitly provides them with a mechanism for reducing financial responsibility for an aging parent. There is also an implied moral obligation placed on the surviving spouse to distribute any property at death to those named contingent beneficiaries. This consequence of the spouse-all pattern is undoubtedly far more important in maintaining intergenerational family continuity than the actual transfer and use of the inheritance.

Implications for Lawyers and Legal Education

Without the support of lawyers and judges who have a vested interest in the practice of probate law, the possibility of legislative reform is nil. Fortunately, knowledgeable lawyers and judges, aware that many of the statutes affecting probate procedure no longer serve either the best public interest or their own, are pushing for reform, either as individuals or through the bar associations. Pressure is also coming in the form of competition in the estate business from banks, insurance firms, and other institutions. If lawyers are to remain in this competitive market, particularly where large estates are involved, the probate procedure must be made more flexible. The numerous articles on probate abuses that for the most part were not substantiated by this study have nevertheless created a climate of public concern. Unless lawyers and judges, through the legislatures, can effect legislation more responsive to the welfare of the individual and the family, they risk being indicted in the public mind. *We recommend* that lawyers, through their local bar associations and national professional organizations, take the leadership in introducing reforms in probate law and participate with behavioral scientists in the development of models and experiments of probate systems that are designed to reduce the time and effort required to effect estate closure and that have provisions responsive to a variety of situations involving economic support of dependent survivors.

Although the lawyer ranks high in prestige ratings, there are both room and opportunity for improvement in his ranking as an important professional.[4] Supporting legislative reform is one way he can accomplish this. Another way is through better understanding of the client's needs and expectations. Lawyers in probate practice need the will-making business in order to develop a steady clientele and a practice that can provide sufficient income from the administration of estates. Will making provides the lawyer with an initial entree to several generations within a family. Although it is not a foregone conclusion that he will obtain the estate-administration business of survivors because he is the lawyer of record for a testator, he nevertheless is in a most advantageous position to demonstrate his capabilities as an estate lawyer and thus optimizes his

4. Albert Reiss, Jr., *Occupations and Social Status* (New York: The Free Press, 1961), p. 263.

chances of being selected by the executor to handle the decedent's estate. Obtaining an entree through the inheritance system may also provide access to other areas of legal practice.

Although lawyers tend to stress the difficulties they have with clients and talk about how little they are rewarded either psychologically or financially for their work in the wills area, it is still an important part of their business, far more important than they openly express. Apart from the interests or needs of the client, this area of legal practice is of sufficient importance to the lawyer to suggest a need for greater classification of the professional values and financial rewards of will making and estate administration. The lawyer should approach estate practice in two ways: (1) he should make the most effective use of his professional skills to meet his client's needs in an area that is likely to be highly charged emotionally and that arouses great concern for the maintenance and well-being of the family; (2) by demonstrating his capabilities in will making and estate administration, he is building a solid practice that in effect will be his own legacy in the later years of his career. *We recommend* that lawyers, through their local associations, organize "probate clinics" to discuss such issues as "will making to estate administration: a continuous process"; "communication problems with clients"; "the fee system in will making and estate administration"; "the lawyer's role in the inheritance system: consultant, advocate, or promoter"; and "strategies in determining the needs and desires of potential will makers."

In order to reach a goal of 100 per cent of will makers, it may be necessary to promote will making as an uncomplicated process. This approach need not negate the desirability for counseling in the actual making of the will, but it would be a point of entry to a close fiduciary relationship requiring one or more meetings between the attorney and the client. The focus should be on the importance of having a will and on simplifying the access routes to the lawyer.

Moreover, the lawyer should consider the possibilities of involving others besides the potential testator in the making of a will. The involvement of other family members need not necessarily violate the traditional confidential relationship of the attorney and his client or reduce the client's expression of testamentary freedom. Assuming that the will maker is primarily concerned with the consequences of his provisions for the family after he dies, there is no reason why they should not be involved in discussions prior to the formulation of the will. The value of this approach is that one can avoid the few misunderstandings among survivors that were detected in this study over specific bequests and reasons for them. If we had found that a veil of secrecy actually surrounded will making and that will makers used their testamentary freedom in disregard of the needs of family members, then we would hesitate to make this suggestion. In the majority of cases, however, there was an openness and concern over doing "the right thing" for family members in property transfers as indicated by deviations from intestate succession made by testators and survivors. Therefore, *we recommend* that attorneys consider experimenting with family group sessions in the will-making phase of the inheritance process.

Insurance plays such a major role in the inheritance system that it is necessary to raise the question of the need and appropriateness of closer cooperation between lawyers and representatives of insurance companies in estate planning. Specialists from both professions can serve the client in planning an inheritance program according to the testator's life cycle stage, income and accumulated equity, and aspirations and expectations. Such coordinated efforts are likely to reduce the antipathy that now exists between lawyers and insurance agents because of competition for the estate business. Their roles should be complementary, with the division of labor effecting the best utilization of specialized talents in behalf of the client. For example, lawyers may write simple wills for complex family situations because the estate is small. They might, however, suggest insurance as a relatively easy and immediate method of building an estate that will meet the needs of a complex family situation. Insurance companies, which have long geared their advertising to both the financial and emotional concerns of clients, also stress the point that an insurance policy which fits the needs of one individual may not fit those of another, thus recognizing the complexity of family situations. Pointing out the importance and advantages of making a will is an additional way of serving their clients. *We recommend* the formation of local liaison committees of lawyers, insurance agents, bank representatives, and others engaged in probate work to exchange ideas related to practice, client needs, developments in the field, legislation, and so forth.

One source of potential conflict between the lawyer and the family stems from misunderstanding over whom the lawyer represents. In actuality, the lawyer works for the personal representative who is responsible for administering the estate of the decedent. Yet other family members believe that the lawyer is also working for them. In order to avoid potential conflict and correct the current ambiguity in the relationships of family members with the lawyer, *we recommend* a formal reading of the will to the assembled heirs and next of kin immediately after the death of a testator. If reading the will becomes a standard procedure, it is our guess that the conflict, anxiety, and misunderstanding over the lawyer's and the executor's roles would be reduced perceptibly. In addition, the assembled devisees and legatees could be provided with an explanation of the administrative processes necessary to settle the estate. This would reduce requests for lengthy explanations at a later time, explanations the lawyer may not be able to provide because of his fiduciary relationship with the executor. It cannot be assumed that the executor will read the will or provide explanations regarding the probate process.

The shortest time in probate is the single best indicator of satisfaction with estate settlement. This suggests that the survivor approaches the probate system with a businesslike attitude. His basic measure of the lawyer's success is his ability to settle the estate quickly. But in addition, he expects the attorney to be an understanding counselor, sensitive to the problems of the human condition. Survivors want service from the court, and it is up to the lawyer to convince them that they are getting the best service, but at the same time that he is effecting a satisfactory business settlement, he must answer questions that deal with the concerns of the human condition. This has implications for legal education. The attorney is aware of the flaws of the probate process; his businesslike activities on behalf of his client and himself must be harmonized with the subtleties of human interaction. Most of his clients are bereaved and must live with memories of what *was* and the tokens that express what *is* in family relationships. The need to reconcile interpersonal and economic demands challenges old methods of socializing the lawyer into his professional role.

We recommend that law schools consider as an integral part of their curriculum a course or seminar covering the social psychology of client-practitioner behavior, with special applications to the probate field.

Traditionally, legal education has emphasized the difficult and unique case in estate planning and settlement just as medical education a decade ago focused on the clever diagnosis. The unusual, difficult, and minority problem has always been used in the training of professionals, while the average case has been largely ignored. The vast majority of estate cases in this study were under $60,000. They generally followed a spouse-all pattern and usually required an uncomplicated will and a modest estate settlement plan. There were very few will contests. These cases require experience and training other than the competencies required to solve difficult problems. The very nature of a will demands a fiduciary relationship and concomitant counseling skills. In estate settlement, the client needs to develop confidence and trust in the lawyer so that the lawyer can function with the highest degree of autonomy. These activities of the lawyer require a high level of competence in handling interpersonal relationships. *We recommend* a program for the student lawyer that will include clinical experience similar to that obtained in the internship of the nurse, physician, and more recently, the minister. The student should be rotated through different types of service and receive experience in handling the different steps of the probate process. This would include the probate court and law office and would cover such situations as appraising, counseling, will drafting, will reading, and estate planning. Record keeping for research uses would also be included in such a clinical program.

Needed Research

The lawyer working with the problems of inheritance engages in varied activities, some of which are of an ordinary business type, such as tasks attached to the examiner role, while others are professional and require mastery of a large body of knowledge and autonomy in practice, such as planning an estate. Inheritance can be conceptualized as a process beginning with the making of a will and ending with the disposition of the estate *n* years later. The fiduciary characteristics and expressions of autonomy are related to the tasks the lawyer is performing at various stages of this process. Consequently, the study of the process can reveal the range and variation in professional and nonprofessional behavior of the lawyer in this area of practice. The circumstances in which client-practitioner relationships occur are controlled by the process. What are the affective and nonaffective responses of lawyers and clients to each other and to others concerned with the probate problem at different steps in the inheritance process? What are some of the principal mechanisms used by the attorney to shift roles (for example, from a fiduciary role to an autonomous one) in daily dealings with probate problems at different stages of the process? To what extent are the nonprofessional tasks of inheritance work delegated by the attorney to others? If such assignments are made extensively, do they help to reduce the ambivalence of the lawyer because he is required to perform simultaneously roles according to business and professional norms?

A large segment of law practice is built around the relationship between the attorney and his client, and this provides a rare opportunity to study the socialization process. The individual who comes to the lawyer must learn the role of client, and the lawyer functions as a socializing agent assisting the client, who is essentially a novice, in acquiring the role knowledge and skills needed in this new role and very often in developing a new personal and social identity. From this lawyer-client relationship it is possible to develop an explanatory model of the processes and mechanisms of socialization in terms of novice-agent interaction.[5] For example, it is possible to study some facets of the widow role within a time sequence commencing with the death of the husband and ending with the final settlement of the estate. The steps in settling the estate provide clearly delineated periods for systematic observations of role learning and identifying with widowhood. Simultaneously, it is possible to examine the influences of family and other systems upon the socialization process, especially their influence on the lawyer-client relationship. It is also possible to look at individual characteristics of the attorney and the client, such as the skills and competence of both individuals in matters of law as well as in interpersonal relationships and the type of experience both individuals have had in such matters.

A third of the lawyers in the sample spent approximately a third of their time in wills-estate practice. These lawyers were basically specialists in probate work

5. Betty E. Cogswell, "Socialization into the Family: An Essay on Some Structural Properties of Roles," *Sourcebook in Marriage and the Family,* ed. Marvin B. Sussman (Boston: Houghton Mifflin Company, 1968), pp. 366–377.

and were, in fact, attorneys of record for one or more cases in the sample. The question is: What do such lawyers do in the remaining two-thirds of their time? Are lawyers truly specialists, and have they developed a pattern of differentiation that is similar to the pattern currently found in medicine? Obviously, most lawyers have a diversified practice, and although lawyers may not wholly specialize in a given area such as probate, divorce, or criminal law, the question is whether a lawyer's practice contains a grouping of cases that allows him to employ a common set of basic skills. For example, if a lawyer develops a body of knowledge and skill in the technology of the law, does he consciously or subconsciously move into a practice such as tax and corporation law where there is a minimum of lawyer-client interaction? On the other hand, if he has consummate skills in interpersonal relationships, does he restrict his practice to personal injury, divorce, estate work, and other areas where he can use these capabilities optimally? Do lawyers who are equally qualified or unqualified in either technology or interpersonal competence have more heterogeneous cases in their practice?

There is a plethora of studies on how medical students choose their specialties, the imagery held by medical students, and their role models for these specializations. On the other hand, there is a paucity of well-designed studies on how lawyers choose specialties such as estate work, which obviously is not a glamorous field and appears to be taken on by older lawyers who use estate work in order to develop their own legacy for retirement. Research is needed on attorneys' choices of particular specializations with special focus on motivations for making such selections and on critical situations and influences, especially the activities of role models, in making such choices. Is the time spent in covering an area of practice in law school related to the selection of a specialty?

Another topic of research concerns uses of inheritance and the sociological implications of inheritance patterns. The finding that there was little dramatic change in the life style of heirs and legatees implies that there is an orderly accumulation and transfer of wealth from one generation to the next. Furthermore, the finding that women who inherited actually controlled the disposition of their new assets adds to the accumulating body of evidence of drastic changes in sex roles in American society and the consequences of this shift for the family. New studies on the uses of inheritance by women will provide data on the mechanisms and processes of decision making, role reallocations, and exercise of power within the family.

Changes in the pattern of intrafamily relationships as a consequence of a woman inheriting should not be viewed as a deterrent to orderly intergenerational transfers within the family system. It can be argued that this adds to the stability of such intergenerational transfers. The wife who inherits from her family of orientation, as a rule, uses her legacy in the best interests of her family of procreation. She maintains her privilege to do this and is more oriented toward providing for the well-being of the children in the family than for meeting current financial obligations. In her view, the latter should be met by those in provider roles in her family, including herself if she is gainfully employed. By her actions, she adds another link in the chain of family maintenance and the orderly transfer of family wealth, identification, and symbolism over generational time.

The facts that inheritance is generally transmitted in an orderly pattern and that service and serial reciprocity underlie the transfer raise a question: What happens to intergenerational family continuity when, in particular situations, distributions are not made according to commonly shared expectations? Major dissatisfaction within the kin-related family network occurs when individuals outside the nuclear family, who have not provided any personal services to the testator, inherit or when preference is given to a favored child, one who provided fewer services and gave less affection to the parent than a sibling did. Surviving children are very pragmatic about this situation and suggest a solution in which they use an economic rather than a social-emotional model. Children hold first to the spouse-all pattern, then they subscribe to the view that the brother or sister who had major responsibility for providing care for the aging parent should receive the largest share of the inheritance when this parent dies. When distributions do not go according to these established patterns of intergenerational transfer, there is disruption in the usual pattern of interfamily relationships within the kinship network, with expressed hostility, ambivalence, and sometimes will contests. The alienation of nuclear-related family members persists through the period of estate administration.

After the estate is settled, is there a reformulation of interfamily relationships in a kinship network of newly defined boundaries based on a new set of expectations of exchanges and reciprocities? The time it takes to reform the kinship network, handle the disinherited and disaffected, and smooth once again the pattern of intergenerational transfers is a question that should be studied. There is an excess of views and flimsy research on alienation between the generations and the breakdown of the family in the modern period. In a minority of cases in this study, disenchantment with family relations resulted as a consequence of distributions that violated the expectations of heirs and potential heirs. This affords an opportunity to determine the viability of the reciprocal principle. Do conditions of interfamily alienation persist permanently or do concerns of familial responsibility and vital mutual interest result in reconstruction of the kin network? It would be possible to revisit in five or ten years members of the broken kin networks in this study to determine the structural properties of the new kinship system and the quality and bases for activities within it.

The use of probate records for sampling covers only that portion of the population which had sufficient assets to warrant the attention of the probate court. There is no information available about the persons with insufficient assets to warrant probate or who decided to evade probate by using legal or quasi-legal means. Sampling a population on a random basis and then conducting extensive interviews would provide information on the percentage of the population who transfer property at the time of death as well as on its value.

In this study, it was found that the typical age for will making was around 40 and that the central issues of inheritance came to the fore during this middle period of the family life cycle. Consequently, further probing into the issues of testacy and the meaning, importance, and expectation of inheritance as related to planning a career and to family would best be served by a study that began from a base other than the probate record. A random sample of one or more jurisdictions limited to individuals over the age of 40 and stratified according to social class would provide sufficient cases of adequate inheritance to determine its meaning in relation to planning a life course and in maintaining a status position within the society and authority within the family.

Where the prospective legacy is fairly large, questions could be asked about expectations of inheritance, and consequential relationships between members of kinship groups could be studied in cases where succession does not occur according to expectations. Also, when estates are large and the clients are fairly well educated, it would be possible to study more fully the types of roles assumed by attorneys and the extent of power they can utilize in relationships with their affluent clients. If such a random sample covered rural as well as urban areas, it would be possible to investigate whether there are any significant differences in patterns of intergenerational continuity primarily involving land as compared with liquid assets. For instance, is there a greater tendency in rural areas to establish a family dynasty in which the eldest son is the prime inheritor?

A further advantage in selecting a population that is over the age of 40 and has financial means is the possibility of investigating the use of the power of attorney as a will substitute, especially for aged persons. This issue becomes increasingly more critical as more elderly people survive and develop intellectual deficits that border on senility. There is no systematic information on frequency of the use of the power-of-attorney technique as a will substitute.

We suggested earlier that the protective aspect of probate law is perhaps too rigid and that adequate protection could be provided under a more flexible system. There is, however, an area in which safeguards of the interests of heirs and legatees appear to be inadequate. The court is inconsistent regarding listing and accounting of tangible personal assets such as cash on hand at death, furniture, clothing, and personal possessions. A car, which requires a transfer of title, is the only such item consistently noted on probate records. It is reasonable to assume that nearly everyone who dies has some kind of tangible personal assets. These may be of either material or emotional value to the heirs and legatees. There are examples in the data of individuals who simply confiscated such assets for their own use to the distress of other interested persons. There appears to be no satisfactory legal recourse to rectify the situation. Moreover, the costs of retrieving such assets are usually greater than the value of the equities. It is our contention that where the assets are of limited monetary value, the legal system is not as interested in protecting the rights of individuals involved as in cases with larger equities where the rewards for the legal institutions and their functionaries are greater.

Further support for this notion comes from the data concerning the decedent estates. Blacks represent nearly 20 per cent of the total population of Cuyahoga County. As in all other metropolitan areas, they are predominantly in the lower class, have proportionately lower incomes than whites, live in poorer housing, and so forth. Thus, the fact that less than 7 per cent of the decedents in the sample were blacks suggests that the poor man is not of major interest to the probate system. The degree to which an institution shapes its practice in terms of the perceived and real returns it receives for the maintenance of its own structure, while presumably acting in the public interest, is yet another question that deserves further study.

Reflections

Two major themes emerge from this study. The first concerns the functions of inheritance and testamentary freedom in American society, and the second is the viability of testamentary freedom. The former provides means for examining family relationships over generational time and along bilateral kin lines within the kin family network. The latter theme furnishes a unique opportunity to discuss a deviant condition—the existence of testamentary freedom in this society—since it does not automatically come into being with modernization and industrialization.

Functions of Inheritance and Testamentary Freedom

Inheritance buttresses the activities of society-wide support systems in providing for the biological maintenance of the aged, the incapacitated, and other dependent family members. This is accomplished by two procedures: the testamentary provisions exercised by the will makers in behalf of needy spouses, parents, children, and so forth, and the redistribution of the estate by the heirs in intestate cases in order to care for needy kin, in most instances the surviving aged widow.

These patterns of distribution aid other family members who do not inherit part of the estate by freeing them of legal, emotional, and moral commitments for the financial support of surviving needy relatives. Community organizations, in turn, are also rewarded. When those persons least capable of being financially independent or semi-independent are provided for through inheritance, the pressure on general welfare and care systems to provide such support is lessened.

Testamentary freedom is sometimes exercised by the benefactor to establish his own security and independence of community organizational systems such as welfare and Medicare by designating as an heir or by giving a larger share of his estate to the person who takes the major responsibility for his care. In this instance and in the case of providing for the maintenance of relatives in greatest need, a high level of independence and autonomy of the individual and family is sustained. The capability of the individual or family to maintain economic independence or something approaching such a state through the use of inheritance has some effect upon general support systems, those especially created to handle the financial deficits of our citizens. Although the inheritance received by individuals in most of the sample cases did not provide for economic independence, it did augment individual or family income from earnings and other institutional sources.

Expectation, exchange, and reciprocity are characteristics endemic to organized groups and provide the bases for interaction among their members. Each group works out its own system of unequal exchange, and the expectation of reciprocation, although disparate in amount or in kind, provides the individual with the rationale and reward for continuing the interaction within the group. Inheritance furnishes a view of these reciprocities, exchanges, and expectations in the holder-heir relationship. Provisions made by testators to provide inheritances of different order, value, and kind according to the individual's position in the reciprocity system and the almost universal acceptance of this distribution by beneficiaries authenticate the notion that participation in interaction within any group is a function of the individual's acceptance of his position in the reciprocity system and the real or anticipated rewards resulting from such participation.

Serial service is another characteristic feature of both society-wide and individual transfer systems. Time accounts for generational transfers; a person gives service and support or receives it according to his position in the life cycle. He receives his due in payment for services already or yet to be rendered, and there is little affect in relation to giving or receiving such services. In situations of individual transfer such as inheritance, who receives and what is acquired depend upon exchanges in relation to the real or perceived needs of the testator or holder. Survivors use criteria embodying exchange and reciprocity in determining the justice of specific property distributions.

Inheritance provides the conditions for examining the relationships that existed between benefactor and heir. This ex post facto analysis of role relationships includes the symbolic meaning of interaction and the affective bases for family continuity. Measures of the symbolic meaning of heir-holder relationships are obtained by examining the transfer of mementos and other items cherished by the testator, such as a favorite chair or art object, and feelings expressed by beneficiaries about these items. The use made by heirs of intangible property in line with the decedent's wishes or expectations is another measure.

These functions (meeting the maintenance needs of family members and symbolic identification) have relevance for the proposition that inheritance helps perpetuate the family through time. Although testamentary freedom per mits the disinheritance of immediate or distant kin in favor of nonrelated persons, this rarely occurs. The continuity of the family is ensured by the setting up of reciprocities and expectations, taking care of family members and providing a symbolization of family continuity. The providing of symbolic meaning and identification cannot be achieved by society-wide generational transfers in effect today or by those to be created in the future. For this reason alone, there is little prospect that the inheritance system as we know it today will ever be abolished.

Inheritance provides one major source of funds for religious, welfare, and other charitable organizations and foundations in American society. Andrée Michel has suggested to the authors that one major reason why there is very little privately funded research in France (where research is controlled largely by the government) is the severe restrictions on testamentary freedom.[6] In contrast, the relatively healthy state of charitable institutions in the United States is in part due to philanthropic giving at death. The consequence is a division and sharing of power over such basic institutional systems as religion, medicine, education, and welfare; the state does not control all these basic systems. Although only a minority of testators make charitable provisions, if this study is representative of populations in other jurisdictions, the total given is reasonably large. It is important to state that these gifts do not deprive the families, since the givers have either already provided for family members or are without an immediate family.

It is difficult to describe the specific contribution of inheritance to economic and political systems. This is because the orderly intergenerational transfer of property in which the ownership is seldom in doubt causes not a ripple in the economic system. Sophisticated mechanisms exist to permit the economy to continue unrestrained and uninhibited by the comings and goings of holders of capital. Political aspects of inheritance are restricted to two areas: (1) patronage in the appraisal system and court appointments of administrators and lawyers and (2) utilization of an inheritance as a means to obtain political office. The study data are scant on both aspects.

Inheritance functions to improve the status of women to the extent that

6. Professor Andreé Michel is on the Faculty of Social Sciences at the University of Ottawa. Private communication, January, 1967.

women are not discriminated against by testators. Whereas will makers do select between kin on the basis of need and services, neither the intestate distribution nor testators discriminate on the basis of sex. Female children are as likely to inherit as male children, and given the greater longevity of women and the likelihood that they are younger than their husbands, female spouses are more likely to inherit than male spouses. Thus, although women may be disadvantaged in the occupational marketplace, they are not disadvantaged in matters of inheritance. The findings that women considered inheritance as their own and that many were successful in their investments of this nest egg have implications for role allocations, distribution of power, and control within the family.

Obtaining a windfall through inheritance may or may not act as an incentive or a damper on mobility and achievement. The societal vision of the effects of inheritance is stereotyped: we see the rich or almost rich passing on their fortunes to children who are willing to live on the income of the inheritance or even to fritter it away and who have little incentive to improve their status; and the less wealthy, those of the middle class, capitalizing on the inheritance and using it to improve the mobility of themselves and their families. The study data cannot support either view, and it is highly doubtful that inheritance functions as either a damper or a spur to achievement. Most beneficiaries in this study inherited too late in life for the windfall to affect their life style. Moreover, few inheritances were of sufficient size to make that kind of difference. Anticipation of an inheritance is clouded by unknown variables: the age at death of the holder, the amount in the will to be received, the testator's perception of need of potential legatees, the beneficiary's position in the reciprocity system, changes in interaction patterns, and emergent but unpredictable situations requiring emergency and long-term care of the aged family member.

The fact that most individuals inherited so late and used what they received for maintenance of themselves and other family members suggests that inheritance is a negative incentive for potential inheritors. A person cannot anticipate any significant assist from inheritance in the mobility race; he has to achieve success by his own efforts.

Wealthy individuals undoubtedly make inter vivos transfers that are important to mobility and achievement of the recipients, an activity indicated but not proved by the study data. These transfers should be investigated more extensively than they were in this study. A study of inter vivos transfers would in effect be a study of the shift of power within family systems. For all individuals except the wealthy, little voluntary relegation of economic power to the spouse or children while the testator was alive was found. A holder could not afford to relinquish such power without jeopardizing his or her position within the reciprocity network.

Recommendations for change or reform of existing practices are always questioned, especially by those who have something to lose if a suggestion is adopted. In this study, our recommendations are derived or inferred from the data. We feel that we have an empirical base upon which to make recommendations; ours are not the result of armchair speculation or philosophical meanderings. Nevertheless, our critics will question the validity of our data and the logical bases of our advocacies for reform and change in laws governing inheritance, probate procedures, and education of the lawyer. We stand fast by our conclusions and recommendations and take the posture that change does not come about painlessly.

APPENDIXES

Statutes from the Ohio Revised Code

Chapter 2105: Descent and Distribution

2105.10 Descent of estate which came from deceased spouse

When a relict of a deceased husband or wife dies intestate and without issue, possessed of identical real estate or personal property which came to such relict from any deceased spouse by deed of gift, devise, bequest, descent, or by an election to take under section 2105.06 of the Revised Code, such estate, real and personal, except one half thereof which shall pass to and vest in the surviving spouse of such relict, shall pass to and vest in the children of the deceased spouse from whom such real estate or personal property came, or their lineal descendants, per stirpes. If there are no children or their lineal descendants, such estate, except for the one-half passing to the surviving spouse of such relict, shall pass and descend as follows:

(A) One half to the other heirs of such relict as provided by sections 2105.01 to 2105.09, inclusive, and 2105.11 to 2105.21, inclusive, of the Revised Code, and in the same manner and proportions as if the relict had left no surviving spouse;

(B) One half to the parents of the deceased spouse from whom such real estate or personal property came, equally, or the survivor of such parents;

(C) If there is no parent surviving, to the brothers and sisters, whether of the whole or of the half blood of such deceased spouse, of their lineal descendants, per stirpes;

(D) If there are no children of the deceased spouse from whom such real estate or personal property came, or their lineal descendants, no parent and no brothers or sisters, whether of the whole or of the half blood, or their lineal descendants, who survive such relict, then this section shall not apply and all such real estate and personal property shall pass and descend as provided by sections 2105.01 to 2105.09, inclusive, and 2105.11 to 2105.21, inclusive, of the Revised Code.

2105.15 Designation of heir-at-law

A person of sound mind and memory may appear before the probate judge of his county and in the presence of such judge and two disinterested persons of such person's acquaintance, file a written declaration declaring that, as his free and voluntary act, he did designate and appoint another, stating the name and place of residence of such person specifically, to stand toward him in the relation of an heir-at-law in the event of his death. Such declaration must be attested by the two disinterested persons and subscribed by the declarant. If satisfied that such declarant is of sound mind and memory and free from restraint, the judge thereupon shall enter that fact upon his journal and make a complete record of such proceedings. Thenceforward the person designated will stand in the same relation, for all purposes, to such declarant as he could if a child born in lawful wedlock. The rules of inheritance will be the same between him and the relations by blood of the declarant, as if so born. A certified copy of such record will be prima-facie evidence of the fact stated therein, and conclusive evidence, unless impeached for actual fraud or undue influence. After a lapse of one year from the date of such designation, such declarant may have such designation vacated or changed by filing in said probate court an application to vacate or change such designation of heir; provided, that there is compliance with the procedure, conditions, and prerequisites required in the making of the original declaration.

2105.21 Presumption of order of death

When there is no evidence of the order in which the death of two or more persons occurred, no one of such persons shall be presumed to have died first and the estate of each shall pass and descend as though he had survived the others. When the surviving spouse or other heir-at-law, legatee or devisee dies within thirty days after the death of the decedent, the estate of such first decedent shall pass and descend as though he had survived such surviving spouse, or other heir-at-law, legatee or devisee. A beneficiary of a testamentary trust shall not be deemed to be a legatee or devisee within the meaning of this section. This section shall prevail over the right of election of a surviving spouse.

This section shall not apply in the case of wills wherein provision has been made for distribution of property different from the provisions of this section. In such case such provision of the will shall not prevail over the right of election of a surviving spouse.

Chapter 2107: Wills

2107.06 Bequest to charitable purpose [in effect since October 6, 1965]

(A) If a testator dies leaving issue and by his will devises or bequeaths his estate, or any part thereof, in trust or otherwise to any municipal corporation, county, state, country, or subdivision thereof, for any purpose whatsoever, or to any person, association, or corporation for the use or benefit of one or more benevolent, religious, educational, or charitable purposes, such devises and bequests shall be valid in their entirety only if the testator's will was executed more than six months prior to the death of the testator. If such will was executed within six months of the testator's death, such devises and bequests shall be valid to the extent they do not in the aggregate exceed twenty-five percent of the value of the testator's net probate estate, and in the event the aggregate of the devises and bequests exceeds twenty-five percent thereof, such devises and bequests shall be abated proportionately so that the aggregate thereof equals twenty-five percent of the value of the testator's net probate estate.

(B) The execution of a codicil to the testator's will within six months of his death shall not affect the validity of any such devises and bequests made by will or codicil executed more than six months prior to his death, except as the same are revoked or modified by the codicil. If a codicil executed within such period increases the aggregate of such devises and bequests to more than twenty-five percent of the value of the testator's net probate estate, such increase by codicil is invalidated to the extent that such increases, plus the aggregate contained in the will and not revoked by the codicil, exceeds twenty-five percent of the value of the testator's net probate estate; and the amount of the codicil's increase of each such devise and bequest in the will and each such devise and bequest contained in the codicil which was not contained in the will shall be abated proportionately.

(C) The portion of any such devises and bequests which is invalid under this section shall be distributed per stirpes among such testator's issue unless expressly otherwise provided in the will or codicil.

(D) As used in this section, "the value of the testator's net probate estate" means the probate inventory value of all the testator's assets which are subject to the jurisdiction of the probate court, less all debts and costs and expenses of administration, but prior to the payment of any estate or inheritance taxes, and "issue" means a child or children, including an adopted child or adopted children, and their lineal descendants.

2107.06 Bequest to charitable purpose [in effect when estates in the study were closed]

If a testator dies leaving issue, or an adopted child, or the lineal descendants of either, and the will of such testator gives, devises, or bequeaths such testator's estate, or any part thereof, to a benevolent, religious, educational, or charitable purpose, or to any state or country, or to a county, municipal corporation, or other corporation, or to an association in any state or country, or to persons, municipal corporations, corporations, or associations in trust for such purposes, whether such trust appears on the face of the instrument making such gift, devise, or bequest or not, such will as to such gift, devise, or bequest, shall be invalid unless it was executed at least one year prior to the death of the testator.

2107.34 Afterborn or pretermitted heirs; effect on will

If, after making a last will and testament, a testator has a child born alive, or adopts a child, or designates an heir in the manner provided by section 2105.15 of the Revised Code, or if a child or designated heir who is absent and reported to be dead proves to be alive, and no provision has been made in such will or by settlement for such pretermitted child or heir, or for the issue thereof, the will shall not be revoked; but unless it appears by such will that it was the intention of the testator to disinherit such pretermitted child or heir, the devises and legacies granted by such will, except those to a surviving spouse, shall be abated proportionately, or in such other manner as is necessary to give effect to the intention of the testator as shown by the will, so that such pretermitted child or heir will receive a share equal to that which such person would have been entitled to receive out of the estate if such testator had died intestate with no surviving spouse, owning only that portion of his estate not devised or bequeathed to or for the use and benefit of a surviving spouse. If such child or heir dies prior to the death of the testator, the issue of such deceased child or heir shall receive the share the parent would have received if living.

If such pretermitted child or heir supposed to be dead at the time of executing the will has lineal descendants, provision for whom is made by the testator, the other legatees and devisees need not contribute, but such pretermitted child or heir shall take the provision made for his lineal descendants or such part of it as, in the opinion of the probate judge, may be equitable. In settling the claim of a pretermitted child or heir, any portion of the testator's estate received by a party interested, by way of advancement, is a portion of the estate and shall be charged to the party who has received it.

Though measured by sections 2105.01 to 2105.21, inclusive, of the Revised Code, the share taken by a pretermitted child or heir shall be considered as a testate succession. This section does not prejudice the right of any fiduciary to act under any power given by the will, nor shall the title of innocent purchasers for value of any of the property of the testator's estate be affected by any right given by this section to a pretermitted child or heir.

2107.60 Oral will

An oral will, made in the last sickness, shall be valid in respect to personal estate if reduced to writing and subscribed by two competent disinterested witnesses within ten days after the speaking of the testamentary words. Such witnesses must prove that the testator was of sound mind and memory, not under restraint, and that he called upon some person present at the time the testamentary words were spoken to bear testimony to such disposition as his will.

No oral will shall be admitted to record unless it is offered for probate within six months after the death of the testator.

Chapter 2113: Executors and Administrators—Appointment; Powers; Duties

2113.35 Commissions

Executors and administrators shall be allowed commissions upon the amount of all the personal estate, including the income therefrom, received and accounted for by them and upon the proceeds of real estate sold under authority contained in a will, which must be received in full compensation for all their ordinary services, as follows:

(A) For the first one thousand dollars at the rate of six percent;

(B) All above one thousand and not exceeding five thousand dollars at the rate of four percent;

(C) All above five thousand dollars at the rate of two percent.

The basis of valuation for the allowance of such commissions on property sold shall be the gross proceeds of sale, and for property distributed in kind the valuation thereof as fixed by the inventory and appraisement.

Should the probate court find, after hearing, that an executor or administrator has in any respect not faithfully discharged his duties as such executor or administrator, the court may deny such executor or administrator any compensation whatsoever or may allow such executor or administrator such reduced compensation as the court thinks proper.

2113.36 Further allowance: counsel fees

Allowances, in addition to those provided by section 2113.35 of the Revised Code for an executor or administrator, which the probate court considers just and reasonable shall be made for actual and necessary expenses and for extraordinary services not required of an executor or administrator in the common course of his duty. When an attorney has been employed in the administration of the estate, reasonable attorney fees paid by the executor or administrator shall be allowed as a part of the expenses of administration. The court may at any time during administration fix the amount of such fees and, on application of the executor or administrator or the attorney, shall fix the amount thereof. When provision is made by the will of the deceased for compensation to an executor, the amount provided shall be a full satisfaction for his services, in lieu of such commissions or his share thereof, unless by an instrument filed in the court within four months after his appointment he renounces all claim to the compensation given by the will.

Chapter 3107: Adoption

3107.13 Legal rights after final decree of adoption

Except in the case of a natural parent married to the adopting parent, the natural parents, if living, shall be divested of all legal rights and obligations due from them to the child or from the child to them, and the child shall be free from all legal obligations of obedience or otherwise to such parents. The adopting parents of the child shall be invested with every legal right in respect to obedience and maintenance on the part of the child, and the child shall be invested with every legal right, privilege, obligation, and relation in respect to education and maintenance as if such child had been born to them in lawful wedlock. For all purposes under the laws of this state, including without limitation all laws and wills governing inheritance of and succession to real or personal property and the taxation of an estate, a legally adopted child shall have the same status and rights, and shall bear the same legal relationship to the adopting parents as if born to them in lawful wedlock and not born to the natural parents; provided:

(A) Such adopted child shall not be capable of inheriting or succeeding to property expressly limited to heirs of the body of the adopting parents.

(B) In case of adoption by a stepfather or stepmother, the rights and obligations of the natural parent who is the spouse of the adopting stepparent shall not in any way be affected by such adoption.

This section does not debar a legally adopted child from inheriting, under a will identifying such child by any name by which he has been or is known or other clear identification, property of such child's natural parent or parents or other natural kin as in case of bequest or devise to any other person.

For the purpose of inheritance to, through, and from a legally adopted child, such child shall be treated the same as if he were the natural child of his adopting parents, and shall cease to be treated as the child of his natural parents for the purposes of intestate succession, except where one of the natural parents of such child has died and his living parent remarries and such child is adopted by such stepfather or stepmother, in which case his right of inheritance from or through his natural parent or other natural kin shall not be affected by his adoption.

Rating Scale for Homes in Cuyahoga County[1]

Class 1

Indicative of "best" housing in the county. For urban areas, probably large single family, set in own grounds with a two or more car garage, well-kept, "best" neighborhood. Note: Not likely to be found in city proper, but in the near suburbs.

Class 2

Similar to Class 1, but "second best," sometimes large older houses in established neighborhoods (these were fashionable a generation ago) or smaller new homes in "best" neighborhoods, but with less grounds than Class 1, but large lot size.

Class 3

"Better than average," but similar in house type to Class 4, only probably newer, or in "better" neighborhood. Well-kept grounds, one or two car garage, smaller lot size than Class 2.

Class 4

"Average housing," probably small, single family or well-kept two family, in "respectable" neighborhood (no business or industry) probably a garage, own grounds, neat and trim.

Class 5

"Below average." Generally single or two family houses, sometimes converted for multiple family use in good condition, but with little land area; neat, but not as well kept up as Class 4; small front yards or none. Some single, small houses, often rows of similar type. On fringes of business and industry, probably no garage.

1. Marvin B. Sussman, *Rating Scale for Homes in Cuyahoga County* (Cleveland: Western Reserve University [privately published], 1960).

Class 6

Single, two, or four family housing often converted to multiple use in poor condition and crowded together, but not in such disrepair as to be substandard. Often in mixed neighborhoods (with business and industry).

Class 7

"Poorest" housing in community. Similar in physical type to Class 6, but in such disrepair that it is easily judged substandard. Usually oldest housing; associated with slum areas of cities; business and industry present in same neighborhood.

Appendix C

Description of the Lawyer Sample

THE CUYAHOGA COUNTY attorneys constituting the lawyer sample were, in large part, locally born and educated. Cleveland, as an industrial area, has also attracted large numbers of foreign-born persons. The lawyer sample had not been geographically mobile. Over 50 per cent of the sample members were born in greater Cleveland; 80 per cent attended Cleveland law schools; and all were first admitted to the bar in Ohio (see Tables C–1 and C–2).[1]

TABLE C–1 LAWYER SAMPLE, BY PLACE OF BIRTH

Place of Birth	Number	Per Cent
Cuyahoga County	36	51.4
Other Ohio counties	8	11.4
Other states	15	21.4
Foreign countries	11	15.7
Total	70	99.9

TABLE C-2 LAWYER SAMPLE, BY LAW SCHOOL ATTENDED

Law School Attended	Number	Per Cent
Cleveland-Marshall Law School (evening, part-time)	38	54.3
Western Reserve University (day, full-time)	18	25.7
Harvard, Yale, Columbia, Michigan, Chicago	6	8.6
Other law schools	8	11.4
Total	70	100.0

1. Lawyers are among the least mobile of professionals. State licensure is apparently more restrictive of mobility for lawyers than it is for physicians. As is true for some other self-employed professionals, lawyers must cultivate a clientele. Jack Ladinsky, "Occupational Determinants of Geographic Mobility Among Professional Workers," *American Sociological Review* 32 (April, 1967):255–258.

Jerome Carlin gives the following figures on law school attendance, taken from a sample of individual practitioners in Cleveland in 1958: ivy league, 4 per cent; other full-time university, 54 per cent; and night school, 42 per cent.[2] As will be noted, there is a greater proportion of night school attorneys (54 per cent) in the study sample of probate attorneys than there was in Carlin's sample of individual practitioners.

In the Cuyahoga County sample, 31 per cent of the lawyers did not graduate from college. Under standards applicable today, they would not be admitted to the practice of law in Ohio. Since 1960, a lawyer must have a bachelor's degree as well as a law degree in order to be eligible for the bar examination.[3] The older attorneys in the sample were predominantly the ones who did not have the baccalaureate degree (see Table C–3).

TABLE C–3 ATTORNEY'S AGE AND COLLEGE GRADUATION
(Percentage Distribution)

Age	College Graduate	Not College Graduate	Total	
			Number	Per Cent
30–39	87.5	12.5	16	100.0
40–59	81.8	18.2	33	100.0
60 and over	31.6	68.4	19	100.0
Total			68[a]	

[a] Two attorneys gave no information regarding college graduation.

TABLE C–4 LAW SCHOOL ATTENDED AND TYPE OF PRACTICE
(Percentage Distribution)

Law School Attended	Type of Practice		Total	
	Full-Time	Part-Time	Number	Per Cent
Cleveland-Marshall Law School	78.9	21.1	38	100.0
Western Reserve University	55.6	44.4	18	100.0
Other law schools	92.9	7.1	14	100.0
Total			70	

Note: $x^2 = 6.44$; $df = 2$; $p = <.05$.

Part-time law practice was associated with the law school the attorney attended. Western Reserve University School of Law had more part-time graduates than would be expected by chance (see Table C–4).

2. Jerome Carlin, *Lawyers on Their Own* (New Brunswick, N.J.: Rutgers University Press, 1962), p. 33.

3. Before January, 1954, the applicant must have completed two years in an approved college. From January, 1954, to January, 1960, three years were necessary. After January 1, 1960, the bachelor's degree was in effect made a prerequisite for law school.

Various studies have shown that lawyers come from the higher social strata and that a large proportion are the sons of lawyers.[4] The Cuyahoga County sample of attorneys contained a greater proportion of blue-collar fathers than was true for the samples in previous studies (see Table C–5).

TABLE C–5 FATHER'S OCCUPATION

Father's Occupation	Number	Per Cent
Professional-managerial	25	35.7
Other white-collar	20	28.6
Blue-collar	25	35.7
Total	70	100.0

A total of 16 per cent of the lawyer sample had lawyer-fathers. There was also a tendency for those with lawyer-fathers to be disproportionately placed in law firms rather than to be in independent practice (see Table C–6). The effect of a lawyer-father was not mediated through the type of law school attended. There was no significant difference between sons of attorneys and others on law school attended.

TABLE C–6 TYPE OF LAW OFFICE, BY LAWYER-FATHER

	Father a Lawyer		Father Not a Lawyer		
Type of Law Office	Number	Per Cent	Number	Per Cent	Total
Independent	3	27.3	35	59.3	38
Small firm (2–5)	2	18.2	15	25.4	17
Medium and large firms (6 or more)	4	36.4	4	6.8	8
Other[a]	2	18.2	5	8.5	7
Total	11	100.1	59	100.0	70

Note: $x^2 = 9.90$; $df = 3$; $p = <.02$.
[a] Those categorized as "other" were not actually engaged in the practice of law (for example, a minister who had a law degree), or they were employed by a corporation or semi-retired. Their probate work was confined to favors for friends and family.

In this study, the nature of law practice in which the interviewed attorneys were engaged was examined, and an attempt was made to determine if they were specialists or generalists. How do the lawyers arrive at an area of specialization? Unlike medicine, where specialization is institutionalized early by specific training in the form of residencies and boards, the lawyer develops a

4. In a sample of 82 New York lawyers with matrimonial clients, it was found that 23 per cent of the attorneys had blue-collar fathers. Hubert J. O'Gorman, *Lawyers and Matrimonial Cases* (New York: The Free Press, 1963), p. 52. In a sample of 84 Chicago lawyers in individual practice, 12 per cent had blue-collar fathers; Carlin, op. cit., p. 25.

special area of practice gradually.[5] After a period of years, he finds himself with a clientele relatively concentrated in one area of practice.

Those lawyers who said their practice was specialized were generally older than those who considered themselves to be general practitioners.[6] Nearly one-half of the older attorneys and just over one-fifth of the younger attorneys had a specialized practice (see Table C–7).

TABLE C–7 TYPE OF LAW PRACTICE, BY ATTORNEY'S AGE

	Age 30–59		Age 60 and Over		
Type of Practice	Number	Per Cent	Number	Per Cent	Total
Specialized	11	22.4	10	47.6	21
General	38	77.6	11	52.4	49
Total	49	100.0	21	100.0	70

Note: $x^2 = 4.44$; $df = 1$; $p < .05$.

The volume of work in the wills-estates area performed by the lawyers in the sample is shown in Table C–8. Not only does the sample include lawyers with substantial experience in probate work, but also the lawyers who work in wills and estates find the area both personally satisfying and financially rewarding. Twenty-one lawyers said probate was the most personally satisfying area of practice, and 24 said it was the most financially rewarding. This is a larger number than for any other area of practice. Only one person said the probate area was the least satisfying, and no one said it was the least financially rewarding. In contrast, 28 lawyers singled out domestic relations as the least personally satisfying, and 31 said domestic relations were the least financially rewarding.

TABLE C–8 YEARLY VOLUME OF ATTORNEYS IN WILLS AND ESTATE ADMINISTRATION
(Per Cent of Attorneys, by Number of Cases Per Year)

				Total	
Wills-Estates	1–19 Cases	20–39 Cases	40 or More Cases	Number	Per Cent
Wills drawn per year	21.7	37.7	40.6	69[a]	100.0
New estate cases per year	69.6	21.7	8.7	69[a]	100.0

[a] One attorney could not recall the number of wills or new estate cases he entered in the preceding year.

5. "The demarcation between specialists and non-specialists in the legal profession is by no means as clear cut as in the curative professions. In general, the lawyer becomes a specialist from the circumstances of location, the nature of the clientele and his particular interests and experience rather than formalized training," Leonard Kent, "Economic Status of the Legal Profession in Chicago," *Illinois Law Review* 45 (1951):326.

6. Ibid., p. 327. "It may be stated that there is a tendency for specialists and concentrating practitioners to be slightly older than general practitioners."

Only one person claimed that domestic relations were the most satisfying, and one other attorney said they were most financially rewarding. Two lawyers said criminal work was the most personally satisfying; none said it was the most financially rewarding. Criminal work was singled out by eight persons as the least personally satisfying and by nine persons as the least financially rewarding.

It is scarcely surprising that a sample of lawyers skewed toward those with probate work should express satisfaction with this area of practice. But the studies of matrimonial and criminal areas appear to indicate that the lawyers who work in these fields are not nearly so well satisfied as the probate lawyers. O'Gorman found that 26 per cent of his sample of lawyers disliked matrimonial clients. The reasons most frequently cited were the emotional strain, inadequate compensation, and the personal nature of the problem.[7] Wood found that 43 per cent of the criminal lawyers have reservations about their area of practice, stating that they would like less criminal work and more corporation or probate work.[8] Their most common criticisms of criminal work are inadequate remuneration, the type of client, and the strenuous work.[9] Lawyers object to matrimonial clients as being too emotional and to criminal clients as being morally objectionable.[10] Of course, there is the possibility that clients in the wills-estates area will be emotional; however, they are apparently not so emotional that lawyers dislike the work. Obviously, probate clients are not particularly morally objectionable.

It is also likely that probate clients are, on the whole, of a higher social class than criminal clients. The lawyers were given brief descriptions of five social classes (upper, upper-middle, middle, working, and lower) and asked to estimate what proportion of their clientele belonged to each class.[11] Seven lawyers refused to make any estimate. The clientele of 15 lawyers was characterized as being primarily upper and upper-middle class. The clientele of 21 lawyers was characterized as being primarily middle and upper-middle class. The clientele of 19 lawyers showed a scattered pattern, with 13 of these lawyers claiming some clients in all five classes, and the remaining six claiming clients in four classes (omitting the lower class). Thirty-six lawyers had no lower-class clients. Twenty-nine lawyers had no upper-class clients. The class of clientele that the probate lawyers deal with is generally average or above. The social gulf should either be minimal or in some instances should be in favor of the client.

7. O'Gorman, op. cit., pp. 117–118.
8. Arthur Lewis Wood, *Criminal Lawyer* (New Haven, Conn.: College & University Press, 1967), pp. 50–52.
9. Ibid., p. 95.
10. O'Gorman, op. cit., p. 117; Wood, op. cit., p. 100.
11. The descriptions were adapted from those found in August Hollingshead and Frederick Redlich, *Social Class and Mental Illness* (New York: John Wiley & Sons, Inc., 1958), pp. 398–406.

Appendix D

Life Cycle and Testacy

THIS ANALYSIS is based on the study's 1,102 interviews, since full family data were not included on the mailed questionnaire. The data were not collected in the ideal manner, that is, longitudinal data over the life span.[1] However, they are consistent with generally known facts on changes in income and family structure over the life cycle.[2] It should be kept in mind that the percentage of testate persons in each category refers to those who had wills at that age and not to when they made their wills.

Here are capsule summaries on the married survivors by age (the data are presented in detail in Table D–1): In their twenties, 69 per cent of the survivors were married. Married women had an average of 2 children, and married men had an average of 1.6 children. Married men had a testacy rate of 26 per cent, and married women had a rate of 17 per cent. Both are low rates in the survivor population.

In their thirties, 83 per cent were married, and the number of children in the home was 2.9 for both married men and women. The married men had a higher rate of testacy than the women: 48 per cent, compared with 39 per cent. The median household income was higher than it was for persons in their twenties: from $601 to $800.

In their forties, married men and women had nearly identical rates of testacy: 56 and 58 per cent, respectively. The women had a lower household income than men: from $601 to $800, compared with $801 to $1,000; but in other respects they were similar. The average number of children in the

1. Reuben Hill, "Decision Making and the Family Life Cycle," *Social Structure and the Family,* ed. Ethel Shanas and Gordon F. Streib (Englewood Cliffs, N.J.: Prentice-Hall, Inc., 1965), p. 119.

2. For a description of the life cycle see Paul C. Glick, "The Life Cycle of the Family," *Marriage and Family Living* 17 (February, 1955):3–9, or Paul C. Glick, "The Family Cycle," *American Sociological Review* 12 (April, 1947):164–74. For a description of income and assets over the life cycle, see Lydall, loc. cit.; or Dorothy S. Brady, "Influence of Age on Savings and Spending Patterns," *Monthly Labor Review* 78 (November, 1955):1240–44; or Janet A. Fisher, "Family Life Cycle Analysis in Research on Consumer Behavior," *The Life Cycle and Consumer Behavior* (New York: New York University Press, 1955), pp. 28–35.

TABLE D–1 MARRIED SURVIVORS: PER CENT TESTATE, BY AGE,[a] SEX, INCOME, AND NUMBER OF DEPENDENT CHILDREN

Age and Sex	Per Cent Testate	Median Household Income	Number of Dependent Children
20–29 ($N = 61$)			
Males ($N = 31$)	25.8	\$401–\$600	1.6
Females ($N = 30$)	16.7	\$401–\$600	2.0
30–39 ($N = 165$)			
Males ($N = 77$)	48.1	\$601–\$800	2.9
Females ($N = 88$)	38.6	\$601–\$800	2.9
40–49 ($N = 249$)			
Males ($N = 126$)	55.6	\$801–\$1,000	2.5
Females ($N = 123$)	57.7	\$601–\$800	2.3
50–59 ($N = 171$)			
Males ($N = 107$)	66.0	\$601–\$800	1.5
Females ($N = 64$)	65.6	\$601–\$800	1.2
60–69 ($N = 66$)			
Males ($N = 35$)	85.7	\$401–\$600	79.1 per cent are living with spouse only after age 60
Females ($N = 31$)	74.2	\$401–\$600	
70–89 ($N = 25$)			
Males ($N = 19$)	100.0	\$201–\$300	
Females ($N = 6$)	100.0	\$201–\$300	

[a] There were 2 married survivors for whom age was unknown.

home was less than for the preceding age group: 2.3 for the women and 2.5 for men. There was also a slight dip in the percentage who were married, 79 per cent of those in their forties.

In their fifties, the percentage who were married was lower than it was for persons in their twenties: 66 per cent. Men had an average of 1.5 children in the home; and women, 1.2. In terms of family responsibilities, the fifties were most like the twenties; however the household incomes were higher. The median for both men and women was from \$601 to \$800, as compared with \$401 to \$600 for those in their twenties. The rate of testacy for men and women was the same: 66 per cent.

Persons in their sixties were the first age group in which the married were fewer than the unmarried: 48 per cent were married. The children were gone and the couple were living alone. Median household income declined from \$401 to \$600. The rates of testacy were 86 per cent for married men and 74 per cent for the married women.

Among those in their seventies, 31 per cent were married. Median household income was lower than in any preceding period: from \$201 to \$300. All the married men and women were testate. There were no married persons in their eighties.

Several conclusions can be derived from these brief summaries. First, women become testate later than men. In their twenties and thirties, fewer women than men were testate. At ages 40 and 50, the rates were very similar. Secondly, the low rate of testacy for both men and women in their twenties cannot be explained by the absence of family responsibilities; 69 per cent were married, and their families had usually been started. Household income was lower than it was for those in their thirties, forties, and fifties. The alternative explanations are that they were intestate by virtue of low economic status, age, or a combination of both factors. Thirdly, the high rate of testacy among persons in their seventies is not a function of present economic status. The median household income was lower than it was for persons in their twenties. At both ends of the age spectrum, age probably explains the testacy phenomenon. For persons in their twenties, age is a negative factor; for persons in their seventies, age is a positive factor that encourages testacy among individuals who arrive at this stage in life without a will. Lastly, it will be noted that the peak of family responsibilities occurs in the thirties and then declines; whereas household income remains the same during the thirties, forties, and fifties, with the exception of males in their forties. The decline of family responsibilities in the fifties implies that this latter period should provide the best opportunity for capital accumulation.

The life cycle framework has evolved in family sociology, and therefore the unmarried have scarcely been considered. They cannot be ignored; they represent nearly a third (32 per cent) of the entire group under consideration (see Table D–2 for detailed data on the unmarried).

TABLE D–2 UNMARRIED SURVIVORS: PER CENT TESTATE, BY AGE,[a] INCOME, AND WIDOWED STATUS

Age	Per Cent Testate	Median Household Income	Per Cent Widowed
20–29 (*N* = 27)	7.4	\$401–\$600	7.4
30–39 (*N* = 35)	25.7	\$401–\$600	28.6
40–49 (*N* = 67)	56.7	\$401–\$600	61.2
50–59 (*N* = 87)	74.7	\$401–\$600	77.0
60–69 (*N* = 71)	74.3	\$201–\$300	83.0
70–80 (*N* = 73)[b]	76.4	\$126–\$200	94.5

[a] There were 3 unmarried survivors for whom age was unknown.
[b] There were 57 unmarried survivors aged 70–79.

In their twenties, only 7 per cent of the unmarried were testate, a much lower rate than for the married in this age group. In their twenties, most of the unmarried were single. The median household income of \$401 to \$600 was the same as the income for the married.

Among persons in their thirties, the rate of testacy was 26 per cent, still substantially lower than the rate of testacy for the married. The median household income was $401 to $600; whereas the married in this age group had incomes of $601 to $800. The single still predominated in the group.

Unmarried persons in their forties had a testacy rate similar to married males: 57 per cent, compared with 56 per cent. Their income remained at the previous level of $401 to $600. The widowed constituted 61 per cent of the unmarried persons in their forties. The percentage of widowed persons in the unmarried group rose steadily in the following decades.

Among those in their fifties, the testacy rate of the unmarried was nearly 10 per cent greater than for the married. The median income had not increased; 77 per cent were widowed.

The unmarried persons in their sixties had virtually no greater testacy rate than those in their fifties: 75 per cent in the fifties and 74 per cent in the sixties. Income declined, as did the income of the married; the median was $201 to $300.

The median income was lowest, from $126 to $200, for those aged 70 and over who were unmarried. In these years, 76 per cent were testate as compared with 100 per cent of the married.

Persons who had never been married predominated in the twenties; they will probably marry in their thirties. The widowed, who were the majority from the forties on, may have made wills during married life or following the deaths of their spouses. In comparing this group with the married group, it is noteworthy that except for the decade of the twenties, the married had a higher median income than the unmarried.

Our conception of the differential impact of the incentives toward testacy over the life cycle is as follows: For persons in their twenties and thirties, death is regarded as improbable and this accounts for the generally low rate of testacy. Those who make wills in this period are those who are most likely to feel the burden of family responsibility: the married men. In the forties and fifties, the income of married persons is high and family responsibilities have decreased. For the married, the incentive may be the accumulation of capital. In the fifties, the testacy rate of the unmarried is distinctly higher than that of the married; the newly widowed may have inherited property or may be suddenly brought to a recognition of the possibility of death. In the later years, income declines and family responsibilities are virtually absent except for the married couple's obligations toward each other; the married regain their lead over the unmarried. However, in this period of life, the rate of testacy is high for all, suggesting that the common factor is the imminence of death.

Appendix

E General Tables

TABLE E–1 CLOSENESS AND INTERACTION OF CHILDREN WITH DECEDENT TESTATOR, BY PER CENT DISINHERITED

Closeness and Interaction	Total Number	Per Cent Disinherited
Closeness		
Close	223	14.3
Average	130	16.9
Not close	39	12.8
Total	392	
Interaction		
Daily	161	14.3
Weekly	167	15.6
Less often	62	16.1
Total	390[a]	

[a] There were 2 survivors who gave no information regarding interaction.

TABLE E–2 CLOSENESS OF CHILDREN TO DECEDENT TESTATOR AND HEIR STATUS (Percentage Distribution)

	Heir		Contingent		Disinherited	
Closeness	Sons ($N = 66$)	Daughters ($N = 85$)	Sons ($N = 83$)	Daughters ($N = 99$)	Sons ($N = 30$)	Daughters ($N = 29$)
Close	57.6	67.1	42.2	61.5	43.3	65.6
Average	31.8	23.5	49.4	26.3	46.7	27.6
Not close	10.6	9.4	8.4	12.1	10.0	6.9

TABLE E–3 INTERACTION OF CHILDREN WITH DECEDENT TESTATOR, BY HEIR STATUS
(Percentage Distribution)

Interaction	Heir Sons (N = 65)	Heir Daughters (N = 85)	Contingent Sons (N = 82)	Contingent Daughters (N = 99)	Disinherited Sons (N = 30)	Disinherited Daughters (N = 29)
Daily	38.5	56.5	26.8	43.4	30.0	41.3
Weekly	44.6	31.8	53.7	41.4	46.7	42.8
Less often	16.9	11.8	19.5	15.2	23.3	15.9

TABLE E–4 OCCUPATION OF THOSE WITH LARGE ESTATES COMPARED WITH TOTAL DECEDENT SAMPLE
(Percentage Distribution)

Occupation	Decedents with Large Estates[a]	Total Sample[b]
Blue-collar	15.2	39.9
White-collar	24.2	36.3
Professional and managerial	60.6	23.8
Total	100.0	100.0

[a] Percentages were based on 33 decedents with gross estates of $60,000 and over. Fourteen were housewives, and occupation was unknown for 1. Total decedents with gross estates over $60,000 was 48.

[b] Percentages were based on 461 decedents. For 198 decedents, there was no usual occupation or occupation was unknown.

TABLE E–5 SURVIVORS' JUDGMENTS REGARDING THE NECESSITY OF A LAWYER AND THEIR SATISFACTION WITH LAWYER, BY SOCIOECONOMIC VARIABLES
(Percentage Distribution)

Socioeconomic Variables	Total Number	Lawyer an Absolute Necessity	Satisfied with Lawyer's Handling and Fees
Occupation			
Unskilled manual	34	26.5	38.2
Semiskilled manual	129	33.3	31.8
Skilled manual	244	33.6	32.4
Clerical, sales, and technicians	203	45.8	32.5
Administrators, small business, and minor professionals	168	36.9	42.9
Managers and lesser professionals	129	47.3	31.8
Major professionals and top executives	113	41.6	30.1
Total	1,020[a]		
Education			
Less than 8 years	69	18.8	37.7
8 years grade school	87	31.0	34.5
Some high school	261	35.2	30.7
High school graduate	388	40.2	35.1
Some college	212	40.1	41.5
College graduate	206	43.7	33.0
Total	1,223[b]		
Monthly household income			
$200 or less	93	23.7	33.3
$201–$400	156	37.2	38.5
$401–$600	317	37.2	31.2
$601–$800	187	39.6	41.7
$801–$1,000	157	41.4	36.3
$1,001–$1,500	129	40.3	34.9
$1,501 and over	82	46.3	26.8
Total	1,121[c]		

Note: The number of survivors in the parts of Table E–5 do not correspond exactly with the numbers found in Tables 4–13, 4–19, and 4–21. Testacy was examined in Chapter 4. Among the survivors, there were 4 for whom testacy was unknown. Of these 4 survivors, income was also not known for all; 1 was not working; for 1, occupation was unknown; and for 2, education was unknown. These survivors were included in the appropriate categories in Table E–5.

[a] For 10 survivors, occupation was unknown, and 204 survivors were not working (widows on social security, students, and so forth).

[b] For 11 survivors, education was unknown.

[c] For 113 survivors, income was unknown.

TABLE E–6 GENERAL ATTITUDE AND YEARS IN PROBATE
(Percentage Distribution)

Years in Probate	General Attitude				Total	
	Favorable	Somewhat Favorable	Somewhat Unfavorable	Unfavorable	Number	Per Cent
Less than 1	36.5	28.4	24.5	10.6	677	100.0
1–2	30.3	24.2	33.2	12.4	380	100.1
Over 2	16.9	20.9	34.5	27.7	177	100.0
Total					1,234	

Note: $x^2 = 60.41$; $df = 6$; $p < .001$.

TABLE E–7 GENERAL ATTITUDE AND COURT COSTS
(Percentage Distribution)

Court Costs	General Attitude				Total	
	Favorable	Somewhat Favorable	Somewhat Unfavorable	Unfavorable	Number	Per Cent
$50 or less	32.8	28.2	28.0	10.9	393	99.9
$51–$100	34.1	25.3	27.3	13.3	684	100.0
Over $100	19.1	23.6	35.7	21.7	157	100.1
Total					1,234	

Note: $x^2 = 23.21$; $df = 6$; $p < .001$.

TABLE E–8 GENERAL ATTITUDE AND LAWYER'S FEE
(Percentage Distribution)

Lawyer's Fee	General Attitude				Total	
	Favorable	Somewhat Favorable	Somewhat Unfavorable	Unfavorable	Number	Per Cent
None listed	36.5	30.9	23.0	9.6	230	100.0
$200 or less	34.1	30.4	28.9	6.6	273	100.0
$201–$500	30.4	23.0	30.5	16.1	514	100.0
Over $500	27.2	22.6	29.5	20.7	217	100.0
Total					1,234	

Note: $x^2 = 37.34$; $df = 9$; $p < .001$.

TABLE E–9 ATTITUDE TOWARD FEES AND YEARS IN PROBATE
(Percentage Distribution)

Years in Probate	Attitude Toward Fees			Total	
	Favorable	Marginal	Unfavorable	Number	Per Cent
Less than 1	31.8	47.0	21.3	677	100.1
1–2	21.1	52.6	26.3	380	100.0
Over 2	13.0	42.9	44.1	177	100.0
Total				1,234	

Note: $x^2 = 54.78$; $df = 4$; $p < .001$.

TABLE E–10 ATTITUDE TOWARD FEES AND COURT COSTS
(Percentage Distribution)

Court Costs	Attitude Toward Fees			Total	
	Favorable	Marginal	Unfavorable	Number	Per Cent
$50 or less	26.5	50.9	22.6	393	100.0
$51–$100	28.4	45.5	26.2	684	100.1
Over $100	12.7	52.9	34.4	157	100.0
Total				1,234	

Note: $x^2 = 20.28$; $df = 4$; $p < .001$.

TABLE E–11 ATTITUDE TOWARD FEES AND LAWYER'S FEE
(Percentage Distribution)

Lawyer's Fee	Attitude Toward Fees			Total	
	Favorable	Marginal	Unfavorable	Number	Per Cent
None listed	29.1	51.3	19.6	230	100.0
$200 or less	29.3	45.4	25.3	273	100.0
$201–$500	24.3	48.2	27.4	514	99.0
Over $500	21.2	47.9	30.9	217	100.0
Total				1,234	

Note: $x^2 = 11.47$; $df = 6$; $p < .10$.

Code of Conduct for Cleveland Banks Regarding Estate Planning

THIS CODE of conduct or statement of cooperation is the result of a recent Ohio case, Green v. Huntington National Bank, 4 Ohio St. 2d 78, 212 N.E. 2d 585 (1965). In this case, a Columbus bank had been offering an "estate analysis" program to its customers that consisted of providing specific legal information relating to a particular person's estate. The court held that by systematically engaging in such activities with the expectation of being compensated, the bank engaged in the practice of law. The lower court's judgment enjoining the bank from offering such advice was modified to permit it to deal with an attorney but to prevent direct bank-customer consultations.

The code of conduct was sponsored by the Cleveland Bar Association and the Cuyahoga County Bar Association and has been agreed to by the major Cleveland banks. It reads as follows:

CODE OF CONDUCT FOR CLEVELAND BANKS PURSUANT TO GREEN V. HUNTINGTON NATIONAL BANK OF COLUMBUS
4 Ohio St. 2d 78, which holds:

Syl. 1. "A bank or trust company which provides specific legal information in relation to the specific facts of a particular person's estate for the purpose of obtaining a more beneficial estate condition in relation to tax and other legal consequences of death is giving legal advice."

1. No bank shall prepare or furnish or offer to prepare or furnish:
   (i) any specific plan for disposition of any person's estate by will or testamentary or inter vivos trust,
   (ii) any gift or death tax computation relating to the planning of any person's estate, or
   (iii) any specific plan for creation of any trust by any person, or
   (iv) any proposed trust agreement, will or codicil,

except upon the prior written approval or request from the attorney for such person, or written confirmation from the bank to such attorney of prior oral approval or request from such attorney. Nothing in this paragraph shall be construed to prohibit a bank either from gathering factual data about any person's estate or from furnishing to any person illustrative examples of estate and gift tax computations or other information of a general nature regarding estate planning, or pension, profit-sharing or retirement trust planning.

2. All specific legal information or legal advice relating to a specific trust, will or estate, shall be given only to the attorney for the person involved. All documents mentioned in paragraph 1 shall be delivered only to such attorney, except and to the extent that such attorney may otherwise direct in writing, or as set forth in a written confirmation from the bank to such attorney, of his prior oral direcions.

3. The foregoing paragraphs 1 and 2 shall also be applicable to any instrument which alters, amends or modifies any existing will or trust.

4. Nothing contained in this code of conduct is intended to modify, restrict, enlarge or increase any rights or privileges which a bank may have under the decision in *Judd v. City Trust and Savings Bank,* 133 O.S. 81.

5. As used herein, the term "bank" includes its officers and employees; the term "trust" includes any testamentary or inter vivos personal trust, insurance trust, pension trust, profit-sharing trust or retirement plan trust; and the term "person" means and includes natural persons, partnerships, associations and corporations.

Probate Court Rules

SUMMIT COUNTY PROBATE COURT RULE 23: REQUIREMENT OF FIDUCIARY TO DESIGNATE ATTORNEY OF RECORD

DESIGNATION OF ATTORNEY: At the time the application is made to this Court for the appointment of a fiduciary, said fiduciary shall file in this Court the name of the Attorney-at-Law who will thereafter represent such fiduciary and perform all legal services required by such fiduciary in all matters relating to the administration and handling of said estate, trust, or other fiduciary proceeding.

In the event of the death or resignation of designated Attorney-at-Law, the fiduciary shall forthwith file in this Court the name of the Attorney-at-Law who will thereafter represent such fiduciary.

FILING OF PAPERS: Each pleading, instrument, application, account, document and paper presented to this Court for filing for and on behalf of any fiduciary acting by virtue of an appointment by this Court in any estate, trust, guardianship or other fiduciary proceeding, shall have been prepared by the Attorney-at-Law designated by such fiduciary, in accordance with this Order to represent such fiduciary to perform all legal services required by such fiduciary in all matters relating to the administration and handling of said estate, trust, guardianship or other fiduciary proceeding, or shall have endorsed thereon or attached thereto a certificate executed by said designated Attorney-at-Law attesting and certifying to the Court that he has examined the same and that such pleading, instrument, application, account, document or other paper is correct and proper; and, in the event such pleading, instrument, application, account, document or other paper is not so prepared or does not bear such endorsement the same shall be refused and denied filing in this Court. Each fiduciary upon appointment by this Court shall be furnished a copy of this Rule and shall thereafter comply therewith. Each fiduciary acting pursuant to appointment made by this Court prior to the entry of this Order shall hereafter comply with this Order as to all pleadings, instruments, applications, accounts, documents or other papers presented to this Court for filing for and on behalf of such fiduciary.

CUYAHOGA COUNTY PROBATE COURT RULE 11:
APPOINTMENT AND COMPENSATION OF APPRAISERS
IN ESTATES AND LAND SALE PROCEEDINGS

The Court is required by law to appoint three disinterested and qualified appraisers. Suggestions as to the persons to be appointed in any particular case will be received by the Court. In making these suggestions, fiduciaries and their counsel will be considered by the Court as vouching for the integrity and ability of those suggested as appraisers. Such suggestions shall be made on a printed form to be furnished by the Court and signed by the fiduciaries or their counsel.

Executors or administrators without special application to the Court may allow to each appraiser, as compensation for his services, any amount agreed upon between the fiduciary and the appraiser, but not in excess of an amount to be computed on the gross appraised value of all assets of the estate (as set forth in the inventory and appraisement filed in the Court), in accordance with the following schedule: (a) One Dollar ($1.00) per thousand on the first Fifty Thousand Dollars ($50,000.00), and (b) Fifty Cents (50¢) per thousand on the balance; provided, however, that where the estate consists in whole or in part of cash; money on deposit; securities listed on an approved stock exchange, as defined in Division (E) of section 1707.02 of the Revised Code; securities as to which there are published quotations and/or tax exempt bonds of state or local subdivisions, an appraiser's compensation, as to such assets shall be Fifty Cents (50¢) per thousand on the first One Hundred Thousand Dollars ($100,000.00) and Twenty-five Cents (25¢) per thousand on the balance of such assets, the compensation of an appraiser as to such assets being limited to Five Hundred Dollars ($500.00).

If by reason of the application of such percentages to the value of assets of an estate a disparity or injustice results, such disparity or injustice may be reviewed on the Court's own motion or upon application of the fiduciary or any party in interest.

In agreeing upon the amount of compensation within the schedule established herein, executors or administrators and the appraisers shall take into consideration the amount of time and work reasonably required in appraising the assets of said estate as well as the type and character of the property appraised.

Additional compensation for extraordinary services performed may be allowed by the Court upon application filed by the fiduciary.

If, by reason of the special and unusual character of the property to be appraised, the fiduciary is of the opinion that the appraisal requires the services of persons expert in the evaluation of such property, such expert opinion may be secured and reasonable compensation paid therefor.

In land sale proceedings the appraisers appointed by the Court may be compensated for their services in the same manner as provided herein for estate appraisers, with a minimum fee of $10.00 per parcel for each appraiser, provided that the amount to be paid each appraiser shall be set forth in the entry of distribution and be subject to the approval of the Court.

An appraiser may waive all or any part of the compensation to which he may be entitled under this Rule.

Where any question arises in the interpretation of this Rule or the amount of compensation cannot be agreed upon, the executor or administrator shall file an application for allowance of compensation to each appraiser. Otherwise, no Court order is necessary and credit may be taken for payment in the next regular account as provided by law, subject to all exceptions which may be thereafter filed.

CUYAHOGA COUNTY PROBATE COURT RULE 26: COUNSEL FEES AND FIDUCIARY'S COMPENSATION FOR EXTRAORDINARY SERVICES [in effect since November 1, 1965]

(a) Counsel fees in administration of a decedent's estate.

(1) The schedules of compensation hereinafter set forth shall serve as a guide in determining fees to be charged to the estate for legal services of an ordinary nature rendered as counsel for the executor or administrator in the complete administration of a decedent's estate. Such schedules however are not to be considered as schedules of minimum or maximum fees to be charged. Further, if by reason of the application of such percentages to values of assets or to amounts of income a disparity or injustice results, such disparity or injustice may be reviewed either on the Court's own motion in respect of any account reflecting such compensation or upon exceptions to such an account.

A. On the appraised value of all real and personal property included in the inventory, unless sold, then on the amount of the gross proceeds from the sale of such real or personal property, on estate income for which the fiduciary accounts, on money actually advanced to the estate to pay debts, taxes, expenses of administration or legacies, and in addition to fees allowable as hereafter set forth where there is a land sale proceeding or petition by the surviving spouse to purchase assets at the appraised value:

6% on the first $2,000.00
4% on the next $13,000.00
3% on the next $15,000.00
2% on the balance
Minimum fee $150.00

B. On one hundred percent (100%) of the value as determined for Ohio Inheritance Tax purposes of all property which is subject to Ohio Inheritance Taxes, and which passes otherwise than under the decedent's will or the Statute of Descent and Distribution, such as joint and survivorship property, property in inter vivos trusts, property subject to a power of appointment, transfers in contemplation of death, annuities, pension and/or profit sharing plan benefits, and other non-probate property (but excluding life insurance proceeds where paid to beneficiaries other than the decedent's estate):

2% of the first $20,000.00
1% of the balance

Where there is litigation or other contest with respect to property in the Ohio Inheritance Tax proceeding counsel may apply for extraordinary compensation as hereinafter provided.

C. Where there are land sale proceedings or a petition of the surviving spouse to purchase at the appraised value, 2% of the gross proceeds of the property sold.

D. The foregoing schedule shall apply whether or not the fiduciary acts as his own Counsel.

E. (a) No application for allowance of fees under (a) (1), A, B, and C above need be filed, but the amounts paid shall be shown in the account of the fiduciary, together with a separate schedule of the computation of such fees, as a condition to the approval of such account.

(b) Counsel fees requiring application for allowance other than in the administration of a decedent's estate.

An application shall be filed for the allowance of counsel fees for services rendered in all matters not otherwise provided for, including services rendered to a guardian, trustee or other fiduciary. Such application may be filed by the fiduciary or his counsel. Such application shall set forth a concise statement of the services rendered and the amount claimed therefor. An itemized statement of the services for which compensation is requested shall be attached to said application.

(c) Compensation for extraordinary services rendered by a fiduciary in the administration of a decedent's estate.

The fiduciary shall file an application for the allowance of compensation for extraordinary services rendered in the administration of a decedent's estate, containing a concise statement of the services rendered and the amount claimed therefor.

(d) Review by the court of fees and compensation.

Counsel fees and the allowance of compensation to a fiduciary for extraordinary services are subject to review upon the consideration of the fiduciary's account reporting such disbursement.

(e) Miscellaneous.

(1) Where all the interested parties have consented in writing to the amount of the allowance of compensation or fees, no application need be made for the allowance thereof, provided such consent is endorsed on the account or evidenced by separate instrument filed therewith.

(2) Counsel fees and fiduciary's compensation will be determined in an ancillary administration in accordance with R.C. 2129.23; in a proceeding on a rejected claim in accordance with R.C. 2117.13; and in a land sale proceeding involving fractional or undivided interests in accordance with R.C. 2127.08.

(3) The Court may require that any application for fees or compensation be set for hearing and written notice thereof be given to interested parties in the manner provided in R.C. 2101.26. Such notice shall contain a statement of the amount of fees or compensation applied for. A copy of such notice, with return registered mail receipt attached in the event registered mail is required, together with an affidavit of the service of such notice, shall be filed prior to the hearing.

(4) Except for good cause shown, neither compensation for an executor or administrator nor fees to the attorney representing such fiduciary will be allowed while such executor or administrator is delinquent in his account or accounting as required by R.C. 2109.30.

(5) The compensation of co-executors or co-administrators in the aggregate shall not exceed the compensation which would have been payable if only one executor or administrator had been acting, except in the following instances:

A. Where the instrument under which the co-executors are serving provides otherwise, or

B. Where all the interested parties have consented in writing to the amount of such fiduciaries' compensation and such consent is endorsed on such fiduciaries' account or evidenced by separate instrument filed therewith.

(f) Counsel fees in a land sale proceeding instituted by a guardian where the ward owns the entire fee.

In respect of counsel fees in a land sale proceeding instituted by a guardian, the following schedule of fees shall apply:

10% on the first $500.00
5% on the next $4,500.00
4% on the next $5,000.00
3% on the next $10,000.00
2% on the balance
Minimum fee $150.00

CUYAHOGA COUNTY PROBATE COURT RULE 26: COUNSEL FEES AND FIDUCIARY'S COMPENSATION FOR EXTRAORDINARY SERVICES
[in effect when estates in the study were closed]

(a) Counsel fees in administration of a decedent's estate.

(1) The schedules of compensation hereinafter set forth shall serve as a guide in determining fees to be charged to the estate for legal services of an

ordinary nature rendered as counsel for the executor or administrator in the complete administration of a decedent's estate. Such schedules however are not to be considered as schedules of minimum or maximum fees to be charged. Further, if by reason of the application of such percentages to values of assets or to amounts of income a disparity or injustice results, such disparity or injustice may be reviewed either on the Court's own motion in respect of any account reflecting such compensation or upon exceptions to such an account.

A. On the appraised value of personal property included in the inventory, unless sold, then on the amount of the gross proceeds from the sale of such personal property, on the gross proceeds from the sale of real estate under a power in the will, on estate income for which the fiduciary accounts, and on money actually advanced to pay debts or legacies:

6% on the first $2,000.00
4% on the next $13,000.00
3% on the next $15,000.00
2% on the balance
Minimum fee $150.00

B. For the preparation of an Application for Transfer of Real Estate, Order of Transfer and Certificate of Transfer, one-half of 1% of the appraised value of the real estate so transferred with a minimum therefor of $25.00; provided, however, that any fee in excess of $100.00 shall be subject to the approval of the Court upon application.

C. On the gross proceeds of real property sold in a land sale proceeding where the decedent owned the entire fee:

10% on the first $500.00
5% on the next $4,500.00
4% on the next $5,000.00
3% on the next $10,000.00
2% on the balance
Minimum fee $150.00.

D. On the gross amount paid for real estate purchased by the surviving spouse at the appraised value:

6% on the first $1,000.00
4% on the next $9,000.00
2% on the balance
Minimum fee $100.00.

E. No application for allowance of fees under (a) (1), A, B, C, or D above, need be filed, but the amounts paid shall be shown in the account of the fiduciary, together with a separate schedule of the computation of such fees, as a condition to the approval of such account.

No further fees shall be allowed in the estate based on the proceeds of real property sold in land sale proceedings under (a) (1) C, above or on the gross amount paid for real estate purchased by the surviving spouse under (a) (1) D, above except as may be fixed by the Court on application.

For extraordinary services rendered in the administration of a decedent's estate or where the fiduciary is acting as his own counsel, the Court will determine the fees on application.

(b) Counsel fees requiring application for allowance other than in the administration of a decedent's estate.

An application shall be filed for the allowance of counsel fees for services rendered in all matters not otherwise provided for, including services rendered to a guardian, trustee or other fiduciary. Such application may be filed by the fiduciary or his counsel. Such application shall set forth a concise statement of the services rendered and the amount claimed therefor. An itemized statement of the services for which compensation is requested shall be attached to said application.

(c) Compensation for extraordinary services rendered by a fiduciary in the administration of a decedent's estate.

The fiduciary shall file an application for the allowance of compensation for extraordinary services rendered in the administration of a decedent's estate, containing a concise statement of the services rendered and the amount claimed therefor.

(d) Review by the court of fees and compensation.

Counsel fees and the allowance of compensation to a fiduciary for extraordinary services are subject to review upon the consideration of the fiduciary's account reporting such disbursement.

(e) Miscellaneous.

(1) Where all the interested parties have consented in writing to the amount of the allowance of compensation or fees, no application need be made for the allowance thereof, provided such consent is endorsed on the account or evidenced by separate instrument filed therewith.

(2) Counsel fees and fiduciary's compensation will be determined in an ancillary administration in accordance with R.C. 2129.23; in a proceeding on a rejected claim in accordance with R.C. 2117.13; and in a land sale proceeding involving fractional or undivided interests in accordance with R.C. 2127.08.

(3) The Court may require that any application for fees or compensation be set for hearing and written notice thereof be given to interested parties in the manner provided in R.C. 2101.26. Such notice shall contain a statement of the amount of fees or compensation applied for. A copy of such notice, with return registered mail receipt attached in the event registered mail is required, together with an affidavit of the service of such notice, shall be filed prior to the hearing.

(4) Except for good cause shown, neither compensation for an executor or

administrator nor fees to the attorney representing such fiduciary will be allowed while such executor or administrator is delinquent in his account or accounting as required by R.C. 2109.30.

(5) The compensation of co-executors or co-administrators in the aggregate shall not exceed the compensation which would have been payable if only one executor or administrator had been acting, except in the following instances:

A. Where the instrument under which the co-executors are serving provides otherwise, or

B. Where all the interested parties have consented in writing to the amount of such fiduciaries' compensation and such consent is endorsed on such fiduciaries' account or evidenced by separate instrument filed therewith.

(f) Counsel fees in a land sale proceeding instituted by a guardian where the ward owns the entire fee.

In respect of counsel fees in a land sale proceeding instituted by a guardian, the same schedule of fees shall be applicable as provided for in Rule 26 (a) C.

Glossary

Administrator—the person who administers the estate of a decedent who leaves no will.

Antenuptial agreement—arrangement in contemplation of marriage whereby the property rights and interests of the prospective husband and/or wife are determined.

Anti-lapse statute—legislation that saves the gift by will to a person who predeceases the testator, provided certain conditions exist.

Appraiser—a person appointed by the court to ascertain and state the value of goods and/or real estate.

Ascendants—persons with whom one is related in the direct ascending line: one's parents, grandparents, great-grandparents, and so forth.

Bastard—an illegitimate child.

Beneficiary—one receiving benefit or advantage; under trust law, one for whose benefit a trust is created.

Bequest—a gift, by will, of personal property.

Civil-law system—the system of jurisprudence held and administered in the Roman Empire, particularly as set forth in the compilation of Justinian and his successors.

Collateral relatives—persons belonging to the same ancestral stock but not in a direct line of descent; for example, brothers, sisters, nephews, nieces, uncles, aunts, cousins, and so forth.

Common law—the body of statutes and juristic theory that originated in England and that exists today in the United States, its basis essentially being court decisions unrelated to any legislative enactments.

Common-law marriage—one not solemnized in the ordinary way, but created by an agreement to marry, followed by cohabitation.

Community property—possessions owned in common by a husband and wife as a kind of marital partnership.

Conditional bequest—a gift that is received from a donor upon the occurrence of a specific event.

Contingency provisions—conditions in a will that are uncertain.

Cotenancy—in a broad sense, co-ownership of property.

Curtesy—at common law, a life estate to which the husband was entitled in all lands of which his wife was seised in fee simple or in fee tail at any time during the marriage, provided that there was issue born alive capable of inheriting the estate.

De bonis non—an abbreviation of de bonis non administratis, *which means "of the goods not administered."*

Descendants—persons with whom one is related in the direct descending line:

one's children, grandchildren, and so forth.

Descent and distribution—intestate succession; intestate laws are frequently called statutes of descent and distribution.

Devisee—a person to whom real property is given by a will.

Disinherit—to cut off by will a person who would have inherited if there were no will; that is, to deprive an heir of his right to inherit.

Dissaving—loss of current or future income by drawing upon capital (negative saving) or going into debt in order to meet expenses.

Distribution per stirpes—succession where there is no will, but by representing a deceased ancestor rather than in one's own right.

Doctrine of ancestral property—tenet favoring the branch of the intestate's family from whom realty was inherited.

Dower—at common law, a life estate to which a widow was entitled, on the death of her husband, in one-third of the lands of which he had been seised at any time during the marriage of an estate in fee simple or in fee tail, provided that the estate was one capable of being inherited by issue of the marriage; today, with statutory equivalents and substitutes, its nature varies from state to state.

Equality—sameness of quantity or degree.

Equity—in a broad sense, fairness or justice; in a technical sense, a system of jurisprudence developed in England collateral to, and in some respects independent of, common law.

Escheat—a reversion of property to the state in consequence of a want of any individual competent to inherit.

Estranged family—general characterization for alienated relationships among members within or between linked nuclear families. Usually refers to the individual's family from whom he is "cut off" because of his or their desires.

Executor—the person (or entity) named in a will as the one to have charge of estate administration.

Family of orientation—nuclear unit in which the individual has been reared, composed of mother, father, and siblings.

Family of procreation—nuclear unit created by marriage with primary functions of childbearing and socialization and composed of husband, wife, and offspring.

Fiduciary—an administrator or executor in estate matters.

Fiduciary fees—compensation paid to an administrator or executor, the amount usually determined by law.

Filius nullius—an illegitimate child; at common law, "the child of no one."

Forced share—a statutory fixed portion of the decedent's estate, which cannot be disposed of by will if the surviving spouse prefers it to what would be received under the will.

Gift inter vivos—an unconditional gift between living persons.

Gift causa mortis—a present gift made in contemplation of immediate approaching death, which is revocable until then.

Guardianship—a legal arrangement where one person has the care and management of the person, or the estate, or both, of another.

Half-and-Half statute—a peculiar Ohio law (Ohio Revised Code 2105.10) utilizing ancestral property concepts.

Half blood—as used in the law of inheritance, the degree of relationship between two individuals who have the same mother or the same father but not both parents in common.

Holographic will—a testament written wholly in the testator's handwriting.

Inherit—*to receive by law from an ancestor at his decease; broadly, to take by intestate succession or by will.*

Insurance trust—*an agreement between an insured and a trustee, whereby the policy proceeds are paid directly to the trustee for investment and distribution to designated beneficiaries in the manner and at such time as the insured has directed in the trust instrument.*

Intestate—*without having made a valid will.*

Intestate succession—*transfer according to a statutory scheme that controls distribution when one dies without a will.*

Irrevocable trust—*an unconditional transfer in trust of property with no power to revoke being reserved.*

Joint bank account—*a checking or savings account in the name of the depositor and another, subject to withdrawal by either party, and in the event of death of one, by the survivor.*

Joint ownership of property with right of survivorship—*possessions owned in some form of co-ownership with the survivor obtaining absolute ownership.*

Joint tenancy—*a form of co-ownership subsisting between two or more persons in respect of an interest in real or personal property whereby such persons own the one interest together and each person has exactly the same rights in that interest as his cotenant or cotenants, including the right of survivorship.*

Laughing heir—*an inheritor who is so loosely linked to his ancestor as to suffer no sense of bereavement at the ancestor's death.*

Legatee—*one to whom personal property is given by will.*

Life beneficiary—*one who has a property interest for the period of his own life or that of another person.*

Life estate—*a property interest whose duration is limited to the life of the party holding it, or of some other person.*

Life insurance—*that kind of insurance in which the risk contemplated is the death of a particular person, upon which event the insurer engages to pay a stipulated sum to the legal representatives of such person, or to a third person having an insurable interest in the life of such person.*

Lineal descendants—see *"descendants."*

Mean—*arithmetic average of a distribution.*

Median—*the midpoint of a distribution where 50 per cent of the cases are above and 50 per cent are below this point.*

Memento—*a token or remembrance.*

Metropolitan area—*geographical division designated by the Bureau of the Census, usually consisting of a city of over 100,000 population and satellite towns, villages, cities, and open country.*

Mode—*the value in a distribution which occurs most frequently.*

Mortmain acts—*statutes that declare charitable gifts invalid unless the will is executed more than a designated time before the testator's death, limit the proportion of the estate that can be left for charitable purposes, or do both.*

Negative saver—*a person who is drawing on capital to meet expenses.*

Norm—*required or acceptable behavior in a given situation.*

Nuncupative will—*an oral testament of personalty made by the testator in his last illness before a sufficient number of witnesses and afterwards reduced to writing.*

Oral will—see *"nuncupative will."*

Parentelic system—*a method for determining the relationship of collateral kin for intestate succession purposes which exhausts the line of the closest common ancestor of the intestate and the claimant before admitting other claimants related through a more remote line.*

Personal property—*all things that are subject to individual rights, whether tangible or intangible, except land and that which is more or less permanently attached to it.*

Personal representative—*an administrator or executor.*

Personalty—*personal property.*

Precedent condition—*an occurrence that must happen or be performed before a particular right accrues.*

Prenuptial agreement—see *"antenuptial agreement."*

Prima-facie case—*a situation that will suffice until contradicted and overcome by other evidence.*

Probate—*the act or process of proving a will.*

Probate docket—*the list of matters to be determined by a probate court.*

Profession—*an occupation requiring mastery of a body of scientific knowledge, a service orientation, and autonomy in work behavior and where members are amply rewarded with income, power, and status.*

Property disposition—*the transference of ownership rights by voluntary or involuntary means.*

"Prove the will"—*probate the testament; the act of proving before a duly authorized person that a document produced before him for official recognition is the last testament of a certain deceased person.*

Purchaser—*for inheritance purposes, one who acquires real or personal property in any manner other than intestate succession.*

Real property—*land and those things such as houses, barns, and office buildings, which are more or less permanently attached to it.*

Realty—see *"real property."*

Reciprocity—*an exchange of goods, services, or acts of behavior between two individuals in interaction with one another under conditions of shared expectations.*

Referee—*a court officer exercising judicial powers, to whom a cause pending in a court is referred by the judge for the purpose of taking testimony, hearing the parties, and reporting to the judge.*

Referee system—*when arbiters are customarily used by the judges of courts.*

Release cases—*decedents' estates exempt from the normal administration process because of their low valuation.*

Remainder interest—*property tenancy limited to take effect in possession and be enjoyed after another tenancy terminates.*

Remarriage—*the act of marrying again.*

Residence rating—*a system of allocating family social status from an evaluation of quality of housing.*

Revocable inter vivos trust—*a trust in which the settlor retains a power to revoke and in which the effect of his revocation is the return of the trust subject matter to himself or the payment of it as he may direct.*

Right of survivorship—*the ability to become entitled to property by reason of outliving another person who had an interest in it.*

Sample—*a subset of a population usually selected in such a matter so that characteristics of it are similar to those of the population from which it is drawn.*

Saving-living index—*a measure of use of inheritance for living expenses or to be placed in savings accounts by beneficiaries or successors.*

Scrivener—*a writer; scribe.*

Settlor—*one who creates a trust.*

Slayer's statute—*legislation with respect to the felonious killing of a testator or intestate as affecting the slayer's rights as the deceased's successor.*

Social status—*a position in a social sys-*

tem that is independent of given actions, such as manager in a factory, senior partner in a law firm, father in a family, and so forth.

Spouse-all distribution—succession resulting in the surviving spouse getting all the decedent's estate.

Statutory share—see *"forced share."*

Subsequent condition—a requirement annexed to a property interest which upon its happening will defeat the already vested interest.

Survivor—a person who outlives another; in this study, the beneficiary or successor who outlives the testator.

Survivor population—all individuals in the sample in this study who were interviewed and who were eligible to take under the will or through intestate distribution.

Takers—successors; beneficiaries.

Tenancy by the entirety—an estate created by a conveyance to husband and wife whereupon each becomes the owner of the entire estate, and after the death of one, the survivor takes the whole.

Tenancy in common—a property interest where there is no right of survivorship between co-owners and where it is accurate to say that the share of each owner is several and distinct from that of his co-owner except that it is a fractional interest in an undivided whole.

Tentative trust—a trust created by the deposit by one person of his own money in his own name as a trustee for another which is a provisional trust revocable at will until the depositor dies; if the depositor dies before the beneficiary without revocation, the presumption arises that an absolute trust was created as to the balance on hand at the death of the depositor.

Testamentary power—a right of appointment exercisable only by will.

Testate—having left a valid will.

Totten trust—see *"tentative trust."*

Trust—a fiduciary relationship in which one party is the holder of the title to property, subject to an equitable obligation to keep or use the property for the benefit of another.

Trustee—in a trust, the party who holds title for the benefit of another.

Unworthy taker—a successor who has wronged the decedent by his misconduct deemed ethically reprehensible.

Verify—to confirm or substantiate by oath.

Will—in general, an instrument by which a person makes a disposition of his property to take effect after his decease, and which is in its nature ambulatory and revocable during his lifetime.

Will substitute—a legal device used to prevent property from passing by testate or intestate succession; for example, gifts, trusts, life insurance, and jointly owned property.

Zero savers—persons who are not saving any of their current income.

Bibliography

Alexander, C. Norman, and Simpson, Richard L. "Balance Theory and Distributive Justice." *Sociological Inquiry* 34 (Spring, 1964): 182–192.

American College Dictionary. New York: Random House, Inc., 1956.

American Jurisprudence, vol. 57, *Wills*. Rochester, N.Y.: The Lawyers Co-operative Publishing Co., 1948.

American Law Reports. 2d ed., vol. 39. Rochester, N.Y.: The Lawyers Co-operative Publishing Co., 1955.

Andrews, F. Emerson. *Attitudes Toward Giving*. New York: Russell Sage Foundation, 1953.

———. *Philanthropic Giving*. New York: Russell Sage Foundation, 1950.

Andrews, Wayne. *The Vanderbilt Legend*. New York: Harcourt, Brace & World, Inc., 1941.

Atkinson, Thomas E. *Wills*. 2d ed. St. Paul, Minn.: West Publishing Co., 1953.

Banton, Michael. *Roles*. New York: Basic Books, Inc., Publishers, 1965.

Bentham, Jeremy. "Utilitarian Basis of Succession." In *The Rational Basis of Legal Institutions,* edited by John H. Wigmore, pp. 413–23. New York: The Macmillan Company, 1923.

Bernard, Jessie. *Remarriage*. New York: The Dryden Press, 1956.

Bird, Roger. "Consumption, Savings, and Windfall Gain: Comment." *American Economic Review* 53 (June, 1963): 443–44.

Blau, Peter M. *Exchange and Power in Social Life*. New York: John Wiley & Sons, Inc., 1964.

———. "Justice in Social Exchange." *Sociological Inquiry* 34 (Spring, 1964): 193–206.

Blaustein, Albert P., and Porter, Charles O. *The American Lawyer*. Chicago: University of Chicago Press, 1954.

Bodkin, Ronald. "Windfall Income and Consumption." *American Economic Review* 49 (September, 1959): 602–14.

———. "Windfall Income and Consumption: Reply." *American Economic Review* 56 (June, 1966): 540–45.

Bogert, George C. *Trusts.* 4th ed. St. Paul, Minn.: West Publishing Co., 1963.

Brady, Dorothy S. "Influence of Age on Savings and Spending Patterns." *Monthly Labor Review* 78 (November, 1955): 1240–44.

Britt, Steuart Henderson. "The Significance of the Last Will and Testament." *Journal of Social Psychology* 8 (August, 1937): 347–53.

Burke, Edmund. *Reflections on the French Revolution and Other Essays.* New York: E. P. Dutton & Co., Inc., 1910.

Calhoun, Daniel H. *Professional Lives in America: Structure and Aspirations, 1750–1850.* Cambridge, Mass.: Harvard University Press, 1965.

Carlin, Jerome E. *Lawyers on Their Own.* New Brunswick, N.J.: Rutgers University Press, 1962.

Carlin, Jerome E., and Howard, Jan. "Legal Representation and Class Justice." *UCLA Law Review* 12 (January, 1965): 381–437.

Casner, A. James. "Estate Planning—Avoidance of Probate." *Columbia Law Review* 60 (1960): 108–40.

Cavers, David. "Change in the American Family and the 'Laughing Heir.'" *Iowa Law Review* 20 (1934–1935): 208–209.

Cheek, Neil H., Jr. "The Social Role of the Professional." In *The Professional in the Organization,* edited by Mark Abrahannon, pp. 9–16. Chicago: Rand McNally & Co., 1967.

Clark, Frank. "The Commodore Left Two Sons." *American Heritage,* April, 1966, pp. 4–9.

Cleveland Trust Company. "The Importance of a Will." *Taxes and Estates,* June 1965.

Cogswell, Betty E. "Socialization into the Family: An Essay on Some Structural Properties of Roles." In *Sourcebook in Marriage and the Family,* edited by Marvin B. Sussman, pp. 366–77. Boston: Houghton Mifflin Company, 1968.

Cohen, Julius, et al. *Parental Authority: The Community and the Law.* New Brunswick, N.J.: Rutgers University Press, 1958.

Cole, G. D. H. "Inheritance." *Encyclopedia of the Social Sciences,* vol. 8. New York: The Macmillan Company, 1932.

Corpus Juris Secundum, vol. 96, *Wills.* Brooklyn: The American Law Book Co., 1957.

Cumming, Elaine, and Schneider, David. "Sibling Solidarity: A Property of American Kinship." *American Anthropologist* 63 (June, 1961): 498–507. Reprinted in *Kinship and the Family Organization,* edited by Bernard Farber. New York: John Wiley & Sons, Inc., 1966.

Dacey, Norman F. *How to Avoid Probate!* New York: Crown Publishers, Inc., 1965.

"The Disguised Oppression of Involuntary Guardianship: Have the Elderly Freedom to Spend?" *Yale Law Journal* 73 (1964): 676–92.

Dunham, Allison. "The Method, Process and Frequency of Wealth Transmission." *Chicago Law Review* 30 (Winter, 1962): 241–85.

Farr, James F. *An Estate Planner's Handbook.* 3d ed. Boston: Little, Brown and Company, 1966.

Fisher, Janet A. "Family Life Cycle Analysis in Research on Consumer Behavior." In *Consumer Behavior,* vol. II, *The Life Cycle and Consumer Behavior,* edited by Lincoln H. Clark, pp. 28–35. New York: New York University Press, 1955.

Freund, Paul A. "The Legal Profession." *The Professions, Daedalus* 92 (Fall, 1963): 689–700.

Friedman, Lawrence. "Patterns of Testation in the 19th Century: A Study of Essex County (New Jersey) Wills." *American Journal of Legal History* 8 (1964): 34–53.

Friedson, Elliott. "Client Control and Medical Practice." *American Journal of Sociology* 65 (1960): 374–82.

Gamson, W. A., and Schuman, H. "Some Undercurrents in the Prestige of Physicians." *American Journal of Sociology* 68 (January, 1963): 463–70.

Glick, Paul C. "The Family Cycle." *American Sociological Review* 12 (April, 1947): 164–74.

———. "The Life Cycle of the Family." *Marriage and Family Living* 17 (February, 1955): 3–9.

Goldfield, Edwin D. *Pocket Data Book USA 1967.* Washington, D.C.: United States Department of Commerce, 1967.

———. *Statistical Abstract of the United States, 1967.* Washington, D.C.: United States Department of Commerce, 1967.

Goode, William. "The Librarian: From Occupation to Profession?" *Library Quarterly* 31 (October, 1961): 306–20.

Habukkuk, H. J. "Family Structure and Economic Change in 19th Century Europe." *Journal of Economic History* 15 (1955): 1–12.

Hall, Oswald. "The Stages of a Medical Career." *American Journal of Sociology* 53 (1948): 327–36.

Harbury, O. D. "Inheritance and the Distribution of Personal Wealth in Britain." *Economic Journal* 72 (1962): 845–68.

Harris, Virgil. *Ancient, Curious and Famous Wills.* Boston: Little, Brown and Company, 1911.

Hays, William L. *Statistics for Psychologists.* New York: Holt, Rinehart & Winston, Inc., 1963.

Henderson, L. J. "Physician and Patient as a Social System." *New England Journal of Medicine* 212 (1935): 819–23.

Hill, Reuben. "Decision Making and the Family Life Cycle." In *Social Structure and the Family,* edited by Ethel Shanas and Gordon F. Streib, pp. 113–39. Englewood Cliffs, N.J.: Prentice-Hall, Inc., 1965.

Hodge, Robert W., Siegal, Paul M., and Rossi, Peter H. "Occupational Prestige in the United States: 1925–1963." In *Class, Status and Power*, 2d ed. edited by Reinhard Bendix and Seymour Martin Lipset, pp. 322–34. New York: The Free Press, 1966.

Hollingshead, August B. *Two-Factor Index of Social Position.* Mimeographed. New Haven, Conn., 1957.

Hollingshead, August B., and Redlich, Frederick. *Social Class and Mental Illness.* New York: John Wiley & Sons, Inc., 1958.

Homans, George Caspar. *Social Behavior, Its Elementary Forms.* New York: Harcourt, Brace & World, Inc., 1961.

Hoyt, Edwin P. *The Vanderbilts and Their Fortunes.* New York: Doubleday & Company, Inc., 1962.

Hughes, Everett. *Men and Their Work.* New York: The Free Press, 1958.

Jenkins, Edward. *Philanthropy in America.* New York: Association Press, 1950.

Jones, John Price. *Philanthropy Today: An Interim Report.* New York: Inter River Press, 1949.

Kadushin, Charles. "Social Distance Between Client and Professional." *American Journal of Sociology* 67 (1962): 517–31.

Kent, Leonard. "Economic Status of the Legal Profession in Chicago." *Illinois Law Review* 45 (1951): 311–32.

Klein, L. R., and Livatan, N. "Significance of Income Variability on Savings Behavior." *Bulletin of Oxford Institute of Statistics* 19 (May, 1957): 151–60.

Komarovsky, Mirra. "Functional Analysis of Sex Roles." *American Sociological Review* 15 (1950): 508–16.

Kounin, Jacob, et al. "Experimental Studies of Clients' Reactions to Initial Interviews." *Human Relations* 9 (1956): 265–93.

Kreinin, Mordechai. "Windfall Income and Consumption." *American Economic Review* 51 (June, 1961): 388–90.

Kreps, Juanita M. "The Economics of Interpersonal Relationships." In *Social Structure and the Family,* edited by Ethel Shanas and Gordon F. Streib, pp. 267–88. Englewood Cliffs, N.J.: Prentice-Hall, Inc., 1965.

Ladinsky, Jack. "Occupational Determinants of Geographic Mobility Among Professional Workers." *American Sociological Review* 32 (April, 1967): 253–64.

Landsberger, Michael. "Windfall Income and Consumption: Comment." *American Economic Review* 56 (June, 1966): 534–40.

Lansing, John B., and Morgan, James N. "Consumer Finances Over the Life Cycle." In *Consumer Behavior,* vol. 2, edited by Lincoln H. Clark, pp. 36–51. New York: New York University Press, 1955.

Lindsey, Benjamin Barr, and Evans, Wainwright. *Companionate Marriage.* New York: Boni & Liveright, 1927.

Litwak, Eugene. "Geographical Mobility and Extended Family Cohesion." *American Sociological Review* 25 (June, 1960): 385–94.

Lydall, Harold. "The Life Cycle in Income, Saving and Asset Ownership." *Econometrica* 23 (April, 1955): 131–50.

Maine, Henry Sumner. *Ancient Law.* Boston: Beacon Press, 1963.

Marx, Karl, and Engels, Friedrich. *Manifesto of the Communist Party.* New York: International Publishers Co., Inc., 1948.

Menshin, Robert S. *The Last Caprice.* New York: Simon & Schuster, Inc., 1963.

Merrick, Frank J., and Rippner, Ellis V. *Ohio Probate Law.* Cleveland: Banks-Baldwin Law Publishing Co., 1960. Quoted in *Cleveland Plain Dealer,* 17 July 1966, under headline "Court OK's Funerals Fit for Kings."

Merton, Robert K., and Barber, Elinor. "Sociological Ambivalence." *Sociological Theory, Values, and Sociocultural Change: Essays in Honor of Pitirim A. Sorokin,* edited by Edward A. Tiryakian, pp. 91–120. New York: The Free Press, 1963.

Missouri Bar–Prentice-Hall Survey. Jefferson City, Mo.: The Missouri Bar, 1963.

Moore, Wilbert E. "Aging and the Social System." In *Aging and Social Policy,* edited by John C. McKinney and Frank T. DeVyver, pp. 23–41. New York: Appleton-Century-Crofts, 1966.

———. "Economic and Professional Institutions." In *Sociology,* edited by Neil Smelser, pp. 273–328. New York: John Wiley & Sons, Inc., 1967.

———. *Man, Time and Society.* New York: John Wiley & Sons, Inc., 1963.

———. *Order and Change.* New York: John Wiley & Sons, Inc., 1967.

Morgan, James N., et al. *Income and Welfare in the United States.* New York: McGraw-Hill Book Company, 1962.

Murphy, John J., and Parkhill, James S., Jr. "Conditional Bequests and Devises." *Boston University Law Review* 42 (Fall, 1962): 520–46.

O'Gorman, Hubert J. *Lawyers and Matrimonial Cases.* New York: The Free Press, 1963.

Parsons, Talcott. "A Sociologist Looks at the Legal Profession." *Essays in Sociological Theory.* Rev. ed., pp. 370–85. Glencoe, Ill.: The Free Press, 1954.

Piaget, Jean. "Retributive and Distributive Justice." *Moral Judgment of the Child.* New York: Harcourt, Brace & World, Inc., 1932. Reprinted in *Sociological Theory,* edited by Edgar Borgatta and Henry J. Meyer, pp. 90–96. New York: Alfred A. Knopf, Inc., 1956.

Plaut, Eric. "Emotional Aspects of Probate Practice." *Practical Lawyer* 5 (1959): 17–27.

Polansky, Norman, and Kounin, Jacob. "Clients' Reactions to Initial Interviews: A Field Study." *Human Relations* 9 (1956): 239–64.

Powell, Richard R. *Real Property,* vol. 6. New York: Matthew Bender & Co., Inc., 1958.

Powell, Richard R., and Looker, Charles. "Decedents' Estates." *Columbia Law Review* 30 (November, 1930): 919–53.

Prosser, William L. *Torts.* 3d ed. St. Paul, Minn.: West Publishing Co., 1964.

Radin, Paul. *The World of Primitive Man.* New York: H. Schuman, 1953.

Rankin, Allen. "Billions of Dollars Unclaimed!" *Reader's Digest,* May, 1964, pp. 77–81.

Read, Harlan Eugene. *The Abolition of Inheritance.* New York: The Macmillan Company, 1918.

Reid, Margaret G. "Consumption, Savings and Windfall Gains." *American Economic Review* 52 (September, 1962): 728–37.

Reiss, Albert, Jr. *Occupations and Social Status.* New York: The Free Press, 1961.

Rheinstein, Max. "Motivation of Intergenerational Behavior by Norms of Law." In *Social Structure and the Family,* edited by Ethel Shanas and Gordon E. Streib, pp. 241–66. Englewood Cliffs, N.J.: Prentice-Hall, Inc., 1965.

Riesman, David, and Roseborough, Howard. "Careers and Consumer Behavior." In *Consumer Behavior,* vol. II, *The Life Cycle and Consumer Behavior,* edited by Lincoln H. Clark, pp. 1–18. New York: New York University Press, 1955.

Robinson, Thomas. *Gavelkind.* London: Henry Battleworth, 1822.

Schwartz, Barry. "The Social Psychology of the Gift." *American Journal of Sociology* 73 (July, 1967): 1–11.

Selltiz, Claire, et al. *Research Methods in Social Relations.* New York: Henry Holt and Co., Inc., 1959.

Sharp, Frank C. "The Criterion of Distributive Justice." *American Journal of Sociology* 2 (September, 1896): 264–73.

Sharp, Harry, and Axelrod, Morris. "Mutual Aid Among Relatives in an Urban Population." In *Principles of Sociology,* edited by Ronald Freedman et al., pp. 433–39. New York: Holt, Rinehart & Winston, Inc., 1956.

Shoup, Carl. *Federal Estate and Gift Taxes.* Washington, D.C.: The Brookings Institution, 1966.

Smith, Adam. *An Inquiry into the Nature and Causes of the Wealth of Nations.* 5th ed. Edited by Edwin Cannon. London, 1930. Cited by T. H. Marshall. *Class, Citizenship and Social Development.* Garden City, N.Y.: Doubleday & Company, Inc., Anchor Books, 1965.

Stehouwer, Jan. "Relations Between Generations and the Three Generation Household in Denmark." In *Social Structure and the Family,* edited by Ethel Shanas and Gordon F. Streib, pp. 142–62. Englewood Cliffs, N.J.: Prentice-Hall, Inc., 1965.

Stouffer, Samuel. *Communism, Conformity and Civil Liberties.* Garden City, N.Y.: Doubleday & Company, Inc., 1955.

Stryker, Sheldon. "The Adjustment of Married Offspring to Their Parents." *American Sociological Review* 20 (April, 1955): 149–54.

Sussman, Marvin B. "Adaptive, Directive and Integrative Behavior of Today's Family." *Family Process* 7 (September, 1968): 239–50.

———. *Rating Scale for Homes in Cuyahoga County.* Cleveland: Western Reserve University (privately published), 1960.

———. "Relationships of Adult Children with Their Parents in the United States." In *Family, Intergenerational Relationships and Social Structure,* edited by Ethel Shanas and Gordon E. Streib, pp. 62–92. Englewood Cliffs, N.J.: Prentice-Hall, Inc., 1965.

———. "Theoretical Bases for an Urban Kinship Network System." Paper presented at the annual meeting of the National Council on Family Relations, October, 1966, Minneapolis, Minnesota.

———. "The Urban Kin Network in the Formulation of Family Theory." In *Families in East and West: Socialization Processes and Kinship Ties,* edited by Reuben Hill and René König. Paris: Mouton, 1970.

Sussman, Marvin B., and Burchinal, L. G. "Kin Family Network: Unheralded Structure in Current Conceptualizations of Family Functioning." *Marriage and Family Living* 24 (1962): 231–40.

———. "Parental Aid to Married Children: Implications for Family Functioning." *Marriage and Family Living* 24 (1962): 320–32.

Thomas, E. J.; Polansky, Norman; and Kounin, Jacob. "The Expected Behavior of a Potentially Helpful Person." *Human Relations* 8 (1955): 165–74.

Turrentine, Lowell. *Wills and Administration.* 2d ed. St. Paul, Minn.: West Publishing Co., 1962.

United States Department of Health, Education, and Welfare. *The Facts of Life and Death.* Washington, D.C.: Public Health Service, 1965.

Wallin, Paul. "Sex Difference in Attitudes Toward In-laws; A Test of Theory." *American Journal of Sociology* 59 (1954): 466–69.

Ward, Edward, and Beuscher, J. H. "The Inheritance Process in Wisconsin." *Wisconsin Law Review* (1950): 393–426.

Warner, W. Lloyd, et al. *Social Class in America.* Chicago: Science Research Associates, Inc., 1949.

———, ed. *Yankee City.* New Haven, Conn.: Yale University Press, 1963.

Warren, Charles. *History of the American Bar.* Boston: Little, Brown and Company, 1911.

Wedgwood, Josiah. *The Economics of Inheritance.* London: George Routledge and Sons, Ltd., 1929.

"Wills, The Subject is Rose's." *Time,* 19 August 1966, p. 49.

Winters, Glenn R. "Pettifoggery and Legal Delays." *Annals of the American Academy of Political and Social Science* 363 (January, 1966): 52–59.

Wolfbein, Seymour L. *Changing Patterns of Working Life.* United States Department of Labor. Washington, D.C.: Government Printing Office, 1963.

Wood, Arthur Lewis. *Criminal Lawyer.* New Haven, Conn.: College & University Press, 1967.

Index

ABRAHANNON, Mark, 54n
Adoption: inheritance rights because of, 20
Alexander, C. Norman, 121n, 144n
Aliens: inheritance rights of, 22
Andrews, F. Emerson, 113n, 116n
Andrews, Wayne, 86n
Anti-lapse statutes, 195–196
Appraisers, 258–259, 282
Appraisers' fees, 241–242
Aquinas, Saint Thomas, 41n
Aristotle, 84n
Assets: general nature of, 1
Atkinson, Thomas E., 19n, 34n, 68n, 121n, 234n
Attorneys' fees, 244–245
Axelrod, Morris, 39n

BANTON, Michael, 56n
Barber, Elinor, 56n, 57n, 214n
Bastard. *See* Illegitimate child
Bender v. Bateman, 195n
Bendix, Reinhard, 55n
Beneficiary: defined, 28
Bentham, Jeremy, 212, 212n
Bernard, Jessie, 93n
Beuscher, J. H., 37, 37n, 38n, 40n, 43n, 63n, 71n, 74n, 76n, 114n, 181n
Bilateral kinship lines, 9
Bird, Roger, 159n
Blau, Peter M., 84n, 128n
Blaustein, Albert P., 57n
Bodkin, Ronald, 159n, 160n
Bogert, George C., 28, 28n
Borgatta, Edgar, 84n
Brady, Dorothy S., 163n, 330n
Britt, Stuart Henderson, 38, 39n, 60, 114n
Burchinal, Lee G., 9n, 39n
Burke, Edmund, 4, 4n
Burke, Kenneth, 44n

CALHOUN, Daniel H., 55n
Capital accumulation, 75–76
Carlin, Jerome E., 43n, 55, 55n, 59n, 325, 325n
Case loss, 52–54
Casner, A. James, 27n
Cavers, David, 138, 138n
Charitable bequests, 113–118
Charitable givers: nature of, 114–116
Cheek, Neil H., Jr., 54n
Civil-law system: defined, 16; utilization of, 16
Clark, Frank, 86n
Clark, Lincoln H., 63n, 163n, 181n
Cleveland, 36
Code Napoleon, 26
Cogswell, Betty E., 306n
Cohen, Julius, 206n
Cole, G. D. H., 153n
Collateral kin: defined, 103; patterns of distribution, 103
Commerce National Bank of Toledo v. Browning, 196n
Common disaster, 22
Common-law marriage, 270
Community property: nature of, 25–26
Community-property states, 25
Companionship marriage, 88
Conception of justice, 13. *See also* Justice
Conditional bequests, 193–195; defined, 192; precedent, 193–194; subsequent, 194
Contingency provisions, 195–199; defined, 195; effect of, 197–199, frequency of, 196–197; kin related, 196–197
Cook County study, 37
Cotenancies, 33
Court fees and costs, 240–241
Credit life insurance, 183n
Cumming, Elaine, 104n

Curtesy: defined, 25
Cuyahoga County study: analysis of survivor response, 49–51; basis, 36; facts about, 36; nature of, 12; ratio of testate estates, 63–64

DACEY, Norman F., 177, 177n, 296n
Dane County study, 37
Daniel's Estate, In re, 126n
Death certificates: as source of data, 53
Death costs, 14
Debts, 180–188; allowance and exemption, 181–182; funeral, 180–181; miscellaneous, 183–184
Decedent sample: characteristics of, 63–64; defined, 62; size of estate, 73
De facto spouse-all settlement, 127
Descent and distribution: chart explaining Ohio statute, 18
DeVyver, Frank T., 85n
Disinheritance: absence of immediate family as effecting, 13; class related, 152; defined, 149n; degree of "closeness" factor, 150; frequency of contact factor, 150; geographic factor, 149–150; position of child, 26; variables, 149–150
Distributive justice, 84–85
Divided ownership: problems of, 127
Doctrine of ancestral property, 22–23
Dower: defined, 25
Dunham, Allison, 37, 37n, 38n, 43n, 60, 60n, 63n, 65n, 67n, 69n, 71n, 73n, 84n, 87n, 89n, 103n, 114n, 127n, 165n, 166n, 179n, 181n, 183n, 193n, 196n, 207n

ECONOMIC class: indicators of, 75–76
Encroachment, 221–223
Engels, Friedrich, 44n
Equity: defined, 84
Escheat, 19
Essex County study, 39
Estate administration: compared with estate planning, 267; dispensing with appraisement, 281; duties of personal representative, 236–237; expenses of, 240–245; lawyers' compensation, 217, 274–276; problems of, 269–273; purpose of, 231; time involved, 237–240, 260–262
Estate fragmentation: due to remarriage, 128–131
Estate of Chadwick, In re, 126n
Estate of Cramer, In re, 234n
Estate of Hoffman, In re, 31n
Estate planning: fiduciary relationship, 214; preventive law, 214
Estate redistribution: intestate cases, 124–143; testate cases, 122–124
Estates: economic characteristics, 44; nature of large, 173–175; nature of small, 174–177; tax considerations when large, 90; tax deductions, 174
Estate settlement. *See* Estate administration
Estranged families, 104–107; defined, 104
Evans, Wainwright, 88n
Executor: client's conception of, 205; corporation as, 236; lawyer as, 235
Extra-probate assets, 177–180; insurance, 179–180

FAMILY continuity, 9–10
Family networks, 85
Family of orientation: disinherited, 111–113
Family of procreation: disinherited, 109–111
Farber, Bernard, 104n
Farr, James F., 224n
Final care: as inheritance factor, 100, 138
Findings: summary of, 286–296
Fisher, Janet A., 63n, 163n, 330n
Forced savings, 5
Forced share, 31, 207
Freedman, Ronald, 39n
Freund, Paul A., 55n
Friedman, Lawrence, 39, 39n, 41n, 60, 92, 92n, 114n
Friedson, Elliott, 57n

GAMSON, W. A., 55n
Generational care, 118
Generational economic transfers, 9
Gift: elements of, 27–28; types, 27
Gift causa mortis: defined, 27, features of, 28; restrictions on, 28
Gift inter vivos: defined, 27; features of, 28
Glick, Paul C., 330n
Goldfield, Edwin, 179n, 180n
Goode, William, 55n
Good faith falsification, 176
Gross estate: defined, 73n
Gross national product: increase in, 2
Guardianships, 191–193

HABUKKUK, H. J., 42n
Half-and-half statute: applied, 141; nature of, 33
Hall, Oswald, 223n
Harbury, O. D., 39, 39n, 60, 174
Harris, Virgil, 41n
Hays, William L., 265n

Heir-at-law designation, 21
Heirs: defined, 121n
Henderson, L. J., 56n
Hill, Reuben, 85n, 330n
Hodge, Robert W., 55n
Hollingshead, August B., 76n, 207n, 329n
Holographic will, 24
Homans, George, 84, 84n, 140n
Howard, Jan, 43n, 55, 55n
Hoyt, Edwin P., 86n
Hughes, Everett, 214n

IDEAL client: estate settlement compared with will making, 272; in estate settlement, 268–269; in will making, 214–217
Illegitimate child: inheritance rights of, 20
Implications of study for lawyers, 302–314
Implications of study for legal education, 302–314
Individual loss, 47–48
Inheritance: economic theory, 159; effects of, 154; effects of industrialization on, 1; fairness of, 146–148; legal restrictions on, 5; meanings of, 166–170; patterns of, 1; perception of, 173; psychological factor, 148, 171; relation to reciprocity, 9–10; symbolic importance, 38; uses of, 158–166
Institutional bureaucratic systems, 2
Intergenerational continuity, 88
Interviews: demographic characteristics, 46; information requested, 46; refusals, 49; test of hypotheses, 46
Inter vivos trusts: features of, 29–30
Intestacy. *See* Intestate succession
Intestate distribution. *See* Intestate succession
Intestate succession: as standard of equality, 84; conditions of, 62; defined, 16; history of, 16; patterns of, 16–17; percent of wills identical to pattern, 101; reasons for, 202; society's image of just distribution, 84; special problems where spouse and minors survive, 131–133; variance relating to survivors, 89
Intestate succession statutes: as theoretically inducing wills, 84n; position of nonrelated inheritors, 112
Irrevocable trust, 29

JENKINS, Edward, 113n
Joint ownership of property with right of survivorship, 33
Joint tenancy, 33–34
Jones, John Price, 113n, 114n, 115n
Justice: decedent's conception of, 121; heirs' conception of, 121; society's conception of, 121

KADUSHIN, Charles, 56n
Kent, Leonard, 328n
Klein, L. R., 159n
Komarovsky, Mirra, 151n
König, René, 85n
Kounin, Jacob, 54n, 55, 55n
Kreinin, Mordechai, 160n
Kreps, Juanita M., 3n, 5n, 39n

LABOR force, 2
Ladinsky, Jack, 325n
Landsberger, Michael, 161n
Lansing, John B., 163n
Lapsed legacies, 66n
Late-life marriage. *See* Companionship marriage
Laughing heirs, 13, 19, 138–142
Lawyer: behavior controlled, 57; choice of, 252–253; client's perception of, 55; compared with other professionals, 57; conflicting loyalties, 57; prestige ranking, 55; role in estate administration, 252–258; role in will making, 217–218
Lawyer-client relationship, 54
Lawyer sample, 58–59; description of, 325–329
Legislative reform of probate process, 296–300
Le Play, 42
Liable-relative law, 144
Life estate, 192–193
Life expectancy: data on, 2
Life insurance, 32–33
Life-style changes, 169
Lindsey, Benjamin, 88n
Lipset, Seymour Martin, 55n
Litwak, Eugene, 149n
Livatan, N., 159n
Local residence rating, 51–52
Looker, Charles, 37, 37n, 38, 38n, 62, 62n
Lydall, Harold, 76n, 330n

MAILED questionnaires: use of, 47–49
Maine, Henry Sumner, 191n
Major marriage: defined, 93n
Marital deduction trust: defined, 189n; "terminable interest" rule, 192n
Marshall, T. H., 257n
Marx, Karl, 44n
Maskowitz v. Federman, 195n
McKinney, John C., 85n
McMillan, Robert, 41n

Mementos: bequests of, 156; burial with decedent, 158; defined, 156; gifts of, 157; symbolic significance, 171
Menshin, Robert S., 41n
Merrick, Frank J., 181n
Merton, Robert K., 56n, 57n, 214n
Metropolitan area, 36
Meyer, Henry J., 84n
Michel, Andreé, 312, 312n
Moore, Wilbert E., 9n, 44n, 85, 85n, 116n, 153, 153n, 154, 289n
Morgan, James N., 155n, 163n
Mortality rates, 2
Mortmain acts: defined, 26; influence on testator, 66; purpose, 66; types, 26–27
Multilineal kinship system, 7
Murphy, John J., 192n, 193n

NEEDED research, 305–310
Negative savers, 63
Net estate: defined, 73n
New York and Kings County study, 37
Next of kin: as determined by degrees of relationship, 19; meaning of "no known," 108
Non-related inheritors: types of, 112
Nuclear family structure, 7
Nuncupative will, 24

O'GORMAN, Hubert J., 58, 58n, 327n, 329, 329n
Ohio Statute of Descent and Distribution, 17
Oral will. *See* Nuncupative will

PARENTELIC system, 16
Parkhill, James S., Jr., 192n, 193n
Parsons, Talcott, 56n, 57n
Per capita distribution, 19
Personal representative: distinction between executor and administrator, 228; family member as, 232–233; lawyer as, 233–236; outsider as, 260; role in estate administration, 259–260
Personal representatives' fees, 242–244
Per stirpes distribution, 19
Piaget, Jean, 84, 84n
Plaut, Eric, 56n
Polansky, Norman, 54, 55, 55n
Porter, Charles O., 57n
Positive savers, 63
Posthumous child: ability to inherit, 20
Powell, Richard R., 20n, 37, 37n, 38, 38n, 62, 62n, 76n
Power of appointment: defined, 189n
Preferred heirs, 181–182
Prenuptial agreements: influence on testators, 91–92
Pretermitted heirs, 15, 66n
Probate court system, 276–284; criticism of, 247; reasons for using, 180; reasons to avoid, 177; reporting of assets, 178–179; role in estate administration, 248–252; suggested changes in, 280–284
Probate records: as source of data, 39–40
Probate sample, 44–45
Probate studies: comparison of previous, 37–39
Probating the will: definition, 229; petition for, 228; procedure for, 229–231
Property exempt from administration, 182
Property transfers as two-step process. *See* Intergenerational continuity
Prosser, William L., 41n
Public education: needed in probate area, 300–302

QUARANTINE, 25
Quid pro quo: estate for old-age support, 85

RADIN, Paul, 83n
Rankin, Allen, 139n
Read, Harlan Eugene, 44n
Redlich, Frederick, 329n
Referees, 276–279
Reflections, 310–314
Reid, Margaret G., 161n
Reiss, Albert, Jr., 302n
Relative deprivation, 85
Release from administration, 175–176
Relict: defined, 141
Revocable trust, 29
Rheinstein, Max, 41n
Riesman, David, 181, 181n
Rippner, Ellis, 181n
Robinson, Thomas, 41n
Roseborough, Howard, 181, 181n
Rossi, Peter H., 55n

SAVING-living index, 163–165; defined, 163
Schneider, David, 104n
Schuman, H., 55n
Schwartz, Barry, 83n, 212n
Selltiz, Claire, 206n, 262n
Serial reciprocity, 118
Serial service, 118
Settlor: defined, 28–29
Shanas, Ethel, 3n, 9n, 39n, 41n, 85n, 100n, 330n
Sharp, Frank C., 84n
Sharp, Harry, 39n
Shoup, Carl, 113n, 175, 175n

Siegel, Paul M., 55n
Simpson, Richard L., 121n, 144n
Slayers: inheritance rights of, 21–22
Smelser, Neil, 116n
Smith, Adam, 257n
Social control system: court as part of, 36
Social status: indicators of, 76
Spouse-all pattern of inheritance: spouse sole survivor, 86–88; lineal kin survive, 89–90
State ex rel. Baker v. County Court, 229n
Statute of Frauds, 23
Statute of Wills, 23
Stehouwer, Jan, 100n
Stouffer, Samuel, 207n
Streib, Gordon F., 3n, 9n, 39n, 41n, 85n, 100n, 330n
Stryker, Sheldon, 151n
Surviving spouse's election rights. *See* Forced share
Survivor interviews. *See* Interviews
Survivor population: average age, 68; characteristics of, 64; defined, 62; testate status, 64; types of kin, 72
Sussman, Marvin B., 3n, 9n, 39n, 46n, 85n, 152n, 306n, 323n

TAX records, 45
Tenancy by the entirety, 34
Tenancy in common, 33
Testacy: conditions of, 62; factors influencing, 72–73; frequency of, 64–81; hypotheses regarding, 64; life cycle's relation to, 330–333; motives for, 69. *See also* Will making
Testacy rate: fluctuation in, 62; marital status related, 69–71; sex related, 71–72; surviving kin related, 72–73
Testamentary capacity, 24
Testamentary freedom, 4–8, 40–41, 202–212; effect of children on, 96–103; effect of surviving kin on, 72; justification, 212; persons favoring, 207
Testamentary restrictions, 211–212
Testate succession: defined, 16
Testators: effect of absence of immediate family on, 113; effect of lineal kin on, 72; legal sophistication of, 209–210; prior wills of, 67; remarried, 91–95; sex differences, 89

Thomas, E. J., 54n, 55n
Tiryakian, Edward, 56n, 214n
Totten, In re, 30n
Totten trust, 30–32
Trust: as testamentary control device, 189–191; defined, 28
Trustee: banks as, 190; defined, 28; duties, 29; importance of continuity, 190; professional, 191
Turrentine, Lowell, 25n

UNIFORM Simultaneous Death Act, 22
Universal care systems, 1
Unworthy taker, 13, 142

WALLIN, Paul, 151n
Ward, Edward, 37, 37n, 38n, 40n, 43n, 63n, 71n, 74n, 76n, 114, 181n
Warner, W. Lloyd, 43n, 158n
Warren, Charles, 55n
Wedgwood, Josiah, 39, 39n, 60, 153n, 174
Wellman, Richard V., 142n, 183n
Wigmore, John H., 212n
Will contest: frequency, 184; nature of, 231; settlement, 184–188
Will making: circumstances affecting, 204–205; deterrents, 204; fees charged, 220–221; influential person factor, 203–204; legal problems, 215–217; motives for, 204; norms, 148; push-pull factors, 203–206; use of standard forms, 219–220. *See also* Testacy
Wills: as expressing testator's value system, 84; change of prior, 67; definition of will, 42, 201; deviation from intestate pattern, 72; execution requirements, 23–25; function of, 73; history of, 23–24; importance of, 83; in relation to large estates, 173; misconceptions regarding, 205; naming of executor, 228; reasons for, 188, 202–206
Wills Act, 23–24
Will substitutes: defined, 27; listed, 27; reasons for, 27
Winters, Glenn R., 56n
Wolfbein, Seymour L., 2n
Wood, Arthur Lewis, 58n, 329, 329n

YEAR's allowance, 25, 181–182